The Mind and Method of the Historian

The Mind and Method of the Historian

Emmanuel Le Roy Ladurie

TRANSLATED FROM THE FRENCH BY
SIÂN AND BEN REYNOLDS

THE HARVESTER PRESS

First published in Great Britain in 1981 by
THE HARVESTER PRESS LIMITED
Publisher: John Spiers
16 Ship Street, Brighton, Sussex

© 1981 by The Harvester Press Ltd. and The University of Chicago

The present volume consists of translations of selections from
Emmanuel Le Roy Ladurie, *Le territoire de l'historien*, vol. 2,
© 1978 by Editions Gallimard

British Library Cataloguing in Publication Data
  Le Roy Ladurie, Emmanuel
    The Mind and Method of the Historian.
    1. Historiography
    I. Title
    907'.2   D13
    ISBN: 0–85527–928–1

Contents

Translators' Note   vi

1 History That Stands Still   1

2 A Concept: The Unification of the Globe by
   Disease (Fourteenth to Seventeenth Centuries)   28

3 The Aiguillette: Castration by Magic   84

4 French Peasants in the Sixteenth Century   97

5 Balzac's Country Doctor: Simple Technology and
   Rural Folklore   123

6 Versailles Observed: The Court of Louis XIV
   in 1709   149

7 The Rouergue through the Lens   174

8 Rétif de la Bretonne as a Social Anthropologist:
   Rural Burgundy in the Eighteenth Century   211

9 The Crisis and the Historian   270

Notes   291

Glossary   307

Translators' Note

IN some of the articles in this book, particularly those concerned with French history, a number of French terms appear for which there are no accurate (or brief) English equivalents. We have therefore left them in French. Sometimes the meaning is clear from the context, or is explained; but in any case a full glossary appears at the end of the book.

S.R.

1

History That Stands Still[1]

As the subject of my lecture at the Collège de France this year, I
should like to consider the economy and society, or rather what
might be called the traditional eco-demography, of a now-vanished
world: one that "functioned", if that is the right word, between the
fourteenth and the eighteenth centuries; more precisely, between
1300–20 and 1720–30. For practical reasons, my research and thus
my acquaintance with this world is at present confined to the hexagon that corresponds to present-day France—an entirely *notional*
entity at that time, and certainly not a national one. In this area
alone, the population throughout virtually the whole period was of
the order of 15 to 20 million, though there are some conspicuous
troughs, as we shall see. Similar studies could and probably will be
undertaken one day, if they have not already begun, in neighbouring countries—Germany, Italy, perhaps Spain; but not necessarily
in the British Isles. Indeed one of the paradoxes of this kind of
project is that England, where P. Laslett's *The World We Have Lost*
was first depicted (with extraordinarily perceptive intuition), was
probably, of all the western countries, the one where that world was
the least typical and the least stable.

The instruments and methods I propose to employ for my purpose are not, of course, those derived from traditional historiography—even, indeed particularly, when it claims to have been rejuvenated by recent transplants. It will be agreed, I think, that the
scientific approach to history can take us a long way beyond a set of
meditations on the role of chance, events and intrigue in the affairs
of man, based moreover on a total disregard for sociology. We
should indeed be reduced to such meditations if we were to lay
history on a Procrustean bed with measurements unchanged since
the days of Aristotle and Thucydides. So, at the risk of being
accused of scientism, I am here today to plead the cause of the noble
savage. Many historians of the *Annales* school, among whom I
would count myself, are quite candid, though not, be it said, naive,
in their championing of Labrousse rather than Rickert, and
Goubert rather than Ammien Marcellin. In our view, chance can-

1

not be studied separately from necessity—even, or especially, when necessity takes the form of statistical regularity or probability.

It is certainly not my intention, in this context, to deny the innovatory possibilities of studying the *event* (even if it does not entirely deserve the rehabilitation *à la Seignobos* which it has been receiving in the last five years or so from a pseudo-revolutionary school of historians who consider even footnotes bourgeois). But the best studies of *l'histoire événementielle* (history in terms of events) in the scientific and non-pejorative sense, are precisely those which, in order to gauge the impact of any given event, seek to locate it firmly within its context, looking both backward and more especially forward in time, to find out whether the event in question really "made any difference" or not. Thus American "clio-metrists" of the Fogel school, for example, seek to discover whether major events in the history of the United States—the War of Independence for instance—really played the role generally attributed to them in economic history. The method is to invent a sort of historico-fictional scenario, in which the great event in question never takes place. The historian then works out from scratch all the chains of chronological consequences. The paradox of this research into events is that it leads its practitioners to quantify, eventually bringing them back—*horribile dictu*—to the good old computer. To paraphrase what Jaurès said about patriotism, a little acquaintance with events sends one away from quantification, but prolonged acquaintance brings one irresistibly back again. As it happens, in the admittedly specialized area of economic history, this kind of testing has not been of great comfort to those who hoped that the event would be restored to its former prominence: the non-occurrence of the American Revolution in the 1770s would not have altered by so much as a shilling one of the pretexts for the war—the price for tobacco paid by the motherland to the planters and colonists across the Atlantic. Rather more encouraging for this approach is the work of the historian Paul Bois who, by working backwards (almost a task of psychoanalysis) through the figures and sequences of major trends in the economic and political history of his chosen region, the *bocage*, has discovered the genesis of the conservatism of western France in the original, short-lived trauma of the Chouan uprising. At the root of what appeared to be a heavily-determined necessity he found an incidental mutation—but the point is that he discovered it by working *a posteriori* and did not make any assumption *a priori*.[2]

As for strictly event-centred or "instant" history—whether written by reactionaries or revolutionaries—it seems to me to cater for a demand which may be legitimate but is often trivial. In an age when, as Marshall McLuhan has pointed out, the mass media sometimes confuse the message with the massage, annihilating the logic of books and thought, it is not surprising that "instant history" easily slips back into the habits of undistanced narrative, characteristic of the old medieval chroniclers before the Gutenberg galaxy.

But there is no reason why such writings—which, incidentally, convey a very good impression of contemporary attitudes—should be regarded, apart from a very few and talented exceptions, as anything other than they are: namely eye-witness accounts, with all the advantages and disadvantages of the genre.

Nor are the instruments and methods which I propose to use necessarily those which a certain fashionable philosophy (one that is demanding and often creative) would thrust upon the historian. From the latest brand of marxism, I would above all draw a lesson which is hardly detectable in it at all: namely that it is, in the first analysis, in the economy, in social relationships, and at a deeper level still, in biological phenomena, much more than in the class struggle, that we must look for the motive force of mass history—at least during the period I am studying and as regards the population that concerns me. It is true that since we are talking about a society "without a motor", i.e. developing very slowly, as in the case of the pre-industrial world, such a heresy may be more pardonable. As for linguistics (which some of my colleagues, mostly non-linguistics experts, have lately been predicting will from now on be the queen of the social sciences), while I would not at all underestimate its immense contributions, these fall outside my area of competence. While recognizing the great interest of studies devoted to vocabulary, I have to confess that up to now pure personal preference has led me to spend less time looking at words than looking at the things the words stand for; even, or particularly, when such "things" as reflected in the archives are in part collective representations: since they have a basis in reality they cannot be reduced simply to the way in which people have spoken of them. I am thinking for instance of land ownership. Perhaps too, when it comes to words, I am rather like the semiliterate of the nineteenth century as described by Jacques Ozouf: I have had my work cut out learning to count, never mind learning to read as well!

So for reasons which, I would stress, have to do with my own area of specialization and not at all with any discrimination or disregard, it is the geology of the layers of rock beneath our feet that has concerned me more than the admittedly fascinating geography of discourse, which is of course crucial to any serious cultural history. The flourishes and contours of language can only figure for my purposes in a preliminary mapping out of the terrain or archaeological survey, preparatory to a deeper probe. Both types of prospecting, archaeological and geological, as it happens, employ techniques of excavation and drilling which may turn out to be remarkably comparable.

Anthropology, though, has always been and will long remain one of my favourite sister-disciplines; but it has to be admitted that in most cases the historian is a very humble practitioner in this field. Card-index at the ready, he has to scan endless numbers of documents, the raw material of social reality, just as the anthropologist has endlessly to question the members of the society he is studying, jotting everything down in his notebook. And yet (as soon as one moves to a higher level of abstraction and the grander schemes of anthropology, structural or functionalist) both history as it used to be and sociology as it still is often turn out to be too poorly equipped to apply all these grand theories in a thoroughgoing way. Several years' teaching in French universities were enough to convince me, through the actual practice of my profession as a lecturer (the ultimate purpose of which was often challenged) of the vanity of the all-out functionalism favoured by Bronislaw Malinowski. Things did occasionally function in our university departments—but Censier was not Melanesia, nor the Jussieu campus the Trobriand Islands.[3] Malinowski's quasi-pre-established harmonies may have worked for coral islands but they did not seem very relevant to our glass and concrete campuses, prone as they often were to attacks of anomie; nor, I suspect, would they be any more pertinent to many other aspects of western society today. Well, you may say, if these days our universities are sometimes deprived of a few of their functions, they do at least still have their structures. Would my work as a teacher, which was driving me irrevocably away from functionalism, bring me closer to structuralism? To tell the truth, I had already long been won over to this position and needed no inducement, biological or personal, so great was my admiration for the efficacity of structuralist method, as applied so successfully to rules governing kinship or mythology in the New World. Alas, these methods cannot always be transposed and reproduced as they stand in the rather different world of the European past. Nathan Wachtel, since he was working in South America, was able to apply Levi-Strauss's techniques to the ancient and sometimes to the recent history of Peruvian society, relating them to myths, institutions and family structures. But in the human groupings of our continent, whether traditional or contemporary, the rules governing marriage for instance (although there are sometimes fascinating exceptions) are too open and unstructured—apart from a certain survival of rural endogamy—for one to be able to use the grids suggested by anthropology; they would defeat the most sophisticated of computers. The European historian will find it difficult to adapt for his own purpose the actual and detailed techniques of structuralism, relating to the exchange of signs: in the present state of research, it seems most applicable to other civilizations. But he will regard as more relevant to himself the general definition of the doctrine which sees itself simply as "a method as old as knowledge itself: it is designed to apprehend phenomena outside their conscious manifestation, and to systematize their relationships and overall transformations, on the basis of a limited number of variables".[4] For half a century, from Marc Bloch to Pierre Goubert, the best of French historians, systematically systematizing away, have in fact been structuralists. Sometimes they realized it themselves; sometimes they did not; all too often nobody else realized it at all.

★

Without being too impertinent, we might also note in this survey of interdisciplinary contacts, how far exploration by a demographer of the past, which is what I should like to consider myself, can take one towards an area of knowledge properly termed psychological—namely psychoanalysis. This field of research is too close to the concerns of the historian for him to be able simply to disregard it. However the sum total of my excursions into such disputed territory is somewhat meagre and the fault is my own. I certainly have nothing to offer to compare with Alain Besançon's rich findings in this field. But my research has twice led me—in a very humble way—close to trails blazed long ago by Sigmund Freud. My work on birth control has inevitably brought me into contact with the observations made by Freud while he was still a young doctor in Vienna, during the last two decades of the nineteenth century. His encounters with his patients led him to consider the beginnings of birth control among the Viennese elites. And it was in this context that he examined the psychological traumas which the earliest attempts at contraception were thought to have inflicted on married women. Such traumas were the result, according to the explanation current at the time, of the crude and unsatisfactory contraceptive techniques of the day. To a psychologist, perhaps, Freud's observations are merely typical of a stage in medical history now past; but for historians, who are not over-provided with documents of this kind for eighteenth and nineteenth-century France, Freud's writings on demographic psychology remain among the most telling items in the very slight corpus of evidence we possess.

To take another example, which again concerns deviant behaviour: I was led, through the history of popular religion in both city and countryside, to study the convulsionaries of the Cévennes and of Saint-Medard in Paris (the former Huguenots, the latter Jansenists). Here, too, the early work of Freud and Breuer on convulsive hysteria, although it may now seem old-fashioned to experts, put me on the track of several interesting hypotheses relating to the sexual and cultural aetiology of convulsive hysteria in times long ago.

In both cases, however, my concern was with the early Freud, before the discovery of the Oedipus complex: the young doctor who wrote the *Letters to Fliess* and the *Studies on Hysteria*. My research has drawn me primarily (and then only occasionally) to Freud's juvenile writings. Such research will therefore be justifiably considered as secondary by real specialists. And in the end, studies like this point to the limitations of the historian's knowledge rather than to the relevance, or otherwise, of Freudian analysis to the development of our discipline—a relevance, indeed, that I feel quite unqualified to gauge. I am reminded of our bewilderment when, about ten years ago, a mighty voice from the Rue d'Ulm[5] woke us historians from the antidogmatic trance in which we sat thumbing through the archives, with the rousing news that "Marx had never been young". Well, of the father of psychoanalysis, I as a historian have to say the opposite: my specific research having had to do only with his youthful writings, I can truthfully say that for me Freud has never been old—or even middle-aged.

★

At this point in my lecture, I may perhaps be permitted to use an expression originally applied by Roland Barthes to certain other groups: as historians we are "the rear-guard of the *avant-garde*". We leave it to researchers in more sophisticated disciplines to embark upon the really dangerous missions. They are the pioneers who, sometimes at the risk of their lives, go ahead and explode the minefields that are holding up a general advance. We historians draw very largely on the wealth created by the established branches of quantitative science such as demography, economics and indeed econometrics. We have shamelessly pillaged—though we do try to give as good a return as possible—the resources of demography, to which we have given a historical dimension. We have drawn, too, on the economics of Marx, Ricardo and Malthus; and the economic theory of our own time; and we have also tapped the resources of anthropology which, from our point of view, has made more positive progress in methodology than in results. In approaching a fairly well-defined field like traditional society, biological models, as proposed by Wynne Edwards for instance, have sometimes been more helpful to us than the latest refinements of semiotics (we do not always understand the idiolects . . .). At the same time, since we are not bitten by the urge to be relentlessly up to date, we feel we are continuing a tradition. After a long period of gestation, the *Annales* school began, as everyone knows, in the 1920s with Marc Bloch and Lucien Febvre. In the 1930s, Ernest Labrousse, following in the footsteps of François Simiand, gave it a quantitative flavour. Fernand Braudel, in succession to whom I am here today, and many other historians now teaching in Paris, Rennes, Toulouse, Aix-en-Provence, etc., conferred upon this by-now polycentric group an unofficial permanence. The school is like the societies it studies: it takes its time. It views its own life-span within the long-term context of the century. And (to borrow an expression) like an old mole, patiently digging its tunnel, it will not willingly desert its underground galleries, but displays a rather remarkable indifference to what is happening on the surface. Epis-

temological breaks may be heard snapping in all directions and
hemlines move from knee to ankle and back; the *Annales* historian
will still be there, imperturbably adding up columns of figures. For
in spite of everything that has been said about history, it does after
all participate in the *cumulative* labour of the exact sciences. It is not
deaf to the sounds of the contemporary world, but it cannot cut its
cloth to suit this year's fashions, whether the imperious summons
comes from the Paris fashion houses or from off-the-peg supermar-
kets.

To have some idea of the impact of the quantitative methods
which are now revolutionizing the way history is written, one has
only to read *Time on the Cross*, the recent book by Robert Fogel
and Stanley Engerman[6] on the economy of black slavery in the
United States. And if you will bear with me, I shall pause briefly to
consider what is for historians something of a test case. The book
was written on the basis of statistical surveys made possible by
census returns and plantation accounts; it also depends on a series
of calculations which would not have been possible without the use
of computers. Its authors' conclusions are all the more paradoxical,
to the point of causing some scandal; so much so that the inattentive
or ill-intentioned reader might even be tempted to see the book as a
disguised apologia for slavery. In fact, the two authors, who are
convinced supporters of black liberation in America today, have
succeeded in demonstrating primarily—and most significantly—
that one of the worst times in the lives of those who had been slaves
coincided with the age of so-called liberty, after 1865. They also
reached the conclusion, after long and painstaking research, that
the thinly-veiled racism of the abolitionists was, in the long run,
almost as disastrous as the undisguised discrimination of the plantation owners before 1860. Fogel and Engerman, who are pioneers of
counterfactual fiction-history, went so far as to calculate what the
price of slaves would have been in 1889, if the Civil War had not
taken place. (It would of course have risen.) Following this up, with
figures to support their claim, the authors have demonstrated that
slavery in North America was an extremely profitable system; that
it was by no means moribund, regardless of what has been said, in
the years preceding the Civil War; and that it was actually more
efficient than the modes of production of the northern States which
depended on the freedom of labour. The black slaves in the south
were very efficient workers, often skilled, and able to tackle urban

as well as rural tasks. They led a normal family life, which was not, in the great majority of cases, interrupted by individuals being sold away. Their material living conditions (though not of course their psychological conditions, since they were deprived of their freedom) were the equivalent of those enjoyed by white workers in the same region. The rates of labour exploitation by southern employers were not high. In 1860, the southern States formed a unit, indeed virtually a nation, which was *economically* advanced in spite of its odiously backward human relations. On economic performance, which is strictly quantifiable, the southern States were well ahead of all continental European countries (France and Belgium for instance). Contrary to the stereotyped image of a region underdeveloped on practically every level, the old South was only outdone economically by the two most advanced regions of the world: Britain and the northern States. Let me repeat once more: by carrying out this potentially dangerous demonstration, Fogel and Engerman did not intend to justify or rehabilitate in any sense the horrors of slavery. They simply succeeded in proving that their predecessors had not necessarily got their history right when they used as source material what they were told by abolitionist pamphlets—even when these were written with the best of intentions. The lesson should not be lost on us European economic historians—young and not so young. If we do not follow Fogel's example and absorb all the elements of the most sophisticated economic theory, the French school of historical research may find itself in possession of a rather overrated capital of knowledge.

★

Having mentioned these considerations by way of introduction, I have now arrived at the object of my lecture: that is, a certain traditional and rural society, between the end of the Middle Ages and the beginning of the eighteenth century. In many ways, this really can be called an *object*, the statistical dimensions of which, despite some sizeable fluctuations, always tended to return to a fixed level which acted as a ceiling. I would by no means claim that "France" (by which I mean the near-hexagon of Vauban's time) was in any sense an organic unit between 1300 and 1700. France, before it became French so to speak, merely serves as a window on the world, thanks to which we can isolate and observe a large sample of humanity. By the time of Vauban's population counts of about 1700, this area contained some 19 to 20 million inhabitants, whom we shall, for the sake of convenience, call Frenchmen (and women). Now it so happens that the very numerous national and regional studies relating to the *count of households* of 1328, and confirmed by a number of provincial monographs indicate that the same area, within the same frontiers (which did not yet exist in 1320 of course, but which we are using for convenience' sake) contained at least 17 million souls in about 1300–40. Over four whole centuries, from 1300–40 to 1700–20, the population increased by only 2 million. (Is this a record?) France has never been as close, except perhaps during the period 1865–1945, to that zero population growth so desperately called for by population experts, but never yet achieved in practice. It is true that the (unintentional) means by which the French system of the classical period achieved this self-regulation would have little appeal in our time: epidemics for instance—they were effectively an element in an eco-system which bound together man and his biological, bacillary and predatory environment. I hasten to say therefore that the model briefly outlined here is factual and eco-demographic—with no claims to be normative or desirable.

The other series of discoveries recently made by the French school of historians concerns the stability of rural techniques and cereal yields between the first agricultural revolution (in the Middle Ages: eleventh to thirteenth century) and the second one, much later, in the nineteenth century. Without discussing for the moment the rather ambiguous case of the eighteenth century, we can at any rate say that subsistence food production was governed, broadly speaking, by stable norms between 1300 and 1720. This discovery reveals an extraordinary ecological equilibrium: though admittedly there were within this period, as there would be in animal demography, a number of upheavals and some massive (but always temporary) backward swings of the pendulum. This overall equilibrium, which was as susceptible to variation and irregularity as an economist's graph, can be epitomized in an image of rural life. Inside the ring of forests spared by the axe, within a space enlarged by the great land clearances of the eleventh to the thirteenth century, a peasant population lived and reproduced itself over twelve or thirteen generations, between 1300 and 1720, in conditions determined by a strait-jacket of numerical possibilities, characterized by certain inexorable constraints. These constraints may have been relaxed somewhat, after 1720, but they did not disappear in a hurry, since even in 1914, on the eve of the war, the active agricultural population in France was still very close to its highest level in 1850. To stay with the crucial period 1320–1720, the virtual stability, over the long term, of the parameters of demography and cereal production enables us to argue with those who insist on the necessity for a conceptual framework as a pre-requisite for analysis. In this case, the figures cannot in any sense be considered reluctant hand-maidens to some concept (which might discard them the moment they disagreed with its analysis). On the contrary, the theory simply leaps out of the overwhelming evidence: it leads us straight back to the old notions concerned with the properties of a virtually stationary state.

This ecologically stable and demographically near-stable society had not always manifested such a degree of equilibrium, at least not in the immediately preceding period. Between the eleventh and the thirteenth century, it had experienced a long wave of real expansion, pushing back the forests and swelling the numbers of human beings. Such expansion had occurred in a world of decentralized powers, wielded by feudal barons in their local fiefs: this old-fashioned world had turned out, after all, to be a favourable environment for the truly prodigious development of society—prodigious, that is, compared to the long periods of stagnation of the four whole centuries after 1300. From the eleventh to the thirteenth century, what was good for feudalism had been good for western Europe as a whole, and more particularly for the population in our selected area, corresponding to present-day France. It was not until after 1300 that the creation of great nation-states, already well-advanced of course, eventually introduced the risk of world wars which were to prove one of the most effective brakes on expansion. They would, along with many other factors, contribute to halting growth in the Gothic and medieval period.

For after 1300, and until 1720 (from Philip the Fair to Law and his system, from a bad inflation to a good, so to speak) the days of heady expansion were over. Human society, which had previously experienced higher levels of reproduction, and the eco-system in general (nature plus agriculture, the fauna of the animal world and the flora of the bacillary world plus the human race) now proved capable, within this geographical unit and in a human perspective,

of secreting certain braking mechanisms (as well as others required
for further take-off). These could block expansion and contain the
flood; or alternatively restore the overall human population
periodically, and not without major upheavals, to the highest point
of equilibrium. This normalization was achieved initially by exogenous sources of braking-power—though such exogenous factors
only appear so at first sight. For it is easy to demonstrate that what
was exogenous to Europe was endogenous to Eurasia, and was to
be endogenous a little later, in the sixteenth century, to the Atlantic
world as a whole. At all events, as gradually, from the eleventh
century on, its demographic dimensions, its trade, commercial,
colonial, religious and military contacts all increased, the western
constellation eventually met and rubbed shoulders with other
equally massive and expanding constellations: China from the thirteenth century and the Amerindian complex from the sixteenth. To
take only the former: the doom-laden regions of central Asia,
infested with rats and plague-bearing fleas, were being crossed early
in the fourteenth century by the silk caravans and by the wide-
ranging Mongol armies, who were free to roam where they would,
thanks to the political and commercial pacification of the heart of
the old continent, brutally achieved by Genghis Khan and his
followers. The increased travels of germ-carriers created a sort of
common market of viruses and other bacilli, first in Eurasia and
later on both sides of the Atlantic: a pooling of resources which still
functions today, to everyone's distress. Germs were thus able to
take short cuts that would have been quite impossible before 1300,
causing most notably the outreak of the Black Death in 1348, the
sequels of which were to cause havoc in France, until the last
recorded epidemic of plague in Marseilles in 1720. And similar
causes account for the unparalleled genocide of the American
Indians after 1492 and 1532, more devastating than any outbreak of
plague in Europe. This disaster was brought about by infections
carried—one can hardly say "in all innocence"—by the *conquistadors* of Castile. They brought back with them, it is true, a disease
which was to be damaging in European demography: syphilis. But
this was no more than a mild reprisal, not to be compared with the
mass extermination of the New World population which the Latin
countries exported to Mexico and Peru. In both cases, in the fourteenth and sixteenth centuries, international agents of contamination had been launched: they have been recorded in precise detail

and their culpability is not in doubt. The Genoese, incidentally, to venture briefly into *l'histoire événementielle* carry a double burden of guilt: first, because of the leading role they played in the Asiatic silk trade, with their counting houses at Caffa, the source from which the caravans carried the plague westwards; and secondly, because Columbus, one of their most illustrious citizens, led the first *conquista*. A great city and a great port, Genoa was also greatly to blame for the spread of sickness.

Global unification in terms of disease, which had been completed at great cost between 1300 and 1650, was one of the most potent stabilizing factors in the eco-system established between these two dates. But stabilization was only achieved, of course, by means of swings of the pendulum to one side or another: at first these were massive (in the fourteenth and fifteenth centuries) but later they moderated. The population of what would today be France stood at 17 million at least, in 1320. This figure had dropped to a mere 9 million by 1440. But by 1550 and until 1715, the late-medieval figure of 17 million had been recovered and even improved upon, for during the "long" seventeenth century, taking the lean years with the fat, the population of the "hexagon" fluctuated somewhere between, or slightly outside, the figures of 19 to 20 million.

But the unification of the world by disease was not the only limiting force. Another very powerful blocking "factor" visibly at work between the fourteenth and the early eighteenth centuries, was war: and pulling the strings of war was the modern, or so-called modern state. More generally, I would also blame the international or inter-state system, since it forms the backcloth against which the different phases of conflict in the west take individual shape.

During the earlier period (eleventh to thirteenth centuries) when old-time wars simply took place within the seamless and very close-ly woven robe of feudalism, there was a good chance that they would remain localized, damaging only a small part of the fabric, in which tears were fairly quickly repaired. But as large kingdoms came into being, the situation altered completely. Great states were driven by their own internal logic; they were led by individuals who were statistically short-sighted—long on ambition and short on vision. They committed themselves to wars on an international scale, which they then proved incapable of ending and which went on for thirty or a hundred years. Such wars were not necessarily very murderous in themselves: after all their power to kill depended on an army whose permanent strength over a long period could hardly have been more than 10,000 (though Louis XIV in his old age put half a million men in the field). So, such killing power was not in itself very destructive. But the little bands of soldiers—"thugs in armour"—had what we would call harmful side-effects. War spread epidemics, carried by the typhus-infected lice or plague-bearing fleas attached to the soldiers, refugees, tramps and beggars of whom there were so many in wartime. One small army of 8,000 men, in the course of an expedition dreamed up by Richelieu, travelled right across France, from La Rochelle to Montferat.[7] Simply through the epidemics it spread in its wake, this tiny army in 1627–8 caused the death by plague of over a million people, who no doubt never suspected that this was the price they would have to pay for subduing the Protestants—the aim of the Cardinal's domestic policy.

War had other side effects too: oxen and horses were requisitioned, villages looted, mills and farms destroyed, granaries full of corn burned to the ground. This could amount to the liquidation of agricultural capital. Such events might be accompanied by mortality of various kinds and by untimely outbreaks of panic which sent the terrified farm workers rushing to safety behind town walls at crucial moments in the farming year—seedtime, ploughing, harvest. The peasant classes, bled white and financially ruined, were in some areas wiped out in this early version of the elimination of the kulaks. In certain circumstances this was enough to make it impossible to reproduce even an *ancien-régime* economy or eco-demography. This was what happened in Normandy in about 1430 and contributed to reducing the population of the province to 28 per cent of its pre-Hundred Years' War level.[8] Guy Bois has described this kind of thing, quite justifiably, as the "Hiroshima model". In the days of Joan of Arc, then, war, pestilence, epidemic and famine accomplished unaided far more than a mere economic recession *per se*, the effects of which we might be inclined to overestimate if we were to be guided by old-fashioned economism. These four horsemen of the Apocalypse between them produced the massive though temporary depopulation of France in the fifteenth century. Or, to be more precise, the late medieval *economic* recession was caught up in a complex of factors and variables in which it was both active and acted upon—but on balance more acted upon than active.

In the period between 1560 and 1715, following the great revival or reconstruction of the population (which took place between 1440–1560), war, with its attendant famine and pestilence, was once more a major regulator of population growth. It set a ceiling on our eco-demographic system and even caused a decline before the recovery that followed. Evidence for this is to be found in the overall study of the product of tithes, for which I am indebted to my friend Joseph Goy.[9] Three major periods of slowdown, accompanied needless to say, by terrible suffering, show up on our graphs: broadly speaking, during the Wars of Religion (1560–95); during the Thirty Years' War and the Fronde (1635–53); and during the wars at the end of Louis XIV's reign (1690–1715).

To speak of war being a "Malthusian check" means of course implicating the standing army, that model of future bureaucracies. But it also leads us to lay responsibility on the "modern" state— monarchic, would-be absolutist, and certainly administrative, repressive and a source of patronage in the shape of "offices". This "modern" state was gradually taking shape between the fourteenth and seventeenth century and it dominates the entire landscape, indeed rather too much if one relies upon the politics-centred historiography of the past. In fact, the monarchic state is thoroughly ambiguous as regards the eco-demographic system that is our present concern. In a Weberian perspective, the state appears initially to have been a modernizing force. By means of what Pierre Chaunu has not been afraid to call its "technostructure", it was able to stimulate certain developments in the economic, cultural and social spheres. But between the fourteenth and the seventeenth century, this growth function was often eclipsed by its stabilizing effect. If one turns to Pierre Goubert's latest book on the *ancien régime*,[10] one finds that the monarchic state was very largely a military institution, itself implicated in the European balance of power. More than half its own budget was swallowed up by an army which became in many respects the graveyard of the nation—much more than the Court of Versailles ever was. So the state and the army must be numbered, between 1315 and 1715, among the principal regulating forces of an eco-demography which engendered them and which they in turn devoured. Not for a moment would I concur with a Panglossian and providential interpretation: namely, that since everything is for the best in the best of all possible worlds (as is

proved by melons coming ready divided for family eating), western
society *needed* to provide itself with rapacious states ready to fall at
one another's throats and organize a holocaust every thirty years or
so, in order to prevent excessive population growth and to reward
the survivors with the fruits of equilibrium: I may attribute such
providentialist notions to a straw man for the sake of argument, but
I have no sympathy for them whatever. I merely wish to point out
that the long-term equilibrium, which seems to me to characterize
the object of my studies, is only fully achieved in conditions of
tragedy, that is—in the past rather more than today—by politics
and therefore by war. After all, the ecology of the animal world
required the existence of predators. Wars in seventeenth-century
France acted as predators, directly in that they caused death, indirectly through taxation, which brought crisis and poverty (as one
can see in the wretchedness that marked the end of the reign of
Louis XIV).

In fact, the State did not completely assume its modernizing,
beneficial and economically expansionist role until after a change of
direction which, for want of a better word, I shall call dialectical:
after 1715, in the era of wars of attrition, of enlightened Provincial
Intendants and of bureaucrats who collected facts and figures. The
age of Enlightenment, as regards the eighteenth-century population boom, was an age of plenty, and the 1789 Revolution, building
a permanent basis for generations to come, provided a final impulse
in the same direction (although during the wars of 1792–1815, the
impulse was sometimes briefly reversed).

These reflections on the State lead me to stress what might be
described as one of the paradoxes of modernization. The State, war
and the army, with their attendant train of scourges, several times
brought the nation to the edge of an abyss in the name of a policy
which, in circumstances of brutal Malthusian discipline, did it is true
help the people to avoid the evils of uncontrolled expansion of
numbers. But politics of similar near-disastrous consequences also
played a part in the major changes of the sixteenth century. I need
hardly remind anyone that the great mass of Frenchmen, apart from
a tiny elite, subsisted from the fourteenth to the seventeenth century, and even later, in a world of comparative cultural stability:
they spoke the local dialect and remained faithful to a Catholicism
still partly composed of folklore, which formed the basis of their
religious sentiments. In such a context, the Protestant Reforma-

tion, which was itself based on the spread of printing and increased literacy among a small percentage of the population, came as a violent explosion, setting off alarming rejection mechanisms. One cannot transplant a Huguenot head on to a body that considers itself Catholic. And a reaction was only to be expected, if one attempted to wean villagers from the cult of the Virgin, and of all the saints who had converted the country people from their age-old pagan worship of trees and objects to the Christian cause. A defensive and punitive reaction—a combination of allergy and panic—convulses the entire national organism (to confine ourselves to France) between 1560 and 1680, until the final expulsion of the foreign body, with the Revocation of the Edict of Nantes, the final triumph of the Papist tradition, refurbished by the Counter-Reformation, and the unity of faith thus redisplayed. In its earliest phase, 1560–95, the rejection phenomenon was of unparalleled violence. It became identified with the backlash of the wars of religion, and set off a massive eco-demographic haemorrhage, thus providing one of the most powerful stabilizing influences in the system. It cut short the previously uncontrolled population expansion of the Renaissance, when people literally multiplied like rabbits. Once again, by this backlash effect, an attempt at modernization ultimately led to the reinforcement of the repressive and stagnant character of the system—which emerged from the ordeal in 1600, stitched up and covered with glorious wounds, but under all the scars still very much the same old body.

It would of course be ridiculous, and indeed stupid, to explain everything in terms of war. This was only a last resort; the *ultima ratio* of our system. During the period embracing the seventeenth century (1560–1715) war only broke out three times (see above). In between there were periods of calm. The period divides roughly into eighty-odd years of crisis and war, and eighty years of peace, or at least semi-peace within the frontiers. So we must recognize that alongside the paroxysms of war, there must have been a peacetime routine which also kept population in check—and indeed there was: the routine of epidemics. François Lebrun's important book on Anjou provides all the necessary detail on this question.[11] His case-study was a particularly rewarding one—if that is the right word. In the eighteenth century, when the rest of France was in the throes of a demographic boom that sent the population from 19 to 27 million, there were some exceptions, enclaves still prey to phe-

nomena that put a ceiling on expansion. Such was Brittany and
especially Anjou, where the population (despite pressures to expand) was held down to zero growth between 1700 and 1789. War
provides no explanation: Anjou was very far from the centres of
military operations and had experienced no fighting under the
reigns of Louis XIV, Louis XV or Louis XVI, and no famine since
1710. So the explanation must lie elsewhere. François Lebrun has
no difficulty tracing it and proving that infectious diseases were
primarily responsible for the failure of the Anjou population to
expand. In prosaic terms, whenever there was a hint of demographic expansion, almost immediately, in this area of poor
hygiene, where people drank the polluted water of the Loire,
amoebic dysentery claimed thousands of victims, wiping out any
recent increase in numbers. And whatever nostalgia one may feel
for the sweet life of Anjou, *la douceur angevine*, it has to be pointed
out that this eminently crude and cruel type of population control is
found in the animal kingdom too: among the higher apes who are
closest to men. Among the island apes studied by a British expert on
animal behaviour,[12] dysentery flourished whenever the population
increased, resulting in more physical contact beween the ever-
growing numbers of individuals. It declined, on the other hand,
when numbers fell after an epidemic, thus affording comparatively
more space for the survivors, who were thus somewhat protected
from harmful contacts. Numbers then rose again until they provoked the next wave of infection, and so on. Dysentery, alas, was to
both the human population of Anjou and the simian population of
the islands, what the centrifugal governor was to Watt's steam
engine.

Does the force of the epidemic argument cast doubt on the
theory, generally accepted in the last thirty years, that urban and
rural populations in France under the *ancien régime* were both
modulated by famine? Not necessarily. It is still true to say that the
famines of the seventeenth century, which had fortunately been
brought under control by 1741, were terrible in their day. Recent
research however usefully reminds us that famine should not be
taken out of context, but is a "total social phenomenon" linked in a
chain of cause and effect. Looking back towards causes, we see that
famine is related to war, which by the devastation it brings both in
immediate suffering and heavy taxation, often creates the conditions against which individual famines stand out.[13] And looking

forward to effects, one finds that famine is related to epidemics, which it may help to cause in two ways: it provides a favourable breeding-ground for them through malnutrition; and it creates large numbers of homeless vagrants who carry germs. All in all, famine seems to me to be a "final solution", so horrific that the mechanisms of demographic equilibrium rarely require to go to such extremes to achieve their ends. In most cases, before there was a real famine in the sense of total exhaustion of resources, both internal and external regulators would already be at work (plague, war, epidemic, late marriage). They planed off, so to speak, the surplus layers of demographic growth before it was too late—and might even themselves have caused a massive downturn in population numbers.

There were even certain other phenomena, generally associated with towns, and which one might therefore assume to be related to modernization, but which in fact acted as brakes on growth, holding it at zero. In one small village in the Paris region, 142 Parisian children sent there to wet-nurses, all died in the space of a single year in the eighteenth century. Even more incredibly, in the same village, so Marcel Lachiver tells me, in the space of thirty months (i.e., the normal interval between two pregnancies) no less than thirty-one babies from the towns were given one after another to the same couple (were they tubercular?) where the wife hired herself as a wet-nurse. All these little ones died, one after another, at a few weeks' interval. This is obviously an extreme, pathological case of organized or at least irresponsible infanticide. But such tragic examples are a sobering reminder that the great towns of the classical age, brilliant though they were, may have deserved their reputations for being "cities of death". To put it another way, they operated as safety valves for the boom in population, absorbing the surplus which came to them in flight from the countryside. A large part of this surplus population was then destined either for death or for sterility—accounted for either by galloping tuberculosis, by the mass export of babies to distrastrous wet-nurses, or by the failure of young women immigrants, whose child-bearing years were either spent in spinsterhood or shortened by late marriage, to reproduce (see Maurice Garden's book on Lyon[14]).

The picture I have painted may seem excessively pessimistic—supposing it to contain a value judgment, which is not the case. It is true that death appears to have played a crucial role in population

control. It is also the case that less harsh means of limitation—
contraception for instance—were practically non-existent during
the four centuries in question. The part-religious part-anthro-
pological taboo which operated for a long time in western countries
against *coitus interruptus* only began to be eroded, among the richer
classes, in the eighteenth century. Among peasants, the taboo did
not collapse until after the Revolution (which was, from this point
of view, something of a demographic Islam).[15]

More significant at first sight, during the period in question, is the
data on late marriage. According to Pierre Chaunu,[16] this custom
was "the contraceptive weapon par excellence of classical Europe".
And indeed, provided it was preceded by a period of strict premarital chastity, the late marriage of girls (twenty-five or twenty-
six) meant three or four fewer pregnancies. It had another advantage too: celibacy until the wedding-day also admirably suited
various ideologies of austerity—puritanism and Jansenism, which
existed and flourished in all parts of pre-industrial Europe between
1580 and 1780. Such rigorous beliefs, if one is to believe Max
Weber, later served as counterpoint to the rise of the petty
bourgeois or capitalist mentality. But in the seventeenth to eighteenth centuries, for lack perhaps of any better purpose, they were
employed at home to justify the enforced period of some ten years'
virginity between puberty and marriage. Before marrying, in a
village of the *ancien régime*, one had it seems to accept a long and
unrelieved waiting period, and either to possess or to inherit a
house, in order to found a home.

The picture of late marriage is a time-sanctioned and tempting
one. It fits, as we have just seen, the Weberian notions of the
austere personality and also matches the discoveries of anthropologists and biologists who, following in the steps of Carr Saunders
and Wynne Edwards, have found many population-limitation procedures among men and in the animal world. Among birds for
instance, it may take the form of a drop in the number of nests. This
line of thought suggests a *general systems theory* of population
control which can be applied either to men or animals. It would ill
become me to question the significance of these efforts to link such
phenomena, since I have myself, in the interests of interdisciplinary research, which I value highly, tried to contribute
something to them. And yet, the most recent research on the failure
of the *ancien régime* population to grow, suggests a rather different

interpretation. It stresses the significant role played in limiting population by death, which seems to have been more significant than the more "intelligent" control procedures based on austerity. And contraception hardly enters the picture at all. Compare on this point the mathematical models proposed by Jacques Dupâquier, which leave very little room for late marriage as a factor in limiting numbers.[17]

★

The theorists of the "stationary state" have defined it as one of perpetual movement, and where there is a tendency for the final, median state to reproduce what are essentially some of the fundamental features of the original state. This theory of *reproduction* is applicable too to our rural eco-system: despite extensive changes in the superstructures, the system eventually (say on the eve of the famines of the Fronde and again before those of 1693 and 1719) found itself very close to what it had been like three or four centuries earlier, just before the famine of 1315. The main parameters— demographic, ecological, even sociological—had fluctuated in between, but they had not significantly altered. For all the apparent movement, things had really stayed much the same. In both cases— 1320 or 1680—the active agricultural population whose total dimensions had persistently observed the same norms, was digging away at its plots of land with techniques that had barely changed, and obtaining yields that had not significantly improved. Such yields were still powerless to prevent some hundreds or thousands of people becoming direct or indirect victims of starvation every thirty years or so. In both cases, it is true, the system was operating close to the limits of its capacity, and in conditions that favoured subsistence crises and the spread of viruses. The ecological disasters which resulted might reduce it to its lowest ebb in terms of population or of surface area under cultivation (as in 1430 for example and, much less seriously, in 1695 or 1711). But such misadventures could not prevent the system from reconstituting itself and healing the scars in accordance with former, internal norms. Such reconstruction or revival was naturally accompanied by certain changes; they could even be quite substantial, provided they remained compatible with the overall logic of the system. One such transformation, though not necessarily an overruling one on a national scale, concerns the crucial commercial sector of agriculture. This was of course represented by the noblemen's estates (*réserves*) which, especially when farmed out, became paradoxically the means of introducing capitalist modernization. Such modernization could occur at various levels: first, the growth of the State and urbanization stripped the feudal seigneur of some of his roles. By the seventeenth century he was often no more than nominal overlord of a political clientele or a local police force. And he had lost something of his function as a petty tribal chieftain in the village. His former powers—virtually those of a State—were now exercised by officials or by the royal or municipal bureaucracy. Secondly, commercialization and urbanization (again) increased the importance of the seigneur's estates, since they produced a surplus of cereals and stock, whereas small holdings were unable to rise above self-sufficiency. As a result the *seigneurie*, while not really losing its identity, was, from the Middle Ages to the eighteenth century, becoming less and less feudal and more and more capitalist, or at any rate "physiocratic". The "reaction" of the nobles in the age of Enlightenment was indeed reactionary in form but its content had to do with making profits. So the 1789 Revolution, with its policy of dividing land up into small peasant holdings was, paradoxically, economically retrograde by contrast!

However these are really nuances and exceptions, dating to some extent from later in time than the historical object under study. On the whole, it is the impression of stability, including of course change within acceptable limits, that remains dominant until 1720. After all, productivity per hectare had hardly increased at all during the period. Precisely because of this low productivity, towns always required a great deal of land, in the form of large properties and feudal estates, to provide for their subsistence. Whatever the changes introduced between 1300 and 1720, they did not alter the mode of production—a combination of smallholdings and feudal estates—which ruled the world of agriculture throughout the period.

Virtual stability does not mean immobility. I have mentioned one area of change. But there were also fluctuations and swings internal to the system. Wilhelm Abel, following Ricardo, has recently studied the major movements of the pendulum in the period.[18] Abel is particularly interested in the shifting network of relationships, formed by means of social structures, between a fluctuating population and the available supply of land. He shows us a rotating circle of variables: in the early fourteenth century these were an objectively high land rent, low wages and land subdivision; then in the period from 1350 to 1450, smallholdings were joined together again, wages rose, the working week fell, and rents dropped, encouraging landlords to go in for gangster-like activities. In the sixteenth century came re-population, more fragmentation of the land and wage poverty; while rents, landlords and bourgeois prospered. Then in the following period, estates and wages were again consolidated and above all rents reached a ceiling at some point in the seventeenth century.

Should the movement of precious metals be mentioned in this connection, the flow and then the drying-up of the treasures of Peru? A recent study, based on radioactivity experiments on coinage, has in fact suggested that the influence of silver on the long-term trends of the economy has been over-estimated to some extent.[19] And technical innovation only appears to have played a minor role in the origins of the various swings of the pendulum described by Abel. Indeed, swings seems to be the word for them: movement to and fro, decline and recovery, rather than any permanent trend towards growth or its opposite.

The major fluctuations of the economy referred to by Abel were produced, over the long term, by massive population changes; that is, allowing for all the intermediary stages, they were determined by biological factors and the rhythm of outbreaks of disease. Economic change was shaped by demographic change rather than the other way about—by the supposed or real effects of falls in living standards. Such change was much more "Ricardian" than "Malthusian". Here I will, if I may, add my own slightly sharp and discordant note to the chorus of (mainly Parisian) opponents of economism. From the fourteenth to the seventeenth century inclusive, the economy was servant not master, dictated to not dictator. Importantly as it loomed in the early stages of our studies, in the last analysis the economy seems to have been fairly obedient to the great forces of life and death. As for the dictates of politics and the class struggle, the age of their power was yet to come, at least in so far as such power is really *specific*.

Seen in a very long-term perspective like this, the system takes on a fatalistic quality: revolts against it make little impression. The run-of-the-mill peasant revolt hardly ever fits the model of the anti-noble rebellion (exemplified by the *Jacquerie* in France and the German Peasant War). Rural rebellions, in France at least, overwhelmingly called for the good old days. They were directed against innovations and above all against that most scandalous of new developments: the gradual appearance, in the centre of the system and around a still-adored monarch, of the proliferation of offices and the "fiscocracy" of tax farmers. The peasant revolt in the seventeenth century, as described in different ways by Porchnev and Mousnier, was essentially a reaction of hostility towards the grasping State, the military-financial complex and the turn of the fiscal screw. After all, between 1609 and 1690, a period which saw several major revolts, the fiscal screw in question brought royal expenditure from 192 tonnes of refined silver to 1,050 tonnes (in precious-metal equivalents).[20] The aforementioned revolts did not attack "feudal" nobles and landlords, whose interests they nevertheless damaged on several occasions; in fact they regularly appealed to the leadership of those natural mediators for the peasant community: the local seigneur, the parish priest or the lawyer. It was not until the cultural revolution of the Enlightenment had reached deep into the heart of the peasant masses and penetrated provinces like Burgundy, already disposed to challenge authority, that uprisings previously aimed at taxation began to direct their fire at the nobility.

An objection could be made: to argue, as I am today, the case for a history that essentially stood still (for all the fluctuations, slow or catastrophic, and all the internal disturbances) might appear to be dismissing rather hastily all the vital new developments that indisputably occurred during the period—whether Newton's theories, Pascal's mystic experience, Papin's cooking pot, the growth of Paris into a great city or the spread of polite manners symbolized by the use of forks at table. No, I would not for a moment deny that all such episodes represented something radically new. But I am concerned here rather with what became—or did not become—of the great mass of people. What was achieved by the elite must be set apart, on a different, higher level; it really matters only in the history of a conspicuous minority—one that did indeed foreshadow the future, but which was not as yet able to lever out of its groove the solid rural mass, still rocking to and fro in its Ricardian pendulum swings.

The powerlessness of the elite only applies, however, to the long period before 1720 (at least in France; elsewhere the chronology may be different). After this date, it is true, the elitist forces of renewal, which had been slowly building up over the centuries, became a "critical mass" or rather avalanche, a surge which carried society on towards real growth of a kind not experienced by the peasant masses since the thirteenth century. The forces of renovation included the State, the modernized Church, the educational system—all more repressive and more efficient; a more plentiful money supply; a more sophisticated nobility and bourgeoisie; better-run estates; greater literacy everywhere; a more rational bureaucracy; more active trade; and urbanization at what eventually became an irresistible rate, forcing nations (whose productivity was not keeping pace) to produce more peasants in order to feed the new mass of townspeople. Wisdom or folly—who knows? But it opened Pandora's box, forcing the agricultural population out of its eco-system, breaking the old medieval norms, unbreached until the death of Louis XIV. The breach stood open through the age of the Enlightenment and of course during the following nineteenth century. In 1328, the French population stood at 17 million; it was 19 million in 1700—still about the same. But by 1789, it had reached 27 million and had risen to almost 40 million by the time of the Franco-Prussian war of 1870. In other European countries, the advance was even more rapid. The demographic upswing, accompanied by the disappearance of famine, made it necessary and inevitable that simultaneously there should be some growth in the gross agricultural product—not to mention the superior methods of transport for grain and foodstuffs. The increase in production of the now generally available fruits of the earth had, if hunger was to be satisfied, to be at least equivalent and probably superior to that of the country's population. On this particular issue, I part company from the paradoxical and brilliant study on which I have drawn so freely earlier in my lecture in order to define the history that stands still. For I do not think anyone would deny the agricultural progress made in the eighteenth century. Indeed one of the most remarkable claims of the work to which I have referred is that there never was an agricultural revolution; a claim backed by detailed evidence from the very province in which that revolution had occurred (the extreme north of France). In fact, unless one admits (and this

cannot seriously be accepted) that France had 27 million inhabitants in 1670,[21] one has to concede that if there was no revolution,
there was at least a very lively development of agriculture in eighteenth-century France. The Unpublished research on inventories drawn
up after peasants' deaths has in any case put paid to the myth of
peasant pauperization during the last century of the *ancien régime*.
(M. Baulant presented her paper to the working party on the study
of consumption at the conference of French economic historians in
1973.)

So the old material constraints, tightly enclosing the growth of
our national Caliban, were cracking under the strain. At the same
time, foundations were being laid for an ideological revolution.
This makes it easier to explain the paradoxes of the militant peasantry which formed the chorus of a non-silent minority in the 1780s.
For the first time, this peasantry was entertaining expectations
relating to equality and the abolition of certain privileges. But at the
same time, it was making a defiant and triumphant last stand for the
defence of small property, against the progress of capitalist production, as represented in the countryside by the noble estates and the
"reactionary" aristocracy. And after all, this twin battle-cry of the
poverty-stricken French peasant had its own logic.

*

By way of conclusion, I should have liked to speak, once more, of
the immense debt which we as historians owe to the social sciences,
in the definition of our object of study. Given lack of time, I shall
instead aim to clear up a misunderstanding. Until the last century,
knowledge was based essentially on the dialogue between two
cultures: the exact sciences and the humanities—mathematics versus intuition, the "spirit of geometry" and the "spirit of discern-
ment". History, from Thucydides to Michelet, was of course included in the humanities. And then along came the "third culture",
unobtrusively at first, but soon becoming visible to all: the social
sciences. For a long time, they coexisted quite cheerfully with the
historian: in the line running from Marx to Weber, Durkheim and
Freud, there was a constant exchange of concepts and much crossing of frontiers between the two. More recently, however, old
Chronos came under attack. The social sciences, wishing to preserve a reputation for hardness and purity, began to operate a

closed shop against history, which was accused of being a "soft"science. The attack was characterized by a great deal of ignorance and not a little gall on the part of the attackers, who affected to forget that since Bloch, Braudel and Larousse, history too had undergone a scientific transformation. Clio had stolen the clothes of the social sciences while they were bathing, and they had never noticed their nakedness. Today at any rate, the move to exclude history seems to be almost over, since it is becoming clear that it has no future. Everyone has eventually bowed to the obvious: it is no more possible to build up a human science without the extra dimension of the past, than it is to study astrophysics without knowing the ages of the stars or galaxies. History was, for a few decades of semi-disgrace, the Cinderella of the social sciences, but it has now been restored to its rightful place. Indeed, it now appears to have chosen just the right moment to withdraw, refusing to become a narcissistic mental activity, rotting away in self-absorption and self-congratulation; while the death of history was being loudly proclaimed in certain quarters, it had simply gone through the looking-glass, in search not of its own reflection, but of a new world.

2

A Concept: The Unification of the Globe by Disease (Fourteenth to Seventeenth Centuries)[1]

THE extraordinary upsurge of interest in the environment, and concern about pollution that characterizes contemporary civilisation, has had the beneficial effect—as often happens—of obliging historians to rethink their ideas on certain important aspects of the past, in terms of present-day preoccupations. But when we look back from the twentieth century to the sixteenth, such "rethinking" requires a total change of perspective, indeed of direction. Despite its progress, for good or ill, towards an antiseptic or aseptic environment, our own civilisation is confronted even now occasionally, sometimes more urgently than in the past, with dangerous outbreaks of infection by virus or germ caused by increased facilities for contacts and transport. Various influenza viruses, for example, from Hong Kong or elsewhere, have already circled the world more than once, thanks to jet airliners carrying infected passengers. Cholera too, though not as terrifying a disease as it was in the nineteenth century, has recently made the leap from the poverty-stricken areas of Asia and Black Africa to the summer tourists in the Mediterranean. But the fact remains that the great environmental problems of the day have more to do with chemicals than with microbes. Our major worries are carbon monoxide, lead in exhaust fumes, and pesticides. There is universal agreement that poison-laden zones are affecting the atmosphere in our cities, the water in our rivers, and the biosphere as a whole. The fear of epidemics, rightly or wrongly, has no place among the major anxieties of the anti-pollution campaigners, despite the very real threat to the health of mankind from the ever-present possibility of diseases being spread by supersonic travel.

Under the economic regimes of ancient or very ancient civilisations, the situation was of course quite different; the relatively simple technologies of those times generated few, if any, pollutant by-products. On the other hand, the earliest forms of growth in the medieval to "modern" era—from the eleventh to the sixteenth century—put the accent very firmly on demography, ground clearance, urbanization, trade, colonization, "Crusades", military campaigns, and conquests. The wealth of contacts thus established carried enormous risks of microbial pollution: to say so is, of course, to state the obvious. I should therefore like to step over the hallowed threshold of first truths and put forward the following concept, applied to a precise period of history, and borrowed, with some modification and extension, from Woodrow Borah: the concept of *the unification of the globe by disease* between the fourteenth and the seventeenth century. This expression, as I shall attempt to show, is much more than a mere formula. It seeks to regroup and incorporate, within a complex but unique ensemble, phenomena apparently very diverse: on one hand, the plague of 1348 in Western Europe with its lethal sequels of the fourteenth, fifteenth and sixteenth centuries; and on the other, the depopulation, amounting to genocide by disease, of the native peoples of the New World during the sixteenth century and afterwards. Such a concept has the added interest, it seems to me, of focussing attention on the most severe and traumatic situations experienced to date by the human populations of America and Eurasia during the second millenium.

★

When I refer to the unification of the globe by disease between the fourteenth and the sixteenth century (from now on for the sake of brevity I shall simply call it "the unification"), I do not of course mean that the process began at midnight on January 1, 1300. Large-scale epidemics were in fact astir and on the move well before that date, though their radius of activity was less extensive than it later became: without going back all the way to the plague of Athens, there was, for example, the great epidemic of the sixth century, which has been studied by J. N. Biraben and Jacques Le Goff.[2]

Nor would I wish to suggest that the process of "unification" ended in the year 1600—or even in 1700: the spread of cholera in the nineteenth century amply demonstrates the absurdity of such a claim. In the course of this essay my aim is simply to draw attention to the existence of a paroxysm: when what might be called global unification by disease or, to put it another way, the creation—first in Eurasia and subsequently in the Atlantic area—of a "common market" of microbes, passed through a particularly intense, rapid, dramatic, one might even say apocalyptic phase, during the period roughly 1300–1600.

The sacrifice of human lives resulting from the global spread of pathogenic agents during these three centuries has had no parallel before or since.

"UNIFICATION" BY PLAGUE

I shall concentrate, to begin with at least, on certain specific categories of disease. As the reader will know, it is not at all easy to identify the illnesses of the past. The parish records which are by far the richest source of information on *ancien régime* demography, can alas tell us nothing. Fortunately, the history of disease is open to investigation with the help of other, often very precise, sources (medical inquests, chronicles, military archives, etc.).[3] Such sources tell us a great deal about deficiency diseases—goitre in mountainous areas, for example—which of course fall outside the scope of this essay. But they are equally informative on run-of-the-mill infectious diseases as they tended to be grouped in former times: small-pox, typhoid, typhus, dysentery, malaria in marshy zones, etc. For the moment, I shall however leave the run-of-the-mill on one side and concentrate first on a bacterial disease: bubonic plague.

It has become commonplace to suggest that plague was one of the inevitable harmful by-products of the expansion in human numbers and activities in the ancient continent during the Middle Ages. But a number of different writers have gone beyond the original, rather too simple formulations and have vigorously explored, developed and refined this idea.[4] With this in mind, I shall begin with the point of origin: the breeding-grounds from which the plague spread to produce one of the major episodes in the unification of the globe by disease. Of the three "natural" varieties of the plague bacillus,[5] the first, *Pasteurella pestis orientalis*, took root in Manchuria and the eastern seaboard of China. "It was responsible for the most recent outbreak of plague, one which spread from China at the end of the nineteenth century." It is not therefore of direct interest to this essay in which our concern is with an earlier period of history. The two other varieties of the "germ" are, however, central to our purpose: *Pasteurella pestis antiqua* which became endemic to various groups of rodents and fleas around the great lakes of Africa, and *Pasteurella pestis medievalis* (the name is a complete story in itself) which established itself in similar conditions in central Asia.

The world-wide ecology of plague ultimately concerns a complex relationship between man and bacillus, a relationship which relies upon the harmonious functioning of a *ménage à quatre* (rat, flea, bacillus, man), or as some writers suggest, of a *ménage à trois* (flea, bacillus, man). The very existence and geographical diffusion of *"ménages"* of this type inevitably leads in the long term to friction and incompatibility of temperament; the "ecological framework" of this cohabitation—which often ends in the death of the three or four partners—is very limited. The flea, for example, needs certain strict conditions of temperature and humidity before it can breed. Such conditions are not always met by man's changing habits, for instance in the matter of heating his houses in winter. For all these reasons, the plague complex with its multiple *dramatis personae* remained endemic in central Africa and central Asia; but in Europe, where it made only sporadic appearances, it proved relatively unstable: in its two visitations (sixth/seventh century and fourteenth/seventeenth century) it never lasted more than two or three hundred years.

Central to these travelling complexes which, at the time of the "unification", made it possible for plague to become established, is of course the flea—and in the first place the rat-flea: bites of an infected flea introduce bacteria into the rat's bloodstream and produce plague buboes in the groin. But the flea can also live on humans and with its bite transfer the plague bacillus to man. It is however repelled by the smell of olive-oil which is therefore an instant prophylactic. It is also driven away by the smell of horses and especially male goats (the role of these animals as counter-agents to the plague was well known very early on: the squire of Gouberville, in the middle of the sixteenth century, thoughtfully presented his sister with a billy-goat when a plague epidemic broke out in her village[6]). The ordinary human flea, *Pulex irritans*, can also pass the bacillus directly from man to man without the intermediary of the rat. (There are, finally, other varieties of ectoparasites associated exclusively with a single species of mammal, dog-fleas for example; but precisely because they are found only on dogs these creatures have had nothing to do with the outbreaks of plague in Eurasia during the past two thousand years.)

With this ecological basis established, the data on the pollution and contacts that account for the spreading of plagues have been researched by two schools of thought: the "rat school" led by the English historian, J.F.D. Shrewsbury, and the "flea school", represented by the Frenchman J.N. Biraben.[7]

Shrewsbury's important book, *A History of Bubonic Plague in the British Isles*, offers the reader what amounts to a complete treatise on the rat, including—much to our purpose—the story of its role in spreading infection and disease all over the globe. Not that Shrewsbury imputes every kind of plague to the rat. He treats pulmonary, or pneumonic plague, accompanied by fits of coughing and spitting of blood, as quite a separate problem when it crops up. This lung disease, "the sickness that spreads terror", is transmitted directly from man to man by the breath and infected spittle; rats play no part in the process. But setting aside this bronchopulmonary form of plague (incidentally an extremely dangerous one), Shrewsbury is at pains to express most forcefully his belief in the crucial role played by the rat in the dissemination of plague. Indeed, if we are to believe him, rats can transfer contagion directly, from one to the other, by cannibalism. But most importantly, the epidemic—or rather, the epizootic—disease induces in *Rattus Rattus* a lethal form of septicaemia: the rat-flea, gorging itself on this poisoned blood, clogs its stomach with a plug composed completely of the bacilli of *Pasteurella pestis*; the obstruction prevents it ingesting its food so the famished flea becomes enraged and bites the skin of any creature it lights upon, animal or human. Thus the epizootic disease of the rat becomes the epidemic of plague in man.

All these phenomena soon become associated with the urbanization and demographic expansion occurring in many places during the period immediately preceding or introducing the plague-ridden phase of the Middle Ages. Fleas hidden away in old rags and blankets carted about by the small traders and pedlars of the time could become very hungry and aggressive from their failure to find adequate sustenance in the cloth bundles that formed their temporary homes. And, in medieval times, the huts and hovels of the poor in both town and country, constituted an ideal habitat for rats and fleas: fleas lodged themselves in the daub and wattle walls, rats in the thatched roofs. The houses of the rich, on the other hand, offered a better defence against such infestations, for stone walls are no sanctuaries for ectoparasites, and an upper floor acts as a barrier between the rats in the roof and attic and the human family living on the ground floor.

From such observations Shrewsbury moves on to a detailed history of rodents and parasites as a by-product, so to speak, of human activity which modified the animal environment. The chief culprit, according to *A History of Bubonic Plague*, is the black rat, *Rattus Rattus*. With its seventeen varieties of fleas, two of which (and in particular *Xenopsylla cheopis*) "are capable of acting as vectors of plague", *Rattus Rattus* is apparently a comparatively timid creature and not much of a fighter: hence its inferiority, from the eighteenth century on, to the more aggressive brown or Norwegian rat, *Rattus norvegicus*. Furthermore, the black rat is a poor swimmer; in northern latitudes it lives in buildings, where it eats its way through stocks of grain. Despite its indifferent performance as a swimmer, it used to go aboard the wooden ships of the old days, putting its remarkable climbing skills to good use in their hulls and timbers (hence the ease and the great range of its travels, in the Mediterranean for example). *Rattus Rattus*, it must be said, is not naturally indigenous to Europe: it was able to spread there only because of the high density of human settlement, with closely-grouped houses, silos, granaries and urban habitats in general. (This brings us back to the original question of environmental pollution by animal.) In his study of England, Shrewsbury has consulted a varied collection of documents and done his best to establish an accurate chronology of the spread of *Rattus Rattus*. It seems to have been comparatively rare in the British Isles before the arrival of William the Conqueror, or shall we say (since it is hardly likely that the rats waited until the very day of the Norman Conquest to cross the Channel), before the year 1000. The manuscript of the *Book of Kells*, however, which dates from an undetermined period between the sixth and the ninth century, shows us "two rats nibbling the Eucharistic bread under the eyes of a pair of cats". In 1187, "large mice, popularly called rats" had been "expelled from the district of Ferns in Leinster by the curse of Bishop Yvor, whose books they had gnawed".[8] By the thirteenth century, still in Britain, *Rattus Rattus* had apparently gained the upper hand: its presence in London is vouched for in a local manuscript referring to "two black rats hanging a cat". Mention of the purchase of rat-traps and rat-poisons is more frequent now, in both account-books and literary texts. It is of course possible to criticize Shrewsbury's chronology and to point out that it uses material from illustrations which may themselves bear little relation to the actual history of the cohabitation of rat and man. Be that as it may, according to Shrewsbury, the introduction in medieval times of the rat into Great Britain amounted to the establishment of an epizootic infrastrucure, providing a base from which the plague of 1348–9 and later, was to take off. It is possible to explain along similar lines certain aspects of the outbreak of plague in the sixth century.[9] This affected southern Gaul, an area already urbanized to some extent and widely colonized by rats, but spared lands to the north of the Loire, which perhaps because of the scattered nature of human settlement in those parts, were not as yet densely inhabited by *Rattus Rattus*. England, being free of rats, was, *a fortiori*, spared this early medieval plague. One might argue that this was one of the causes of the economic, demographic and indeed political and military advance of the north, from the seventh century on. Charlemagne owed his triumph, one might say, to an absence of rats![10]

To return to fourteenth-century Britain: Shrewsbury seeks to establish his entire theory of plague on the geography of rat infestation. In the 1340s, the densely populated and industrious England, which was also to become the England of plagues and epidemics, lay "south-east of a line from Exeter to York"; a privileged zone indeed, but one that was to pay dearly for its privilege!

In this England which, including Wales, had a population of approximately four million in 1300–30,[11] it was indeed south and east of that line that the great majority of towns of more than 5,000 inhabitants were situated. According to Shrewsbury's theory, this figure of 5,000 constituted the lowest possible basis upon which rats could breed in sufficiently large numbers to maintain an epizootic murine plague, capable in turn of contaminating human populations in epidemic proportions; the spread of plague in humans, says Shrewsbury, calls for a constant traffic of infected fleas from man to rat and back again, if the pestilence is to maintain its fullest momentum. In the south, too, lay some of the most prosperous and most densely populated rural areas; here were the major networks of roads for the transport of grain, hay, straw, and above all, wool, providing opportunities for rats to ride the carts from town to town, while the traders in their flea-ridden furs also played their part in transporting the parasites who were the chief propagators of the bacillus. Here too were the fairs, and the great shrines such as Canterbury cathedral, visited by crowds of pious pilgrims in conditions of dangerous and verminous promiscuity. Turning once more to the central fact of urbanization, though still somewhat undeveloped in fourteenth-century England, it was yet again south of the York-Exeter line that town houses were to be found in sufficiently large numbers, stacked and huddled together, for the plague to be able to spread from one household to another. At the same time, these houses were still primitive enough in construction (wattle and daub, with thatched roofs) to support colonies of rats and fleas: rats in the thatch, fleas in the mud walls. The town houses of more modern times, which replaced these old hovels, were built of brick, baked in either wood or coal furnaces; consequently they offered a better defence against vermin, their brick and stone presenting a daunting obstacle to feats of burrowing or climbing. And it was again south of the "York-Exeter line" that there lay, in the Middle Ages as in the eighteenth century, those areas of England with the best grain farmlands and the highest yields of corn,[12] the rat's favourite food. It was in the south-east of Great Britain, broadly speaking then, that human settlement of both urban and agricultural areas created a habitat for *Rattus Rattus*, man's fellow food-consumer and privileged form of vermin. So it was entirely logical that the great English plague that broke out in the fourteenth century should establish itself in this part of the country. The regions situated to the north and west of this famous line, on the other hand, where people were fewer, urbanization less highly developed and rural settlement more scattered, provided nothing like so good a breeding-ground for this devastating plague.

★

Such then is Shrewsbury's theory, with the rat as chief culprit. The French expert on plague, J.N. Biraben does not challenge the Englishman's thesis as such, but his own research has led him to lay greater stress, as far as the West is concerned, on the independent role of the flea. The number of historic plagues in Europe in which the rat has played any significant part, have actually been very few.

It is true that in his novel *La Peste*, (*The Plague*), set in Oran, Albert Camus mentions the corpse of a rat. But this was in the Maghreb, and in any case, he may well have been influenced, if only

indirectly, by the work of Yersin who, commenting on conditions in
the Far East, refers to "the role of the murine epizootic preceding
and accompanying the human epizootic".[13] Did some popular version of Yersin's research set Camus on the wrong track? It is quite
possible. For as far as genuinely historical evidence is concerned,
references to "murine" plague are very rare and we never glimpse
so much as the tail of a rat in the corpse-countings of the chroniclers.
There is one text, however, which seems to point in that direction:
in 1348–9, the Greek historian Nicephore Gregoras[14] noted that
"the plague invaded the islands of the Aegean; it attacked the
inhabitants of Rhodes and Cyprus alike . . . ; dogs, horses, and *rats
in the houses* died". One would give a great deal to lay hands on a
few more texts of this kind in the West. The fact is there are scarcely
any to be found. This gap in the archives (but is one justified in
arguing *a silentio*?) led Biraben to draw attention to the special role
of the human flea (*Pulex irritans*) as the direct carrier of plague from
man to man without the intermediary of the rat.

With this in mind, Biraben suggests two possible theories to
account for the ways in which the plague may (or may not) have
spread:[15]

1. "In areas where human ectoparasitism is rare (this is the case in
many tropical countries where the natives wear very little clothing),
the incidence of plague is sporadic and infrequent". "Such cases as
do occur [in X or Y village] are the result of accidental bites by
rat-fleas (*Xenopsylla cheopis*) which have abandoned dead rats".

2. "If, on the contrary (as in the case of the clothed, indeed
heavily clothed, populations of the *anciens régimes* of the past) flea
infestation of the human body is common, epidemics on a vast scale
may be unleashed, their favoured breeding-ground being every sort
of place where people gather in crowds—town centres, fairs,
armies, processions," and also the main roads, thronged with traders and soldiers on the march; such were the factors, it would seem,
that on a number of occasions during the sixth century and certainly
during the fourteenth century and later, led to the pollution of
Eurafrica and subsequently of Eurasia.

It is no easy matter (for a historian who is not himself a specialist
in medical history) to decide between Shrewsbury and Biraben. In
the pages that follow, therefore, I shall take into consideration the
various possibilities—often tending towards the same conclusion—
that the two theories suggest.

A PRECEDENT: THE SIXTH CENTURY PLAGUE[16]

Shrewsbury or Biraben, flea-infested rats or fleas alone, Yersin's
bacillus was not an entirely new visitor to Europe. Eight hundred
years before 1348, the "plague of the early Middle Ages" had
reached Gaul in 543 A.D., ushering in a series of catastrophic
epidemics which were to continue until at least 760 A.D. It then
died out, thus proving, for the first time, what the later, comparatively short-lived epidemic cycle (fourteenth-eighteenth century)
was to demonstrate quite emphatically: namely, that plague is not
spontaneously persistent in the countries of Western Europe.[17] Is
this incapacity to establish itself definitively in our part of the world
attributable to the complex conditions[18] of ecological equilibrium
necessary for the maintenance of the *ménage à trois* (rat, flea,
bacillus), on the cohesion of which the persistence of an epidemic in
one locality depends? Whatever the explanation, it is a fact that in
the course of the early Middle Ages, as in the later medieval and
modern eras, plague tended, after a few centuries of repeated
outbreaks, to die out in the West and withdraw to African and
Asian bases: with the possibility of launching another lightning
offensive some eight hundred years later.

It is also worth noting—and this relates to our ecological and
environmental problem—that a map of the plague in the sixth to
eighth century would correspond, broadly speaking, to the geography of the urbanization, demography and trade networks of Gaul
and the West in the early Middle Ages. Originating in Pelusium in
Egypt, the plague made its way west through the Mediterranean to
those classic reception centres for plague, the cities of Marseilles
and Narbonne. It then moved on into the northern parts of Gaul, at
the limits of its expansion reaching Trier in 542, the middle reaches
of the Loire in 560, the middle reaches of the Rhône and the region
of Albi in about 580. As Biraben and Le Goff put it: "the zones of
activity of this early-medieval plague reveal some of the fundamental features of western Europe during the Dark Ages of the
sixth and seventh centuries. The maintenance of an urban life-style
favourable to the wider dissemination of epidemic disease; the
continuance of trade-links between Alexandria, Byzantium, Africa
and Genoa, Marseilles, Narbonne—gateways to the plagues since
they were gateways to the East (Venice and Marseilles were to
continue to pay the price on into the seventeenth and eighteenth

centuries); the importance of river communications, particularly the Rhône-Saône axis; all of these features show up in the geography of the epidemics. The northern limits of the plague—the Loire, the Marne, the Rhine, the Alps—correspond to the frontier enclosing the area of communication and urbanization, and to the terminal points of the oriental trade-routes."

Now the plague of 1348, too, eventually encountered just such structural frontiers as its predecessor in the days of Justinian. The sixth century blazed the trail, so to speak, for the fourteenth. But as a result of developments that had taken place during the intervening centuries, the northern and eastern limits were much wider in 1348 than they had been in 542. The contagion on this occasion spread far beyond the Trier-Rheims-Tours-Agen line which had offered a solid barrier to any further advance in the age of Theodebert and Chilperic. In 1348–50 this *cordon sanitaire* of former days, which incidentally owed nothing to the conscious efforts of the authorities, broke down all along the line: from south to north, the whole of France and the area corresponding to all of ancient Gaul (with certain notable exceptions in both cases) crumbled before the onslaught of the bacilli. And this time too the vast human settlements of England, Germany and Scandinavia, which the sixth century plague had spared or barely touched,[19] fell victim to the terrible onslaughts of the Black Death[20] as the Middle Ages waned.

The differences in the radius of expansion of the two plagues demonstrate all the more forcefully the logical similarities between the two cases. On both occasions (sixth century and fourteenth century), the outermost waves broke and died on those imaginary yet perfectly real shores, marking the extreme limits reached by demographic expansion, by a dense and much-used system of roads, and by the networks of towns.

The Merovingian plague, as we have seen, exhausted itself and expired when it met the great belts of forests barring its progress towards the plains and plateaux of the Paris basin. The plague of 1348–9, however, surged on in full flood to the now hedgeless fields of Normandy and the open countryside around London; and on it went, further still, to Scotland in the north and the Elbe in the east without encountering an obstacle of any consequence. The great ground-clearances of the centuries after the year 1000 had in fact paved the way for it by improving communications, opening up isolated areas, felling the forest barriers, and by creating new centres of population. Both the open clearings and the new or expanding towns now became infested by various species of disease-bearing rats: all of them, whether they were country rats preying on the harvest, or town rats living off refuse, were flea-ridden.[21] And when the time was ripe, they turned into sowers of pestilence of a kind the healthy, unpolluted Merovingian woodlands had never known.

Beyond the Oder and the mountains of Bohemia, (well outside the area discussed here) the picture is not so straightforward. Here, in 1349 and 1350, the dense forests and semi-deserts, comparatively empty of villages and cornfields, slowed down the onward march of the army of rats, fleas, and men afflicted by the plague. As a result, the advance of the twin fronts of plague, bubonic and pulmonary, was to some extent checked. The factors that in the sixth century had limited the spread of the catastrophe beyond the Loire were therefore found at work again in the fourteenth century: this time in areas further to the north and especially the north-east, well beyond the Germanic population centres which had greatly increased in size in the interval, and which because of their earlier scattered nature had been spared by the first, Merovingian outbreak of plague. It was only when it reached the Slav lands, as Frantisek Graus has shown, that the 1348–50 plague finally encountered the conditions of sparse human settlement that were henceforth to check its progress, without however, succeeding in halting it altogether.[22]

THE EURASIATIC "SHORT-CIRCUIT" OF THE FOURTEENTH CENTURY

A comparative study of the medieval plague in France and the West thus tends in the first place to stress the importance of multiplicity of contacts as a condition for the occurrence of catastrophe. An analysis of this type, which helps us to understand the various ways in which the plagues spread, is even more useful when our aim is to solve the fundamentally important problem of origins with which we shall be concerned in the pages that follow. For, an explanation of the arrival of plague in Europe is to be sought in the establishment, long before the germ itself appeared in Italy or southern France, of a number of trade routes which became "short-circuits" and excellent conductors of disease between Eurasia and the Mediterranean.

At this point, if we are to understand the manner in which a process of crucial importance to mankind was triggered off, I must give a brief outline of the establishment of the conditions that set the scene for disaster. Without it, some of the significance of this essay on pollution-by-microbe would be lost.

The sixth century plague—and also, so it is said, the plagues of antiquity—probably came originally from the great lakes of Africa.[23] It was certainly around their shores that the natural variety of Yersin's bacillus, *Pasteurella pestis antiqua*, was widespread, and this is the germ thought to have infected the Merovingian population. Having travelled from the great lakes and Ethiopia as far as Egypt and the delta port of Pelusium, via the Red Sea or possibly the Nile Valley, the Eyptian plague of 541–2 eventually made its way in the natural course of events to all the great Mediterranean cities, from Alexandria to Marseilles. And then, in successive waves of persistent contamination, it gradually infected the whole of southern Gaul over a period of two centuries.

The nature of the 1348 pandemic suggests a break with this distant past and the establishment of very different bacillus-itineraries. For this plague came not from the Red Sea, but from the Black Sea, not from Pelusium in Egypt, but by way of Caffa in the Crimea, having originated far beyond this Genoese counting-house, in the depths of Tartary and the Nestorian communities of central Asia.

In the heart of the Asiatic continent there lived then, and still lives now, widely disseminated, another natural strain of *Pasteurella pestis*, classified in commemoration of its most remarkable accomplishment, as *medievalis*.[24] Medical specialists have described[25] the various species of animals that ferry the carrier-fleas of *Pasteurella pestis medievalis* from both sides of the Urals across immense distances. They are: *tarabagans*, or giant marmots from Manchuria, Mongolia, Russian Turkestan and Transbaikalia (Siberia); little *spermophiles* (ground squirrels)[26] or *susliks*, a species resembling tiny marmots, whose habitat is southeast Russia and whose incredibly hardy fleas can survive temperatures of $-25°C$, and can fast for up to ten months on a meal or two of blood.[27] Other storehouses of the bacilli, through the intermediary of parasites, are colonies of *gerbils*, or desert rats, from southeast Russia, Iranian Kurdestan and regions beyond the Caspian Sea. When they die in

their underground burrows, their fleas and the bacilli survive on
their dead bodies, waiting to pass on the disease, sooner or later, to
human beings. Baltazard, and after him Biraben, both refer to
these lethal chambers and their favourable micro-climates in which
the germs hibernate. When summer returns, they infect other gerbils who, thinking they have struck it lucky, move in as squatters
into the former homes of their deceased fellow-creatures; "meanwhile, other rodents may have moved into the burrow and serve as
blood donors to fleas, thus ensuring the survival of these infected
parasites".[28]

The distant equivalent of these species of Asiatic marmots and
gerbils, according to Shrewsbury's theory at any rate, were the
great sedentary colonies of black rats that had established themselves in Europe: these creatures, like that other rodent, the rabbit,
had also multiplied prolifically since the tenth century so that their
numbers had increased prodigiously in the open spaces created by
the great ground-clearances. Urbanization and the demographic
"take-off" had swollen their numbers immeasurably in the towns,
villages and ports where they prospered uninhibitedly and without
competition until their partial extermination by the brown rats in
the eighteenth and nineteenth centuries. Between these two teem-
ing populations of rodents, the Asiatic and the European, history
from 1330–50 onward was to throw an unforeseen bridge of
fraternal mortality. The staging-posts of this plague-bearing short-
circuit, destined to unite the West and the East in the same fate, had
gradually been placed in position beforehand by two groups of
"sorcerer's apprentices": the builders of the Mongol empire and
the bazaar merchants of the silk caravans. Both became the unwitting agents of a process of international pollution.

How did this happen? Between 1200 and 1260 the Mongols,
under Genghis Khan and his successors,[29] achieved the unification
of Asia and a part of Europe, from China to Russia; they were thus
opening the way to the microbial integration of the ancient world on
both sides of the Urals and the Caspian Sea, and setting up a
common market of bacilli.

Very quickly, trade-routes were established across these wide
open spaces where the frontiers had been removed. In about 1266,
the Genoese founded the colony of Caffa on the southeast coast of
the Crimea. The *pax mongolica*[30] enabled the pioneers of this new
trading-post[31] to make safe and regular use of a route which "for the
first time in history enjoyed absolute security"[32]—an unthinkable

situation before the unification and pacification of central Asia by the forces of Genghis Khan. This new safe route[33] carried the Mediterranean and Black Sea trade of Genoese merchants all the way to the Far East. It crossed the Sea of Azov from Caffa to Tana at the mouth of the Don, after which it bore the Genoese traders on their seemingly interminable journey by ox-cart and then by camel, donkey and mule, and by boat when they came to the rivers and the Caspian Sea, into the heart of China,[34] the source of silk. This route was in constant use in those two fatal decades, the 1330s and 1340s, the very time it was described by Francesco Pegolotti in his book *Pratica della Mercatura*. It was a successful route swarming with men and convoys ever moving to and fro, since Chinese silks brought this way to the bazaars of Constantinople cost much less than if they had come in the traditional manner along the ancient routes travellers took before the establishment of this great Genoa-Mongolia road.[35] But this new trail, the creation of the thirteenth-century spirit of invention, brought both good and ill in its wake. Indeed the royal road of Chinese silks of the first half of the fourteenth century seems, from 1338 onward, to have become the plague-trail of contagion.

New light was thrown on this crucial itinerary by an archaeological dig towards the end of the last century. In 1885, the Russian archaeologist Chwolson[36] was engaged in excavating the remains of some ancient Nestorian cemeteries near Lake Issuk-Kul in the district of Semiryechensk at the extreme eastern corner of Kirghizistan. This region which, as we now know, was situated at the epicentre of one of the original sources of the plague, was also, in an entirely different context, towards the end of the Middle Ages, an important focus of Nestorian propaganda. In the course of his excavations, Chwolson uncovered three tombstones on which contemporary epitaphs bore witness to the fact that the persons buried beneath them had died of the plague in 1338–9. Furthermore, the discovery of a whole row of graves of similar date was proof that the death-rate for the two years (1338–9) had been extremely high. "It is certain therefore", writes Pollitzer[37] "that plague was conspicuous in central Asia a few years before the Crimean ports became infected (Caffa, 1346), and the disease was carried from there by ship to Europe".

So, if Pollitzer is right, the Mongolian road played a prominent part in the story. Semiryechensk, Przevalsky and Lake Issuk-Kul, the first *known* cradles of the plague, are situated near the approaches to the Tian-Chan mountains, not far from the little towns of Almaligh and Kachgar, each of which was an important staging-post on the two alternative branches of the Genoese route from Caffa to the hinterland of Asia and from there on into China.[38] That the plague-germs should have swept through this region in ‚1338, the first known zone of infection, and then spread westward by flea-hops from victim to victim along the great axis of the Turcoman caravans, the Mongol armies and the Italian merchants, is surely a plausible hypothesis, consistent with all that we have learnt, with the passage of time, of the regular trajectories of the plagues as they spread on their lethal way.[39]

We know what followed: how the contagion was conveyed in 1346 by plague-stricken soldiers of a Tartar army to the gates of Tana and Caffa, which lay at the Crimean terminus of the China-Genoa road. The Tartars laid siege to Caffa and used catapults to hurl a number of diseased corpses over the city walls, with the result that the fatal infection spread to the Italian defenders of this Black Sea port; alternatively, a number of infected rats may have made their way into the town by burrowing under the gates. At all events, healthy or sick, those who survived the siege embarked on the last remaining ships and made their escape to Byzantium, Genoa, Venice and Marseilles, contaminating in turn these great cities and, through them, the whole of the West.[40]

There now exists a whole series of important research studies on the progress of plague in western Europe, relating to Italy, Catalonia, England, Portugal and the Germanic countries. In France, while several excellent monographs have shed light on certain regional or local epidemics, there is still a need for some kind of national synthesis. In the next few pages, therefore, I shall attempt to draw up a balance-sheet of outbreaks of plague in France as a whole. This is no more than a preliminary sketch and cannot claim to replace the major synthesis which we still await. I shall look principally at the quantitative and demographic aspects of the problem.

★

By November 1347, then, or at latest by January 1348, the plague had reached Marseilles (by way of a Genoese cargo boat from the

Crimea?). The Bishop of Marseilles died of it, as did all his canons, so it is said, together with countless numbers of mendicant friars. Off the Canebière, phantom ships, their crews all dead, drifted on the tide, tossed by the waves; no one was interested in the precious merchandise still in their holds.[41]

This Provençal plague hit not only sea-ports and towns but the surrounding countryside as well. And it also rapidly gained ground, spreading within months to towns and rural communities in Languedoc, to the crowded mountain settlements of Dauphiné and on into the villages and townships of Forez and Burgundy. It also rediscovered the route along the Rhône-Saône axis it had already followed once before, in the sixth century pandemic. In Provence, in town and village alike, the plague assumed apocalyptic dimensions. The statistics on households all tell the same story:[42] in the district of Moutiers where we have the population figures for five localities, the number of households fell by 75.4 per cent between 1345 and 1354; the town of Grasse lost 45.7 per cent of its households between 1341 and 1351; three village communities coming under the jurisdiction of Grasse experienced similar losses—a decline of 46.5 per cent between 1345 and 1352. In all, in ten localities, villages, and townships whose fate between 1345 and 1355—roughly the period of the Black Death—we are able to piece together, the number of households fell from 8,511 to 3,839, i.e., a drop of more than a half (− 54.9 per cent).

For thirty or so other villages and country towns for which we have the necessary documentary evidence, the starting date is a little earlier—about 1340—and the finishing date somewhat later—about 1365. In these cases, the demographic statistics cover at least two separate outbreaks of the plague, those of 1348 and of 1361, but without distinguishing between them. The total number of households in this sample fell from 7,860 (in about 1340) to 4,069 (in about 1365)—a drop of 48.2 per cent.[43]

In short, it seems reasonable (if reasonable is the right word to apply to so cruel an episode) to estimate, that by the end of the two first epidemics, those of 1348 and 1361, Provence had lost, at a low estimate, 40 per cent of its pre-plague population, the majority of deaths resulting from the first outbreak in 1348. How can we possibly account for this appalling catastrophe, the equivalent—*mutatis mutandis*—of a present-day medium-sized nuclear holocaust?

We find the answer to this question in the words of Guy de Chauliac, a brave eye-witness of the Provençal plague in Comtat:

The great death toll began in our case in the month of January [1348], and lasted for the space of seven months. It was of two kinds: the first lasted two months; with continuous fever and spitting of blood; and death occurred within three days. The second lasted for the whole of the remainder of the time, also with continuous fever, and with ulcers and boils in the extremities, principally under the arm-pits and in the groin; and death took place within five days. And [it] was of so great a contagion (especially when there was spitting of blood) that not only through living in the same house but merely through looking, one person caught it from the other.[44]

So there can be no question about it: the Comtat epidemic occurred in two distinct stages. During the first, winter stage (January-March 1348), pulmonary (or pneumonic) plague launched a devastating attack: it was characterized by fever, spitting of blood, ultra-rapid death causing wholesale slaughter; the infection was transmitted directly, person to person, by the breath (not simply by looking, as Chauliac—who was mistaken on this point—seemed to think). This pneumonic phase, it goes without saying, invests the events of 1348 in Provence with their own particular dimension of horror, never to be equalled in any subsequent period of time. On the other hand, the following five months of the spring and summer of 1348 were marked by outbreaks of bubonic plague only—and bubonic plague, highly dangerous though it may be, is less of a killer disease than its pulmonary counterpart. And looking to the future, it offered a warning of things to come, heralding as it did a type of epidemic that was to become common, for from the fourteenth century onwards, hundreds of outbreaks, for the most part bubonic only, with a small percentage of pulmonary complications, were to recur in Provence and elsewhere in the West in the course of the plague-ridden era between 1348 and 1720.

*

The question left unanswered by the events and documents of Provence in 1348 is easily defined, not so easily resolved. Why, in a word, did it ever happen? What caused this massive and complex

wave of plague, first pneumonic, then bubonic? What was it that set
in motion this uncontrolled bacteriological disaster producing a
demographical impact in the West which has so far had no equivalent in the last thousand years (and never will have, let us hope, in
the future)?

A question of this type[45] probably calls, first of all, for purely
epidemiological answers. Always supposing that historical and
medical science could provide them, which at present they cannot,
such answers would concern the changing patterns of behaviour of
the plague bacillus down the ages, the mutations it may have
undergone, and the competition it has encountered from other
types of bacteria; in a word, the changing pattern of infectious
diseases about which we know so little, save that it does indeed
exist, and that it has, to some extent, determined certain key-dates
in the demographical fluctuations of mankind. Since present-day
research is as yet incomplete, these purely biological factors still
constitute the concealed but crucial face of the Black Death. Other,
more superficial, aspects are comparatively better understood. As
such, they offer a useful approach, helping us to at least a partial
understanding of the different factors that led to the ultimate catastrophe.

Firstly, climate. In the Comtat in 1348, as in Manchuria in 1921,
the pulmonary or pneumonic form of plague was a winter phenomenon which disappeared at first signs of spring. Diseases that
attack the lungs are greatly affected by a rise in the temperature, be
it seasonal as in these two cases, or geographical (as in the instance
of Madagascar: the epidemics of plague on this large island were
bubonic on the coast, pulmonary in the cooler regions of the high
inland plateaux). The introduction of pulmonary plague to the
south of France during the disastrous winter of 1348 followed a
time-honoured pattern. Firstly, it must be emphasized that
pneumonic plague—*and not only the bubonic!*—may well have
sprung fully armed from the famous Genoese vessels responsible
for the introduction of the germs.[46] Secondly, the probability of the
disease spreading to the lungs in an area recently infected with
bubonic plague, as was the case in Provence in 1348, is always likely
in the winter season. Since respiratory complications and secondary
infections are more frequent and more serious between December
and March, as is only to be expected, it was sufficient in January

1348 for an inhabitant of Provence to contract a straightforward attack of bubonic plague, followed by septicemia, for the germ to settle upon the lungs, which are particularly vulnerable in the winter season. A single victim, or perhaps a few individuals, scattered here and there in several different places in Provence, would be enough to set up a chain reaction, and this, indeed, is what occurred. The first person to fall victim to this pulmonary form of plague was no doubt someone who had plenty of contacts (this was gregarious Provence). And he no doubt had a cough (because it was winter). With his breath and saliva droplets freely laced with germs, he must have bombarded his family, his friends, passers-by, his confessor, and his notary, and they in their turn passed on the infection to their nearest and dearest. From that moment on, a chain reaction set in, from which the only escape was isolation. But in these southern villages whose poverty-stricken inhabitants crowded together for comfort, solitude was the last thing their house-builders had thought about.

For such a sequence of events to have been set in motion there is no need to suppose that the winter of 1348/9 was particularly severe.[47] A normally keen winter, such as Languedoc and Provence still experience about every third year, would have been sufficient to launch the deadly cycle of pulmonary plague. Once on its way, it developed spontaneously through countless agents of contagion. Proof *a contrario* is that with the arrival of the milder temperatures of spring and the consequent decrease in coughs and colds, the respiratory organs became less vulnerable to attack: the plague in Provence, Chauliac records, at once ceased to be pulmonary and reverted to the simply bubonic.

*

Unpredictably, perhaps, social history has something to say on the question of assessing the effect of wintry conditions accompanied by a pneumonic epidemic. The coldness a person senses is not necessarily the same thing as the temperature shown on a thermometer; it also varies in inverse ratio to the effectiveness of heating and clothing. In this respect the inhabitants of Provence and the south of France generally in the fourteenth century were rather badly off. Without question, heating was pitifully inadequate in

Provence in the first part of the fourteenth century, when the forests had been ravaged[48] by the high concentrations of people, goats and sheep. In the trade records of the region, we find more references to staves needed for barrels, planks and beams for the building-sites and charcoal for the kitchen-stove[49] than we do to logs for fireplaces, which as yet scarcely existed, or if they did took the form of simple open hearths.[50] During the preceding decade, Marseilles (from where the plague was to spread in the January and February of 1348), was by no stretch of the imagination a sparsely populated city, but it was deprived and chilly in winter judging by the scanty deliveries of fire-logs. As for the average Provençal home, this too was quite inadequate (even measured by the undemanding norms of the fourteenth century) to protect its occupants from the cold. A few years ago, excavations were carried out in the now abandoned village of Rougiers which dates back to somewhere between 1200 and 1400.[51] The houses discovered by the archaeologist were no more than shacks with neither stairs nor chimneys, with uneven earth floors and smoky fireplaces hollowed out of the living rock, all set in a maze of narrow alley-ways where much of the social life of the village took place, so that the close crowding of the settlement was complemented by promiscuity. The 1348 epidemic was to deal harshly with the poor folk on this site—as in other parts of Provence, more than half the villagers were wiped out. Their fate is comparable, in fact, with that of the agricultural workers of Manchuria who fell victim in their thousands, in their chilly huts, to the pulmonary plague of the winter of 1920–1.[52]

The people of Provence then were poorly housed and poorly heated. Were they poorly clad as well? It seems quite likely. In Marseilles, the trade in leather and textiles of all kinds (from Languedoc, northern France and Flanders) had been in decline throughout the period from the 1260s to the 1340s.[53] True, the textile trade was more closely linked to the sea-borne commerce of the Mediterranean; the leather trade was rather more regional. Nevertheless, taken as a whole, the statistics we have for leather and textiles all tell the same story; they suggest that many of the natives of Provence in the fourteenth century were not only without adequate heating or comfort in their houses; they also lacked warm woollen clothing and stout boots for their feet. In 1348, a winter plague, *ipso facto* pneumonic, would have caught these unfortunate people unawares. They would provide ideal breeding-ground for the bacteria and for the chain reaction of pulmonary complications that followed; and they would be unlikely to survive the winter.

The broncho-pulmonary slaughter of that winter is not our only concern. We have also to account for the virulence of the bubonic outbreak that flared up in Provence and Languedoc in early spring 1348 just as the last flickers of the lung disease were dying out.

In this second stage, we must look to vermin, and to the promiscuity that favours the breeding of vermin, for one of its fundamental causes. Bubonic, septicemic plague is transmitted to man not only by parasites of the rat but also by the species of fleas that prey on man (see above). Thus it is not the relatively slow cycle— *rat-flea-man-flea-rat-man*, etc.—that we find, but a much speedier rotation of the bacteria—*man-flea-man*, *etc*.

What conditions did it take, in the spring and summer of 1348, to produce bubonic catastrophe on so vast a scale? In the first place, a certain degree of crowding, easy enough to find in Provence in 1348 as a result of population growth, the development of towns, especially the little country towns, and the proliferation of roads and trade-routes. In the second place, much depended on the degree of hygiene, or rather non-hygiene practised at that time. In the detailed account of the daily life of the people of southern France, to be found in the Inquisition registers compiled by Jacques Fournier in about 1320,[54] the only reference to bathing in the life of the ordinary village folk is to the hot mineral baths taken both by the lepers in Ax-les-Thermes, and by the parish priest of Montaillou on occasions when he turned up there hoping for good fortune . . . Not very much. To which we might add that the spread of bubonic septicemia, helped considerably by such inadequate attention to hygiene, may also, on occasion, have resulted from the locally prevalent practice of nit-picking! The southern French of the fourteenth century were much addicted to this form of warfare upon their parasites: one of the greatest proofs of affection that his mistresses—he had more than one— could show the *curé* of Montaillou, was to pick at his fleas as he lay upon a table or at a window-ledge, expounding some Cathar mystery or listing the charms of young girls as they went down the village street. This practice was so prevalent in Languedoc that one finger was specially assigned to it and given the name of "louser" (*"tuepoux"*).[55] Now of course, squashing parasites—bugs and fleas—in this way could be dangerous, for if the "squasher", male or female, happened to

have a scratch on his or her "louser", the bacilli of bubonic plague
(or typhus) of which the tiny creatures are carriers, could easily
enter the bloodstream.

To conclude this review of the possible or actual causes of
epidemics of the plague, perhaps we should also ask ourselves
whether, throughout the vast region known as the Midi, extending
from Toulon to Port-Vendres, or more broadly from Genoa to
Barcelona, deficiencies in the diet of the common people on the eve
of the Black Death weakened them, ruined their constitutions, and
so prepared the ground for the pulmonary epidemics? This
apparently plausible point of view is put forward by Pollitzer apropos of the plague in Manchuria.[56] He suggests that diet deficiencies
in both calories and vitamins may have cleared the way for the lung
infections that afflicted the poorer agricultural labouring population in and around Harbin in 1921. These diseases in their turn
prepared the ground for the pulmonary plague that carried off these
unfortunate people, month by month, throughout the winter.
Mutatis mutandis, one is tempted to apply this Manchurian model
retroactively to the Midi of Languedoc and Provence, which also,
between 1300 and 1348, suffered from repeated shortages of food
and from chronic poverty,[57] affecting not only the housing and
clothing of the poorer classes but also their diet. Honesty however
compels us to say that present-day specialists in the history and
epidemiology of the plague, Biraben and others for example, are
reluctant to accept the notion of malnutrition as a determining
factor in the pulmonary outbreaks. Without discounting completely
this "food deficiency" theory,[58] perhaps it would be better for the
moment to put it to one side. One day further documentary evidence may make it possible to take it down from the shelf to which
we provisionally consign it.

★

Despite these uncertainties, it seems clear that in Provence, as
elsewhere, in town or country, the Black Death was the outcome of
a culture of poverty, dirt and promiscuity. Poverty was reflected
both in housing and clothing (if not in diet) making all the more
cruel the bite of winter's cold; there was dirt from the filthy living
conditions and the fleas they harboured; and there was promiscuity
both on the international scale (via the great trade-routes between

Eurasia and the Mediterranean), and at local level (rising population, expansion of the towns and the larger villages, trade and
migrations of every kind). This triple "culture", the potential dangers of which were exposed by the hazards of a harsh winter, had
been slowly maturing over the centuries in the bright sunshine of
Provençal expansion. The problems of the early decades of the
fourteenth century, which were severely felt all round the Gulf of
Lions[59] had served to mitigate some of these features (e.g., the
decline of large-scale trade); but other characteristics of the
"plague culture" had emerged, stronger than ever, thanks to the
hardships of 1310–40. Foremost among these was poverty, as can be
ascertained from the repeated food shortages, the incessant pro-
tests of villagers (against usury and deflation),[60] and the low wages
of the farm-workers, gardeners and vine-dressers.[61] Everything in
1348 was ripe for the unleashing of a catastrophe: it might never
have happened, at least not on so cataclysmic a scale, if the accident
of a severe winter had not lent maximum strength to the onslaught
of the plague bacilli. Is it possible that the winter of 1347–8 was wet
as well as cold—a paradoxical combination of weather conditions,
rarely experienced in the south of France? Such a hypothesis would
no doubt help to explain the rapid spread of the broncho-
pulmonary diseases which furnished the appropriate breeding-
ground for the most virulent forms of the plague.

★

Beyond the Rhône and the High Alps, the mid-fourteenth-
century plague in northern France appears only as a mild and more
shadowy replica of the Provençal original. The shadowiness, to take
that first, stems from our ignorance of the relevant statistics. This
may disappear when some scholar does for other provinces what
Baratier has done for Provence: a mass count of households before
and after 1348. The mildness is a matter of historical fact: in its
travels from south to north, from one end of France to the other, the
plague seems to have lost some of its virulence. This progressive
weakening can, I think, be explained: in Provence the epidemic
occurred in the winter season; it was therefore pulmonary and as a
result devastating in its effect; the plague did not reach northern
France, on the other hand, until a little later, in the spring and
summer of 1348. Consequently it was the bubonic form that pre-

dominated here, and its impact, excruciating though it must have been, was more limited than in the south. If there has to be a plague, better the bubonic than the pulmonary. To confirm this theory of lesser evil, one has merely to follow the epidemic's progress from the south of France to the north.

At the point of departure, in lower Languedoc, just as in Provence, the pulmonary offensive was at its most severe; the death and destruction it caused here were overwhelming. The same was true of the other Mediterranean areas east of the Rhône. Towns like Castres and Albi lost some 55 per cent of their populations (but Toulouse only 30 per cent apparently). We know less of what the effect was in the country districts, either because there are no documents, or because the necessary research has not yet been carried out. But in the few Languedoc country towns for which we do have statistics the death toll was the same as in Provence: more than 50 per cent of the households, i.e., more than half those eligible for assemblies of electors, were sent to their family tombs or the communal grave as a result of a single outbreak (1348), or of two outbreaks (1348 and 1361). In Narbonne and the surrounding districts, the winter or "Lenten" plague of 1348, (in other words the pulmonary plague) carried off a quarter of the population, according to one witness; the bubonic plague that followed in the spring continued the massacre.[62] The Occitanians, whether from Languedoc, Provence or the Comtat, were completely defenceless against this winter pulmonary plague; they were a little less so against the bubonic: to draw out the poisonous buboes they employed the old wives' remedies of mountain peasants and applied poultices of boiled onions mashed together with figs, yeast and butter.[63] Agents of the King of England were accused of having introduced the evil and three other very significant categories of people were also singled out as scapegoats: Jews, nobles and lepers.[64]

Moving further north, however, towards the high plateaux of the Massif Central, the plague gradually lost some of its harmful potential. Mountain people are not, of course, immune to Yersin's bacillus simply by virtue of their place of birth—as we know from the experience of the *gavots* of the High Alps. These ragged and poverty-stricken peasants descended on Avignon in 1348 to earn good money burying the dead; but, writes one of the chroniclers, the ghoulish desperadoes did not survive to make old bones[65]: after one or two safely accomplished burials they too caught the infection and perished in their turn. The comparative immunity of the mountains, if indeed there is such a thing, derives therefore not from singularly blessed constitutions but rather from the particularities of the environment. This can be demonstrated by the examples of the Forez and Savoy mountains.

Moving up the Rhône valley, which seems to have played a vital role in the course of this north-bound pilgrimage, the plague reached Lyon in May 1348. From Lyon it exploded in every direction like a bomb, creating centres of infection to the west, east and north; in Forez, Savoy and Burgundy.

Once again, it was the big cities, and then, in descending order of size, the small towns that acted as distributors of disease. Lyon, where the plague first struck in late spring, transmitted the contamination over the mountain range between Beaujolais and the Cévennes to the Forez basin known as the "Little Limagne".[66] Feurs, the central market-town of this "Limagne", was the first place to succumb. Then, via Feurs, the villages on the rim of the basin were each contaminated in turn by bubonic plague during the summer of 1348. Gradually, from one settlement to the next, the epidemic spread out into the Soir mountains on the eastern borders of Forez: it crept on through these hills during the winter of 1348–9, reverting once more from its bubonic to its pulmonary form. In its final fling in this area, the plague reached up into the highest and least populated regions on the outermost rim of the basin, the Bois-Noirs and the Forez mountains. Here, taking its time, killing insidiously, the plague continued to exact its toll of deaths from the latter part of the winter of 1349 until November 1350.[67] But the highest and most isolated mountain areas, far from any highways and byways (Mount Pilatus, Mount Madeleine and other remote heights) were spared: they were quite untouched by the great epidemic wave, either in 1348 or in the years that followed.

So the plague fell like a meteorite into the centre of the Forez mountain region. The concentric circles marking the spread of its influence reached to the base of the mountains bordering the basin, and then progressively died away. The loss of life (in Forez mainly from bubonic plague) did not reach such enormous percentages as in Provence and Languedoc where the destruction was the result of pulmonary complications. The Forez in 1348 lost between a quarter and a third of its inhabitants, whereas only a few months earlier, the

Mediterranean provinces had lost a half or more in many places. And in the Forez mountain regions the percentage was even lower, with death claiming less than a fifth of the population.[68]

So in the Forez region in the mid-fourteenth century, only 20 to 33 per cent of the native population were sent to the tomb or the communal grave—a low figure indeed compared with the death-rates for the Marseilles and Montpellier regions. But it was enough to inspire, in both Forez and the Comtat, spontaneous outbreaks of mass flagellation in a panic-stricken and devout population, despite the opposition of the clergy. Several different southern texts describe these extraordinary events of 1348: barefoot, in sackcloth and ashes, groaning, tearing out their hair, the flagellants of the lowland regions lashed each other with sharp whips, believing that by so doing they were drawing upon themselves the scourge of the world, sent by God in the form of a plague, as a punishment on the human race for its sins.[69]

In Savoy, the plague seems to have struck in much the same manner as in Forez, in country villages and small towns alike. It is true that in 1348 fully half of the village people of Savoy seem to have disappeared from the limited area of the province for which we have documentary evidence. At Saint-Pierre-de-Soucy, the number of inhabitants fell from 108 in 1347 to 55 in 1349; and in seven other parishes from 303 to 142. But did 50 per cent and more of these householder "parishioners" really perish? We may well doubt it, for three years later, in 1352, the number of households in Saint-Pierre and the seven other villages rose again to four-fifths of the 1348 total, where it subsequently remained.[70] Those who had "disappeared" in 1348—a certain number of them at any rate—were not dead and buried at all. Used to migrating as Savoy peasants always have done, they had simply decamped to return later to their chalets as soon as the plague seemed to have been cast out for good.[71]

So, judging from these figures, the plague in Savoy, probably bubonic and not pulmonary, was relatively mild in comparison with the cataclysm that struck Provence. Nevertheless, since it killed at least one in five of the population of Savoy, it produced in the survivors psychological traumas of incalculable consequence: from mid-summer day 1348 and on into August, the villages and small towns of Savoy (e.g., Yennes, Aiguebelle), whether suffering from the plague or under threat from it, killed all their Jews, whom they accused of having poisoned the wells. The Jews in Chambéry were in turn thrown into prison in December 1348, and later they too were massacred by the townsfolk.[72]

After Savoy and Forez it was the turn of Burgundy to feel the lash of the plague. But in the Burgundian plains the calamity, horrific though it was, did not necessarily lead to pogroms as in Savoy or to a holocaust as in Provence. It broke out in summer and was almost entirely bubonic. In the large village of Givry,[73] the plague which had come by way of the Rhône and the Saône, set to work in the second fortnight of July 1348; it was very active in August and reached its climax in September of that year, with a tally of ten dead every day (all records broken on September 10: 24 deaths). Still very severe in October, it finally petered out on November 19. From its August-September maximum we deduce that it was not the pulmonary form of plague. It therefore claimed "only" 615 victims, not quite one in three of the 2,000-strong population of Givry on the eve of the epidemic.[74] Here again, as in Savoy and Forez, the axe had fallen; but not so savagely as to cause the wholesale slaughter (nearly one person in two) commonly experienced in Provence and Languedoc a few months earlier during the pulmonary plague of the winter season.

Further north, this impression of weakening and abatement was even more marked than in Burgundy. This becomes clear as we follow the plague bacillus on its onward march—progressively less and less of a triumphal progress—across the Paris basin and into Flanders. It has long been remarked that between the western and eastern halves of the Netherlands, a wide area containing both urban and rural communities was either hardly touched by the Black Death (Brabant?) or even completely spared (Limbourg and Hesbaye).[75] It is as though the two arms of the "pincers", one closing in from France in 1349 and the other from Germany in 1350, never completely closed: they marked off and preserved, as it were, in this crucial year at the mid-point of the fourteenth century, a territorial "sanctuary" around Bruges and Ghent, at the gates of which the infection petered out. It also seems likely that there were other "sanctuaries" of a similar type, in 1348 and later, in the south of France: one of these, as it happens, seems to have been situated—at the height of the pulmonary phase—in the very heart of

Provence and the Camargue, around Beaucaire and Tarascon
where the number of households remained constant.[76] The same
thing occurred in Béarn[77] and throughout extensive regions in the
Pyrenees, the mountains, as was often the case in 1348, acting as a
protective shield and insulator against the plague. (The Pyreneans
did not escape so lightly in the long run, however: the 1385 census
returns show Béarn to have been as depopulated as the regions of
Aquitaine on its northern border. We can only assume that the
inhabitants of this Pyrenean province, spared by the 1348 epidemic,
succumbed all the more easily to the contagions of the succeeding
decades, to the "mountain plagues", as they were specifically
designated;[78] or perhaps they emigrated to neighbouring regions to
take up the vacant lots left in the wake of the first plague.) In some
of the country areas around Paris too, just as in Flanders, Béarn and
the Camargue, there seem to have been certain clearly-defined
districts that remained virtually untouched by the plague. Why this
should be is a mystery.

In the Ile-de-France and in Champagne at any rate, the Black
Death was awaited with the utmost anxiety: in the Champagne
countryside, if we accept the word of a contemporary doctor,[79] the
disaster was heralded by hot winds from the south, unhealthy mists,
spring maladies and various other "poxes", dysentery and typhus:
all the regular epidemic diseases of the fourteenth century.[80] And
when it arrived, the plague justified all the anguish that had preceded it. The infection reached Paris through the village of Roissy-
en-France: the capital, over-populated and therefore especially
vulnerable, was hard hit. At the height of the onslaught it is said that
there were about 800 deaths a day in the city and in the eighteen
months the contagion lasted, a total of some 50,000 persons
perished. These figures may not be altogether reliable, but they
suggest that in the course of these critical months, the lower-class
population of Paris was cut down ruthlessly—a suggestion confirmed by documentary data on rents, and above all on earnings. At
the hospital of Saint-Jacques-aux-Pèlerins the building workers'
wages, which had been stable in nominal and in real value from 1339
to 1348, doubled within a year; the increase was maintained and
even improved upon up to 1360. But the price of grain, despite
occasional fluctuations, did not rise during the period.[81] Real wages
therefore increased enormously, thanks of course to the plague
which, by killing workers in their thousands, unbalanced the labour

market and sent up the earnings of the survivors in compensation. The working classes suffered the Plague of Paris in their flesh; their higher wages were small consolation.

The capital's upper class citizens, however, lost only a small percentage of their numbers.[82] And the country districts of the Ile-de-France sometimes survived the ordeal without coming to too much harm. Some communities suffered badly, of course: Saint-Denis, for example, which had the ill luck to be a staging-post between the source of the plague in Roissy-en-France and the capital. A number of villages were so reduced in numbers as to be abandoned by their priests; others were caught by the epidemic just as they were congratulating themselves on being safely out of it, and had organized great rejoicings with dancing, pipes and drums in celebration of their fortunate but precarious immunity.[83] But in other parts of the old Capet domain of the Ile-de-France, people continued to lead untroubled lives throughout the reign of the great plague: it either merely brushed them in passing or ignored them altogether and left them in peace. This is what happened, for instance, in the villages of the valley, plains and forests of the *baillage* (district) of Senlis, where the middle years of the fourteenth century seem to have been a curiously euphoric era with the plague only passing by in the distance like a bad dream.[84] Much the same thing occurred in a few parishes or localities in the countryside around Paris, where we are fortunate enough to possess census returns for pre- and post-plague years; in Garges, for example, near Pontoise, in 1327 there were 90 tenants paying rent to the Grand Prior of Saint-Denis; in 1351, the records show 86 still paying. Losses due to the Black Death, if indeed there were any local plague victims, were minimal in comparison with those recorded in Provence and Burgundy.[85]

These results, obtained from a single parish which, thanks to the documents, we can examine in the closest detail, confirm what is suggested, here and there, in across-the-board estimates of the national population. In Garges, and no doubt in other villages around Paris and Senlis, the Black Death may well have been active, but much less so than in the south,[86] less than in Marsillargues (Languedoc) or in Givry (Saône-et-Loire). It made few inroads into the total number of rent-paying tenants.

In conclusion, I should like to use an inexact but nevertheless instructive comparison. When one looks at the final toll of the Black

Death between the Rhône and the Seine, one is inevitably reminded of a nuclear explosion: its effects are always horrific but are
more varied and less intense the further the distance from the point
of impact. It seems that in the area under discussion, the devastating blast of the plague was most strongly felt in the Mediterranean
south, where, to the lasting detriment of the Occitanian civilization,
the form it took was pulmonary. The highly dangerous "fall-out"
subsequently scattered as far afield as the Ile-de-France, Picardy
and Normandy, was bubonic rather than pulmonary and its effect
varied according to region, social group, or district—urban or rural.
So pronounced were these inequalities of effect that they occasionally provoked from the luckier ones ferocious mockery of the
victims: "1348 . . . fut la mortalité si grande parmi la Normandie que
les Picards se moquaient des Normands pour cela."[87] ("So great was
the mortality among the Normans that the Picardians made fun of
the Normans for it".) In the very heart of the Capet kingdom, in the
Ile-de-France, it is clear that the plague bled the capital far more
seriously than it did the rural areas. Ten years after the plague had
come and gone, in 1358, on the eve of the epoch-making act of the
peasants' revolt in Paris—known in history as the Jacquerie—the
revolutionaries' purses were singularly empty, but in many a village, their numerical strength was as great as ever, or nearly so.

★

After this predominantly French account of the first "short-
circuit" of the bacilli from central Asia to Paris and the Ile-de-
France, it is outside the scope of this essay to describe in detail the
subsequent incursions of the plague. (According to Biraben, between 1348 and 1530, such incursions were geographically widely
dispersed, but there was usually at least one outbreak a year).[88] I
should prefer, instead, to attempt to draw up a balance-sheet, still
confining myself to France, of the demographic consequences of the
resulting depopulation which lasted over a century. I shall look first
at the pre-plague era in France when the population figures reached
their peak in about 1330; and then at the final term of those evil
times, the "*Wüstungen*" of pestilence and death, when the figures
touched bottom, in about 1450.

A DEMOGRAPHIC BALANCE-SHEET:
FRANCE IN THE YEARS BEFORE THE PLAGUE

In the period before the Black Death, in about 1330 or 1340—a century before the disastrous figures of the mid-fifteenth century—France was swarming with people. The Paris basin, upper and central Normandy, Picardy, Dauphiné, central Languedoc, were all registering rural population densities already the equivalents of census returns in the same regions four and five centuries later, in the age of Louis XIV, or even Napoleon. Rouergue, Savoy, Provence, and the Nîmes region, did not reach such high peaks in 1330: the figures in these areas were slightly less than they would be in the eighteenth century, but certainly much higher than the demographic "lows" recorded in these regions in about 1440. And in the kingdom as a whole, the 1328 register of households confirms the local figures. First of all, in terms of the number of communities: in 1328, in the areas directly controlled by agents of the King, the number of parishes was approximately 24,000. This enormous figure indicates a very high density of population, and in itself represents a peak that was never subsequently exceeded. Within the same territorial limits, the number of parishes in 1585 was 23,000; at the end of the eighteenth century, 21,000 to 22,000; in 1794–5, 23,117. As for the number of households, in 1328 in the areas controlled by the agents of the King, it was 2,470,000, equivalent to 84.6 per cent of the total figure for the same area towards the end of the seventeenth century (2,919,316 households).[89] Another method of calculation, based on the average population of a typical parish (99.93 households in 1328; 114.27 households in 1720) gives a roughly similar percentage. Reckoned by this method, the population of France, in the regions for which we have the census figures for 1328, amounted to 87.5 per cent of the total for 1720.[90] This is a field full of pitfalls: to be anywhere near the truth, we must be prepared to be no more than approximate: let us say then, that bearing in mind that the provinces annexed at a later period (Provence, Dauphiné, Savoy, Alsace) were also densely, even overpopulated at the start of the fourteenth century, the estimates proposed in Table I may be taken as reasonably accurate. (The figures used as a comparison are those suggested by Vauban for the years 1690–1700. They are by no means infallible but they enable us to make some retrospective calculations.)

Table I

	A Population of France circa 1700 (late seventeenth century frontiers)[91]	B Estimate of population circa 1328 (same frontiers)
Improbably high hypothesis	20.9	18.3
Medium hypothesis	19	16.6
Least probable low hypothesis	17.1	15

(Figures in millions of inhabitants)

With such statistical parameters in mind, it seems not at all absurd to suggest that in 1328, a time of high population, after the rather dizzy demographic upsurge of the thirteenth century, "France" within boundaries approximately those of today, had a population of some sixteen or seventeen million. The mass of human beings alive in 1328 was enormous, when one considers how inadequate were the means available to sustain all these people: not only did they lack the resources of the highly productive agriculture we have today, but they were also partly or entirely deprived of those simple additional elements which in the eighteenth century enabled French populations of twenty, and later, twenty-five million, to maintain an adequate standard of living. Among these additional elements, some were vital, others secondary: foreign and colonial trade, monetary supply, urban and rural industries, the network of cities, administrative offices and capitalist enterprises; and also, impossible to evaluate statistically, but certainly stimulating, the *savoir-faire* and competence of economic experts. All these factors, which were either absent altogether or only present in modest form in the first half of the fourteenth century, were to count so much in the eighteenth century that even without any technological revolution the national economy prospered.

These over-populated communities of the first forty years of the fourteenth century, despite the heavy tolls exacted from time to time by famine, logically invited calamity. Admirable regional accomplishments such as wine production in Bordeaux and cereal-growing in the great landed estates in the Paris basin did not prevent the picture from looking on the whole rather gloomy. The great ground-clearance operations, long since completed, had stopped short at the marginal lands and forests which it was considered vital to preserve for timber and fuel requirements. The medieval "frontier" which for so long had moved forward, opening up new territories for farms and market-gardens, advanced no further. Grain yields reached a ceiling and levelled off: the resulting unfortunate stability—or rather stagnation—in the economy is not difficult to explain: the agricultural revolution of the late Middle Ages, bringing such innovations as the mill, the wheeled plough and the horse collar, had had beneficial repercussions over a long period on the economy of the Roman and Gothic eras; but subsequently, and for some time to come, agricultural technology seems to have run out of inspiration.

The early decades of the fourteenth century, when a large population was faced by this lack of growth in the economy, were times not so much of crisis—in the somewhat vague sense of that over-used word—but rather of a predominantly agricultural society whose expansion was blocked, or nearly so. It was all the more vulnerable to short-term hazards such as the famine of 1315, which brought unprecedented hardship. In this hostile environment the peasants bowed before the storm and at times, in true Ricardian and Malthusian fashion, lay down and died under the triple burden of high rents, wretchedly low pay, and inadequately tiny plots for cultivation. Landowners took advantage of the high demand for land, resulting from the increase of the peasant population, to put up dues of every kind: land rents, seigneurial dues, tithes and taxes. The surplus labour supply contributed to a drastic lowering of wages, whether in cash, goods or a mixture of both. And lastly, the demographic boom of the preceding centuries was the cause of an excessive subdivision of the land into individual plots, creating a permanent chequer-board pattern across the country; these individual plots had to coexist alongside the huge *réserve* of land farmed directly by the *seigneur* or his tenant—a source of friction, as may be imagined. Such private estates were not perhaps as extensive as was once thought,[92] but they were certainly not negligible.

This accumulation of hardships was not necessarily intolerable. The peasants of France were to experience many more, for example during the worst moments of the tragic seventeenth century; and their society did not collapse under the strain. But in 1340, the gods were against them. After a number of military encounters, familiar to us from history books, that ushered in the Hundred Years War, the plague of 1348 set in motion a whole series of catastrophes, wholly or partly attributable to the bacillus, which spelt disaster for the population figures. A hundred years passed by, bringing wave after wave of trials and tribulations; finally, in about 1445, the demographic decline reached its nadir, setting a "bench-mark" for future time against which to measure new "lows" in post-Plague population counts, whether long past or more recent.

A DEMOGRAPHIC BALANCE SHEET:
MINIMUM POPULATION FIGURES (CIRCA 1445)

Once again, we start in the south and move north: in Provence, in the areas for which we have comparable figures, before the Black Death, there were 70,000 households; in 1471 30,000 heads of families; in 1765 130,000 houses.[93] The units referred to (households, heads of families, houses) are not strictly comparable. But there can be little doubt that the late medieval minimum (30,000) in this large province in the extreme South was lower by at least a half than either of the quoted maxima of the earlier and the later centuries. In Languedoc too, all the available data tend to confirm a similar assessment:[94] electoral rolls, registers of communicants, tax lists. Fifteenth-century documents (between 1410 and 1480) invariably indicate population figures down by 50 per cent, broadly speaking, on those for the pre-Plague or the post-Renaissance eras ("post-Renaissance" referring to the second half of the sixteenth century, the seventeenth century even at its worst period, and of course the eighteenth century).

For the diocese of Geneva[95] (part of which covered areas in present-day Savoy) we have statistics of the numbers of households, varying according to the dates, of some 200 to 500 villages. Taking 100 to represent the demographic minimum (1443–5), two methods of calculation—the first taking into account the 1470 data, the second omitting them—enable us to reconstitute, by compiling a sequence of indices, the fluctuation of the population figures between 1339 and 1518 (Table II).

These unequivocal figures reveal the dizzy fall in numbers between 1339 and 1411, followed by the continuing descent until we come to 1443 (the population of the diocese in these middle years of the fifteenth century was only 42.5 per cent of what it had been in 1339). Subsequently, stagnation or stabilization—call it what you will—was the order of the day and lasted until about 1470–82. The

Table II

The Diocese of Geneva

Years	Population index (First method)	Population index (Second method)
1339	234.8	234.8
1411–4	115.2	115.2
1443–5	*100*	*100*
1470	98.5	
1481–2	99.5	101.2
1518	128	130.1

modest recovery that began in the 1470s turned into a positive boom of rapid expansion between 1482 and 1518; but even at this latest date the Genevan villages remained far below their 1339 peaks.

To return to the period of decline and stagnation around the shores of Lake Geneva in the fifteenth century: one should note that the hardships that were its root cause are not to be attributed to armed conflict of any kind. The diocese of Geneva was at peace throughout this whole period of demographic decline, from the middle of the fourteenth century until 1475. There must therefore be some other explanation for the decline in numbers in these country villages. Rural exodus perhaps? If so, it was only marginally responsible, for though Geneva was in the process of developing in the fifteenth century, it was still quite small, and capable of absorbing only a tiny fraction of the missing population. The blame therefore must be attributed to the least replaceable of the phenomena that preceded the population collapse—the plague and other epidemic diseases, combined with the vicious circle of economico-demographic decline which set in almost everywhere in Europe at the time; and also the disastrous market recession which was itself the consequence of the swathes cut through the population by the continuous high mortality. For evidence of the effects of the plague in this region we need only consult the unhappy childhood recollections of the schoolmaster Thomas Platter, who describes the persistent ill-health he saw all about him as a boy in Switzerland, ill-health he claims to have been still prevalent at the start of the sixteenth century. "My father was in the district of Thun in the territory of Berne, buying wool. There he was attacked by the plague and died. Of my brothers and sisters, I knew only two sisters

[Elizabeth and Christina]. Christina died above Stalden, at Burgen, of the plague, with eight persons of her family".[96]

The Geneva area provides historians, seeking an accurate picture of population trends, with a detailed set of statistics. The picture that emerges seems to have been fairly typical (even in percentages of decline) of the fate overall of the northern Alps: in Dauphiné and Faucigny, for example, the records for 1475 show a number of households representing a mere 47.7 per cent of the total figure for 1339; and the mountains along the valley of the Isère figure in the lists as regions most completely abandoned by their inhabitants: the survivors of the epidemics and other disasters of the times simply left their poor patches of soil and settled in the richer plains below, filling up the empty places created by the plague.[97]

Thanks to the numerous *counts of households* in Burgundy, further to the north, we should soon have at our disposal a synthesis of the late medieval demography of the province similar to that which Baratier has supplied for Provence. We already know that Burgundy was sorely tried by the Black Death which, in the little market town of Givry, for example, wiped out a third of the inhabitants (see above). Subsequently, in the fifteenth century, a few random but convergent items of information indicate, as expected, a population minimum compared to the maximum of the latter part of the thirteenth century. In four villages of the *châtellenie* (manor) of Saint-Romain (in the present *département* of the Côte d'Or) in 1285 there were 119 households, i.e., about 500 inhabitants: in 1423 there were only 36 households, and the figure stayed somewhere between 30 and 50 from 1430 to 1460[98]—a fall of more than a half. In Ouges,[99] another Burgundian village, there were 70 to 80 households in 1268; about 50 (of which one quarter to two-fifths were occupied by beggars) between 1375 and 1400; 13 households (only 3 of whom were solvent) in 1423, after a series of particularly disastrous years; then 15 households in 1430, 28 in 1436, 34 in 1444, 42 in 1450, and finally the figure was back to fifty or so by 1470. The trough of the wave, therefore, comes somewhere between 1420 and 1430; in any case, until 1445 the figure remains at only half that of the demographic peaks of the end of the thirteenth century. All in all, whether one looks at the five previously-mentioned villages or the urban or suburban zones of Chalon-sur-Saône,[100] depopulated by approximately 58 per cent between 1360 and 1413, Burgundy as a whole touched bottom around 1420; and the province was still in poor shape demographically—despite a few revivals here and there—between 1425 and 1450.

These Burgundian figures are fully confirmed by Marie-Thérèse Caron's recent study. In ten villages in the Tonnerre region (Yonne) she found 352 households in 1423 (a figure well below that of 1400–2). Yet in these same ten villages, there were 940 households in about 1700, as I was able to verify on consulting Saugrain,[101] proving that the late Medieval minimum in the Tonnerre district amounted to only 37.4 per cent of one of the modern peaks—and not one of the highest either.

In the Paris region (in approximately 80 parishes included in the Deanery of Montmorency and the Archdeaconry of Josas) depopulation between 1328 and 1470 was at the rate of at least two-thirds; it reached similar and equally frightful levels in the *bailliage* of Senlis and in the Beauvais area.[102] In Normandy it was worse still: by 1450, according to one of its recent historians, the communities in the Caux region had lost up to three-quarters of the numbers recorded there in 1315.[103] The immediate cause of this well-nigh incredible fall in population was of course war; but much of it (since war brings in its train other forms of mortality) was due equally to hunger and to our particular concern—epidemics. Hunger was the result of the plundering of harvests and the destruction of agricultural capital. Epidemics were caused by fleas carried on the soldiers and wandering beggars.

Let us leave for the moment Normandy and all its sorrows (Guy Bois's theory of the "Hiroshima model" is inspired by this period in its history). Westwards, in Brittany (a province, unlike Normandy and the Ile-de-France, situated well away from the "witches cauldron" of France during the Hundred Years' War), there were between a million and a million and a quarter inhabitants in about 1390 (the pre-Plague figure is not known). By 1450 these numbers had probably fallen by about a quarter: one house in four was empty. But the point to bear in mind is that this figure of a million Bretons in the middle decades of the fifteenth century should be set alongside figures of some two millions by the end of the seventeenth century.[104]

In the Bordeaux region, there are no precise figures available for the latter part of the Middle Ages. But a survey in 1459, carried out by the Archbishopric of Bordeaux,[105] shows that of a sample of 330 parishes, one quarter had been completely or largely abandoned.

The majority of these village communities would recover and flourish later on, but with such conditions prevailing, how can one avoid the conclusion that the level of the population here in 1459 was far lower than in the previous age, in the days of the English domination, before the wars and before the plagues? According to certain recent studies it is possible that the population fell by as much as two-thirds.

I have reserved for the end of this section consideration of the special problems which affected the extreme north of France, and the French-speaking zones outside France, in the fifteenth century. Everything suggests that the crisis in this region, though sometimes less marked than in other regions, was no less serious. In thirty-two villages in Artois, the records list 2,121 households in 1229; in 1469 there were only 1,222.[106] The fall in numbers is less dramatic than in the Ile-de-France or in Normandy (losses of 72 per cent), yet it indicates a decline of 43 per cent in the population compared with the "good old days" of the Middle Ages. In the Cambrai area the population was lower in the fifteenth century than in the more fortunate sixteenth century: in 1444 there were 495 households in twelve villages compared with 563 in 1469 and 640 in 1540.[107] But once more it is evident that this fifteenth-century "trough" (compared with the sixteenth-century peak) was nowhere near as pronounced in the area around Cambrai as it was in Provence or Languedoc.

To turn to Hainaut: certain reputable historians have thought it wiser to play down the losses that followed the *Wüstungen*—the evil times—of the latter part of the Middle Ages. In fact these losses were probably heavy: as the Black Death pursued its deadly course, a number of villages where records have been preserved lost half their households (G. Sivery). Subsequently, the population of Hainaut continued to fall, steadily if moderately, from 31,000 households in 1365 (the date of the first known low post-Plague figures) to 22,000 in the two bad patches in the fifteenth century (1400–24 and 1479–1501).[108] These two troughs were separated, it is true, by a fortunate period of recovery which temporarily restored the Hainaut population, by about 1450, to 28,000 households, a figure approaching that of 1365, but still much lower than the pre-Plague high "ceiling".[109]

So, despite these slightly better figures, we see that Artois, and even more so Hainaut, also suffered during the crisis. To find populations less seriously affected we have to go further north. In Brabant, which was apparently almost untouched by the Black Death, the number of households fell from 92,000 in the middle years of the fourteenth century to 75,000 towards the end of the fifteenth, a moderate loss—all things considered—of 19 per cent.[110]

With the help of these recorded figures, varied as they are, we can now draw up an overall balance-sheet, allowing for the usual reservations and approximations, and taking into account the fact that the scale of the catastrophe was less severe in the extreme north. Here then are a few suggestions on the subject of the fluctuating population of France over the ages.

During its peak periods, the population of France is known to have reached something like 17 million in about 1330, 19 million in about 1700. At its lowest, in about 1440–70, it was probably no more than 10 million, if indeed it reached this figure at all. At a modest calculation, too modest no doubt, set against the probable peak of 1328, 10 million represents a fall of 42 per cent.

Ten million—of whom eight to nine million would have lived in the rural areas—is the reasonable estimate. And, in any case, it is the absolute *maximum* that would have been possible at this time of depressed population figures at the very end of the Middle Ages.

The major culprit, portrayed in many a "danse macabre", was Death, since there is no reason to believe that fifteenth-century France was particularly infertile, or deliberately and systematically unwilling to reproduce. The age of marriage (about which we know very little for this period) was probably no higher than between 1600 and 1800. The fact that in these later centuries girls in many parts of the country did not marry until they were 25 or older was no bar to the population increasing by leaps and bounds—in the eighteenth century at least, thanks to its lower death-rate. So, to return to the fifteenth century, it was not late marriage—always supposing marriages *were* late—that caused the population figures to stagnate or to plummet.

In that case, can the low demographic levels of the fifteenth century be explained by a deliberate refusal to have children, some primitive form of birth-control maybe, or possibly amenorrhoea in young women brought on by famine, poverty or anxiety? The very little information we have on this subject does not suggest that this was the case. Using available data on the distribution of extra provisions of food for the mothers of newly-born babies, Hugues

Neveux has calculated the average interval between births in a particular village in the Cambrai region; failing anything better, his study offers a rough guide to the level of fertility in the area.[111] He sets the interval at 29.5 months, at a time when population figures were low (1468–82) as compared with 30.5 months when times and figures were better (1559–75), from which we see that in the declining years of the Middle Ages women in the Cambrésis were no less fertile than their highly prolific sisters in the Beauvaisis in the seventeenth century. And yet, despite such praiseworthy efforts, the Cambrai women failed to halt the decline, or check the stagnation affecting the population figures in the age of Louis XI. Some other factor, therefore, must have been at work to frustrate their endeavours. Can we doubt that this factor was the high death-rate of the times, with the consequent shortened life-expectancy of marriage partners, one or both of whom might die before the wife had given birth to her full quota of children? Here surely is the explanation why, despite completely normal fertility—"pre-Malthusian" we might say—the number of births per household in the same village in the Cambrai region (a rough guide to the birth-rate) was 2.2 between 1476 and 1481–2, compared with 3.1 between 1559–60 and 1574–5. Couples in the fifteenth century were separated too quickly: despite their abundant fertility they produced, *in toto*, fewer offspring than their counterparts of later generations.

★

A high death-rate was the chief culprit in these episodes of population decline. And among the causes of death in the late Mediaeval era it was plague, always plague, that led the field, flourishing on vermin and fleas, those twin agents of human contamination.

In any given area in the fifteenth century, the plague might be expected to strike every ten years, on average, as for example in the Chalon-sur-Saône region,[112] but in some places it was every two, three or four years, or even as often as annually (as in the Toulouse area, for instance,[113] which like the whole of the South was much more plague-ridden than the North of France). On the whole, the towns suffered more seriously, but the country was by no means spared—throughout France in the fifteenth century, plague was an

Table III
Population during the
"demographic trough" of the fifteenth century

Regions situated wholly or partly in present-day France	Fall in numbers compared with the pre-Plague figures	Decline compared with the seventeenth century
Provence	57%	
Languedoc	50%	same
Grésivaudan	60%	
Diocese of Geneva	57%	
Burgundy	50% +	
Paris region	fall of ⅔	
Normandy	fall of ¾	
Brittany		50%
Artois	43%	
Hainaut	probable fall of ½	

ever-present fact of life. Every year, without exception, it was active somewhere or other in the kingdom. Viewed nationally, the cycle of disease enjoyed only brief intervals of remission (never of more than two or three years at a time throughout the period 1350–1540). There was always a trouble-spot somewhere, near Caen, or Béziers, or Beauvais, depending on the year. It was this same demonic rhythm, maintaining plague as an ever-present uninvited guest, that certain Islamic countries were to experience until as late as 1840, long after its disappearance in the West. Somewhere about that date, a few simple prophylactic measures (quarantine, etc.), similar to those that had been adopted in Europe in the middle of the sixteenth century, reduced the numbers of the plague epidemics in the Muslim world.[114] Judging from this comparison, it seems that in the fifteenth century, European and in particular French populations were still almost defenceless against the scourge; but later, they were to combat it rationally and, eventually, in the seventeenth century, successfully. At the latter end of the Middle Ages, people were still far too inclined to rest their hopes of salvation in processions to St Roch, or else to confine their activities to acts of senseless bravado. At times, they behaved as if there were nothing to worry about, often failing to put into practice the energetic measures of disinfection, evacuation and isolation that health officers, public administrators and eventually the military authorities increasingly adopted in the sixteenth and above all in the seventeenth and eighteenth centuries. The result was that each succeeding decade of the late Middle Ages witnessed a series of hecatombs that vastly depleted the stock of humankind and prolonged demographic stagnation by a kind of slow torture—without however succeeding in preventing the eventual recovery which took place, at different times and in different parts of the country, during the second half of the fifteenth century.

★

The reader may object that in France both wars and famines, as well as plague, played an important part in accelerating depopulation. But comparative history must be our guide: and in the other countries of Europe, this combination of factors was not present. It is true that between 1340 and 1450, Germany, Italy, England, the Scandinavian countries, Catalonia and Portugal all experienced war in one form or another; but their peoples escaped the worst of the devastation during the Hundred Years' War, which was fought on French soil. (Indeed the very term *Hundred Years' War* has no real meaning for the majority of continental countries other than France.) And yet, towards the end of the Middle Ages, every one of these countries experienced a century-long period of depopulation, by a third or a half, very similar to that of France. In Germany, pollen-graphs from the peat-bogs of the Rhön valley show that the *Wüstungen* or bad times of the second half of the fourteenth century were the worst and most prolonged on record between the year 1000 and the eighteenth century.[115] Since war as an overall factor on the European scale is ruled out, we must look for some other explanation. Famine, perhaps—or, more generally, the secular series of successive subsistence crises? Surely not: famine on its own could never explain the disastrous decline, in a single century, of the populations of the West. For successive famines in the medium or long run inevitably create the conditions of their own alleviation: the fewer mouths there are to feed, the more food there is to go round. So when we talk of a massive, century-long crisis of depopulation, famine is highly unlikely to have caused it. More generally, the over-population of 1280–1310, the "peaking" that produced a surplus of people at the beginning of the fourteenth century, not only could, but did, culminate (as Postan, in the Malthusian tradition, has demonstrated) in demographic stabilization, and indeed in a modest decline in the late Medieval population figures. (We find a similar stabilization later, under somewhat similar circumstances, in the seventeenth century, after the population explosions of the sixteenth.) But there is no intrinsic reason why the overpopulation of the early years of the fourteenth century should, simply because it preceded them, have engendered the calamitous sequence of events recorded from 1348 on. For this to have occurred, some additional factor must have been present: one which in all the countries of the West *made all the difference*. This factor, external in origin to Europe, internal to Eurasia, was Yersin's bacillus. Without the intervention, as an additional factor, of this deadly scourge from outside Europe, it is difficult to see how the surplus populations of the early fourteenth century could have found *within themselves* the dialectical impulse to transform themselves—by some sort of Hegelian pirouette—into their opposites: producing the strikingly low levels one finds almost everywhere by 1450, and which differ so radically from those of the pre-Plague era.

So we are left with one antecedent, for which no substitute seems at all possible, one common factor in a general and drastic demographic collapse: death from epidemic disease, and more particularly from repeated outbreaks of plague, as a result of the "short-circuit" of plague-germs in circumstances I have tried to outline above. Every outbreak of plague, as it occurred regionally, would of course take its place within an overall and much more complex process (brilliantly described in works of synthesis by Abel and especially by Postan). Depopulation, brought about in the first place by outbreaks of plague, could lead to a series of economic crises of slump and stagnation, which might in turn lead to a kind of "gang warfare" (Postan's expression), thus contributing further to the population collapse. But secondary factors could not have accounted on their own for the extraordinary and indeed absolutely unprecedented character of demographic developments in western Europe between 1348 and 1450. So unprecedented were they that the only possible comparison would be with the hypothetical results of a modern nuclear or bacteriological war. The nature, at once universal and horrendous, of the biological catastrophe that occurred towards the end of the Middle Ages cannot be understood unless proper recognition of its primary importance in the causal chain is accorded to the plague bacillus.[116]

WOODROW BORAH'S RESEARCH ON THE GENOCIDE
OF THE AMERICAN INDIANS

It is fairly well known that the microbial unification of the fourteenth and fifteenth centuries certainly affected Eurasia west of
Tibet and more particularly western Europe. It may also have
affected China where ominous signs of a demographic shortfall
were evident towards the end of the Middle Ages (to use European
chronology).

But beginning in the very last years of the fifteenth century and
during the next hundred, or at least fifty years, the processes of
epidemic contagion took a giant step westwards, across the Atlantic. From this time on, large tracts of the American continent felt
the impact of "unification"; its devastating properties were experienced on a scale beyond anything Europe had known, shocking
though that had been. To discuss this apocalyptic event in the
history of America, obviously we must consult the work of Woodrow Borah.

Borah, of Berkeley University, California, revised, or it would be
more correct to say, demolished the theories of Soetber, a fellow
historian who refused to believe that any post-Conquest catastrophes had taken place in Mexico.[117] To produce his devastating
rebuttal, Borah drew upon a mass of documentary evidence of
many different kinds: pictographs dating back to the Renaissance,
the work of native Mexicans; surveys and census returns of Spanish
origin; and tax data which, with the aid of fairly simple calculations
based on overall tax receipts, tax assessments per family, and
numbers of persons per household, enable one to estimate reasonably accurately population figures for the times such taxes were
levied. Complete accuracy is of course impossible and the final
figures, in millions and in hundreds of thousands are, in Borah's
own words, only "a guess at the mid-point of a probable range".

By the use of this method, however, Borah and his team produced some impressive estimates of the population figures of pre-
Conquest Mexico. It is true that long before the arrival of Cortez,
the cultivation of maize had made it possible to supply the needs of a
considerable population, but there were already signs of a Malthusian saturation point: several instances of famine are known to have
occurred in the course of the fifteenth century, and the persistence
of the practice of human sacrifice might, after all, be interpreted—

why not—"as a sign that the local culture contained elements favourable to population limitation".

But having said that, the worst outcome is not always the most probable; the catastrophe that finally occurred was by no means inevitable. But for contagious contacts from outside, the acknowledged Malthusian tendencies in fifteenth-century Mexico might well have led to nothing more than a long-term period of population stagnation, such as that on record in many parts of Europe in the seventeenth century.

It was the shock of conquest from without—accomplished by Cortez at the expense of the Aztec Empire in 1519–21—which caused this demographic collapse; admittedly the population figures were not in too healthy a state, but they would have remained relatively stable in an endogenous context if only the country had been able to remain free from external contamination.

In a preliminary assessment, S.F. Cook and L.B. Simpson[118] proposed the figures given in Table IV for the post-Cortez "haemorrhage" of the population of Central Mexico.

These numbers are already astonishingly high at the earliest date and terribly depleted at the lowest point (1650); they convey more effectively than any long commentary the impact of the Spanish invasions and occupation. Subsequent research carried out by Borah in follow-up studies to his first book extend still further the upper and lower limits, confirming this impression of collapse. A close study of the *Suma de Visitas*, compiled in 1547, persuaded Borah to revise *upwards* the figures relating to the first half of the sixteenth century.[119] Together with those for the latter half of the century they should now read as in Table V.[120]

Table IV

Date	Inhabitants (million)
1519	11.0
1540	6.4
1565	4.4
1597	2.5
1607	2.0
in about 1650	1.5
1700	2.0 approx.
1793	3.7

Table V

Date	Inhabitants (million)
1518	25.2
1532	16.9
1548	7.4
1568	2.6
1580	1.9
1595	1.4
1608	1.1

Figures like these point to a continuous rate of demographic decline between 1518 and 1608 of something between − 3 per cent and − 6 per cent *per annum*. Calculated regionally, the rates concerned were particularly bad in the low-lying coastal areas in central Mexico, which were more exposed than other areas to contagious diseases and outside contacts. The higher Mexican plateau was comparatively healthy and in parts less subject to contamination than the lower-lying territories. Measured in percentages rather than in absolute figures, the decline began to slow down after 1580. After this date, immediately following the holocaust of *matlazu-huatl*—the worst of all the outbreaks of disease—the epidemics became slightly less catastrophic in their effect. It was in the course of the last twenty years of the sixteenth century, then, that the lowest point was reached. From this baseline, very much later, after 1650 in fact, that recovery once more became possible. But for a very long time such recovery was no more than limited and partial.

Monographs such as the one dealing with the Mixteca Alta region,[121] complement and confirm Woodrow Borah's overall estimates (Table VI).

In this case again, the rate of decline was at first absolutely catastrophic; but from 1580 onward it began to slacken—if that is the right way to put it—once the demographic low-point was reached. The slow, painful recovery in the Mixteca Alta area did not get under way until after 1650; it did not really take off until after 1850, from which time it became very marked indeed.

★

Borah's calculations on overall numbers are backed up by a series of complementary indices which he has carefully studied for the

Table VI

Population of the Mixteca Alta region (Mexico)

Date	Inhabitants
1520	700,000
1532	528,000
1540	100,000
1569	57,000
1660–70	30,000
1742	54,000
1777	74,000
1803	76,000
1826	65,000

period 1520–1650. He draws attention first of all to a startling contrast: the Indian population figures collapsed but the white settlers were immune to or better protected against, the various epidemics and diseases which, however, they brought and spread. In 1570, there were 60,000 Whites in central Mexico; in 1646 there were 125,000, in 1742 565,000 and in 1772 784,000. At the same time, this Indian genocide was accompanied by a critical shortage of foodstuffs, normally supplied by the coloured subject people for the needs of their white masters: towards the end of the sixteenth century, supplies of chickens and turkeys diminished, and tithes in the form of cereals fell. *Latifundia*—large ranches—managed by the Spanish colonists were created to try to make up for the increasingly serious deficiencies of native agriculture, which eventually failed altogether through lack of manpower. There was some slight consolation: as the American Indians became fewer on the ground, cattle and sheep by the million came to take their place. (The consequence of this invasion of livestock, replacing men, or rather, the corpses of men, was an irremediable process of soil erosion.) Systems of forced labour, of semi-slavery in payment of debt, and of tied-labour on glebe-land became the established practices by which the colonists hoped to remedy the drastic shortage of native manpower. As in the case of the Europeans in the fourteenth and fifteenth centuries, the Spaniards in Mexico found that as a result of its increasing scarcity, the cost of Mexican labour grew faster than the price of raw materials and agricultural produce. Wages, which therefore rose sharply, were not the only problem. Textiles, highly labour-intensive, multiplied in price twenty and thirty times between 1520 and 1610; on the other hand, in the grain market, which was more dependent on purely natural factors, inflation was markedly less pronounced. Another case of shortage of manpower after 1580–1600 in Mexico was in the silver mines. As a result, this local population deficit in the first half of the seventeenth century became one of the causes of the silver shortage, which gradually began to choke the economy of the far-off Mediterranean countries and continued to do so until at last, after 1670–1700, demographic and mining prospects picked up again. Even the building of churches closely conformed to the population trends in New Spain: during the first decades of Spanish domination in Mexico, says Borah, there was intensive building to the greater glory of God, just as, in a later age, in Europe, there was a building boom to the greater glory of profit in the halcyon days of the Industrial Revolution. To the singing of hymns, Indian manpower was lavishly deployed on the holy building sites. Then after 1576–9, the cathedral builders had to abandon their projects, not so much because their credits had run out but because there were no masons and above all no labourers to build the house of God—nor enough of the faithful to fill it.

Borah briefly investigates the causes of this demographic decline and its train of secondary phenomena, and finds that in the main they are attributable to the incidence of epidemics that followed on the "unification of the world by disease". There is, of course, no question of absolving or of whitewashing the Spanish colonization which was as cruel as any in history; nor of denying that, in certain instances, the Indians adopted frankly suicidal attitudes, either simply lying down and dying or refusing to have children. But causes of this nature can only have been additional or partial; the central factor was disease. The proof of this is that in those regions of Asia and Africa that were later to come under European colonial rule, there is no record of genocide or ethnocide on anything like so drastic a scale. Native populations in the old continents remained stable and then expanded. The relatively benign nature of colonial contact in the Ancient World was not due to any particular kindness of treatment on the part of the conquerors but to the immunity, or at least partial immunity, enjoyed by the subject native peoples to the microbes that had been in circulation over a long period of time throughout Eurasia and Eurafrica. The native populations of the West Indies, Mexico and North and South America, by contrast, had to absorb the shock, all at once, of a whole host of pathogenic agents that had been roaming about the older continents for centuries, but were unknown until about 1500 in the recently discovered territories that were to form the empire of New Spain. For this reason, mild or not so mild diseases such as measles, smallpox, various forms of influenza and scarlatina, newly introduced from Europe, created havoc on the other side of the Atlantic. The epidemic *matlazahuatl*, which towards the end of 1570 killed off a large percentage of the remaining native population "was possibly only a form—harmless to the whites—of influenza".[125] At a later period, about 1700–50, the Indians of Baja California, already subject to syphilis, were to fall victim to plague, smallpox, typhus, dysentery and measles.[123] The Europeans had brought with them both plague and influenza—the serious and the not so serious. Both types of disease flourished at the expense of the local population, which for the most part had had no previous experience of them. By joining forces, indiscriminately, they delivered what was virtually the *coup de grace* to the native peoples of America.

For it was not only Mexican territories that were affected. Recent research by Nathan Wachtel has clearly demonstrated the local effects of the "unification" upon the Cordilleras of Peru. Wachtel points out that from the time of Pizarro's conquest until the end of the century the death-rate was appalling.[124] Within its traditional boundaries the Inca Empire, in about 1530, (in 1524, to be precise) before the first epidemic struck, had a population of some seven or eight million (perhaps as many as ten million). But by 1560 the figure was two and a half million—a fall of at least 60 per cent in 30 years. And by 1590 the population was between 1.3 and 1.5 million, a fall of a further 40 per cent in the next thirty years. These figures suggest that on the whole the fall was less catastrophic in Peru than on the Mexican plateau, where within the same time-span 95 per cent of the native population perished. They also indicate that in Peru, as in Mexico, there was a slowdown in the demographic "landslide": from 1560 to 1590 the rate of decline is less steep compared to that of 1530 to 1560; after this date the worst was over, though from a demographical point of view the situation still remained catastrophic until the end of the century.

The brief paroxysms of the epidemics in Peru occurred:

(a) in 1524–6: measles and/or smallpox. These infectious diseases were rife even before the conquest of the country, for the germs had already spread through the native populations: from Mexico where the Europeans arrived first, all the way to Peru. The white men had sent on their microbes before them.

(b) in 1546: an undiagnosed disease, contagious and deadly, characterized by pains in the head and ears.

(c) in 1558–59: smallpox.

(d) in 1585–91: combinations, spreading in different directions and at different times, of smallpox, bubonic plague and typhus; also coughs and colds accompanied by fever, probably influenza.

When they were questioned, in the presence of the investigators, as to the causes of their depopulation, the Indians courageously spoke out against the harsh treatment and forced labour imposed upon them by their conquerors. But they too laid most emphasis on the fatal and all-important role played by epidemics. As their numbers decreased, the natives were progressively better fed as the century wore on (a similar sequence of events had already been observed in Europe after the Black Death of 1348–50). The Peruvians even, mistakenly, regarded this more abundant allocation of food as one of the causes of their higher death-rate. They were nearer the mark, surely, when they apportioned part of the blame to the harmful effects of alcohol to which they had been introduced by the colonists; they pointed out, rightly, that this too had contributed to the death toll.

DEATH IN THE CARIBBEAN ISLANDS

Thanks to Borah and Wachtel, we now have a general impression of the problems created by "microbial unification" in the most densely populated territories of the American continent. Borah's work in this field has also reached out across a broader area, to the insular fastnesses of the Caribbean: long protected against bacterial infection, these islands were suddenly and rudely subjected to the shock attack of pathogens brought to their shores by sailors and colonists from the West.[125]

Borah's investigation of these islands demonstrates that during the phase of world conquest by Europe, there were certain cultures whose demographic pattern resembled that of continental America, that is, they tended to collapse like a *soufflé*, indeed to disappear altogether except for minute traces in the form of crossbreeding with the invaders; they were in effect "physically liquidated", by microbe. Other groups by contrast, held firm, or even tended to expand when they met with the invaders from the white man's world. The line of demarcation between these two types of demographic behaviour leads to the heart of the concept of microbial unification.

★

The populations which disappeared altogether were those of the Caribbean islands, notably of Hispaniola (Santo Domingo). Even between the best of historians, estimates of the pre-Columbian population of this large island differ wildly: in 1964, Pierre Chaunu[126] suggested a figure of three million inhabitants for Santo Domingo in 1492: Woodrow Borah, however, in a powerfully documented study, puts forward a figure of *seven to eight millions!*[127] and appends a table showing the progressive decline of the population which I now reproduce (Table VII); they are truly appalling—responsibility for their accuracy I leave to him.

Charles Verlinden, on the other hand, writing in the Braudel *Festschrift*,[128] believes that there was only a total of "55,000 or 65,000 inhabitants on the island of Haiti before Columbus set sail".[129] It is true that Verlinden did not have the benefit of Borah's latest research (1971) which confirmed, proposed precise figures for, and even enlarged upon Chaunu's estimates. It is also true that the assessments of the two historians—Borah and Verlinden—differ greatly in their evaluation of the rate of population decline.

Table VII
Decline of the population of Hispaniola

Date	Inhabitants
1492	probably 7 to 8 millions
1496	3,770,000
1508	92,300
1509	61,600
1510	65,800
1512	26,700
1514	27,800
1518	15,600
1540	250
1570	125

According to Borah, during the worst period of Haiti's total de-population, between 1492 and 1570, 40 per cent of the surviving natives died *every year*—a truly geometrical progression of decline! Verlinden, however, without offering any further explanation and basing his estimate on pure guesswork (?) will only allow a *total* decline of 33 per cent in the population of Haiti during the first phase of the Conquest, i.e., between 1492 and 1509, and a total drop of 50 per cent between 1492 and 1514 ("which is certainly frightful enough", as he rightly concludes).[130]

As a non-specialist, I shall avoid taking sides with either Verlinden or the Chaunu-Borah combination. But it is worth noting that these three writers are in agreement upon a point of importance for our concept: the total, or near total, extermination (apart from small groups of half-breeds) of the native population of Hispaniola between 1492 and 1570. Equally, all three are agreed that infectious disease was the chief cause. Hispaniola—like so many other islands, well protected at first, then suddenly thrust into the front line of contact—fell victim, in an area of the world unfortunately not immunized beforehand, to a veritable onslaught of pathogenic microbes.

Now for a change of oceans: concerning the islands in the Pacific, Borah's comprehensive study proposes percentages of population decline sometimes less radical but almost always catastrophic (Table VIII).

Table VIII

Australia:	300,000 aborigines before 1780; 80,000 in 1937
Tasmania:	2,000 natives before colonization; none at all in 1876.
New Zealand:	300,000 to 500,000 Maoris before colonization; 40,000 in 1900.
New Hebrides:	Possibly one million inhabitants before colonization; 40,000 in 1939.
Hawaii:	400,000 inhabitants circa 1778 71,000 in 1853; 40,000 natives in 1890–1900.
The Marquesas:	80,000 inhabitants before colonization; barely 2,000 in 1939.
Guam:	70,000 to 100,000 in 1668; 1,654 in 1733.

These Oceania territories therefore followed the same pattern of demographic collapse as America in the sixteenth century, though much later owing to the time-lag in colonization. A complete contrast can be observed between this behaviour pattern and that of the populations of Asia (China, Japan, India), and even of Africa: despite periods of stagnation, or indeed of temporary or prolonged decline (especially in Africa because of the slave-trade), we find nothing comparable, among these colonized populations of the Ancient World, to the bacteriological genocides in the American and Pacific island territories. Particularly remarkable from this point of view is the case of Indonesia and the Philippines. These archipelagoes, although comparatively close to the great civilizations of the neighbouring continent, have an "Asiatic" and not a "Pacific" pattern of demographic behaviour: their populations did not collapse "like a *soufflé*". Despite some temporary setbacks, they experienced phases of healthy growth even during the heyday of colonialism, dating from various points in the eighteenth century. The reason for this state of affairs is very simple: the Philippines and Indonesia, through numerous lines of communication, were in constant contact with their neighbouring countries in the continental Far East. The two large groups of islands were therefore included in the microbial community which covers a large part of densely populated Asia from India to China, and which has also had links with Europe dating back over many centuries. So the arrival of Westerners in person did not, from an epidemiological point of view, prove any more dangerous for the Filipinos and the Indonesians than it did for the Japanese, the Chinese and the Indians. The Pacific islands situated very much further to the east, on the other hand, had not benefited from the partial immunization that had come by way of the age-old contacts; they were, therefore, from the eighteenth century onwards, submerged beneath the bacteriological flood, as the Americas had been two centuries earlier.

I should like to end on this note, by paraphrasing Woodrow Borah's trenchant conclusion, condensing and simplifying it a little here and there: the correlation to be made, he writes in essence, is not one between primitivism and depopulation: but between the *degree of isolation* or isolationism before contact with Europe, and the *size of the demographic destruction*, once that contact had been established. This suggests that the most important factor making for demographic destruction has been the spread of infectious diseases.

Regions linked to the long-distance trade routes from Europe to the Far East absorbed the impact of a varied number of diseases over long periods of time; it was thus possible for them to recover and to build up immunological resistance. The peoples of the New World and later those of Oceania, who lived in complete or almost complete isolation, absorbed, in a few decades, the impact of every infectious disease that could be spread. They received in a very brief period of time the series of shocks that Europe and the Far East had had the opportunity to absorb over several thousands of years.

Bacteria and viruses, in fact, had brought about the unification of the world before man succeeded in achieving it on his own account.[131]

CONCLUSION

In conclusion, let me take up again that last sentence of Borah, hoping that I shall not deform it too much to suit my purpose.

My point of departure in this essay was the notion that a "community of disease" had once upon a time existed: it did not extend to the whole of Eurasia, and had not reached America at all. This being so, accidents—"short-circuits"—were always *possible*, and in fact the *probability* of such accidents increased in the course of the later Middle Ages and the years immediately preceding the Renaissance. It grew ever greater as the large mass populations of the world expanded—the Chinese, the Mediterranean and European races, the American Indians—and also as vast networks of roads between these great masses (and attended by armies of rats and fleas) opened up, stretching across the forbidden zones of endemic disease in central Asia. The danger became urgent the moment those redoutable disseminators of epidemics, the Genoese, began to cross the Black Sea and press on towards central Asia, now newly unified under the Mongols—those other guilty parties; and then once again, when one of those selfsame Genoese set sail westwards at the head of the Iberian conquistadors. One is tempted to draw a comparison with our own age, now that the proliferation of nuclear weapons has made the risk of accidents at any time not only possible but indeed probable.

But, to concentrate on the crucial phase of the fourteenth, fifteenth and sixteenth centuries: the risk of an ecological and biological disaster on a major scale was all the greater since the threatened populations were in *a state of least resistance*, partially in the case of Europe, almost totally in the case of America. And this was so whatever the nature of the agent of destruction: in Eurasia chiefly plagues; in America (and later, in the Pacific), infectious diseases of every kind. Thus a large part of the human populations of the world, especially in Europe and America (but leaving out, for the moment, Oceania, where certainly the same thing occurred, but later and on a smaller scale) perished, between 1348 and 1600, in the flames of a microbial holocaust—causing loss of life on a scale serious in Europe, devastating in mainland America, and total, or near total, in the Caribbean. The shape of the demographic curves, with their precipitous swoops in the fourteenth and fifteenth centuries in Europe and the sixteenth century in America, followed by painfully slow upturns (in the sixteenth century in Europe, and the second half of the seventeenth in Mexico), has inevitably influenced all the rhythms of world history up to the present, so great is the role of demography as one of the fundamental and crucial variables shaping the development of mankind. And looking beyond demography, we find ourselves confronted by a disaster of cataclysmic proportions, too extensive to be confined in Postan's purely economic categories. It was not only the nourishing root-system, but the tree of life itself that was axed.

By 1530 in Europe, and 1650 in America, the time of major and universal demographic collapse seems to have passed. Subsequently, it was essentially on a regional scale that catastrophes of bacteriological origin occurred, some, it is true, on a vast scale: the wholesale destruction in Germany, for example, resulting from a combination of epidemics and violence associated with the Thirty Years' War; and instances of genocide of the remoter races, more offensive to the world's conscience than decisive in the world's history—I refer, of course, to the extermination by bacteriological infection of the native populations of Oceania from the eighteenth century onwards (see above). But the spread of cholera in the nineteenth century is proof that the era of *microbial unification* is not yet over—far from it, even in the countries of Eurasia. At least its effects are not as apocalyptic as they were on both sides of the Atlantic between 1348 and 1650. Unification by disease as the evil concomitant of expansion and trade has gradually, in modern times, lost its capacity to fashion the destiny of mankind.

3

The Aiguillette: Castration by Magic[1]

FREUD'S relationship with history is a complicated one; even more problematic is his relationship with historians. In the first place, he terrifies a fair number of them: is a historian who has not himself been psychoanalysed competent to use psychoanalysis as a tool of research in his investigation of documents? Scholars have different views of the ethical niceties of this question and I shall be careful not to intrude my own point of view, which is not only that of a layman but probably sacrilegious too. Setting aside this not inconsiderable problem, we still have to define the areas in which historical psychoanalysis could usefully be applied. Erik Erikson, in his well-known study of Luther, was tackling one of history's outstanding personalities: his own great talent made the undertaking a plausible one. Alain Besançon chose to examine, in the same spirit, a long cultural tradition—that of Russia; and in another book he applied psycholanalysis not to history but to the historian: in this case Michelet, who had himself chosen to study the revealing topic of witchcraft. Here too, the results are promising.

I am not a psychoanalyst, nor have I been analysed myself; so I have decided to tread very warily in presenting the following cultural example of collective abnormality. This article brings together many items of evidence relating to magical castration by *aiguillette*, a phenomenon found particularly in the sixteenth and seventeenth century in France. Morbid fear of the aiguillette corresponded to certain specific kinds of panic that affected the people of the *ancien régime*, including the lowest classes of rural society. An obsessive fear of this kind seems to relate to a castration anxiety-complex, whether inflicted on others or experienced by the victim. My incompetence to take the question further need not prevent others from going beyond this article, which aims to present in a straightforward and erudite form the documents concerning such fears and dating from the heyday of the aiguillette: I shall let the texts speak for themselves.

★

To begin with then, here are a few dictionary definitions, some of them very down-to-earth. According to the *Nouveau Petit Larousse illustré*, an aiguillette is a cord with metal tips at both ends, like a shoelace. It can also be a lanyard, a military uniform decoration (*aiguillette de fourragère*), or a thin strip of meat (especially duck, or according to another reference book, rump steak).

Other meanings for the word, some of which are now obsolete, are to be found in Littré, sometimes linked with the similar term *ligature*: the aiguillette was a braid or lace used to fasten hose or doublets; while a ligature in surgery is a suture of variable thickness tied round tumours or veins to check the flow of blood.

Littré also has some curious quotations: "Libertines, i.e., freethinkers, refuse to believe in the aiguillette" (J. B. Thiers, *Traité des superstitions*, IV, p. 500 ff.); "To excommunicate these people as they do locusts and those who tie the aiguillette" (Voltaire); "Is it possible that a man may lose his virility if this aiguillette or Satan's cord is not snapped?" (Pierre de Lancre).

A curious echo to Lancre's question (he was the torturer of Basque witches) is found in a text by Bossuet, also quoted by Littré, in quite a different context: the ligature, Bossuet writes, is a *suspension of potency* occurring in mystics.

Lastly, Littré refers to the now obsolete meaning attached to the dreaded words aiguillette and ligature: they are used, he says, in connection with "evil spells intended to bring about a sudden suspension *of some bodily function, such as the consummation of marriage*." In this last sense, the aiguillette was therefore a magical device to induce impotence.

Two monumental works provide us with our first detailed information on the subject: first, the *Encyclopédie théologique* by the Abbé Migne, in fifty volumes, published in the middle of the nineteenth century;[2] and second, a learned and still useful book, the *Traité des superstitions qui regardent les sacrements*, (Treatise on the superstitions concerning the sacraments) compiled towards the end of the seventeenth century by Jean-Baptiste Thiers, one time *curé* of Vibraye.[3]

According to both Migne and Thiers, the aiguillette was one particular form (relating to sexual functions) among the many kinds of ligatures, magic rituals and evil spells "by means of which some physical faculty in man or woman can be restricted".

Such ligatures were among resources generally attributed to the devil. If we are to believe the theologians of the seventeenth century, a man made impotent by a witch's aiguillette was comparable to one struck dumb, to a horse checked in full gallop, or to a bewitched bolt in a faulty cross-bow.

> Daily experience teaches us, writes Fr. Fevret in his treatise on Abuses, that it is as easy by magic arts to render a man impotent in the marriage act, as it is easy by spells to bind the tongue and remove the power of speech, and to stop in an instant the course of swift horses, to fix and jam the geared wheels of a turning mill, to charm the bolt of a hunter's cross-bow, to loosen or to arrest the wind, and other similar feats that sorcerers perform with the aid of the devil.[4]

Migne quotes various historical precedents taken from Classical or Biblical antiquity: Shem, Plato, Virgil, Ovid, and many others are said either to have practised or at least to have referred to rituals of magical impotence, and binding of the private parts; "O Amaryllis, bind fast with three knots these strips of cloth and say: bonds of Venus, I tie you . . ." Virgil writes in the eighth eclogue, in his account of a magic spell intended to render one person insensitive to the pangs of love, while inspiring in another the most frenzied of passions. (But as I intend to show technically, the aiguillette as such does not appear with any certainty and precision until the Middle Ages when it figures in the list of secrets of the "great Albert".)

Rituals to induce impotence, though, are found in modern times in all parts of Europe, and even far to the east. The author of a book called *Nouveau Voyage vers le Septentrion* (New Journey to the North), published in 1708, tells of an experience he witnessed in Russia: "I saw a young man come out of his wife's chamber like a mad man, tearing his hair and crying out that he was bewitched. Masters of "white" magic cast out the spell and untied the aiguillette" (in Migne, under *ligature*, 1846).

However, it was neither in Antiquity nor in Peter the Great's Russia that witchcraft causing conjugal impotence exercised its most terrifying mischief. In the opinion of demonologists and the most discerning of experts in the practices of superstition, it was in sixteenth and seventeenth-century France, in the Europe of the late Renaissance, the Baroque and the Counter-Reformation.

Tying the aiguillette has become so common a practice, wrote Pierre de Lancre in 1622, that there is hardly a man who dares to marry except in secret. One finds oneself bound without knowing by whom and in so many different ways that the most skilful have no knowledge of how it is done. Sometimes the spell is on the husband, sometimes on the wife, sometimes on both. It lasts a day, a month or a year. One partner loves but is not loved in return. Couples bite, scratch and repulse one another. Or else the devil interposes an evil spirit between them.[5]

The sex-obsessed Pierre de Lancre, the ruthless burner of witches, is a notoriously suspect witness. But he is not the only person, at the end of the sixteenth century, to affirm the universal belief in the aiguillette and "ligatures" or bindings. Montaigne, an observer we can trust, speaks of *ces plaisantes liaisons de mariages, de quoi le monde se voit si plein qu'il ne se parle d'autre chose*[6] ("the absurd 'ligatures' of marriages, so frequently seen as to be the sole topic of conversation"). The great essayist refuses to attribute any demonic or supernatural origin to this epidemic of impotence. Clear-eyed amidst the general obscurantism of his age, he defines *ligatures* quite simply as "impressions of apprehension and fear". But one only has to read his essay, (which is actually called "On the Force of the Imagination"), to realize that his contemporaries believed in the aiguillette, and in their marriage-beds frequently thought themselves its victims. Noël du Fail, the delightful sixteenth-century teller of tales, agrees with Montaigne: in the days of François I, he writes, stories about the aiguillette were not as frequent as they are today.[7] People did not fear, as they do now, to offer hospitality to any caller who happened by, for in those days they did not fear sorcerers and magicians casting the blight of misfortune and sterility upon the marriage-bed. But Fr. Crespet, Prior of the Celestine Order and author of *Deux livres sur la haine de Satan* (1590),[8] provides us with an even more valuable chronology. In his opinion it was from 1550–60 that the aiguillette epidemic became generally widespread. And by way of explanation, the pious father naturally blames the heretical Huguenots and the sacrilegious atheists: "Our forefathers did never experiment so much with charms and evil spells against the sacrament of marriage as we have now seen these last thirty and forty years since heresies have proliferated and atheism has been introduced into our midst."[9]

The period that separates Noël du Fail and Montaigne (sixteenth century) from Fléchier (second half of the seventeenth century),[10] is one that sees the aiguillette, an old country ritual, emerge from the rustic obscurity of village witchcraft, to become a well-known cultural phenomenon, written about at length in literature, told about endlessly in stories, and frequently invoked in law: it was the age *par excellence* of the aiguillette of which Jean Bodin, Pierre de Lancre and other experts in the wiles of the devil were the formidable witnesses, in their capacities as writers and as burners of witches.

In the opinion of Jean Bodin and the other demonologists of his day, the devil had, on the whole, no power over the organs and senses of man.[11] Satan could not deprive man of his appetite, nor cause him to lose the use of his legs and arms.[12]

There was one exception however, one single function subject to the devil's power: sexuality. "And it is a fact well to note that neither the Devil nor his Ministers in sorcery . . . have power to take from a man (the use) of a single member save only the virile parts: which is what they (female witches) do in Germany, causing to be hidden or to be snatched out of his belly the private parts".[13] The allusion to Germany tells us where Bodin acquired the idea that the genital organs were particularly vulnerable to the devil's machinations. It was from the *Malleus Maleficarum*, published in 1488 by Jacques Sprenger, a monk from Cologne and a great seeker-out of witchcraft. Sprenger it was who first identified the parts of the human body that had been chosen as the devil's prime targets; and he justified this geography of selection by reference to the serpent: "The Devil by God's permission has great power over the genital organs, for the serpent which trails over the earth signifies the serpent of lust . . . the serpent, in an allegorical sense, signifies lust, which trails over the belly".[14] The serpent was simply made in the image of one of the two sex organs.

It was in Touraine, Languedoc and above all in Poitou that Bodin, through contact with local witchcraft, formed his ideas on the subject of the aiguillette. In 1567, when the extraordinary assizes were being held in Poitiers, and the future author of *Demonomania* was serving as the deputy *procureur du Roi*, a young woman of virtuous reputation, demonstrated before both him and his friend Jacques de Beauvais, the fifty different ways of tying the leather lace that the public, in fear and trembling, called the *aiguillette*.[15] In one of such ways the witch could bind only the wife, leaving the husband in full possession of his powers; in another, it would be the husband who was bound, while the wife retained in full her conjugal appetite. (This second case, with the husband impotent, was thought to be the more frequent.) One can easily guess at the suits for adultery for which such magic rituals were responsible.

Other variations could decide not only which of the marriage partners was to be affected but also how long the spell was to last. With practice the magician could "bind" a couple for life, for a year or even for a day: Bodin quotes the case of a couple in Toulouse who were so bound; "nevertheless, three years later, they recovered and had many children".

The particular form the impotence could take was subject to infinite gradations among which the knot-tiers could choose: the most refined type of ligature consisted of binding the couple in such a way that they continued "to love one another passionately"; but when they were about "to come together, they scratched and fought each other most violently".

Lastly, under the influence of a certain type of aiguillette, physical love was still possible but was sterile and never resulted in the conception of a child: "A couple might sometimes be prevented (bound) from conception and not from intercourse"[16]—a truly magical form of contraception that certain modern people would greatly welcome! But for "ancients" such as Bodin and de Lancre, fertility remained the supreme goal; this spell-binding form of birth control seemed to them totally damnable.

The leather lace known as the aiguillette was certainly synonymous in the highest degree with sterility; as long as it remained knotted to bind a married couple, all along its length would appear certain wart-like swellings. Each one of these warts or verrucas, protruding like a pimple on the cord of the aiguillette, was the symbolic representation of a child who would certainly have been born, had the couple not been bound by black magic.

Unborn children were thus the chief victims of the aiguillette; so much so that Bodin thought the use of this spell quite as serious as abortion or even the murder of a living child: "it cannot be denied that he (the aiguillette sorcerer) is a murderer: for he who prevents the procreation of children is no less guilty of murder than he who cuts their throats".[17]

As well as child-victims, there were child-practitioners: children "who had no knowledge whatsoever of sorcery" were able to learn the awful secrets of ligatures and so take vengeance on adults by bewitching their marriages. We read, for instance, of a very young child who tied the aiguillette to bewitch his parents' servant-girl who had just got married; she had to beg the little rascal on her knees to undo the spell.[18] And Riolé, the Deputy General of Blois, told Bodin "that a woman in church saw a little boy tying the aiguillette under his hat while two persons were being married": the little boy was caught in the act but he succeeded in running away.[19]

The aiguilllete, being a device of black magic was also, of course, susceptible to magical cure; sorcerer and spell-lifter might be one and the same person. In 1560, in Niort in sixteenth-century Poitou, where ligaturing was a very common practice, a young wife whose husband was "bound" laid the blame for the magic spell upon her next-door neighbour. Without more ado, the Niort magistrate sentenced the neighbour "to a dark dungeon" and threatened to have her locked up for life unless she "unbound" the couple. Frightened our of her wits, the sorceress obeyed. She commanded the man and his wife to *lie together* (*qu'ils couchassent ensemble*). Learning that the spell had been lifted, the judge at once had the imprisoned woman released—an edifying story, ending for once without a burning at the stake. The moral is plain: he who "tied" could also "untie". And the Catholic Church was so well aware of this fact that it was obliged to battle on two fronts: against the sorcerers who *tied* the aiguillette and against those who *untied* it—good magic was just as reprehensible as bad.[20]

The reader understandably may be sceptical about taking the word of Bodin, the demonomaniac and burner of witches; but other writings from unprejudiced witnesses confirm his allegations.

In 1596, the Swiss doctor Thomas Platter, whose accuracy and acuteness of observation I have checked on a number of occasions, was staying in Languedoc. On March 23 of that year he was a guest at the wedding of a merchant called Rouvière, a native of Montpellier.[21] Platter followed the ceremony from start to finish, even being present when the bride was being led into her chamber. "As she passed, a young man stole her garter. When she was seated on the bed in her nightgown, all the guests, men and women, young and old, came to her and kissed her on the mouth, with many compliments and good wishes".

A dark shadow, however, lay over this intimate scene: the daytime religious ceremony preceding the evening's jollifications had been conducted in secret. "The merchant Rouvière was married secretly without witnesses, in the church of a village outside Montpellier. This was a custom in Languedoc, to prevent the knotting of the aiguillette".

Was this a custom in use in Montpellier only? Not so. Two years later, on July 16, 1598, Thomas Platter was a guest at another wedding, this time at Uzès.[22] Same panic. To the doctor's great ‚astonishment the young couple were not married in the church at Uzès, but secretly, in a nearby village, to prevent anyone tying an aiguillette "which engenders hate between man and wife".

And Platter describes in detail the diabolical ritual: the sorcerer (or sorceress) chooses the precise moment when the priest says: "Whom God has joined together, let no man put asunder"; Satan's servant then adds under his breath "but let the devil do it", at the same time tossing a "*patard*" (a small coin) over his shoulder. If no one succeeds in finding the coin—in other words, in restoring the bridegroom's virility—all is lost; the new husband is impotent, at least insofar as his own marriage is concerned. His potency in regard to other women, however, remains unimpaired. One may well imagine the instances of adultery to which this led!

The people do not doubt, adds Platter gravely, "that the Devil himself has made off with the farthing and will keep it until the last day of judgment, to ensure the damnation of the guilty".

The penalty for this "crime", according to the Swiss doctor, was burning at the stake; yet the ritual was practised very frequently in Languedoc, for this was how spurned suitors avenged themselves upon their preferred rival. "Therefore not more than ten marriages in a hundred are performed publicly in church", notes Platter, probably exaggerating. Couples received blessing in secret in some nearby village and then returned to the town for the wedding feast.

The aiguillette, Platter concludes, was one of the reasons why there were so few marriages in Languedoc—with this unforeseen consequence: "it is why the country is less populous than ours, and there is more land for each of them".

Platter's on-the-spot witness is particularly convincing, for the ritual he describes (aiguillette *and coin*) was not mentioned by anyone else at the time writing on the subject of ligatures. Platter must have noted it down from some local Languedoc informant. And his testimony as to the widespread nature of this casting of spells on marriages bears out Bodin and de Lancre: "Of all these

filthy evils, there are scarcely any more frequent than the aiguillette
. . . Everyone knows that in France this wicked magic is so commonplace that it is held to be a mere pleasantry (*gentillesse*)".[23]

So what does the aiguillette really amount to in this primitive
practice described by Bodin, Platter and de Lancre? A technique to
induce impotence, of that there is no doubt. But to put it more
precisely, it was a technique of inducing an artificial and psychological form of impotence as opposed to natural or congenital
impotence. Pierre de Lancre makes a clear distinction between
these two states. On the one hand, there is natural frigidity, "which
resembles crystal, water condensed by the cold, ensuring that the
organs of generation can never be warmed".[24] On the other hand,
there is magical frigidity, the work of the aiguillette, and so common in the France of his day that men of honour did not dare to
marry by day, but had their unions blessed by night to escape the
devil and his minions.[25]

On this point, de Lancre makes a distinction of crucial importance. The aiguillette, he says, is not just an impotence spell. The
aiguillette is well and truly a means of *castration*. "Who is there who
doubts", he says, "that the devil cannot teach his minions the arts of
castration, elision, interruption, desiccation and frigidification".[26]
There were many such forms of castration, and in his *Incrédulité du
sortilège* he lists ten of them.[27] The most extreme forms involved
actual and complete mutilation: he quotes the case of one of his own
compatriots, a gentleman of Bordeaux who, at the devil's bidding,
"had completely emasculated and castrated himself".[28]

But even in de Lancre's opinion, this ultimate form, self-
castration, represented an extreme situation. What interests me is
the normal form, the aiguillette ritual as it was currently practised.
How was it possible that the symbolic act of tying a cord during a
marriage service could be considered, by all concerned, to be a
magic ritual of castration?

A first answer to this question was supplied seven centuries ago
by Albert le Grand in Book 22 of his treatise *De Animalibus*. Maître
Albert, a great authority on magic, was the first, as far as I know, to
provide a relevant description of the aiguillette ritual:[29] *Si virga
lupus in alicuius viri vel mulieris nomine ligetur, non poterunt coire
donec nodus ille solutus fuerit*. A popular translation of this work,
the *Admirables secrets du Petit Albert*, tells us: "Take the penis of a
newly killed wolf, go to the door of him you wish to bind and call

him forth by name. As soon as he answers, tie the penis with a length of white thread and immediately the poor man will become impotent".[30]

These texts make quite clear the purpose of the aiguillette knot. It is not a completely arbitrary act or empty ritual. The ligature is a knot specifically intended to mutilate the genital organs—actually in the case of the wolf, symbolically in the case of the man.

And this mutilation was simply an imitation of standard veterinary practices.

A very old practice, dating as far back as 1590 at least, and probably much further back still, consisted of castrating rams by the method of tying with a thong (*fouettage*), and bulls and foals by twisting (*bistournage*). In both cases, in one way or another, the testicles of the animals together with the scrotum, or simply the scrotum alone, were tightly tied with a length of hemp or wool or leather. Throughout the whole Languedoc region where the aiguillette ritual was endemic, *bistournage* had been the practice since time immemorial. And in the sixteenth century, the two methods— the magical and the veterinary—were both vouched for as being in use simultaneously, in about 1595–60, the one by Platter and the other by Olivier de Serres. A farmer about to castrate a bull or a Camargue pony would begin by twisting and forcing the testicles into the upper part of the scrotum ("he stuffs them up into the belly", to quote Olivier de Serre's earthy expression).[31] Then he would twine the wool or hemp three or four times round the scrotum, immediately above the testicles, tug hard and tie a double knot, thus blocking the *vas deferens* of the testicles.

Bistournage (literally "twice turning") therefore consisted of two actions, one after the other: first, forcing the sex organs upwards, second, the actual ligature. In similar fashion, in the Languedoc aiguillette ritual, the sorcerer began by throwing upwards, over his shoulder, the coin (the symbolic equivalent of the testicles or contents of the *bourse*—which in French has two meanings: purse, and scrotum).[32] Then he would tie the knot, sometimes a double knot.

But veterinary castration of animals and human castration are two very different things, you may say. Not at all—the correlation of the two operations is quite close. Human castration by *ligature* is a practice attested from very long ago: one of the heroes of ancient Greece carried out the experiment on himself. In Toulouse, in the twelfth century, it was by this ligature method that the urban community punished citizens convicted of adultery.[33] And in cultures other than ours, in Africa and in the Americas, primitive theory and practice progresses easily from animals to humans: Talayesva, the Hopi Indian chief, whose personal reminiscences were recorded by Simmons, tells of an incident during his boyhood, at the time of the year when horses were being castrated: by way of a cruel joke an adult member of his tribe threatened to do the same thing to him. Talayesva was so terrified that later, when he was a grown man, he revenged himself upon his persecutor by snaring him in a lassoo. Nearer home, in certain African tribes, if the witch-doctor wants to prevent a woman becoming pregnant, he takes the oviduct of a chicken, *ties a knot in it*, boils it and eats it. The Yaos in the former German colonies of southeast Africa, make a rope from the bark of a tree, rub it over an egg and *tie several knots in it*—their way of laying the curse of sterility upon a woman. In both these cases, among the Rifs and the Yaos,[34] we see all the characteristics of the aiguillette ritual. The notion of the *castrating knot* is therefore either part of a folk-inheritance common to the peoples of Europe and Africa, from Virgil's shepherds to the Yaos of southeast Africa; or—and this is another plausible hypothesis— the magic knot that castrates must be assumed to have been invented independently in the various cultures of the two continents north and south of the Mediterranean.

★

The list of magic remedies to *counter* the aiguillette is characterized by a fairly obvious symbolism. Here are three such remedies, each having features in common:[35] if a "tied" husband wished to be cured, he should tap a full barrel of white wine and direct the first jet through his wife's wedding ring. Or else he can simply "piss through the ring". A third solution would be to urinate through the key-hole of the church in which he was married. The common elements in these three "remedies" are so obvious as to be self-evident. They presuppose a magical equivalence between the "ritual" so practised and the desired sexual intercourse between man and wife; given a male and a female element, the one has to direct a jet-stream through the ring of the other.

This magical symbolical pharmacopoeia is very ancient; it is vouched for, according to Thiers, by Arnaud de Villeneuve, a Montpellier doctor of the Middle Ages.[36]

There were other symbolic practices: "In many places, future husbands put marked coins in their shoes as a precaution against the aiguillette being tied in their names".[37] Thiers, who described this practice, does not attempt to explain it. Platter's text, which was unknown to Thiers, provides the key: the coins were the magic equivalent of the testicles.[38] Putting marked coins into his shoes was a husband's way of placing the most precious parts of his virility, safely hidden and marked, out of the reach of the sorcerers. Or, to be more accurate, this was the foundation on which the ritual was formed. Subsequently, young couples must often have performed the ritual without knowing the reason for it.

The counterpart of the ritual of the coins was the ritual of the ring:[39] the bride did not put coins in her shoes, but she did put her ring in her shoe, and it remained there for the duration of the ceremony. She took it out only when it was time to kneel before the altar for the celebration of the mass.

★

So the aiguillette constituted a "peril" which, despite its mythical character, was dreaded by many people: almost everywhere in France, couples married in secret to avoid the evil spells of the aiguillette sorcerers. So widespread did the custom become that a series of provincial ecclesiastical councils considered it their duty to condemn nocturnal marriages performed in this spirit: Thiers cites a number of such councils in the northern half of France who, between 1583 and 1640, roundly denounced the practice.[40]

Another propitiatory practice which consisted of dropping the wedding ring before placing it upon the bride's finger was also denounced by six councils between 1606 and 1647, five in the north of France and one in the north of Italy.[41] As we see then, fear of the aiguillette was widely attested, both socially and geographically. But to what deep-seated psychological phenomena did this fear correspond? I am at a loss to answer this question except by repeating something that everyone knows: the considerable role that fear of castration plays in Freudian theory. In this field, historians of my kind must honestly acknowledge their personal incompetence and hand over to someone else. From now on, it is up to the psychoanalysts, whether historians or not, to exploit and interpret the data that history places before them—if such a thing is possible (or desirable).

BIBLIOGRAPHY

BODIN, J., *De la démonomanie des sorciers*, Paris. (I have used the 1580 and the very similar 1581 editions.)

CRESPET, FR. PIERRE, *Deux livres de la haine de Satan*, Paris, 1590.

HIMES, N., *Medical History of Contraception*, New York, 1963.

LANCRE, P. DE, *L'Incrédulité et mécréance de sortilège pleinement convaincu*, Paris, 1622.

LE GOFF, J., *La Civilisation de l'Occident médiéval*, Paris, 1965.

MIGNE, ABBÉ, *Nouvelle Encyclopédie théologique,* vol. 20, Paris, 1846; vol. 20, the work of M.A. de Chesnel, is entitled *Dictionnaire des superstitions, erreurs, préjugés* . . .

PLATTER, THOMAS, *Journal of a Younger Brother*, trans. Seán Jennett, Muller, London, 1963.

THIERS, J.B., *Traité des superstitions qui regardent les sacrements* (several editions, Paris, particularly those of 1679, 1700–4, 1777; see especially vol. IV).

4

French Peasants in the Sixteenth Century[1]

THIS article looks at the history of the French peasants in the sixteenth century: their economic and social history and—as far as possible—the history of their mentality. In a sense, this is not new ground for me; though what is really important is that in some respects it may well be a new—or renewable—subject for at least some of my readers. For, over the past few years, there have been several valuable fresh studies in this field (J. Jacquart's thesis, for example, which has now been published); and it may prove interesting to examine the problem in the light of these new findings.

I propose to begin, somewhat abruptly, with the subject of population: the rural population in this case, of course. Demographic growth in the sixteenth century, in France that is, (in the case of Spain the chronology would be different, and earlier in time) demographic growth in the 1450–1560 period then, i.e., from the end of the Hundred Years' War to the start of the wars of religion, is a well-established fact. But a few figures that have recently come to light, in parts of the country previously only slightly explored, if at all, now enable us to develop in detail certain aspects of this question.

Let us take, for example, the case of the Ile-de-France region and the great zone of the open plains around Paris. We have known for a long time, from Yvonne Bezart's already dated book on the subject, that in the villages in these areas there was, between 1460 and 1560, a massive increase in the rural population; in that single century the demographic level returned to what it had been before the Black Death (1300–40), or not far from it.[2]

But what Jacquart in his recent comprehensive thesis has demonstrated,[3] is that the total figure for the rural population around Paris in about 1550–60 was higher than any figure subsequently attained by the same population in the seventeenth century. In other words, demographic growth had, by the middle of the sixteenth century, produced a total number of people exceeding by 20–30 per cent or more any population total reached in the seventeenth century within the same boundaries.

To give just one example among others: in Bagneux, Arcueil and many other parishes on the outskirts of Paris, the number of baptisms in about 1542–50 exceeded by 50 per cent its corresponding number, in the same villages, in any decade of the seventeenth century.

We may define mid-sixteenth century France, then, as having been in a state of over-population, whereas, in the seventeenth century, at least around Paris, there was to be simultaneously a situation of crisis (depopulation) and, paradoxically, an increase in rational behaviour: migration from the rural areas into the great city, tending to empty the Ile-de-France of its surplus of inhabitants. This process was finally to bring about a more reasonable and more modern balance between the rural population and its urban counterpart. But that is a remark that applies to the seventeenth century. In the sixteenth century this point had not been reached.

As for other regions: according to Bois, Croix, Lebrun, Goubert and other writers, in the area around the Loire (not the upper Loire) which we may define geographically as median France, the tendencies in the sixteenth century were much the same: the demographic ceiling of the sixteenth century, in about 1560 and even 1580, was as high or even higher than that of the seventeenth century in about 1640. In Normandy, too, after the population growth, a peak was reached in the 1570s.

In the sixteenth century, again, towns like Nantes foreshadowed the Parisian pattern of development: Nantes grew more quickly than its surrounding countryside and in a more continuous and consistent fashion. Thus after 1560, the town continued to acquire more inhabitants, and the country round about to lose a certain number, partly as a result of the devastations of the wars of religion and partly because of the rural exodus. Nantes and Paris then played essentially similar roles vis-à-vis the rural population.

The general notion of a demographic maximum and a state of relative overpopulation in the 1550s has also been corroborated by recent research on the situation in the south of France. The population boom of the pre-Black Death era, and the overpopulation of the years before 1348, had come to an end in Provence and elsewhere as a result of the plagues and wars of the fourteenth and fifteenth centuries. By 1471, the population of Provence had fallen to less than half of its 1320 level. By 1540, it had partially recovered and this growth was to continue. As far as Languedoc is concerned, Georges Frêche recently presented a thesis on the Toulouse area in which he gives an account of a census he discovered for the year 1536. The figures demonstrate that after two generations of outstanding growth, the population of upper Languedoc was greater (in 1536) than it would subsequently be in any period of the seventeenth century or early eighteenth.

Naturally, there were several possible patterns and regional variations, since French demography is no more all of a piece than was the French Revolution. The most frequent trend was towards rapid growth. Between 1450 and 1560, it is possible that the population doubled, which is another way of saying that the level returned to what it had been before the Black Death. Or, to put it another way again, by 1560 it had reached a peak in a huge area of France— from Beauvais to Montpellier and from Lorraine to Normandy— that surpassed all subsequent levels until about 1720.

On the other hand, in the extreme north of France, in the area around Cambrai researched by M.H. Neveux, and also in the French-speaking zone of Belgium (Hainaut, Wallonia), the trend may have been a little different. Instead of a growth of 100 per cent between 1460 and 1560, as was the case in most of the regions that made up the kingdom of France, there was an increase in the rural population of these northern provinces of only 40–50 per cent between 1450 and 1550 (assuming an index of 100 in 1450).

But these discrepancies represent only an apparent contradiction. If these French, or French-speaking areas in the extreme north, and other regions close to them, had an apparently less spectacular pattern of growth and recovery in the 1450–1560 period, compared to that of provinces situated further to the south, it was because their demographic decline in the previous 1340–1450 period had been less pronounced than that experienced further south, in *la pauvre France d'oïl et d'oc*, so ravaged by the Hundred Years' War. In these two apparently divergent cases—the bulk of France on the one hand and the Walloon and northern French provinces on the other—what happened between 1450 and 1560 was the restoration of an "ecosystem", the same ecosystem that had been in operation before 1340. But this restoration, naturally enough, was less impressive when the devastation of the intervening period—1348 to 1440—had been less pronounced: and this appears to have been the case in the northern French-speaking complex, the extent of which I have just defined.

*

I shall now, if I may, suggest a few overall figures: what was the total strength, during the various periods under review in this article, of the "French" population within the boundaries of the geographical hexagon, or rather the quasi-hexagon of 1700 (in other words within the boundaries of France as they were in Vauban's time, which makes a good period of reference for demographers)? In 1328, this figure (based on a count of households) was probably at least 17 million (85 per cent of whom lived in rural areas). At its point of greatest decline, in about 1440, as the Hundred Years' War was coming to an end, it had fallen to *less* than 10 million. For the years 1568–80, some 130 to 150 years later, thanks to some Genoese merchant bankers, we have one isolated estimate of figures.[4] *A priori*, such a source is not necessarily unreliable: these financiers were well-informed and were quite capable of carrying out their own approximate informal census-takings so that they could assess, tolerably fairly, the mainly indirect taxes they were authorized to levy. We also have a few overall figures supplied by one Froumenteau, a somewhat eccentric statistician of the 1570s, who attempted, among other things, to calculate the number of prostitutes and homosexuals ministering to the personal needs of members of the clergy! He went so far as to determine the numbers in both of these categories, not only per diocese, but also per individual priest, monk or bishop! But having said that, it would be wrong to condemn Froumenteau out of hand: he was genuinely interested in questions of demography: for example the number of households in each diocese and in the kingdom as a whole, at the end of the 1570s. Alas however, his figures for the dioceses (in *Secret des finances*), some of which are not too wide of the mark, are spoilt by an unfortunate failing on his part: for some reason or other, whenever it comes to deciding the total number of households in a given diocese, he has a predilection for the numbers 52,000 and 58,000! Not only this, but after totting up his own figures, he states that in 1580 there were 3,500,000 households in the kingdom. Now as it happens, this overall figure is vitiated by a glaring error! With the aid of an ordinary calculator, I re-totalled

Froumenteau's figures, using his own tables of statistics for the numbers in each diocese, and immediately discovered an error of one million households (i.e., of four to five million inhabitants) due to simple carelessness on his part. His own figures correctly totalled show 4,500,000 households and not, as he has it, 3,500,000.

But for all that, if we group together every possible source of information, sources I have no time here to go into,[5] it is reasonable to suppose that in about 1550–60, "France" within the quasi-hexagon of Vauban's early eighteenth-century boundaries, had a *minimum* population of 17 million, at least equal therefore to the minimal estimate for 1328. This probable count is nearer to 20 million, perhaps even more: making due allowance for a considerable margin of error, 20 million is by no means a ridiculous hypothesis.

There are two comments to be made about these overall estimates. First, once the process of demographic growth and recovery, extending from 1450 to 1560, had come to an end, the population, especially its rural majority, would in the course of the subsequent period (1560–1730) reach the state of zero population growth—the state in fact that modern population experts are so anxious to attain but are so incapable of realizing.

In this respect, the population of France was altogether different from that of England: the latter, in the interval between the Middle Ages and the seventeenth century, tended to some extent to increase, whereas the former, the French, though subject to huge fluctuations upwards and downwards, in the very long term, i.e., between 1300 and 1720, achieved a state of near-stability. Second, the above remarks apply particularly in the case of the rural population. The urban population, taken as a whole, tended to increase somewhat between the fourteenth and the seventeenth centuries (and therefore throughout the sixteenth century). But the overall totals of the "purely" peasant population remained almost stationary: from 15 million—the lowest estimate—in the early part of the fourteenth century, to 17 million—again the lowest estimate—in the seventeenth century. This transition towards stability, after the profound "troughs" of the fourteenth and fifteenth centuries and the positive upturn of the sixteenth, is of the highest interest to demographic historians: Jacques Dupâquier, for example, is working on a simulation project by computer of this stable phase in the population between 1560 and 1730. He started off with a population of a certain fixed figure; he has infected it with plague and small-pox; and is carrying out calculations based on age at marriage, and inter-birth intervals, to see what happened and to determine which were the decisive factors—births or deaths, entrances or exits—that produced this state of stability.[6]

But I should now like to return to the sixteenth century proper, and submit a brief analysis of the structures governing the rural demographic growth that occurred between 1450 and 1560. It is true that we have far fewer reconstitutions of families based on the village as a unit for the sixteenth century than we have for the seventeenth. But all the same, it is possible that certain conclusions may present themselves; and it will be in order at least to suggest a range of possibilities, or plausible hypotheses, all of which may not necessarily have occurred at the same time.

First of all, let us take a look at the mortality figures. Between 1480 and 1540, the death-rate seems to have been lower than it was in the seventeenth century. Food was plentiful until about 1520, when demographic pressure triggered off the first severe food short-age; from this third decade of the century onwards, when the food situation was becoming serious, fortunately the impact of plague was beginning to wear off, or at least the waves of plague were becoming less frequent—one every ten years instead of every two. This was due, if we accept the evidence of a study by Biraben, to certain administrative measures, enforced both inside towns and between towns, such as removal of refuse and quarantine precau-tions. Thus, for the first time, it became possible to prevent, or at least diminish, the spread of plagues, whereas before the 1520s they had broken out almost every year without interruption in certain parts of the country.

A second structural feature of the demography of the sixteenth century was the marriage age, manipulation of which, according to Pierre Chaunu, constituted the contraceptive weapon *par excel-lence* of the Classical Age in Europe. Guy Bois tells us, in his book on Normandy, that in about 1550 Norman girls married when they were 21, whereas in the seventeenth-eighteenth centuries they mar-ried at 25 or 26. The early marriage age of the sixteenth century was the reason for a higher birth-rate and helps to explain the demo-graphic growth of this period.

Discussing this question, Bois suggests the following pattern: in the Middle Ages, couples married very young, since life expectancy was short, and yet it was essential to find the time to produce and rear the one or more children who would one day succeed the parents on the family plot. After 1450, death came later, people died older, but the habit of early marriage continued more or less for a hundred years: hence the increase in the numbers of the population.

As for the *interval between births*, in the Cambrai area at least, it seems to have differed very little in the 1550s from what it was to be in the second half of the seventeenth century: one child every twenty-five months, in other words every two years.[7] Thus, in our present state of knowledge, the fact that the demographic growth of the sixteenth century changed to the stagnation of the seventeenth is explained better by changes in the death-rates, or by a raising of the marriage age, than by alterations in the fertility pattern which, from the little we know of it, does not seem to have varied very much.

Several other factors explaining the demographic growth of the sixteenth century have come to light thanks to recent studies by A. Croix and other researchers.[3] In the first place, it seems that certain aspects of the model of sexual austerity, based on the teaching of St. Augustine—which the Catholic Church later imposed in the seventeenth century, and which was to prove a not ineffective means of limiting population growth—had already been in operation in the sixteenth century. (This bears out Noonan's findings based on purely theological evidence.) For example, in the pious province of Brittany, where Catholicism had roots in pagan-cum-Christian folklore, sexual abstinence had been the rule during Lent from as early as 1526–1600, long before the Tridentine Counter-Reformation and before its application in other regions. Quantitative history thus teaches us not to exaggerate "non-Christian" factors as influences on the size of pre-Counter-Reformation populations.

However, certain other features of this model of austerity, which were to prove so effective in the seventeenth century had perhaps not been in operation in the sixteenth century. For example, the illegitimacy rate was probably fairly high, especially among the nobility, in about 1550 (as many as 24 bastards might be sired by three male members of the nobility, according to researches into

the Fontanges family in the Auvergne; and also into the Gouber-
villes in Normandy). By contrast, the seventeenth-century illegitimacy rate would be kept considerably lower, thanks to the energetic discipline maintained by the confessors of a stern and
rejuvenated Catholic Church.

★

Faced, then, with a growing or recovering population, what was
the trend in production, revenue and consumption in the rural
sector? (It may seem somewhat rash to group together notions so
heterogenous and hard to classify as those of production, revenue
and consumption; but in discussing a peasant economy, it is legitimate to consider them as a group, since much of the agricultural
output of the time was consumed on the spot, "auto-consumption"
so to speak, by the producers themselves, while another portion of
the output was consumed locally, by the inhabitants of country
towns and villages and by peasant workers not themselves engaged
in cereal production, who bought their wheat from the local farmers.)

Peasants, and *a fortiori* country-dwellers in general, made up, at
the lowest estimate, 85 per cent of the total population. Their ration
of cereals, consisting as a rule of the coarser grains, was as great as
or greater, per head or rather per stomach, than that of the upper
classes and the urban bourgeoisie, who had every opportunity to fill
themselves with meat. One may well conclude, therefore, that at a
minimal and deliberately cautious estimate, 80 per cent of the total
output of cereals, or very nearly so, was consumed by the rural
community itself. This is the reason for saying that consumption
and production were close to each other. Furthermore, at the
national level, exports of cereals in good years and imports in bad,
balanced out nearly enough in the medium term, so it would be true
to say that production and consumption of grain in France
amounted to much the same thing.

So, one is justified in tackling the production/consumption of
cereals as a single problem. A large collective study, *Le Produit des
dîmes* (*The Product of Tithes*) has been published by the 6th Section
of the *Ecole Pratique des Hautes Etudes*, and I shall draw on this in
my remarks on the subject for the period 1450–1560.[9]

Let us consider first the question of productivity in cereals: Morineau, in a book published in the *Cahiers des Annales*, has provided us with a critical reappraisal of the work of Slicher Van Bath (which still remains important in the field). Van Bath diagnosed a large rise in grain yields (the return on seed-corn) from the thirteenth/fourteenth centuries to the sixteenth/seventeenth centuries. He is right, within limits no doubt, in the case of England and the Low Countries. But for countries like France, underdeveloped perhaps by comparison with their northern neighbours, Van Bath's data are too scattered to be considered positive proof that such an increase really did take place. On close investigation, it seems that yields on cereals in France remained by and large stable and unchanged from the thirteenth/fourteenth century until the 1840s. On the whole, they appear to have remained fixed at somewhere about 6:1 or 8:1 in the alluvial soils of the north-east and even in Brittany, and about 4:1 or 5:1 in the south. In fact there was no great agricultural change in France before the nineteenth century (although some growth occurred in the eighteenth). The dominant characteristic of cereal productivity from the Middle Ages until the seventeenth and eighteenth centuries was stability; grain productivity was "frozen" during this period.

As far as the production of grains is concerned, from our collective study of the tithes, it would seem reasonable to advance the following conclusions:

(a) there was a minimum, a clearly defined "floor", of cereal production that was reached after the plagues and the Hundred Years' War, some time in or around the 1430s (a little earlier perhaps in the south). In any case, it was clearly marked both in the south and in the north of the French "Kingdom" (cf. the work of Stouff, Fournial, Fourquin etc.). The only exception (partially outside our boundaries, in any case) was in the French- and Flemish-speaking far north (Wallonia, Flanders, etc.) which had hardly been affected by the Hundred Years' War, and which maintained a fairly healthy production of grain in the 1430s.

The "low" in French grain production during the 1420s–1430s was responsible for famines on a massive scale, the repetition and intensity of which were never again to be equalled, even during the bad years of the seventeenth century.

(b) This "minimal" period was followed by an era of growth and recuperation in the production of cereals, when the peasants reoccupied the deserted countryside. The abandoned fields had, for the most part, become covered over with scrub, and since the forest had often not had time to take them over again completely and grow back to its eleventh-century level, the recovery of grain production was speedy, efficient and not too costly. From 1440 to 1520, cereal production seems to have progressed, or rather to have re-established itself at a rate exceeding, or at least equalling, the rate of population growth and the increased overall demand for cereals. The positive result of this synchronization of rates was the almost complete absence of large-scale famines or subsistence crises during the period 1445–1505. The cereal price curve was extraordinarily steady during these sixty years, whereas after 1520 (and until 1740) it was to undergo terrifying fluctuations as overall demand, resulting from the now permanent increase in the population during the first half of the sixteenth century, kept coming up against the Ricardo-Malthusian ceiling of cereal production.

In fact, (according to the latest graphs based on the statistics of tithes and the farming of noble estates) the overall production of cereals continued to increase for some time after 1520, but at a much slower rate than in the 1450–1520 period. The famines of the 1520s mark a turning-point: from a period of rapid or relatively rapid increase in cereal production *before* 1520, there followed a period of slow increase *after* 1520. Eventually, increased production of cereals ceased almost completely after 1560 (during the wars of religion).

So, in about 1510–20, we enter a Ricardo-Malthusian situation, that is to say, a phase in which the demographic upsurge and the overall, especially the urban, demand for staple foods were rising more rapidly than the supply from the country.

This is the explanation for the new wave of subsistence crises I have just referred to. It is also an explanation of the price revolution of the sixteenth century, or at least certain aspects of it. In this connection, see Ramsey's *Price Revolution in the Sixteenth Century*,[10] and also Baulant's article on wages (*Annales*, 1971) with their comments on the differential evolution of prices as compared to wages.[11]

When it comes to the price revolution, there is, of course, no reason to jettison the quantitative theory. The influx of silver from America probably contributed—directly or only indirectly—to raise prices and promote inflation. But the differential rises in the different price categories (cereal prices, non-cereal food prices, and prices of commodities other than food) are less convincingly explained by the theories of Jean Bodin or Milton Friedmann on "monetary history" than by the contrasting trends in the economy and the demography of the time. As Ingrid Hammarstrom[12] has shown (and her demonstration is equally valid in the case of France), from the first or second decade of the sixteenth century, the population, particularly in the towns, was expanding faster than the production of cereals and the means of their distribution and sale; demand for wheat accordingly rose steeply, proportionately more steeply than that of noncereal foods and of goods other than food; in both of these two latter categories, either demand was less acute or supply was more plentiful than was the case with grains (see the figures quoted in Baulant's article in *Annales*, 1971). These attractive, bullish cereal prices proved to be a great stimulus for the development of a vast grain-producing agriculture, but one which in the event proved incapable of maintaining the required rate of growth. Stock-raising, on the other hand, tended to stagnate and even in some areas (the Languedoc for example) to decline in the sixteenth century; market trends led farmers to concentrate their efforts and any investment (despite the falling yields) on the most profitable crop—grain—throughout the sixteenth century. This policy ruled out any agricultural revolution, since an advance of this nature—in the West at least—depended on stock-raising and the use of cattle-manure as fertilizer.

The agricultural revolution in western Europe in fact took place in countries where urban demand for meat and dairy products coincided with a temporary pause in demographic growth: for example, in Holland in the fifteenth century (according to Van der Wee), and in England after 1650 (Hoskins).

The case of France in the sixteenth century, with its increasing overpopulation, was completely different: the demand for grain was paramount, paralyzing the expansion of stock-raising and blocking any chance of an agricultural revolution.

*

On the question of the total tonnage of cereal production in France in the sixteenth century, it can be stated that this reached a ceiling, in about 1560, which should be compared with two other secular "ceilings" of similar type:

1. The maximum, or ceiling, in cereal production recorded in the late thirteenth century and early fourteenth—almost the whole of the first half of the fourteenth century in fact (before the Black Death): something like 55 million quintals of grain, which had to cater (not very effectively) for 17 million people (plus their livestock) and also to provide seed corn.

2. The "second ceiling", which begins precisely with the 1550 maximum, and was to last, despite a number of ups and downs, some quite violent, until the 1720s : 65 million quintals for a population of approximately 20 million (plus, of course, livestock and seed corn).

After 1720, grain production began to increase very gradually; in time, it succeeded in breaking through the apparently impenetrable ceiling of "65 million quintals" which had lasted so long (see above, thirteenth to eighteenth centuries).

In terms of productivity and cereal production, as in terms of population growth, what we see starting between 1450 and 1550 and being practically achieved in about 1550–1560, is the restoration of the medieval eco-system, which drew its second wind, so to speak, between 1550 and 1720. (From 1720–50 onwards, a new eco-system, based on slow but steady growth and partial renewal, would take the place of the earlier one whose characteristics, demographic or cereal-producing, I have attempted to outline here).

Incidentally, when I use the word "eco-system", it is not just a figure of speech. As it happens, the labour-intensive agriculture, employing many people but producing comparatively low yields, that we find in France between the fourteenth and the eighteenth centuries was remarkably conservationist in terms of soil and ecology. The only exceptions were perhaps certain southern regions (the *garrigues* or scrubland areas for example) where erosion gained the upper hand over thin soil and vulnerable belts of forest.

So far, I have dealt mainly with subsistence foods—cereals. But of course in the sixteenth century—and even in the fourteenth— there was a form of agriculture aimed at the market. I am thinking principally of vineyards and wine-growing. Here, as in the case of cereals, there was not only a recovery in the sixteenth century but sometimes a real increase of output which exceeded the medieval maximum of the pre-Plague era.

Such, for example, was the case in the Nantes region (according to Tanguy, and also according to Trocmé-Delafosse). In this area, viticulture achieved a real breakthrough between 1550 and 1570: exports from Nantes rose to almost 300,000 hectolitres of wine around this date, far exceeding the much lower figures of the late Middle Ages, or of the early sixteenth century. But this was an isolated instance. If we take a look at the Bordeaux region, with its famous vineyards exporting their wines to England, we find that in about 1550 the volume of wines produced in this area, as measured in exports from the port of Bordeaux, was certainly much greater than it had been in 1470; but it was distinctly less than it had been very much earlier, in 1300–20, when 850,000 hectolitres of wine left the Gironde every year en route for England and northern Europe (Bernard).

*

In general then, although there were some important, if sometimes short-lived exceptions (see G. Caster's study of the problems of the dyers' woad trade in Toulouse), what we have in the sixteenth century is not so much a process of real growth, but rather a movement of recovery, within the framework or within the course of a homeostatic system—at least insofar as the agricultural sector is concerned. (In the urban sector, on the other hand, the picture is very different: here one may find innovations and changes radically affecting the pattern of medieval urbanization, characteristic of the years immediately preceding the great plagues).

*

At this point, I should like to review the problems not only of the production but also of the distribution of the agricultural product which, after the interruptions of the Black Death era, eventually in the 1550s returned to its "normal" level for the medieval and modern period.

The first type of distribution occurred "horizontally", in the system of land-ownership and tenure. In my *Peasants of Languedoc* I have already indicated how land-tenure in the sixteenth century was evolving in two directions.

On one hand, there was a dividing-up (*morcellement*) of small estates and holdings as a result of demographic growth and successional subdivision. Despite precautions taken by the regional Commissioners who did what they could to preserve a certain proportion of undivided properties in the name of one only of the holder's heirs, the relatively large families at the end of the fifteenth century and the first two-thirds of the sixteenth, tended over time to subdivide and parcel out their estates among heirs whose numbers increased from generation to generation. For this reason, land in the sixteenth century became more and more fragmented. The countryside began to look like a jigsaw puzzle or mosaic of tiny plots gradually growing ever tinier.

But on the other hand, at the same time—and very often on the same lands, the opposite was taking place: the combination of several estates into one! Wealthy citizens, merchants, the old and the new nobility, churchmen as individuals or in groups (chapters, etc.) bought up and pieced together farmlands on the open plains; in this way they acquired the habit of expanding their already large estates; or else, out of separate lots, they created "foreign" properties in the midst of "native" properties in villages up and down the land.

And so the peasant lost on both counts. He saw his own property shrink by virtue of the continuous subdivision of the family holdings; while at the same time he was being alienated from land ownership by this practice of land-purchase by outside (or sometimes local) property-accumulators.

The first problem—the subdivision of the land—raises certain specific questions of French regional anthropology, questions that are splendidly treated by Jean Yver in his book, *Géographie coutumière de la France* and in two further articles.[13] The book gives a comprehensive survey, by province or groups of provinces, of the inheritance customs of France and its frontier regions. A few words, then, on the subject. To take the north or extreme north of France first: here among populations with solid ethnic traditions (Normandy, Flanders), equal distribution of property was the rule: the family wealth was distributed in equal shares to each of the children (or alternatively to any heirs entitled to it by their position in the line of descent), when a succession became vacant, following the death of the father of a family, or of some other person of property.

This custom encouraged subdivision. In this respect it was at the same time archaic (since it was linked to ethnic custom, Flemish or Norman), and modern (since it was egalitarian). In the south, on the other hand, notably under Roman law, the sovereign power of the *paterfamilias* prevailed: a father was empowered to hand over his land, *undivided*, to one of his sons—not necessarily the eldest— the intention being to preserve the estate intact. On closer inspection, however, in the south and also in quite large areas of the north, the following principle is commonly encountered at the time of the Renaissance: land belonging to the family or household was not to be divided: the land was to be handed on by one married couple living in a given house to a following couple—the next in line. The inheritance passed therefore either from a father to a son or, failing a son, from father-in-law to son-in-law. Any other married children were excluded from inheriting, receiving only a settlement (*une dot*) on marriage. In other words, there were basically two systems: in the first, the inheritance was divided according to the structure of the family; in the second, the property, preferably intact, passed in succession from an older couple to a younger. One system set greatest store by *consanguinity*, the other set more by *marriage*.

But in the long run, in the sixteenth century, demographic pressure proved too strong. Although "anthropological" distinctions of the kind mentioned above were not entirely eliminated, there was a general move towards dividing up inheritances into smaller plots of land, especially in the Paris region and even in the south.

*

I mentioned in an earlier paragraph, with reference to Languedoc, two major concurrent and concomitant trends: alienation of the peasant from the land, and the subdivision of properties. It is interesting to discover that Jean Jacquart, in his thesis on the countryside round Paris in the sixteenth century, encountered the same kind of bi-polarization at work: it was even more marked here than in the south of France.[14]

In about 1550, in Hurepoix, south of Paris, the average size of a peasant holding (using the word "peasant" in the sense of "native of a rural area") was 1.30 hectares (a little over 3 acres). This was considerably smaller than would be theoretically needed to support a family: our peasant was therefore well below the level of "minimum self-sufficiency" or even of "minimum subsistence". This was the result of the subdivision of land.

As for the other trend, sixty per cent of the land, in a region like Hurepoix near Paris, did not belong to the peasantry, which as we have seen was already impoverished by land division, caused both by demographic pressure and inheritance customs.

Of this "sixty per cent" of land which did not belong to the peasants, thirty per cent was accounted for by the seigneurial *réserves*, (in other words, the part of a *seigneurie* which was retained and farmed directly). And thirty per cent (the other half) consisted of former peasant holdings: they had been bought (at different times, often recently) by city folk, members either of the bourgeoisie or of the nobility, from Paris or elsewhere.

We can put these figures in another way. Of this "sixty per cent" of non-peasant property, one third (that is to say, twenty per cent of the "complete total", inclusive of peasant and non-peasant land) belonged to groups of the traditional Establishment (clergy, nobility old and new); forty per cent (the remaining two-thirds of the "sixty per cent") belonged to the bourgeoisie, whom we may legitimately subdivide in turn into two sub-groups, as follows: (a) twenty per cent "office holders"; (b) twenty per cent merchants and other non-office holding bourgeois.

So we see that, in the event, the peasants were not crushed by the traditional forces of oppression,[15] for in the last analysis this sector—the clergy and the nobility—seem to have exercized moderation, taking only twenty per cent of the villagers' land. Modernity more perhaps than tradition caused the peasant to suffer. He appears to have been a victim to some extent of progress, since forty per cent of his lands passed into the hands of the bourgeoisie and the office-holders, those pillars of "modernity". In a general sense, the fact that a large part of the land passed out of the possession of the rural classes seems indeed to have been, in England as in France, one of the essential pre-conditions for the early development of capitalism. But this development, even in relatively advanced countries such as England, and the north of France, was not to attain its full "capitalist" momentum in the rural sector until the second half of the seventeenth century in England, and not until the eighteenth century—some would say the nineteenth—in France.

Referring once again to Jacquart's remarkable study, what has he to tell us about the way in which the agricultural activities in Hurepoix were shared out among the different property-owning classes—the nobility, bourgeoisie and peasants—in about 1550–60?

In the case of the peasants, their property consisted in the main of vineyards and wheatfields. The nobles and the clergy, inasmuch as they owned seigneurial *réserves*, possessed practically all the forest land, or at least all of it that did not belong to the King, the first nobleman and first seigneur of the realm. *N'a pas des arbres qui veut*, (trees are not for all and sundry): the *privilégiés* (i.e., the nobles and the clergy) were on the right side of the barricades—the side of those who owned forests: they just watched their timber grow. As for the bourgeoisie, because they did not have the money, and also because they were excluded from the "society of the orders", they were debarred from acquiring forest property: but we may spare our tears on their behalf, for they descended on the vineyards and the wheatfields; some of them eagerly turned to the literature of rural economy which at this time was beginning to circulate in Paris and elsewhere under the influence of two of their fellows, Étienne and Liebault.

*

So far, through a few examples drawn from the Languedoc and Paris areas, I have been discussing the problem of the *horizontal* sharing out of agricultural revenue, as it operated through the structures of land tenure. From what has emerged, it is certain that subdivision on the one hand, and expropriation to the profit of non-rural groups on the other, subjected the peasant community to forces of pressure and disintegration that were difficult to withstand.

After this "horizontal" review, what can we say about the levels of "vertical" distribution of the revenue (land rent, profit, wages)? To take land rent first, I propose to interpret this term, or rather concept, in its widest sense: to include seigneurial dues and tithes, as well as land rent in the strict sense, viz. rent obtained by a landowner who let property on short-term leases (for a few years, or for two or three *triennes*—three-year periods). Quesnay's term "the proprietorial class" includes these various aspects of "land rent" in the broad sense.

To take seigneurial dues first: the sixteenth century (1450–1560) was on the whole a pretty bad time for those entitled to such dues. Inflation, as is well known, operated a sort of euthanasia on any dues the seigneur received in the form of cash. Over the very long term (from the mid-fifteenth century until the end of the eighteenth) such payments, effected in the smallest denominations of coins, lost 95 per cent of their real value: the reason was the rise in the price of grain as expressed in *livres tournois* (a money of account). Grain prices in fact rose twenty-fold during this period. The *seigneurie* then might be said to have been the victim of a series of monetary heart attacks, to which 1789 provided a welcome *coup de grâce*. So it seems to me, though I have not the time to develop the point here, that some very widely-held notions such as "aristocratic reaction" and "re-feudalisation", whether applied to the sixteenth century or the eighteenth, do not really make much sense. (In the eighteenth century, what may have been happening was a delayed struggle, waged in the cause of fixed dues, against price inflation: on this subject, though in a slightly different context, see Paul Bois' *Paysans de l'ouest*, in which he refutes the idea of seigneurial reaction.)

In the sixteenth century, at all events, what was going on was a process of "de-seigneurialisation" and "de-feudalisation" of society, following the gradual demise of seigneurial dues in cash form.

And what about the *champart*—tribute in kind ? (We know that this often represented the most burdensome element of all the seigneurial levies, outside the *réserve*.) On this point, too, Jacquart's thesis seems to suggest that the *champart* was much less widespread than has been thought up to now, at least within the parts of the country he has so scrupulously studied.

An exception must, of course, be made for provinces such as Brittany and Burgundy that were still, in the sixteenth century, relatively backward and firmly under the heel of the *seigneurie*. At that time, the Burgundian aristocracy *as such* defended itself better than did the Parisian.

But now, turning to the subject of tithes, the picture is rather different: at the end of the fifteenth century and in the early part of the sixteenth, tithes increased in value proportionately with the growth and recovery of agricultural production, especially cereal production. The higher clergy therefore (*the* great tithe-takers) grew richer and richer; which was one cause, among many, of the anti-clerical feelings which later gave rise to the Reformation.

Lastly, we turn to land rent proper, rent the landlord obtained from leasing a property to a farmer for three, six or nine years. This naturally increased during the sixteenth century, in the years before the wars. By the hectare, it eventually amounted to the same as the cost of the seed required, (i.e., 2.5 hectolitres of grain per hectare); but it never rose to the dizzy heights that it was to reach in the course of the seventeenth century, when it really would crush the farmer.

The taxes levied by the State in the sixteenth century, were not exorbitant, at least in comparison with those that would be levied in about 1640–60. And interest on borrowings too, although very high (9–10 per cent), was gradually whittled away by the inflation that was the logical accompaniment of the price revolution.

On the whole, we can say that the general share of the revenue that was levied by the upper classes, the Establishment, or the "proprietorial class" (the nobility, the landowners, the clergy, the State) was not yet excessive in the sixteenth century. To put it another way: if the "horizontal" pressure was great (see above), the "vertical" pressure was not too heavy. In about 1550, the overall seigneurial levy might have amounted to somewhere between a sixth and a third of the produce of a given piece of land, depending on whether the peasant was a lease-holder, owner, or only a tenant-farmer (on whom the levy weighed heaviest). In the seventeenth century, on the other hand, the levy, similarly defined and under the same conditions, might represent anything from a fifth to a half of the gross product of the land.

From the point of view of dues at least, then, the peasants of the middle years of the sixteenth century, though slightly worse off in some respects than their predecessors of the end of the fifteenth century, enjoyed more of a "breathing-space" than their descendants and successors in the seventeenth century would ever get.

With wage-earners well on the way to pauperization in the course of the sixteenth century, such a situation was basically profitable to the large landowner or tenant farmer; both were able to benefit from the relatively low land rents and yet pay out (real) wages which, as the century progressed, shrank to almost nothing. Consequently, their business revenue or "profits" accumulated and even grew.

This state of affairs proved to be the case particularly in the years 1540–1560, when wages touched rock bottom. This seems to have been the time when the rich tenant-farmers first reached prominence—as their profits went up.

After 1560 however, and even more so after 1580, the demographic increase which, against a background of sluggish growth in cereal production, had been the essential motivating force behind the reduction of wages to pauper level, and of the fall in the marginal productivity of labour, came to an end.

In these changed circumstances, although real wages (which hit rock bottom in 1540) did not actually recover, their rate of fall slowed down in the Paris region. (In Languedoc however, they continued to fall for some time still during the wars of religion.) The rise in entrepreneurial profits, which depended on this background of depressed wages, gradually slowed down too, during the second half of the sixteenth century.

*

From the point of view of social demography, however, we should introduce some weighting to these general considerations, and ask ourselves what was the statistical significance of the numbers of well-to-do tenant-farmers, compared to those of the impoverished peasants. Such a question is difficult to answer at national level. Once again, we shall have to turn to a regional monograph. And we shall have to reconsider also the familiar concept of a dual structure governing village life, dividing the inhabitants into two separate groups: first, the well-to-do *laboureurs* (peasant farmers) who, while quite numerous, are usually considered to have been the minority; and then the great majority of farm-workers or labourers (*travailleurs, manouvriers*) owning no ploughs, or horses or oxen of their own.

In fact, Jean Jacquart's expert investigation of the archives of his chosen region compels us to modify this concept to some extent, at least when we are talking about the "fortunate sixteenth century". (He has a different story to tell about the seventeenth century, which turned out to run much truer to type.)

In his sample of parishes typical of the open plains of northern France, Jacquart too finds both farmers (*laboureurs*) and farmhands (*manouvriers*) but the latter, according to the documents he cites, seem to have occupied a different place in the rural society of their times from that to which historians have hitherto assigned them.

The pinnacle of peasant society in Hurepoix, we find on reading Jacquart, was composed of a small group of people (less perhaps than 5 per cent, and maybe only only 2–3 per cent of the total active peasant population): this, of course, consisted of the rich tenant-farmers and the seigneur's tax-gatherers; they made up the tiny elite of this rural community. They were among the very few people in the villages who benefited from the rise in profits in the sixteenth century; they also benefited from the formation of large or medium-sized estates by the land accumulators who, as we know, were either members of the bourgeoisie or of the nobility, and generally from the towns. Within the framework of rural society, this upper crust of rich farmers was outclassed in the local hierarchy only by the gentry, when the latter were resident—when they were content, in other words, to be country gentlemen. In Hurepoix this squirearchy was neither very numerous nor very well-to-do: Paris was too close at hand, absorbing the upper classes into its web, and dissuading the lesser nobility from residing permanently in their country mansions. But as soon as one ventures into the *bocage*, or the ancient lands of Normandy and Brittany where towns were few, one finds plenty of country gentlemen. One such, the Sire de Gouberville, who lived in the Cotentin in about 1550, was the recognized chieftain, almost in the tribal sense of the word, of his little community; he was judge and jury in all disputes; he was the local doctor or barber-surgeon; he lanced boils and dispensed herbal concoctions; armed with an unofficial but powerfully effective *droit de seigneur*, he seduced the local farmers' daughters and lived in the midst of a family of bastard children, his own or his father's. Although inclined to Protestantism, the Huguenot ethic was not for him—its austerity appalled him; nor, *pace* Max Weber, do we find in him any rudiments of the "spirit of capitalism" that his religious convictions ought to have inspired. As a matter of fact, he scarcely knew how to set about marketing his sacks of grain. Yet he never seems to have gone short, and apparently lived out his life without ending up bankrupt.

But leaving aside these picturesque but essentially marginal instances of squirearchy, and turning our attention once again to the basic core of peasant society as formed by the *laboureur* group, we find beneath that thin layer of rich farmers just referred to, the main mass of ordinary *laboureurs*—small farmers who made up the *majority* of the active agricultural population, not only in the Paris region but elsewhere, and even in the far south. These farmers were not all, as a too rapid and superficial reading of the works of Georges Lefebvre would have one believe, opulent rural capitalists or village entrepreneurs (apart from the small minority of rich farmers already mentioned). They were quite simply and straightforwardly peasants, often very humble peasants, owning as a rule just one horse (hence their designation of *"laboureur"*—literally "ploughman"). If they did own more than one horse (two or more) it was because they were a little better off, or rather a little less poor than most. In the typical Ile-de-France village, one finds alongside the *laboureurs*, two groups of specialist workers, either vine-growers or artisans. Both groups were fairly poor, but enjoyed a social status or prestige that was not unequal to that of the *laboureurs* which was not very great in any case. Lastly, on the lowest rung of the village social ladder in about 1550, we find the farm-hands (*manouvriers*), a *minority* group and sometimes a very small minority. A marginal group, their social status was very low, their possessions, in land or effects, a bare minimum. And yet, in the Paris region, this "poorest of the poor" group had before it an even worse future, the future of the seventeenth century.

At the level of the majority of the peasant farmers, who set the tone, the French village of the sixteenth century can be considered to have been a relatively well-integrated unit (notably by reason of the local inbreeding that was so prevalent). Acknowledging the existence of this village "unity" is not to show proof of reactionary romanticism, nor is it to deny that there were often instances of internal conflict and spleen within the village community. But it must be said that the main fronts of the class struggle in the rural world, before as well as after 1560, did not run through the middle of the village, nor did they set *laboureurs* against farm-hands. These fronts, when they did appear (which was not very often) usually lined the village up against enemies from without (the State or the profiteers in the towns) more than they divided it against itself.

But the villagers—apart from the happy few on the larger farms—*were* affected by the sixteenth century plague of pauperization. The peasant farmers *en masse* suffered, in greater or lesser degree, from this creeping impoverishment: they suffered from the process of fragmentation of inherited properties; they suffered even from the slump in labourers' wages to poverty level, for some of them, in order to make ends meet, had to take part-time jobs themselves.

And yet, I repeat, before 1560 inside the village itself there was scarcely ever any sign of the class struggle. The farmers accepted their lot, which was far from brilliant, with sleepy resignation (it was commonplace for travellers to depict them "snoring away in their little houses like so many wheezy harmoniums"). They came to life only, or particularly, when some danger from outside the village— demands from the State, or from the groups of plutocrats, finan-ciers, and sharks who were becoming entrenched in the State— threatened the financial and economic security of the peasant com-munity (as during the *gabelle* (salt tax) revolt in 1548 in Angoumois, for example). On this question, Paul Bois' analyses of the *Chouan* uprisings apply with almost equal validity to the *Nu-pieds* in Nor-mandy in 1639, or to the *Pitauts* in Angoumois, Saintonge and Guyenne earlier in 1548. Against oppression in its varied forms, against "feudal" and "seigneurial" domination, or more frequent-ly, against "bourgeois" exploitation in the form of income and salt-tax extortion and land-grabbing expropriation by urban specu-lators, the village, its fighting spirit roused, developed a strategy of attack on all fronts.

Under these conditions, how would the peasant world react to the mental transformations the sixteenth century brought with it? We have seen how, from the point of view of material and economic history, the dominant feature was a return, demographically and economically, to the previous equilibrium: a "rural eco-system" that had been rudely disrupted by the great leap backwards of the fourteenth and fifteenth centuries, had been re-established. A tendency towards restoration of the *status quo ante* was hardly compatible with sympathetic welcome for cultural innovation.

And indeed, as a general rule, the Reformation was either unre-marked or accorded a cool reception by the peasant community. In the main, it only affected those members of the urban and, more rarely, the rural classes who had become contaminated by "reading and writing", that is those who were semi- or wholly literate: the bourgeoisie, the nobility, office-holders, the artisan class—in short the elites, mainly from the towns. As for the ordinary peasants, they showed little interest in the new religious developments; except of course in the case of a minority, principally in southern France, where the following particular factors affected the issue.

(a) *a good communication network between town and country*: we know for instance that in Mediterranean Languedoc, life in the villages followed a pattern similar to that in the towns (see Maurice Agulhon's writings, many aspects of which are equally relevant to the modern period). A structure like this made it possible for the tiny elite, influenced by new cultural currents (whether the political left of the nineteenth century or the Reformation converts of the sixteenth), to make contact with a rural/urban mass of people who were, in the circumstances, inclined to accept new ideas.

(b) *the peculiarities of local religious life*: despite certain widespread exceptions (but which do not seem to me to invalidate the rule), such as the Marian cult in the sanctuary of Le Puy, one is struck, on the whole, by the comparatively slight significance (in the lower Languedoc, for example) of ancient cults of the Virgin. Calvinism, which was so scornful of the feminine bias of papist piety, was thus able to establish itself without too much difficulty in the Cévennes: as early as 1500, witches here regularly blasphemed the name of the Virgin, whom they referred to as the Redhead (la Rousse).

(c) *the group strategy of the Occitanian elites* who, for reasons more or less consciously political or "regionalist", were interested in reinforcing Protestantism, which presented itself as a means of combating the crushing political, administrative and institutional influence exerted by the north against the south. Earlier even than the Montmorency affair, the Protestantism of the south had done its part to build—and readers will pardon me the expression since I know no other that suits the case more adequately—a *"regional power"* in the southern provinces. The local elites were therefore powerfully motivated to swing the peasant masses towards the Reformed Church. Their efforts were only rarely crowned with success; but it was not altogether out of the question (as, for example, in the Cévennes).

But if we except questions of regionalism, found mainly to the south of the La Rochelle-Geneva line, the great mass of the peasant population of France, whose numbers were great in the north, was little, if at all, interested in Protestantism in about 1560; here again, we have only to turn to Jacquart's thesis. He makes it abundantly clear that the Reformation, between 1550 and 1575, passed right over the heads of the peasant community.

Naturally, "fall-out" from the Huguenot movement necessarily affected the peasants. Some of them tried to buy up the *biens d'Eglise* when Church land, by order of the King, came up for sale at intervals between 1561 and 1595. Temptation to acquire land was particularly marked among the wealthier peasants who farmed in the region round Paris, which was being taken over by large-scale agriculture from about 1550. But when such properties came up at auction these cocks of the dunghill had to leave the field beaten: in competition with the really rich, the placemen, the bourgeoisie, the merchants, the nobility, they lacked weight. They were only able to buy a small percentage of the ecclesiastic property on offer.

On the other hand, when one looks at the movement against tithes, historical analysis does show a rather different picture. Starting in the 1550s and reaching a climax in the 1560s, this was a genuine peasant movement; it was particularly active in the Languedoc and also in the Paris basin, culminating in 1565–7. But after 1570, this wave of tithe "strikes" spent itself, lost impetus and finally collapsed. One of the causes of this final failure of a genuine enough movement towards peasant independence, was the stubborn opposition, not only of the bishops, canons and abbots (whose objections were only to be expected), but also of the lower clergy and parish priests. More hard-working, more pious, more closely in touch with their flocks than has been said of them, these *curés*, the spiritual and cultural guides of their villages, made short work of leading their parishioners back onto the right path. This was especially the case in the Paris region. In their way, they too contributed towards the stabilization of the eco-system and towards blocking innovation in the countryside. The peasant anti-tithe movement was just a flash in the pan.

★

In the last analysis, I see the French peasants of the sixteenth century as the objects rather than the subjects of history. The final outcome of their activities as producers and reproducers was the restoration of a system that oppressed them and sometimes crushed them: the restored equilibrium of the regime which was to dominate—though not without some huge fluctuations—the period from

1550 to 1720, was achieved only at the very Ricardian cost of property subdivision, land expropriation, and wage-depression to pauper levels. Apart from a handful of wealthy big farmers, the vast majority of our peasants were affected by one or other, or even by several, of these three scourges. And yet, the great majority remained fundamentally silent, prisoners of their provincial dialects and folklore customs, incapable of participating, save by fits and starts, in the stirring events of the 1560s: the Reformation, the tithe war, the sale of Church property.

We must except certain groups of regional activists: the peasants of the Cévennes, of course, but also their rebellious counterparts in Gers and Agen who, in the first years of the 1560s refused the seigneurial yoke, and jeered defiance of *le petit reyot de merde de l'oïl* ("the little shit of a northern king"). These extremely tiny minority groups excepted, it becomes clear that the peasants did not mobilize, in any considerable numbers, until after 1575, in fact not until between 1580 and 1595. Then, and only then—in a sort of dress-rehearsal of the "Porchnev model"—do we witness great anti-fiscal, and occasionally even anti-seigneurial, anti-urban, or anti-profiteer revolts (*Tard-Venus*, *Gautiers*, above all *Croquants*— three great peasant risings). And certain regions—often but not always the most backward—even began to dabble in the authentic peasant counter-culture of witchcraft. But that is another story.[16]

5

Balzac's Country Doctor: Simple Technology and Rural Folklore[1]

THE first chapter of Balzac's *Le Médecin de campagne* (*The Country Doctor*) has a rather flat title, vaguely reminiscent of geography books: "The Country and the Man". A certain flatness also marks the opening descriptions of Alpine landscapes for which the author has little feeling, and none of the generous vision of a Rousseau or a Horace de Saussure. And his first paragraph ends with a platitude of national sentiment: *Enfin c'était un beau pays, c'était la France!* This accent on Frenchness is somewhat out of place, since the setting of his novel—the Dauphiné—is a border province which, from the point of view of physical appearance, economy, and even the language spoken by the majority of its inhabitants (a fact passed over in total silence by Balzac) had, at the time, little in common with French France, the domain of the Capet kings.

But none of this really matters. Despite these lapses, the essentials, as always with Balzac, are there from the start, in the very first pages. Here is the Dauphinois saw-mill with its wooden troughs and its stripped fir trunks. The ramshackle cottages of the poor labourers are immediately contrasted with the solid houses of the better-off peasants and the local bourgeoisie. The vines described here are correctly staked *en hautains* (using dwarf elms), while the herdsmen feed bales of leaves to their flocks, as was local practice. The baskets holding little cheeses (Saint-Marcellin perhaps?) hanging to dry above every doorway, are duly pointed out in the first paragraph by the author, and his observer of the scene, the new-comer Pierre-Joseph Genestas, an ex-army captain. All these visual details, *choses vues*, are confirmation of Balzac's unfailing and instant (perhaps too instant) sureness of observation.

In 1832, Balzac had crossed the Alps, in squally weather, in the vain hope of seducing Madame de Castries; but despite the failure of his mission, he kept his eyes open. Some of the on-the-spot observations he made at the time turn up in *Le Médecin* (1833), jumbled up with a host of other more or less relevant details remembered from previous journeys through various provinces in his youth. A scrupulous anthropologist of today would be horrified at the hotch-potch this method produces. But when Balzac wrote, there were no scrupulous anthropologists about.

★

Pierre-Joseph Genestas, an ex-army veteran in his fifties, and the first character we meet, is a gallant and courageous fellow, whose arrival in the mountain valleys serves as a peg for Balzac's reflections. The orphan son of a soldier, brought up in the regiment, Genestas has risen through the ranks in Napoleon's *Grande Armée*, which is known to have been a powerful engine of promotion up the social ladder, provided the climber did not fall victim to a cannonball or sabre-thrust. We can take Balzac's word for it that this old soldier could have existed. The memoirs of Captain Coignet, another orphan promoted in the wars, guarantees the authenticity of Genestas' career, one built entirely on his own achievements.

The first peasant farm that Pierre-Joseph comes across in his wanderings in the Alps (technically the pre-Alps[2]) is the poor smallholding which affords a meagre living to the *gardeuse d'enfants*, one of the village foster-mothers to whom abandoned children were farmed out at random by the poorhouse in Grenoble. In his book on eighteenth-century Lyon,[3] Maurice Garden has described in some detail the practice of baby-farming, which was one of the secrets of growth in the countryside between 1700 and 1850. To look after a poorhouse child (or indeed one from a city family), to wet-nurse and then spoonfeed it, was a stroke of luck for a nursing mother, a chance to taste the delights of a little ready cash. Thanks to these foundlings who were farmed out right and left, coins found their way to even the poorest of households, which would otherwise have known only a bare subsistence economy, with very little cash element in it. But alas, defensible though it may have been from an economic point of view, the practice was very much less so demographically. Garden has shown that the farming out of foundlings amounted in fact to a form of organized infanticide, of which the authorities were dimly—or fully—aware. In every village to which these babies or young children were sent, literally hundreds of them died within days, weeks or months, at the breast or in the mercenary arms of the nurses, wet or dry, to whom they had been entrusted by what then passed for "Public Assistance".

The good foster-mother Balzac describes, living on her wretched smallholding, is a widow, already old at thirty-eight and wrinkled like an Eskimo; their exhausting way of life aged such women before their time. She takes in children, but only after they have been weaned. She is capable and kind; with her they survive, they do not die, for she is one of the heroic minority among these child-minders who genuinely and humanely care for the little ones placed with them. She keeps them alive and brings them up, instead of making money by letting them die. In the real, non-fiction world of social history, good nurses of this kind did exist; but as Garden points out, they were few and far between, forming only a small minority compared to the vast army of uncaring foster-mothers who were as mercenary as they were infanticidal. All of which serves to remind us that novelists—even, or perhaps especially, those who like to be thought of as faithful witnesses of their times—often, without warning their readers, choose to describe the untypical, perhaps flattering exception instead of the normal run of life's daily tragedies. In this respect, Zola was, if not better inspired, at least truer to the evidence of statistics than Balzac: in *Fécondité*, he showed what charnel-houses these foster-homes really were, temporary halting-places for town babies on their way to their final destination in country graveyards. Balzac had his reasons for idealizing the picture: he wanted Genestas' meeting with the baby-minder to be a kind of premonition, a happy Annunciation as the old army captain entered the district under regeneration at the hands of the Good Doctor Benassis.

When it comes to recreating a way of life and its setting, on the other hand, Balzac once more becomes a reliable and skilful observer. In describing interiors, expecially dining-rooms, he has no equal. Not a gaiter-button is missing from Genestas' outfit. And in his description of the one and only room where the *gardeuse* and her little charges live, sleep, prepare and eat their food, not a spot of grease escapes his eye as it ranges over fireplace, bed, milking stools, chest, open-barred door . . . (oddly enough, there is no mention of a table, though there probably was one, or of a cupboard, or even a chair). This, effortlessly recreated for us, is the smoke-blackened setting in which a good half of the peasant population of France (the poorer half of course: about ten million) lived out their lives. Even a single-roomed cottage like this might well have other quarters: outbuildings and areas which served as annexes for farming purposes: a dairy, a shed to store fruit, a yard for manure. The *gardeuse* and her infants survive on the money supplied by the poorhouse, together with the yield from her two cows; by gleaning at harvest-time, weaving in the evenings and gathering wood in "winter". (It should have been autumn: Balzac seems to have been unaware that in winter the Alps are covered in snow.) This late season activity, in areas where there was no coal or other kind of fuel, was a source of extra but indispensable income for the old-style proletariat. One way or another, this poor "old woman", not yet forty, manages to get by—but is never free of debt. In Louis XIV's time she would have died of hunger. In the reign of Louis XVI, all the children would have died. In 1830, this exceptional woman saves both herself and her charges. She is always in arrears, but not disastrously so; almost all the poor peasants are in arrears under the "Old system" B.D. (Before the Doctor) but somehow or other they survive—just.

The *gardeuse* draws inspiration for her life of good deeds from a painted plaster Virgin (with the infant Jesus) which stands in the place of honour above her mantelpiece. This cult of the Virgin Mary was a survival from the Counter-Reformation religiosity instilled with great perseverance by the clergy into the minds of their flock, down to the level of the very poorest.

★

The foster-mother, desperately poor but devoted to saving life, is herself the epitome—the distillation, so to speak—of the characteristics of the two villages, one good, one bad, on the slopes of the Chartreuse, which now pass under the scrutiny of Genestas' military eye. First, the old-time village, the embodiment of the "predoctor" barbarism that had reigned before the arrival in the area of Benassis, the archetypal country doctor. Its main street has both open sewers and mountain torrents crossing it at intervals. Its roofs are an extraordinary mixture, some thatch, some shingle; some tile, some slate. (Slate roofs were apparently the privilege of the upper crust of this rural community—local dignitaries, the parish priest etc., though as far as I know, *lauze*, the only slate known in the Alps, is not considered to be particularly "aristocratic" material.

As a matter of fact it is often seen in this area on the roofs of hay-barns, not on the houses of the bourgeoisie and gentry.) This mixture of roof-top materials that catches Genestas' eye seems to me to have been a composite figment of Balzac's imagination. The Chartreuse mountain, which is the scene of the regenerative exploits of Doctor Benassis, is a semi-fictional backdrop made up of bits of Alsace, fragments of the Parisian and Touraine countryside, elements from the Cantal and the Pyrenees—and a few actually from the Alps! *Le Médecin* is constructed rather like an old-fashioned work of anthropology (of the kind now superseded by minutely-researched monographs written by specialists who often spend years in their chosen corner of *the field*). Reading this comparatively youthful work by Balzac reminds me of Frazer's *Golden Bough*, or of certain essays by Marcel Mauss, in which the customs of a tribe in Africa are solemnly compared with those of a Melanesian kinship group. The Balzac of the 1830s had none of the passionate accuracy of a Rétif de la Bretonne, who had the good sense in *Monsieur Nicolas* or *La Vie de mon père* to confine himself to speaking only about the rustic affairs of his native Burgundy. The less scrupulous author of *Le Médecin* does not hesitate to jumble together, on the rooftops of Savoy and Dauphiné, shingles from the Alps, slate from Anjou, tiles from Provence—and thatch from everywhere else. Should we object? I do not think so. The point is that Balzac has something to tell us about the condition of the French peasant in certain undeveloped areas, especially south of the Loire. The picture he paints for us of his Alpine setting, though showing his usual talent, is a little too cavalier perhaps, tending to simplify and generalize.

From the village of variegated rooftops, buried in the gloomy hollow of a valley, the view opens upwards. Balzac takes us up into the air and Genestas allows his gaze to wander to the summit of the nearby mountain. Up above him, not far from the newly-created farms and ground recently cleared of trees, the "new look" workshops established in his heroic wisdom by Doctor Benassis are in full swing, files rasping, hammers tapping. And yet as everyone knows, after about 1815, people in the Alps were tending to move *down* not up. This "descent" was particularly true of the small-scale nineteenth-century metal works in the Alps which were powered by water. Balzac paid no attention to that. Ignoring all the laws of historical gravity, he decrees that the new enterprises, which his correct observation of reality had suggested to his novelist's imagination, should be located halfway up a mountain. The economic growth in rural areas, which really did take place in the period 1815–35, is literally exalted by the author in a mood of Utopian creativity and wish-fulfilment.

The physical opposition between the two villages, with Nature down below and Culture up above, establishes one of the fundamental themes of the novel. The same kind of contrast figures in one or two other quasi-ethnographical or semi-fictional works about the French countryside, written in the sixteenth and eighteenth centuries. Noël du Fail, writing in 1540, portrayed two parishes close together in time and space. In his *Propos rustiques*,[4] the villages of Flameaux and Vindelles, respectively, embody two conceptions of the world: the Golden Age of the past (Flameaux) and the decadence of modernity (Vindelles). Rétif de la Bretonne and Balzac, both of whom have as much confident enthusiasm for the future as Noël du Fail has for the past, take the opposite point of view. Placing two peasant localities side by side is a device to present a theory of the passage of time very different from that of the sixteenth-century story-teller. Sacy, the village of adoption of the Rétif family, knee-deep in Nature and its past, is contrasted with Nitry, birthplace of the writer's father, forward-looking, open to development and capable therefore of giving Sacy a transfusion of Culture which would transform Nature. In Rétif, the optimism of the eighteenth century prevails over the pessimism of the impoverished Renaissance era we detect in Noël du Fail. There is the same forward-looking attitude in *Le Médecin*: in Balzac, the contrast between the two types of habitat, scattered over several sites, serves to bring out a number of important contrasts: past/future, backwardness/progress, sickness (goitre)/health, underdevelopment/development, barbarism/civilization, obscurantism/education, superstition/Christianity. (The Christianity implied in the religious aspects of these oppositions is one purged of heresies, stern, and comparatively modernized.)

*

After the two villages, we have the two houses: the priest's house and the cretin's.

(a) *The priest's house*: after his first contacts with the local population, now embarking on a new way of life under Doctor Benassis, Genestas becomes a boarder in the house once owned by the parish priest, now the good Doctor's home. This provides an opportunity for a brief glimpse of the bourgeois comfort enjoyed by the previous owner—the parish priest and consequently a well-off and eminent local figure. This comfort continues to be the prerogative of the new occupant: with his personal fortune, his well-appointed house and the despotic ministrations of his housekeeper, Benassis enjoys a relatively high standard of living.

(b) *The cretin's house*: it is to this house that Genestas comes for his first meeting with Benassis, who is on a round of calls to some of his worst cases. In a cottage bare of all furniture, a mere hovel, the army captain and the doctor begin their acquaintance. Both are from the south, but their different careers, the one in the army and the other in Paris, have removed all traces of their southern origin. They each strike the other as being, in their various ways, typical representatives of a culture both French and bourgeois, whether acquired easily or with difficulty. Together they are engaged in exploring one of the very worst features of mountain region poverty at that time—the goitre-afflicted villages of the northern Alps. Nothing new for the doctor, a frightful revelation for the old soldier.

The rural population of Savoy and Dauphiné were the victims, in statistically significant numbers, of specific dietary deficiencies: their drinking-water, coming from the mountain springs or from melted snow, lacked iodine. The poverty of the people and the high cost of carriage meant that deliveries of salt water fish—herring, dried cod—were few and far between; and this was the only food which could have compensated, by providing the minute amounts of iodine essential for the healthy growth of young children. For this reason, many children in the mountains presented the simultaneous symptoms of idiocy, goitre and myxoedemia: swollen thyroid and neck glands, gnome-like heads, baldness, retarded mentality, etc. Many Alpine valleys were transformed, by these deficiencies, into pockets of lunatic cretinism peopled by dribble-mouthed idiots, who became peepshows for the sick curiosity of travellers lured there in a disreputable form of tourism. But Benassis is no gaping tourist. He sets about remedying the disease, scouring out this affliction, eliminating it once and for all. Introductions over, he explains to Genestas what is happening while, at his side, in this wretched little cottage, his patient, the last surviving cretin in the canton, is breathing his last. Perhaps nowhere else in Balzac's racially-determined world is the confrontation between Enlightenment and the forces of a lumpen- , almost brute-like obscurantism pushed to such lengths as in this dramatic death-bed scene. Genestas, for our benefit, views both doctor and dying boy as they face one another. On one side, lit by the flames from the hearth, we see Doctor Benassis, his face satyr-like, his brow significantly protuberant: a great man for the ladies in his youth, he has now, in later life, turned away from such pursuits, but without renouncing his powerful progenitive proclivities which have simply been diverted, employed to better advantage in the tasks of improving the medical, economic and social lot of a community of Alpine peasants. At his side the poor monster-headed cretin gently expires, his feet dangling in a bowl of brown stream-water placed for him by his poor soul of a mother.

The Doctor's method of combating cretinism is deliberately repressive. Before his arrival among them, the local peasants, old and young, male and female, thought of their cretins, in social terms, as so many Christs at liberty in their midst. They bore kindly with the goitrous youngsters destined to so short a life; they venerated them and gave them alms, in the hope of ensuring themselves a reward in heaven. They left them free—in the open air—to look after the sheep, instead of locking them up in asylums to die. The approach of country people to these cretins was very different from that of the educated city-dwellers. In Grenoble and Chambéry, for example, the authorities had already adopted the cruel, modern practice of locking up imbeciles. (And yet there was a good remedy to hand for these goitrous regions of the Chartreuse: all that was necessary was to improve the diet of the people, and in particular see to it that they had supplies of salt-water fish.)

When Benassis arrives on the scene, he is by no means opposed to the notion of improving the food supply as a solution to the problem. But he is unaware—and how could he have known?—of the body's need for regular doses of iodine. In any case, his diagnosis and his therapy follow a very different path. Our good Doctor, in matters medical, is not always up with the avant-garde; he treats his goitrous cretins according to the precepts of the "fresh air" school of thought, a philosophy already out of date. "If goitre spread in the deep valley where the peasants of this canton used to live", Benassis tells Genestas in the course of their first meeting "it is because the valley is never lit by the light of the sun, nor swept by a healthy wind". Condemned to perpetual shadow and stagnant air, the natives of the valley are also at risk from their drinking water, which comes directly from mountain torrents produced by the melting snows (on this point, the Doctor was quite right).

In the second place, in his attitude towards cretins, Benassis is drawn along in the immense racialist current that the eighteenth and nineteenth centuries had already set in motion (long before the excesses of the twentieth century). Cretinism and goitre, in his opinion, are caused as much (or more) by heredity as by diet deficiencies. The risk, therefore, is that the disease will spread throughout the canton simply as a result of intermarriage and the consequent population increase. Altogether, the Good Doctor's attitude is traditional on two counts: he professes (a) *constitution* medicine, based on the state of the air breathed by the patient; and at the same time, (b) *species* medicine, the logical conclusion of which would be the castration of cretins. It cannot be stated too often that racialism, which since ancient times, has been a canker in Western culture, is nourished, in all innocence, by a whole range of agricultural and social practices, from selective cattle breeding at one end of the scale to defence of hereditary aristocracy at the other. Hence the popularity, which takes many forms, of a pseudo-scientific kind of genetics: it is found in the novels of Balzac and in the anthropology of the nineteenth century—to say nothing of our own time.

Such are the premises, then, of Benassis' social and medical experiments (often reminiscent of one of Molière's doctors)— destructive, repressive, morally castrating. Far be it from me to underestimate his day and night devotion to the care of his poor patients, but it has to be acknowledged that the remedies he prescribes often seem to derive from some old-wives' pharmacopoeia (couch-grass soup!), while his therapy at times is no advance on that of Molière's Purgon whose only cure-all was fasting. And this, in spite of his peasants' reasonable pleas: in normal times never having enough to eat, they beg the doctor to let them eat their fill on the only occasion when traditional custom allows it, that is when they are ill. They plead in vain, the Doctor remains adamant. *A la diète!* (Nothing to eat!)

In other ways, too, his regime is well and truly "destructive and repressive", as we hear him actually boast to Genestas: despite popular opposition—from the clergy, the women, the children and the old, who all vainly try to thwart his plan, Benassis has had the cretins, living in the canton of his experiment, *taken away by night*. They have been moved far away to asylums in Aiguebelle, where the poor creatures are "humanely treated" and prevented from sexual intercourse and reproduction.

Worse is to come: the great Saviour-Castrator is not satisfied with uprooting the cretins from the community. He also takes it upon himself, in all good conscience, to strip them of their possessions: to seize their family plots and, without further ado, transform them into communal property. From now on, irrigated in the Alpine or Limousin fashion, these plots become grassy meadows, a godsend for the healthy survivors who can now practise mixed farming, using their own and the common land, in the once-cursed canton. The end justifies the means. The better to achieve it, the Doctor employs a system of values which turns out to be double-barrelled. In the first place, he attacks the friendly, easy-going manner in which the cretins have habitually been treated—according to age-old attitudes—by women, children, the poor, the elderly, and by the former *curé* of the parish. This he does by invoking the new petty-bourgeois ethic based on avarice, a manoeuvre which rouses the "rich" (or the less poor) members of the municipal council, and prompts them to veto spending any money on the "Idiots": they point out that the small local budget may run into the red. Consequently the "rich" are all for the concentration-camp type deportations he is organizing against those who are weak in the head.

After Mammon, God (second barrel): Benassis calls for a change from the old obscurantist religion to a more enlightened new one. Old-fashioned Christianity teaches that poor unfortunates should be kindly treated, individually helped, supported and loved for what they are; but now this ceases to apply, being nothing but superstition, unworthy of our century! Benassis therefore approaches the bishop of his diocese, and asks him to dismiss the local *curé*, who is resisting the regeneration of his flock. The new man will be a more understanding priest altogether, one who will be aware of the need to reconcile the imperatives of true religion, essential to social progress, with the harsh necessities of carrying out drastic surgery on the *commune*. It will then at last be possible, with the new *curé*'s blessing, and no misgivings, to proceed with the eradication of cretinism, thus guaranteeing, for the benefit of all uninfected members, the health of the communal body. Here Balzac is harking back to a certain ecumenicalism, sometimes encountered in the eighteenth century, whereby the parish priest, the natural instrument of authority, is the indispensable agent of the spread of Enlightenment and Progress among the mass of the peasant population. At each other's throats in the towns, Voltaireans and Clericals often settled their differences in the villages: who better than a good churchman to teach country yokels respect for citizens' property, and to thunder from the pulpit about observing restrictions on rights of way? Thanks to such restrictions (say Benassis and the *curé* Janvier) there will now, for the benefit of the whole community, be a new network of paths through the village, to channel the trampling feet of wandering flocks of sheep that used to be so harmful to farmers' property. Genestas, old soldier that he is, may well voice his scepticism of the "waffle" (*salades*) preached by the *curé* from the pulpit, but Benassis sets very high store by the value, both spiritual and material, of ecclesiastical teaching.

Perhaps I may be pardoned if I, too, express a certain scepticism on this point. I should like to suggest that the utilitarian Christianity championed by the Doctor was not really so very effective in the education of the peasants: if we are to believe the findings of research on this subject, it appears that in the period from 1815 to 1833, parishes in France where the Church was dominant were neither more progressive, nor more backward, economically, than those where the peasants were hostile or resistant to the Church. On the whole, and on this point I venture to contradict Benassis and his colleague Janvier, the civilizing role of the rural clergy seems to me to have been more characteristic of the seventeenth century or possibly the eighteenth, than of the nineteenth.

★

The first cut of the scalpel, putting paid to cretinism, may rather take our breath away. As Balzac sees it, though, this is only the first phase of "operation Benassis". In order to launch itself into the adventure of economic growth, the Alpine village must first pay its pound of flesh. This has been done. From now on, biologically decontaminated, purged of its goitres, local society can expand. With the village now protected from the rear, the good Doctor can give free rein to his economic miracle.

The "take-off", as economists would call it, of this canton of the Chartreuse happens in broadly four stages:

First stage: there is no question of "innovation for innovation's sake". And in any case, the canton has no providential natural resources—no coal or metals. Nor does it have any noble landowners who are rich, enlightened, blessed with capital, and prepared to invest it locally. The territory of *Le Médecin de campagne* is a region with no seigneur, no lord of the manor. This is a "peasant economy" in the neo-populist sense of the term as used by the Russian economist Chayanov: characterized by a patchwork of small plots; backward, share-cropping agriculture; illiteracy; notables who are few and far between, and in any case ignorant, lazy and stupid; or else absentee landlords with no rich family connections. None of these is capable of offering any sort of leadership to the peasantry, who are themselves equally unenterprising. Unless, that is, Benassis himself takes these notables in hand, reshapes them, and out of this very unpromising human material, fashions an elite after his own heart. And this is precisely what he does.

After the *coup* against the cretins, the good Doctor proceeds therefore to attack the task which Balzac considers the most crucial: the establishment, using the means already to hand, of a modest market economy. This means directing towards the rapidly expanding town of Grenoble, fortunately only a few leagues away, the little saleable surplus there is of local agricultural produce. This is the only hope of extricating the peasants from the obscurantist squalor in which, without even putting up a struggle, they vegetate.

The opening-up of the little region operates, to begin with, along two different lines. The first is not particularly significant: an osier bed is planted and—thanks to the injection of a little capital, a dowry from an outside source—a basket factory is established. Now the villagers can make little containers for their cheeses—a local delicacy—and send them down to Grenoble. The townspeople go wild about them. Next, again at the Doctor's instigation, and partly with money that comes out of his pocket, they build a road over the mountains. The former mayor, the proprietor of a saw-mill, can now deliver his timber to the regional capital.

One thing leads to another. The development strategy takes shape of its own accord: to transport this timber, horses are needed; to shoe the horses, blacksmiths. And before long, even bakers are needed because the villagers are now much too busy transporting timber to make their own bread, as they used to in the old days.

Second stage: this revolution on the bakery front, a little far-fetched perhaps, leads Balzac and his spokesman Benassis on to the second phase in their joint programme of growth. The intention is to introduce large-scale agriculture. This is a difficult problem for, as I said, there is no local noble, no country gentleman, no *ci-devant* lord of the manor, no royalist landowner, no wealthy gentleman-farmer with money to invest, to set an example. The civilizing mission of the Comte d'Angeville, who was at the time in the process of rehabilitating his native Bugey, has no equivalent in our Chartreuse country. In the Alps, it is a case of starting from scratch—which implies the usual advantages of a clean sheet: thanks to Benassis, the village will pass directly from the swing-plough to the wheel-plough. The old implement was inefficient, barely scratching the soil, so the Doctor has ploughs, on the model of those in use in the north of France, manufactured locally. But the real problem lies elsewhere: land, buildings, capital. By great good fortune there appears a *deus ex machina* in the person of a certain "Monsieur Gravier, a clerk at the *prefecture* of Grenoble", a wealthy public servant of private means. Bored with sitting in town, surrounded by his unemployed money, his bureaucratic files and his bird-brain of a wife, he is converted to the religion of progress by Benassis, and lays out large sums of money for projects of ground-clearance, building, rehousing, and leasing of untilled, under-employed land in this canton of the Chartreuse. Stirred to emula-tion, the Doctor follows the bureaucrat's lead, and with his own money, in more modest amounts it is true, plays his part in the ground-clearance schemes. Altogether six farms are created, four by Gravier, two by Benassis, each of about 40 hectares (100 acres approximately) making a total of 250 hectares (600 acres). The farms are now rented out to tenant-farmers: this makes a welcome change from the old backward share-cropping system previously predominant in the canton. And then comes another miracle: an extra 250 hectares, produced as a result of further ground-clearances, are added to these conquests, but this time they become the personal property of the farmers. Here we find ourselves in the part of the novel which, if not the silliest, is nevertheless the most utopian, jumping way ahead of itself. We might almost be on the U.S. frontier, or the Canadian prairies in the nineteenth century. For while Benassis and Gravier are busy winning the battle in the wheatfields, demography appears to be having a field day too. In one year, seventy houses are built. In *six weeks*, the local population increases by several hundred! Pure science fiction! These 500 hectares of large farms, created in a few years out of land hitherto brush and scrub, are enough to take away the breath of any economist who knows what the nineteenth century was like. And as for the demographic "take-off", no sooner are the goitrous cretins out of the way than we have the inhabitants of the canton multiplying like rabbits. Numbers in the village increase *more than tenfold* in a space of time scarcely sufficient for Benassis's hair to turn a little grey. Well now, are we to laugh this off? Yes and no. Like many a visionary, Balzac *is* overdoing it—in the short term. But in the medium term, and *a fortiori* over the long term, he has not got it wrong. Great advances in farming techniques and increase in the population were indeed among the important factors making for agricultural growth in the first half of the nineteenth century. But the scale was more modest than Balzac has it—particularly in the case of the Dauphiné.

Third stage: this phase in the regeneration of the canton is more convincing than the "great leap forward" of the preceding stage. This time, small-scale agriculture, semi-commercialized and accompanied by artisanal production, makes its reappearance. These two elements had inaugurated the "take-off" during phase I. The reason they were able to do so was the providential proximity of the Grenoble market, on the doorstep of the Chartreuse. They had taken a back seat during phase II, which had been marked by massive injections of capital coming from outside sources, and particularly from the town—Grenoble once more. They recover their importance in phase III; thanks to them, there now takes place something similar to those development models (founded on simple technologies and exploitation of local resources) which "reason-able" prophets of growth are calling for almost everywhere today.[5] The primitive accumulation of capital, exemplified by the successive investments of Gravier and Benassis, had been made possible by outside finance. A sudden change now takes place: capital investments of this kind now give way to slower, more laborious, more petty-bourgeois transactions. They disturb me less, I confess, than the capitalist explosion of phase II. They are more in line with the homely, humdrum progress that was typical of French provincial life under Louis-Philippe's umbrella. In phase III, everything becomes possible—on the small scale. The demands of the market, the availability of labour, and the contagious virtues that flow from the example of the innovatory agriculturalists, stir the local inhabitants, free now of their poor cretins, to expand and diversify their output. Their family farms *à la Chayanov* start producing goods for door-to-door sales or market stalls—selling the traditional cheese in Grenoble is no longer enough. Now the villagers take in their eggs and poultry, their fruit and vegetables as well. Local forests provide wood which they dispatch, in all shapes and sizes, to the city. With the money they earn, they buy iron for the local young blacksmiths to make tools for the farmers and craftsmen. In this step-by-step progression through the stages of economic growth, we next see the establishment, in the heart of the Chartreuse of food and clothing shops—grocers, butchers, drapers. They take their rightful place in the community, as consumers in the mountains are spurred on to emulate the more "affluent" life-style of the townspeople and their own local notables; no longer are they content to dine on the simple old soups and wear the old-fashioned breeches of their forebears. Meanwhile, the agricultural revolution proceeds apace: as early as phase II, it had replaced the buckwheat of the old days (more Breton than Alpine, in fact), good only for gruel and *galettes*, with the superior bread cereals: wheat and rye. Now the revolution even begins to turn its attention to stock-raising. Breeds of cattle are improved, and in the construction of their cowsheds, the farmers imitate the Swiss or "Auvergnat" models. (On this latter point, Balzac is not entirely convincing: the Auvergne, a very underdeveloped province, was hardly likely to be able to provide a *model*, even in the construction of cowsheds.)

The secondary artisan or craft sector has just begun to make headway, thanks to the success of the small metal-works, the craft industries and the food and clothing shops. This now calls into being a tertiary sector, on a small scale of course, but real enough for all that. From all directions, a multitude of scribblers converge on the experimental village created by the seminal actions of the Doctor. In come the hacks and pen pushers, pettifogging lawyers and part-time clerics, anyone short of a job, a wage or a pension. After bread, meat and iron, education is the first requirement of the people. And the more education the people get, after all, the more likely it is that they will later produce even greater quantities of iron, meat and bread. So the village, in a radical break with its backward past, gets a schoolmaster: abominably paid, of course, scarcely as much as the *garde champêtre*, the village constable, and only one-third as much as the village priest. But then, says Balzac, the sermons preached by the local *curé*, the poor man's Fénelon, are indispensable (thanks to the prospect of bliss hereafter with which they dazzle the parishioners) for the morality of a fast-developing community. A champion of the happy mean *à la* Louis-Philippe, Benassis is well aware of the problem involved in the appointment of the schoolmaster. Therefore, conciliating both the Church and the Revolution, he sees that the post goes to a former *curé assermenté* (i.e., a priest who had taken the Revolutionary oath), whose acceptance of the Civil Constitution of the Clergy had estranged him from the clerics of the diocese. The canton is also to have a schoolmistress: to her will fall the task of teaching the daughters of the wealthier farmers, the beneficiaries of the capital-ist Revolution, (girls who will one day become the little Madame Bovarys of the region). Lastly, there is never any rise in the stan-dard of living without a corresponding rise in the consumption of wine—and the conviviality that accompanies it. The slopes of the neighbouring village, as unsuited to wheat as they are to the good Doctor's heavy ploughs, take very well to the hoe, the hand-plough and the vine—and with vines they are covered. Simultaneously, taverns appear, right on the doorstep of Benassis-ville. They are not yet thought of as dens of alcoholism against which the prohibition-ists will one day fulminate. They too are included in the torrential flood of social progress, in which wine, business and new ideas all mingle. Tourism which will later become an important feature of Alpine life now makes its debut with the building of an hotel to serve the needs of visitors to the Grande Chartreuse.

At the heart of this fast-growing little world there now springs up a profitable forest, planted on the land of which the cretins were forcibly dispossessed. Balzac's trees grow quickly, too quickly to be taken altogether seriously, but we must remember that he has to make them keep up with the headlong pace of the various enterprises of our Good Doctor, whose time is limited. Little by little, this tall stand of trees with its layers of green foliage, covers up the memory of the original sin: the cruel expulsion of an innocent, feeble-minded and defenceless group of people. Reading *Le Médecin*, one could be forgiven for thinking that trees of all kinds flourished abundantly in great forests which sprang up spontaneously all over the mountain. But on this point Balzac is hopelessly unrealistic: his fiction transcends reality and forgets even to keep within the bounds of possibility. In this fast-developing Alpine world, the Doctor seems to have wrought a change in the climate! Not so much as a flake of snow ever falls! Balzac's geography is a little vague too: from this imagined Chartreuse, looking *south* through a gap in the mountain, one sees what in fact lies in an area from west to northeast, viz. the Lyonnais (to the west), the Dauphiné (this really is to the south) and the Maurienne and Savoy (north and northeast respectively).

Dr. Benassis, the one-man-band, after completing in magnificent style the first three movements of his regional revolutionary symphony, is now in a position to tackle the fourth movement, which will take his canton to industrial maturity. The starting-point for the local manufacturing sector had been a humble saw-mill; next came the establishment of a number of little workshops whose products rarely went further than Grenoble. Now, after a phase which sees a revolution in agriculture and land tenure, "modern" industry is about to appear—or at any rate a modest version of it. For there is more to the village economy than food and clothing: feet must be shod, heads covered, families housed. So, starting from scratch, a few enterprising businessmen, some from outside, some local, set up various establishments: first a brick and tile factory (which seems to have been launched at the outset with firewood that the proprietor used to go out and steal during the night); next hat and shoe factories, which in turn lead to the establishment, as natural corollaries, of tanneries and hat-fairs linked to markets in Switzerland and the French Alps. The first features of an embryonic urbanization also begin to appear, as evidenced by the brand-new shops of the chemist, the bookseller, the watchmaker and the furniture dealer. We catch a glimpse of the time, not so very distant now, when this once-cursed village will compete with Grenoble, Chambéry and Allevard-les-Bains.

Despite the Faustian energy by which it is driven and the novelist's licence to exaggerate, the model of agricultural and manufacturing development that Balzac proposes does actually conform to the pattern of evolution in "traditional" France, south of the Cherbourg-Paris-Mulhouse line during the first three-quarters of the nineteenth century (except of course for the genuinely capitalist developments about this time in Saint-Etienne, Alès and Decazeville). Up here, in Dr. Benassis' mountains, as yet no blast furnaces or chemical factories have arrived to pollute the skies of Balzac's imaginary Dauphiné. The manufacturing industry, based on simple technology, which crowns the efforts of the Redeemer of the Chartreuse, has been grafted on to a background of small-scale enterprises, part-agricultural, part-artisanal, which helped to launch the economic take-off. Such complexes are typical of a certain type of growth: petty-bourgeois, non-polluting. One finds it in many regions of Europe in the nineteenth century, especially in the south. We have lost sight of it today, through a kind of teleological blindness, due to the more "successful" achievements of large-scale industrial and financial capitalism, which unduly occupies the front of the stage. And yet it was on small-scale developments of this kind, efficient and unspectacular, that much of modern society was built—in central and Mediterranean France, in Italy and Spain—but not of course in the smoke-laden zones where the "real" industrial revolution, Lancashire-style, took place. Only the latter kind of industrial development is recognized in the history books, because this was the one that won out in the end. *Le Médecin* celebrates the artisanal path to modernization: it is at the opposite end of the spectrum from *Germinal*, the harrowing epic of another type of growth.

Such petit-bourgeois features do not, however, prevent this society, created over a period of twenty years by the good Doctor, from being profoundly inegalitarian. Benassis himself is conscious of this fact: in this little Chartreuse community, after the great changes he has brought about, there are a few families who are rich, though not extravagantly so; a further minority who could be termed well-to-do; the vast majority who are poor working people; and in theory (though it seems unlikely) not a single beggar, so well policed is the process of growth. The medical and social enterprises fostered by the local Redeemer result in a mixture of small-scale family farming, whose produce is hawked locally; larger-scale tenant-farming;

craft production; self-financed manufacture, and a slightly disgruntled petty-bourgeoisie. The mixture more closely resembles provincial reality south of the Loire than do the grandiloquent descriptions written by Karl Marx later in the century. He predicted the disappearance of this small-scale economy. In the event it survived well beyond Marx's lifetime. The theorist of socialism was overhasty in prophesying the victory of large-scale capitalism. Small plots of land, small shops and workshops were destined to remain essential components of the western economy until at least 1910, if not 1950 or later.

It would, however, be wrong to paint too idealized a picture of the Benassis recipe for growth: it has its weaknesses as we have already seen, and even its harmful by-products—low wages for example, the result of the low prices of agricultural produce which had persisted since 1818. Low wages were particularly rife in this expanding little corner of the Chartreuse. Not without a tinge of cynicism, Balzac considers them to be a panacea for the economic development of France.

Balzac's account of rural life mentions cases of destitution or marginality, in addition to straightforward poverty—whether caused by low wages or not—and in so doing sometimes transfigures them: the old couple who eke out a living by clearing a patch on the wild mountainside; and *la Fosseuse* ("Ditch-dweller"), the beggar girl, who is the only representative of child or juvenile vagrancy resulting from villages having become derelict. In the case of this girl, Balzac attempts and once more brings off, the task of transfiguration he previously accomplished, apropos of the foster-mother who is not a baby-killer. In a novel by Dostoyevsky, *la Fosseuse* might have been one of the infinitely pitiful characters like Marie, the Swiss village child, in *The Idiot*. But with Balzac, the bourgeois apologist of redemption by work, *la Fosseuse* achieves her salvation more prosaically in the drudgery of her tasks as a linen-maid, a post procured for her by Benassis, and in the affection he constantly showers upon her.

Another marginal character is Butifer, the chamois hunter and shoe-smuggler from the Mandrin country.[6] Balzac, who came from Touraine, is usually uninspired in his descriptions of the Alps and the Alpine people, subjects with which he is unfamiliar. But in his portrait of Butifer, he is on sparkling form: the sporting prowess of the mountain people and their incredible climbing feats on the

rock-face genuinely fascinated him, so we are treated to a brief
flight of lyricism. Butifer's age-old way of life, however, based on
poaching and smuggling, is well suited to the ecology of the mountains but it no longer fits in with the norms of a well-ordered society
as prescribed by Benassis. A reformed character, thanks to the
good Doctor, Butifer is now obliged to take up another calling: he is
to train Genestas' son (who later goes on to become a student at the
Ecole Polytechnique) in the manly virtues of the Savoyard moun-
taineers; after that he comes down to *terra firma* and transfers his
talents to the army, that last refuge of society's misfits, there to earn
a soldier's pay and, in the end, a hero's grave.

Butifer's place is with the wild animals and the harsh life of the
mountain peaks. But with another villager, Gondrin, we move in
quite a different direction, into the sophisticated areas of political
conflict. A crippled survivor of the *Grande Armée*, by some miracle
Gondrin had managed to save his skin from the icy waters of the
Beresina. Back home in his native country, he finds himself deprived, by bungling bureaucrats, of the disability pension he ought
to be receiving. The anti-government recriminations of the tired
war veteran introduce, for the first time so far in the novel, the
contagion of political protest to a region which does not otherwise
appear anxious to participate in history, or to draw attention to
itself. Until this point, the book seems to suggest that justice and
welfare are dispensed from above by Benassis, rather than demanded from below by the peasants. (On this point, Balzac's version is quite different from the real Dauphiné, which was a very
revolutionary province, even at grass-roots level, after 1789.)

But let us look at the incident from the viewpoint Balzac thought
most appropriate: a peace-loving one in almost every respect. True,
Benassis is aware of, and can gauge exactly, the gulf of incompre-
hension that separates the bourgeois from the man of the people,
and even more from the peasant. It takes the Doctor a good deal of
time and tact before he succeeds in holding a dialogue with lower
orders—a paternalist dialogue naturally: they will never turn him
into a supporter of universal suffrage. But on the peasant side of
"the gulf", which remains a deep one for everyone except Benassis,
resignation rather than revolt reigns. It requires the experience of a
Gondrin, who has become urbanized by military service, for a
mighty fury to burst out from this peasant community against a

Power that could refuse a Wounded Soldier his few pence of a pension. It is not without significance that this malcontent had ended his career as a soldier in the *Grande Armée*. In these remote regions of France, the Napoleonic legend produced, in its own peculiar way, a certain political awakening and consciousness among the peasants.

Gondrin stands out as one of the spots and blemishes of the new regime. Another of these has a rather different origin: the revolution in cereal production, Benassis' pride and joy, brings in its train money-lending and money-lenders, since there is no agricultural credit system in operation. A certain Monsieur Taboreau makes a fortune by providing loans for purchase of seed-corn against subsequent repayments at exorbitant rates of interest. Benassis takes no exception to such practices, which he sees as the unavoidable consequences of the system of self-sustaining development that he has inaugurated. He has succeeded in obtaining the cooperation of the people in order to do so—but it never occurs to him to ask their opinion.

*

According to some of today's experts, there are cases in which development takes place not by means of some sudden change of habits, but by the action of a few elements present in the traditional culture which lend themselves to economic growth. Japan and Indonesia are convincing examples in support of this theory, and have fascinated students of economic "take-off". Balzac, as a purely amateur *ethnographer*, dashing off in holiday pursuit of amorous escapades, but imbued nevertheless with a remarkable capacity for anthropological synthesis, sensed all this by vivid intuition as he explored, at breakneck speed, one or two mountain or rural regions. He understood it long before Albert O. Hirschmann and Clifford Geertz expressed in more scholarly (and sometimes more ponderous) terms this now self-evident truth.

*

Attitudes towards the family, lineage and death are of crucial importance in bringing into play pre-existing factors, favourable or not to the take-off of an economy, particularly when the take-off, as in the case of *Le Médecin*, operates within a framework that remains rural, traditional and regional.

Let us allow ourselves once more to be guided by Benassis and Genestas: down below in the valley, which everyone thought for ever cursed, where the sun rarely penetrates and the air is heavy with poisonous vapours, the poverty-stricken, incompetent peasants soon forget their dead. Beside the corpse of a father or husband, the poor housewife weeps out of one eye and looks hard with the other at her neighbours, who have come running with their condolences, to remind them that they owe the bereaved family a shilling or two. A few sprinklings of holy water over the mortal remains, a hurried burial, and in a week the departed is forgotten.

But socio-geographical variations are possible in community attitudes towards death. Let us follow the Doctor up the slopes of the Chartreuse. Here, high up on the mountain, Balzac locates the "little Beauce"[7] (sic) which Benassis has manufactured for the use of the inhabitants. An unnaturally elevated plain, this fictional and archetypal Beauce serves as the well-prepared ground on to which Balzac unloads the sociological concepts he has constructed from a number of particular cases, and raised to the status of general propositions. On these rolling Alpine "open-fields" (sic), which are nevertheless unsuited to cereal-growing (in theory the proper use for them), Monsieur Gravier has now established a number of large farms given over entirely to livestock. In the model cowsheds, there are ingenious drainage channels for the urine and liquid manure; and in winter, family and farm hands can warm themselves at no cost between the double rows of cattle. None of this would have functioned properly, nor would Monsieur Gravier receive his annual rent of a thousand francs—the return from each farm on the capital invested by him—if there were not powerful dynastic structures and, not to put too fine a point on it, structures for handling death, which sustained the efforts and hopes of individual members of the clan who worked in this collective enterprise of tenant-farming. The death of the head of one of these families, a major lease-holder, is the signal for a long ritual ceremony. Traces of such ceremonies are still to be found in folklore and archival records in many parts of the country. The funeral rites over the corpse of this wealthy farmer, as described by Balzac in *Le Médecin*, are no doubt drawn from personal observation, or from information supplied by someone who had witnessed such an event, but are not necessarily peculiar to the Dauphiné. We may sum them up as follows: a long wake around the corpse; family gatherings in the dead man's house, going on for more than a week after his death; lamentations, sincere yet at the same time ritualized, by his wife who will remain alone as the widowed mother of the family; participation in the ceremonial mourning by the farm servants who, unless and until dismissed, are members for better or for worse, for sorrow or for joy, for blows received or for food shared, of the extended family of the late farmer. The farm-hands too, assembled around the recumbent corpse, cry out at regular intervals: *the master is dead* (understood: *long live the new master!*). This collective ritual, enacted at times of death and burial, derives directly from family rites promoted by the Counter-Reformation.[8] It offers the double advantage of consolidating family cohesion and family continuity; while at the same time ensuring, for the reasonable profit of the land-owning bourgeoisie, the maintenance on the land of a peasant family of tenant-farmers, who expect to farm the same soil from father to son, but without the sovereign rights over it which belong to the landowner. In the view of Balzac, the utilitarian philosopher, the presence or absence of family rites for the dead is synonymous with the presence or absence of large capital-intensive, efficient and soundly-based farms.

★

In peasant culture, the folklore of death culminates in thoughts of the hereafter, thoughts not always wholly Christian. During the long wake in the barn, the women spin and sew; the men do nothing; but all of them, men and women, listen raptly to the story-teller. This vigil is one of the highspots of Balzac's anthropology. The listening audience thus gathered together for the night-time ceremony in the barn are in this respect no different from the Burgundian peasants in Rétif de la Bretonne's stories, or the Pyrenean peasants of the fourteenth century. What really matters for them all is the post-mortem journeying of the dead man's soul. The tale of the murdered traveller, to which Genestas surreptitiously listens from his hiding-place above the assembly, is very edifying in this respect. The story-teller relates:

After the murder, the corpse of the traveller was thrown to the pigs and eaten by them; then it came back down to earth again, piece by piece, by way of the flax-seller's chimney: this flax-seller had been the horrified witness of the murder; but fear had sealed her lips and she had revealed nothing to the law. The corpse implores this woman to do her duty. Finally, she complies: she denounces the assassins to the Judge. They will be broken on the wheel in the public square. And the dead man, thus avenged, will be able to find his place of rest and his soul's salvation. Glory be! The house[9] of the flax-seller, because she succeeded in recovering her courage, will henceforth be rewarded with the finest harvests of flax that have ever been seen, and also by the birth of a male child.

Thus, in rustic folklore, of which Balzac is a faithful witness, fertility here below, and the just repose of the dead in the hereafter, are revealed as logically complementary. One will not happen without the other; and if each man keeps to his proper place, dead or alive, everyone will be well served.

Conservative, reactionary folklore? Yes and no. In passing, the narrator of the flax-seller story has a dig at the lords and masters of earlier days who used to "put the peasants in pies". But real, live, flesh-and-blood lords and masters had long since disappeared, it seems, from Benassis' canton. So the anti-seigneurial propaganda in these tall stories was only a symbolic attack, a mere pinprick at authority. A very different kind of folklore appears when the reader turns to the second panel of Balzac's diptych. We are still at the interminable wake in the barn—a wake that has to be considered, once more, as an "ideal type". Such a ceremony may not have taken place exactly as Balzac describes it, but it represents a composite of various observations he had made, or which some informant told him about.

This time, during the second part of the all-night vigil, thanks to Goguelat's narrative skill, the whole of the Napoleonic legend comes to life. A former infantryman who has returned to the village, Goguelat is now employed as the *piéton*, or rural postman, in Benassis' reformed canton. Does the "people's Napoleon", described for us in great detail by the postman, convey to the listeners the most subversive of legends? Yes, in the sense that the second story told in the barn attacks, both obliquely and directly, the powers of the King of France, restored in 1815; and also in that the enthusiastically-told legend heralds the triumphs to come, in the still distant future beyond 1850, of the Second Emperor. It would be wrong, however, to exaggerate the theme of progress in the legend surrounding the Imperial Eagle. The legend is above all magical and supernatural: it is turned into folklore by the peasant imagination. It stresses, first and foremost, the *lucky star* of the Corsican soldier, and the mystical good fortune that attends him throughout his consular and imperial career. This star goes on shining as long as the mysterious "man in red" who helps the Bonapartes, continues to look favourably on them. In 1814–15, the man in red abandons his protégé and transfers his favour to the Bourbons. Then comes Waterloo and after that Saint Helena.

Napoleon was already a folk-hero in the French countryside, more than a century before the legendary tales brought back to their villages by the soldiers of the Great War, and long before the imported fantasies of cowboys and Indians. Later than Charlemagne, earlier than the *poilus* and Buffalo Bill, the Little Corporal is one of the most charismatic of historical figures in French rural folklore.

★

As a historian of rural society, I have laid particular emphasis on those aspects of the novel that relate most closely to village life. A less-than-scrupulous anthropologist, and a rather inaccurate geographer, Balzac made up for this by being a first-class reporter and creator of anthropological syntheses. Casting his eyes rapidly over the Alps as he hurried through, he seized on the really important problems, assembling a number of scattered observations into a unified whole, for the benefit of his city-dwelling readers. The countryside, in spite of everything, remained for him an alien, strange and primitive world. Bearing this in mind, we can see that the particular attitude of *Le Médecin* to the peasant community lies somewhere between the intuitive sympathy of a Rétif de la Bretonne and the racist scorn of a Maupassant. The outsider's account, as written by Balzac, starts from a plausible point of view: to go and live in the country, after bidding a farewell to arms or to the city was, Balzac thought, the kind of thing a retired soldier or jaded lover would do: when one had tired of killing or kissing, of battles or mistresses, one retired to a village, there to invest one's surplus creative talent in civilizing missions. In this sense, notwithstanding several remarkably perceptive insights, Balzac remains on the margin of the theme of rural society, whereas Rétif is able to bring it to life from within. A real-life case from the 1830s, that of the peasant Pierre Rivière (whose own story was published in 1973 by Michel Foucault) tells us more about private life in rural France than do Benassis and Genestas. Rivière, a boy from Normandy who murdered his own parents, wrote his autobiography, which sheds much light on the hitherto hidden face of the French peasantry.

Balzac can do no more than take us by the hand and lead us to the threshold of village mysteries; he does not altogether succeed in taking us over it.

His real virtues lie elsewhere: with the lightest of touches *Le Médecin* provides administrators, city-dwelling philistines, and the bourgeoisie almost everywhere, with information about the *maieutic methods* that can be used to help the peasant community to rise above itself. Benassis, the General Practitioner par excellence, is also the obstetrician of a new social order. The techniques of social manipulation that he sets in motion are neither "capitalist" nor "socialist" : they are family-based, artisanal, proprietorial. It would be wrong to see this as *poujadisme*. *Le Médecin de Campagne* merely stresses the importance of simple technologies, born out of the needs and habits of the countryside. It puts the demographic expansion of the time to good use: it ignores the blast furnace and the railways in which the Saint-Simonians put their hopes; and it turns its back on grandiose but empty projects, stuck like band-aids on to the permanent reality of under-development. *Le Médecin* is rather like a handbook, without the jargon: it describes techniques of social development in the old-fashioned nineteenth century. It could still be a useful handbook today for specialists in the field of economic growth, who think that small is beautiful. Pragmatic, modest, *Le Médecin de Campagne* would be extremely instructive for twentieth century technocrats—if only they would bother to read it.

6

Versailles Observed:
The Court of Louis XIV in 1709[1]

A STUDY of the Court of Versailles combines a number of themes encountered in various types of research: the study of small groups, for instance, or of closed communities (containing perhaps several thousands of people, of whom only a few hundred or a few dozen are influential at any given time); and an understanding of the problems of power, or at any rate of influence (the Court had no powers itself, but it constituted the physical environment surrounding the exercise of power as embodied in the person of the King, and the action of his ministers; it can therefore be described as a pressure group with an impact upon the "decision-making process" that was far from negligible). The present essay may be considered as a contribution to a potential "political science" of the *ancien régime*.

The point of departure of the present case-study is the Court of Louis XIV during the latter part of the reign, as it is described in the *Mémoires* of the Duc de Saint-Simon. We shall find here the "subjective" picture painted by the "little duke"—a picture that does not necessarily correspond to the facts of the real world. Ideally, one should follow this with a critique of the data Saint-Simon provides, but that would take us beyond the deliberately restricted boundaries of this study, which aims simply to suggest a model. My text is a section of the *Mémoires* for the year 1709, in which Saint-Simon describes the "cabals", that is, the factions at Court.[2]

> It is hard to find the right word for what I wish to express. The Court, through the great changes in the state and fortune of Vendôme and Chamillart [both of whom had recently fallen into disgrace] was more divided than ever. To speak of cabals would perhaps be putting it too strongly, and an exact word for what was happening does not readily come to mind. So although it is too forceful, I shall use the term cabal, with a warning that it overstates the case. . . . Three parties split the Court between them, embracing all the principal personages . . .

There follows a commentary on the egoism or (rare) lack of it among the members of these different parties.

To simplify the picture which the reader may form of these three parties, I have set them out on a vertical or generational axis. This diagram represents the "molecular structure" of the Court, which also has a horizontal axis.

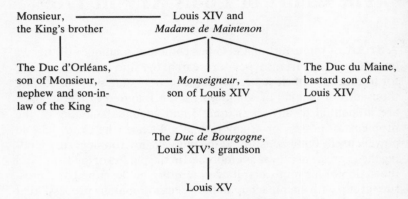

Monsieur, ——————— Louis XIV and
the King's brother   *Madame de Maintenon*

The Duc d'Orléans,   The Duc du Maine,
son of Monsieur, ——————— *Monseigneur,* ——————— bastard son of
nephew and son-in-   son of Louis XIV   Louis XIV
law of the King

The *Duc de Bourgogne*,
Louis XIV's grandson

Louis XV

At the top of the diamond, then, we have Louis XIV and his wife, Madame de Maintenon, whose marriage, though clandestine, was a secret to nobody. In the centre of the geometrical figure is Monseigneur, Louis XIV's legitimate son and heir presumptive (though in fact he was to die a few years before his father). Monseigneur, occupying the centre of the diagram, can be regarded as the centre of gravity of the system. At the bottom of the diamond comes the Duc de Bourgogne (married to the Duchesse de Bourgogne), son of Monseigneur and second in line of succession to the throne. At the bottom of the figure, what must be a dotted line leads to the future Louis XV, as yet unborn but whose birth was shortly to occur—in 1710.

The passage of Saint-Simon's text immediately following, refers to the three key points on the vertical axis (Louis XIV-Madame de Maintenon; Monseigneur; Duc and Duchesse de Bourgogne):

> The first [cabal] came together under the wing of Madame de Maintenon; its principal members, anxious to derive what they could from the fall of Chamillart [a disgraced minister] and encouraged by that of Vendôme [a marshal, also in disgrace] whom they had also egged on as much as they could, courted and were courted in return by Madame la Duchesse de Bourgogne, and were on good terms with Monseigneur.

THE GODMOTHER

Next, comes a description of the first cabal, that of Madame de Maintenon; giving a list, with brief or not so brief comments, of the persons and personalities who were members of it:

They [the members of this cabal] stood well in public opinion and basked in the reflected glory of the Maréchal de Boufflers. The others in the group rallied round him, to enhance their own reputations and to make use of him. Harcourt, even from his post on the banks of the Rhine, was the pilot of this group; Voysin and his wife were both the tools of the others and at the same time drew support from them. In the background was the Chancellor, [who had been] exceedingly chagrined by Madame de Maintenon's suddenly taking an aversion to him, and by the consequent coolness of the King. Pontchartrain [the Chancellor's son] lending support from a distance; the first master of the horse [Beringhen] who had long experience of intrigues and who had engineered the alliance between Harcourt and the Chancellor, and who egged them all on; his cousin Huxelles, to outward appearance philosophical; a cynic and an epicurean, throroughly deceitful and whose character I have already described on p. 380 [i.e., in the manuscript of the Memoirs]. He was gnawed by the darkest ambition. Monseigneur had formed the highest opinion of him through Mademoiselle Choin [Monseigneur's mistress] whose head had been filled with his praises by Beringhen, his wife and Bignon; the Maréchal de Villeroy, who although deep in disgrace had never fallen from favour with Madame de Maintenon, and who for this reason and because the King's former liking for him might be revived by her offices, was still treated with respect by the others; the Duc de Villeroy [son of the marshal] who was encouraged by his father, but had a rather different approach; La Rocheguyon [François de la Rochefoucauld] who was always laughing to himself, without saying anything, and laying traps. Through Blouin, [the first valet of the King's bedchamber] and other secret communications, they knew everything, and were accorded full credit by Monseigneur; they had not been without influence, indirectly, on the fall of Vendôme and Chamillart and attached to their group was the Duchesse de Villeroy, whose lack of wit [i.e. intelligence] was made up for by her sense [i.e. common sense], great prudence, impenetrable secrecy and the confidence of Madame la Duchesse de Bourgogne whom she could lead however she pleased.

This, then, was the Maintenon cabal which we can now pause to inspect. Because of the conjugal relationship between this group's First Lady and the King, the cabal can be considered as being very close to Louis XIV. Janine Field-Recurat and I have worked out a diagram showing the network of the three cabals. For reasons of clarity of exposition, we have placed the Maintenon group in the top left-hand section of the network.

In the top left-hand corner, then, we have Madame de Maintenon; Blouin, the King's head valet; the Maréchal de Boufflers; the Duc de Villeroy, who was Louvois's son-in-law; the Duc de la Rocheguyon (François de Rochefoucauld) also a son-in-law of Louvois. These two, we might note in passing, represented the remains of the Louvois clan. Madame de Maintenon was on bad terms with the minister, but being a shrewd politician, she had integrated his sons-in-law into her cabal.

Still in the top left corner, we find other names: the Chancellor, Pontchartrain, and his son, also a Pontchartrain; relations between these two (especially the father) and the King's wife, were very complex; and Beringhen, Bignon, the "Maréchal" d'Huxelles, and Voysin. Between them they formed a group, drawn together and bound to each other in varying degrees by ties of friendship (close or casual), or even paradoxically of enmity; by relations of kinship, clienthood or love (see the key to the diagram).

Simultaneously devout and a *précieuse*, a sort of universal mother superior of the church, the wife of a king who saw himself as a champion of the faith, Madame de Maintenon had extremely close, numerous and varied relations with the other members of the group. When studying her entourage, one comes first upon her "general staff"—which was also, in practice if not on paper, *the* general staff, or at least a good part of it. First of all, there was Harcourt, commander of the Rhine army, and the patron of an enormous clientele in Normandy: apoplectic, a schemer, and most resourceful in secret dealings and subterfuges. He was connected with the Louvois clan, or what remained of it, by an old friendship with Louvois himself and with Barbezieux, his son (later on, Harcourt's eldest son was to marry Barbezieux's daughter). Harcourt's relations with the royal Council (on which Madame de Maintenon, whose protégé and adviser he was, tried to find him a place) would repay further study. He fairly systematically took the opposite side

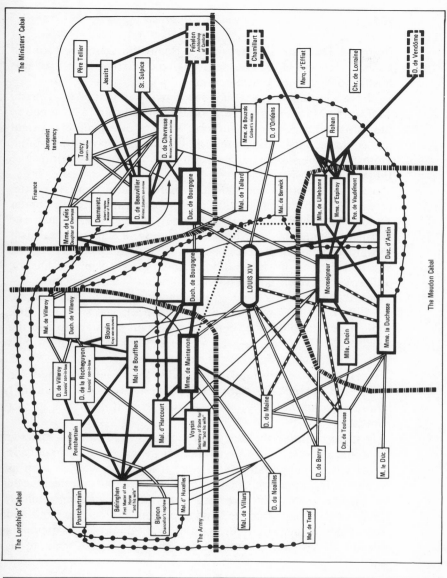
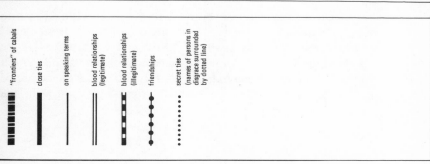

The Ministers' Cabal

The Lordships' Cabal

The Meudon Cabal

Père Tellier

Jesuits

St. Sulpice

Fénelon
Archbishop of Cambrai

Chamillart

Marq. d'Effiat

D. de Vendôme

Chr. de Lorraine

Jansenist tendency

Finance

Torcy
Colbert's nephew

Desmaretz
Colbert's nephew, Minister of Finance

D. de Chevreuse
Minister, Colbert's son-in-law

Mme. de Bouzols
Colbert's niece

D. d'Orléans

Rohan

Mme. de Lévis
Daughter of Chevreuse

Mme. de Villeroy

D. de Villeroy
Louvois' son-in-law

D. de la Rocheguyon
Louvois' son-in-law

Chancellor Pontchartrain

Pontchartrain

Béringhen
First Master of the Horse "and his wife"

Bignon
Chancellor's nephew

Mal. d'Huxelles

D. de Beauvillier
Minister, Colbert's son-in-law

Duc. de Bourgogne

Mal. de Tallard

Mal. de Berwick

Duch. de Bourgogne

LOUIS XIV

Mme. de Maintenon

Mal. de Villeroy

Duch. de Villeroy

Brouin
King's valet de chambre

Mal. de Boufflers

Mal. d'Harcourt

Voysin
Secretary of State for War "and his wife"

D. du Maine

D. de Berry

D. de Villars

D. du Noailles

The Army

Mal. de Tessé

Mlle. de Lillebonne

Mme. d'Espinoy

Pce. de Vaudémont

Monseigneur

Duc. d'Antin

Mlle. Choin

Mme. la Duchesse

Cte. de Toulouse

M. le Duc

Legend

- ▮▮▮▮ "frontiers" of cabals
- ▬▬▬ close ties
- ─── on speaking terms
- ═══ blood relationships (legitimate)
- ▬▪▬▪ blood relationships (illegitimate)
- ●●●● friendships
- ·········· secret ties (names of persons in disgrace surrounded by dotted line)

from the Ducs de Chevreuse and Beauvillier, members of the Colbert clan and of the Duc de Bourgogne's party—in other words hostile to Madame de Maintenon.

I have mentioned what could "objectively" be called the general staff of the Maintenon party: another marshal should be added to the list, the Maréchal de Boufflers, who was outstandingly upright and could be outstandingly foolish, but was popular in the capital. He brought the support of a certain kind of Parisian patriotism to the Maintenon side.

There were other marshals too—hardly more than chocolate-cream soldiers: Huxelles and Villeroy. Huxelles, a deceiver "under a cloak of probity", had connections with the Phélypeaux, the Beringhens and the Louvois clan. Villeroy, a stage general, was incompetent and in disgrace because of his military defeats, but he still had the ear of Madame de Maintenon. His son, the Duc de Villeroy, Louvois's son-in-law, did not have the problem of disgrace to contend with; and as for his daughter-in-law, the Duchesse de Villeroy, (little wit, but common sense), she was one link, though not the only one, between the Maintenon group and the Duchesse de Bourgogne—who was herself linked, at least through her husband, to an opposing cabal.

If Harcourt represented Normandy, the Villeroys stood for Lyon, and Huxelles to some extent for Alsace. One should not ignore regional connections, power bases and clienteles in this context.

It might be noted that the other marshals were either connected to Monseigneur's cabal (Vendôme, for instance), or were outside Court cabals altogether (there were a few lone wolves, such as Vauban). It is interesting in this connection to note that the Duc de Bourgogne's cabal contained practically no high-ranking soldiers; indeed it was, as it happened and as personified by Chevreuse and Beauvillier, a pacifist group. In order to obtain peace, its members would willingly have abandoned the Bourbon King of Spain to his sad fate.

"Voysin and his wife were both the tools [of Madame de Maintenon and Harcourt] and at the same time drew support from them". Voysin came from one of those families of *maîtres de requêtes* (appeal judges), who provided so many councillors of State, intendants, and senior bureaucrats in general, and who were so important in government and at Court. Voysin's shrewd wife had launched his career, if one is to believe Saint-Simon, by the carefully-judged hospitality she had offered Madame de Maintenon in Hainault, where her husband was the provincial intendant, during the 1692 campaign. After taking Chamillart's place as war minister, he later became minister of state, and was to play an important role in Madame de Maintenon's scheme of things. The permanent objective of the "godmother"—since the King did not automatically follow the advice she whispered in his ear (far from it)—was to have one of her own lieutenants as a minister in Council, one who could pass on the messages she wished to be conveyed indirectly to the King when he was in session with his ministers. The role she tried, but in vain, to have conferred on Harcourt, who was a favourite of hers, was eventually filled by Voysin. He was to play a vital part, at the very end of the reign, in getting certain "pills" swallowed—the King's will and codicils. After becoming Chancellor, he kept his position as secretary of state. His wife, by making a good impression on Madame de Maintenon, had given his career a decisive boost.

> In the background [of the Maintenon cabal] was the Chancellor [Pontchartrain] who had been exceedingly chagrined by Madame de Maintenon's taking an aversion to him, and by the consequent coolness of the King; Pontchartrain [the son] lending support from a distance.

Here, Saint-Simon unveils one of the rules of his description of the cabals: one might no longer be in favour with the leader of the group, in this case, the "godmother" herself. And yet by reason of one's position, one's links and counter-links with other important persons at Court, one might find oneself "stuck" in the network one had originally joined, obliged now to take a back seat. The Phélypeaux-Pontchartrain case is of general interest in several respects: this was one of the great bureaucrat-producing families of the seventeenth century who were, in the eighteenth century, to be found occupying a place among the very highest aristocracy. What was more, the younger Pontchartrain had jurisdiction over Paris: he was therefore a party to all the police secrets of the city, which he passed on to the King. For him, then, (although his relations with the Paris police in the shape of d'Argenson, their head, were actually rather complicated) this was an indubitable source of power.

"Through Blouin and other secret communications, they knew everything". The Pontchartrains introduce us to the question of the police, one of the keys to the power of the Maintenon group. Louis Blouin, head valet of the King's bedchamber, and an intimate friend of the Ducs de Villeroy and La Rocheguyon (two pillars of the group) brings us once more to matters of spying, this time at Court rather than in the capital.

Blouin, as governor of Versailles, had under him the Swiss guards, as well as other informers or domestic staff of the Château of Versailles. Reports to the King on all courtiers passed through his hands.

With Beringhen, the Premier Ecuyer (First Master of the Horse), known as Monsieur le Premier, who was in charge of the smaller stables, we come, on paper at least, to a lower rank of services than the police. But at Versailles, the smaller stables were in a state of permanent rivalry with the great stables, under the command of Louis de Lorraine, the Grand Ecuyer de France (Grand Master of the Horse) known as Monsieur le Grand, and an intimate friend of Louis XIV. In spite of the rather pointless rivalry between the two lobbies, Beringhen occupied one of the key positions in the network of friendship on the Maintenon side. He was on familiar terms with Huxelles and acted as go-between for the Maréchal d'Harcourt and the Chancellor Pontchartrain: "The first master of the horse, [who] had long experience of intrigues and [who] had engineered the alliance between Harcourt and the Chancellor, and egged them all on."

La Rocheguyon (François VIII de la Rochefoucauld) "who was always laughing to himself without saying anything and laying traps", is another interesting counter on the board. This man was the son of François de La Rochefoucauld, another intimate friend of the King, like Monsieur le Grand, but on bad terms with Madame de Maintenon. But the son was a son-in-law of Louvois, brother-in-law of the Duc de Villeroy, and friend of Blouin; he was on bad terms with Beauvillier and Torcy, that is the Colbert clan, and consequently with the cabal of the Duc de Bourgogne. He therefore found himself, through the inevitable processes of attraction and repulsion—of valencies, so to speak—in the Maintenon cabal.

THE "MINISTERS"

Let us turn now to the second cabal:

On the other side, living in hopes nourished by the birth, virtue and talents of Mgr le Duc de Bourgogne, and entirely devoted to him was the Duc de Beauvillier, the most conspicuous figure; the Duc de Chevreuse was the soul and moving spirit of this group [both dukes were married to daughters of Colbert]; the Archbishop of Cambrai [Fénelon] from the depths of his exile and disgrace was its pilot; subordinate to these were Torcy and Desmaretz [both related to the Colbert clan], Père Tellier [the King's confessor] and both the Jesuits and Saint-Sulpice, who were in other respects so hostile to each other. Desmaretz, who was friendly with the Maréchal de Villeroy and the Maréchal d'Huxelles and Torcy, on good terms with the Chancellor [Pontchartrain], at one with him over matters concerning Rome [i.e. gallican], and consequently opposed to the Jesuits and Saint-Sulpice and thus in difficulty over this matter with his cousins Chevreuse and especially Beauvillier, which led to embarrassment and often awkwardness between them. The latter [Chevreuse and Beauvillier] presented a joint front if necessary, and grew ever closer, having continually occasion to see each other without appearing to seek each other out, [because they were both brothers-in-law and ministers *in partibus*] rendered immune by their positions to the slings and arrows of enemies; having immediate knowledge of everything, they were in a position to tease others with fantasies and with a wave of the hand to make a fantasy of reality . . . so true was it of the whole reign that the ministry ruled in all matters, however much confidence Madame de Maintenon had usurped within it. [There follows a description of the actions of the two brothers-in-law.] Their piety lent itself easily to ridicule [this was a religious cabal]. The fashionable, the elegant and the ambitious were all on the other side with Mademoiselle Choin and Madame de Maintenon. These two cabals [that of the Duc de Bourgogne, the grandson, and that of Madame de Maintenon, the "grandmother" so to speak] viewed each other with respect. The Bourgogne cabal went its way in silence; the other on the contrary made much stir and seized every opportunity to harm its opponent. All the top people in the Court and the army were on her [Maintenon's] side and their numbers were swelled even further by exasperation and disgust for the government. Many right-thinking persons were attracted by the probity of Boufflers and the talents of Harcourt.

Who were the prominent members of the second cabal? First of all there was the Duc de Bourgogne himself: the son of Monseigneur and grandson of Louis XIV, the duke is said to have been an aimless youth, who spent his time absent-mindedly swatting wasps or crushing grapes. But it seems that he grew up during the last years of his youth (and indeed of his life). The bright royal destiny which may have awaited him was cut short by his untimely death, at the age of thirty, in 1712. He was a pious young man, bigoted even.

The Duc de Beauvillier, Colbert's son-in-law, was a man of regular habits, an early riser, pious, humble, punctual, not given to fancy (I am merely repeating or paraphrasing what Saint-Simon says about him). A Minister of State, Beauvillier was one of those rare individuals who, although born into the very highest aristocracy (non-mandarins), sat on the Council of Ministers. It was his indisputably ministerial presence as well as that of Desmaretz, Torcy and even Chevreuse (minister "in partibus") which earned the Duc de Bourgogne's group the nickname of "the Ministers' cabal". The Maintenon group, on the other hand, (much worse off as far as access to the ministry was concerned, despite the powerful influence of the First Lady), was dubbed "the Lordships' cabal"— apparently because of the rather large number of dukes it included.

Another prominent figure was the Duc de Chevreuse, brother-in-law of Beauvillier, son-in-law of Colbert, unofficial adviser to the King, to whom he had access at any time "by the back stairs", and in whose ear he whispered his opinions, enjoying the royal confidence to such an extent that he received the consideration due to a minister of state, although he was not in fact a member of the Council. According to D. Van Elden,[3] Chevreuse (whose arguments were, in fact, unreliable) was the Pascalian prototype of the "spirit of geometry" as opposed to the "spirit of finesse" to be found in many of the Mortemart family, especially Madame de Montespan and her children, who were all blessed with the famous "Mortemart wit" (*l'esprit Mortemart*), which so fascinated Marcel Proust.

Fénelon was, of course, a crucial member of this group. He represented the man of the liberal opposition par excellence, whether of high noble birth or not. Saint-Simon did not entirely like

Fénelon, whom he considered (not quite correctly) as a man of agreeable and cultivated mind, who turned it "on and off like a tap", dispensing to each the appropriate dose of intellectual, moral, or worldly honey or vinegar. In fact, Fénelon was a man of the highest intelligence: of all the cabals, the Duc de Bourgogne's was the one that could lay the most claim to ideas.

We can pass briefly over two other people in this group, both important and ministerial members of the Colbert family clan: Torcy, minister for foreign affairs—who had a good memory and a talented pen; and Desmaretz, controller general of finance. The latter was also to some extent a representative of high finance (at least through his contacts with a prominent financier, Samuel Bernard, which were useful to the State). It goes without saying, in any case, that the most powerful financiers had their entrées, and their ability to intervene everywhere: the capitalist circles of the great seaports, for instances, were connected with the Pontchartrains— and so, indirectly, with the Maintenon clan (however strained the relations between Pontchartrain *père* and the First Lady had become over time). And Monseigneur himself, the centre (still or moving) of the third cabal, was thought to be on good terms with the financial world.

It is surprising, at first sight, to find the King's confessor, Père Tellier or Le Tellier, in the cabal of the Duc de Bourgogne. This Jesuit, who was, according to our noble informant, the son of "poor (?) Normandy tenant-farmers", came therefore, by Saint-Simonian standards, from "the dregs of the people". A hard man, obstinate, cruel, brutal, he was a practised dissembler and a terrifying figure, inaccessible even to the other Jesuits, only four or five of whom dared approach him—a man born to harm, thought Saint-Simon.

It appears from the *Mémoires*, then, that the elements constituting the cabal of the Duc de Bourgogne included an intellectual and aristocratic opposition, a ministerial clan, and a financial lobby. For good measure it contained two clerical lobbies, which were indeed rivals: the Jesuits (divided even amongst themselves), and Saint-Sulpice (mentioned frequently by Saint Simon, who had nothing but scorn for these "grubby and unshaven priests" (*les barbes sales*); they had so much influence in the seminaries that they could be considered the nursery-gardeners of the lower clergy). But we should note that the Duc de Bourgogne's cabal also contained those who, like Torcy, were gallicans or even Jansenists[4]—in spite of the aversion Jansenists felt for both the Jesuits and Saint-Sulpice, and which was reciprocated in both cases. But the Jesuit/Jansenist division did not coincide with the frontiers separating the court cabals.

This, then, was the "Ministers' cabal", the group surrounding the Duc de Bourgogne; we have placed it in the top right-hand section of the diagram.

The further one pursues this analysis, the clearer it becomes that the cabals were determined by patterns of kinship, crystallizing at certain points in the genealogy of the royal family: after the clan around the King's wife (Louis XIV: *Madame de Maintenon*), and the group attached to the royal grandson (*Duc de Bourgogne*), we turn now to the galaxy surrounding the King's son (*Monseigneur*).

THE MEUDON CONNECTION

> D'Antin, Madame la Duchesse, Mademoiselle de Lillebonne and her sister, their uncle, who was inseparable from them, and the inner circle of the court at Meudon, made up the third party.

These lines reveal the two poles of Monseigneur's group: one formed by sibling, or rather half-sibling ties; the other, the Lorraine connection. Madame la Duchesse was, in fact, the ("natural") half-sister of Monseigneur, Louis XIV's legitimate son, since she was the illegitimate daughter born of the "tender love" (Saint-Simon) between Louis XIV and Madame de Montespan. She was also the half-sister of D'Antin—another influential member of the group, who was none other than the *legitimate* son of Madame de Montespan and Louis-Henri de Pardaillan, the Marquis de Montespan. As for Mademoiselle de Lillebonne and her sister (always accompanied by their uncle Vaudémont), who had at one time been protégées of Louvois, they were princesses and prince of the house of Lorraine. As in the time of the Guises, but with less flamboyance, panache and bloodshed, the house of Lorraine was a force to be reckoned with in the cabals at court, making contact with the royal family at the nodal point in the line of succession represented by Monseigneur.

The inner circle of the court of Meudon was articulated along these two axes. This created problems for the would-be "perfect courtier" who was anxious to get on. One could not be everywhere at once: one followed the King to Marly, of course, but one ought also, with an eye to the next reign, to spend some time at Meudon, paying court to Monseigneur. (No-one knew, of course, that he was to die before his elderly father.) So, one had to arrange to "fit Meudon in between visits to Marly"—and indeed this was one of the major preoccupations of the reign, or rather of the King-cultivators of Versailles.

To return now to the words of Saint-Simon, his text continues as follows:

Neither of the other two [*parties*] would have anything to do with them, both feared them [*that is the persons in Monseigneur's cabal*] and mistrusted them, but all maintained polite relations with them because of Monseigneur [*the "future king"*], even Madame la Duchesse de Bourgogne herself. D'Antin and Madame la Duchesse were but a single mind [*they were half-brother and sister*]; they were equally badly spoken of; but they were at the head of this party. D'Antin, by his private conversations with the King, which increased daily, and which he excelled at displaying to the best advantage; and both D'Antin and Madame la Duchesse by their private contacts with Monseigneur. Which did not stop the Lorraine princesses retaining his confidence just as much, and that of Mademoiselle Choin [Monsigneur's mistress] at least, more than the other two. They also had another advantage, which was not known at the time, or indeed for long afterwards, and of which I have already spoken: the contacts with Madame de Maintenon, so shamefully but so solidly established and for that very reason so well concealed [one of the princesses of Lorraine acted as an informer for Madame de Maintenon and regularly sent her letters about what was happening at Meudon] but they were still reeling from the twin thunderbolts that had just struck Vendôme and Chamillart [who were both now in disgrace]. Boufflers, Harcourt and their principal supports hated the arrogance of the former [Vendôme] and the high rank and command to which he had been elevated. . . . This third cabal [that of Monseigneur] was really the cabal of Vendôme.

I shall try to take my commentary a little further, introducing a few complications. The third cabal, Monseigneur's, was a group which brought together not only the foreign princes (of Lorraine) but also, a greater achievement, the families of the princes of the blood, Conti and Condé—both married to bastard daughters of Louis XIV, who were intimates of Monseigneur. Practising both endogamy and polygamy, the monarch had so arranged matters that during his lifetime he succeeded in marrying off four of his natural children, three girls and a boy to princes and a princess of the blood, the males of whom were all eligible to succeed to the throne. Condé or Conti, they were all descended from Charles de Bourbon, grandfather of Henri IV. Marrying off all the cousins to each other was an ingenious way of settling family quarrels, however unsound it might be genetically.

In the circumstances, then, the ties between Monseigneur and his group (or cabal) on the one hand, and the Condé-Contis and their wives on the other, were far-reaching, having ramifications that even touched upon the private life of the crown prince. Monseigneur was closely attached to his mistress, Mademoiselle Choin: according to Saint-Simon's various portraits of her, she was, when young, a solid, rather squat girl, dark and ugly but witty; as she grew older, she became excessively fat, aged and foul-smelling; but she was modest, sincere and disinterested. (I am paraphrasing his own words.) Now, Mademoiselle Choin, who was so to speak the Madame de Maintenon of the Grand Dauphin (i.e., Monseigneur) and of his cabal, had originally been a lady-in-waiting to the first ("dowager") Princesse de Conti, the illegitimate daughter of Louis XIV and Louise de la Vallière. This Princesse de Conti was thus Monseigneur's half-sister, and long remained his intimate confidant, until she was replaced in this role by their shared half-sister, Madame la Duchesse (Monseigneur evidently could not do without at least one of his half-sisters in attendance). And it was through the senior Princesse de Conti that Monseigneur first formed a liaison with Mademoiselle Choin.

The "Monseigneur network" was criss-crossed with even more internal links. I have already mentioned the Princesse de Conti, married to a Conti prince, who died soon after. Alongside this widow, I have placed the Grand Dauphin's other half-sister, Madame la Duchesse, daughter of Louis XIV and Madame de Montespan. This second illegitimate child of the King, who remained a daughter of the royal house of France "even on her commode", married not a Conti, but a Condé known as Monsieur le Duc. (Whether Condé or Conti, did not signify much: it was still a family affair.)

The Condé-Conti-Bourbon connections, in Monseigneur's immediate, or not-so-immediate circle, were further reinforced by other marriages or even extra-marital relations. For the younger

Prince de Conti (the younger brother, that is, of the one who died) himself married a Condé girl, the sister of Monsieur le Duc. And to crown it all, Conti junior was the lover of Madame la Duchesse. Monsieur le Duc was therefore being cuckolded by his sister's husband, who was also his cousin, as well as his wife's cousin and lover. It is a tangled web indeed—but at least in Monseigneur's circle it could be said that affairs were kept in the family.

Fifteen years earlier, in about 1692–4, there had been a similar set of intrigues in the Grand Dauphin's set. At that time, the Maréchal de Luxembourg, anxious to influence the man he was already considering as Louis XIV's successor, dispatched to his side his aide-de-camp and kinsman, Clermont-Chaste, as a sort of *alter ego*. Luxembourg had originally propelled him in this direction with the idea that he should become the lover of the dowager Princesse de Conti, the better to influence her, since she in turn had a strong influence over Monseigneur. Later, by an even more crafty manoeuvre, Luxembourg had succeeded in placing Clermont-Chaste as the lover of Mademoiselle de Choin herself—thus obtaining an even more direct line to Monseigneur. Louis XIV ruined the whole plan by reading out to the Princesse de Conti (who burst into tears) her love-letters, which had been intercepted by the secret police (the *Cabinet noir*).

It would take too long to explain how Vendôme, one of the great military commanders and grandson of a bastard son of Henri IV, for a while came to represent the Meudon cabal, which through him became identified with a section of the military lobby.

Seen from the outside, the Meudon cabal, with members who were bound together by all manner of relationships, with its impossibly complicated intrigues, might look something like a octopus with a tangle of tentacles. Seen from the inside, it looks more like a jellyfish: Monseigneur, as we have seen, was the soft underbelly, the low centre of gravity of his group and of the entire system. Monseigneur, Saint-Simon says in essence, was about as unintelligent as a man can be; fat but not robust; possessed of some common sense, but no wit; a web of pettinesses put together; amiable through stupidity, and mean to his mistresses. What little brains he had, had been overwhelmed by an excess of education, and all he ever read was the Court circular, or the obituaries in the *Gazette de France*.

SPLITS AND LIAISONS

So much for the elucidation (rather a brief one) of the three cabals. Next, Saint-Simon describes how the stars and lesser lights at Court disposed themselves around them. I shall confine myself chiefly to the right- and left-hand corners of the family diamond of Louis XIV. These corners correspond to the Duc de Maine (bastard son of Louis XIV) and the Duc d'Orléans (the King's nephew and son-in-law), both located on the same horizontal and generational axis as Monseigneur.[5] Maine was, in fact, his (illegitimate) half-brother, while Orléans was his cousin-german and half-brother-in-law, since he had married his half-sister, Mademoiselle de Blois (bastard daughter of Louis XIV and Madame de Montespan), who thus became by marriage Duchesse d'Orleáns. "Monsieur du Maine, who reigned over the hearts of the King and Madame de Maintenon, while humouring everyone, owed allegiance to none but himself, mocked at many and harmed everyone as much as he could. Everyone feared him and knew him for what he was." As Saint-Simon saw it, Monsieur du Maine was so well-protected and so influential that he did not need to be a member as such of any of the cabals. As for "Monsieur le Duc d'Orléans [he] had neither the desire, nor was he in any position to enter into anything at all." Orléans, who was in disgrace with Louis XIV, and who had some contacts with the Meudon or Vendôme cabal, was "in reserve", so to speak, for what was to happen later. Located on the same horizontal axis as Maine and Monseigneur, he was biding his time.

The text also indicates a wealth of distinctions relating to possible splits within each cabal. Such splits could arise from the different attitudes adopted by various people towards Jansenism: in the inner circle of the Colbert group, attached to the cabal of the Duc de Bourgogne, there was a division between Chevreuse and Beauvillier (Colbert's sons-in-law) who were anti-Jansenists, and Torcy (Colbert's nephew) who was pro-Jansenist. "Chevreuse and Beauvillier, who had no secrets from each other, did not discuss everything with their families and although they were cousins german of Torcy, a whiff of Jansenism made them steer very clear of him." If Torcy had a weakness for Port-Royal, Beauvillier was more inclined towards the Jesuits.

There were also the divisions, in Monseigneur's cabal (Meudon-Vendôme), arising from the ambitions of various sub-groups which tended to focus on the future of the Grand Dauphin, heir presumptive to the kingdom (though in fact his destiny was cut short by his early death). The two sub-groups lined up in (unacknowledged) rivalry were, on one hand, the Montespan children (the half-siblings D'Antin and Madame la Duchesse, who was herself Monseigneur's half-sister though out of wedlock); and on the other hand the group formed by the two princesses of Lorraine and their uncle:

> D'Antin and Madame la Duchesse, who were as one in their views, their mutual needs, their vices and their *haunts*, greatly distrusted the two Lorraine princesses, although to outward appearance they were on terms of confidence and intimate friendship, terms which would only be maintained as long as the King was still alive, as they would afterwards be at each other's throats, to gain sole possession of Monseigneur, once he was King.

We should also note the presence of certain elements who acted as go-betweens for the various cabals, "roving atoms" so to speak. One such was the astute, subtle and charming Duchesse de Bourgogne. Through her husband the duke, she belonged to the third cabal; but she was a great favourite with Madame de Maintenon (first cabal): "Madame la Duchesse de Bourgogne . . . floated between the two cabals."

The Duchesse de Bourgogne, then, was an amphibian with two habitats. Another person who played the role of go-between, this time for the second and third cabals (Monseigneur's and Duc de Bourgogne's), was Marie-Françoise Colbert de Croissy, the Marquise de Bouzols, ugly, spiteful, and charming.

> As for the Ministers' cabal [i.e. that of the Duc de Bourgogne] it was extremely hostile [to Monseigneur's cabal] although Torcy [third cabal] and Madame la Duchesse [second cabal] and consequently D'Antin [*ditto*] both treated and were treated by Madame de Bouzols with respect; she was Torcy's sister and a longstanding and intimate friend for all seasons of Madame la Duchesse; despite her hideous face, she was a delightful conversationalist with the wit of ten demons.

And Saint-Simon concludes his masterly sketch of the Court as follows:

> Such was the internal appearance of the Court, in these stormy days heralded by two such mighty collapses [the disgrace of Vendôme and Chamillart] which seemed to point the way to others.

FROM POLITICAL SCIENCE TO ORGANIC CHEMISTRY

It is now time to turn once more to the original question: what can a text like this, and indeed Saint-Simon's *Mémoires* as a whole, contribute to a discipline with which, I confess, I am not wholly familiar, though I have occasionally been asked to examine students in it: political science? It is a discipline which, for some reason, possibly the incomplete nature of its results, is not very popular with historians, except those studying the very recent past. Their general distaste for political science is even more marked where the *ancien régime* is concerned. Everyone would agree, for instance, that in the seventeenth century, coteries, factions or even parties certainly existed—rather different ones, of course, from the twentieth-century political party as charted by Siegfried and others. But the environment in which such structures were shaped is too different from our own; the lessons of contemporary political science, whether American or French style, are of no great assistance to us in this case.

I have tried to re-open the question, by putting aside all contemporary considerations, and taking the text of Saint-Simon, analysed above, as a starting-point. This text is based on a concept, central to the thought of the duke and also, of course, to the reality of the Court of Louis XIV: the concept of the *cabal*. A cabal is a temporary structure—although it may last for two decades or more—the aim of which, in Court circles or in the higher reaches of the State, is to obtain certain advantages such as power, prestige, money, appointments to high office in the church or high command in the army, or the promotion of its members in the order of precedence of dukes, princes, etc. For Saint-Simon, the study of the cabal, together with the inevitable character-sketches of its members, is in fact one of the principal objects of writing history. Indeed, he reproaches Père Daniel, the author of a history of France written in about 1714, with having sacrificed everything else to "battle-history"—neglecting "cabal-history" or "character-study history", so to speak.

Independently of the centre to which the cabal is attached—in this case the royal dynasty—the cabal itself takes the form of a network, woven among its participants by bonds of kinship, clienthood, friendship, etc. Negative relationships created by enmity, quarrels, perhaps within the same family, can contribute, through the intermediary of any given person, to the alienation of one cabal from another. The cabal may derive support from various groups or subgroups, corresponding to different social, socio-political, institutional or religious forces, such as the army for instance, the church, finance, the bureaucracy, the aristocracy, the princes of the blood, the dukes and peers.

However, the essentially individualist approach—atomistic, with a possibility of becoming molecular, to use chemical terms—which Saint-Simon displays towards the cabals and the cabal system, makes my own analysis, which aims to introduce some sociological perspectives, appear rather superfluous. On the other hand, it could be argued that for comparative purposes it is imperative to study cabals which operated within a system where there was no official or organized opposition, or where such opposition as there was never succeeded in taking power. One could use the same approach to study various contemporary systems, different from each other and very different from the *ancien régime* in France: systems where access to power is controlled by an established hierarchy, rather than by a process of permutation, in the course of which government and opposition change places. Examples of such contemporary systems where the basic element is continuity (not to be identified with "pre-established harmony") could be found, for instance, in the various communist régimes, about which something is known through the analysis of bureaucratic elites—a study known as "Kremlinology". Another instance, in a very different setting of course, might be seen in gaullism and post-gaullism or "giscardism": here, too, various complex mechanisms of *succession* have always operated so far (1977) by means of established processes that imply a certain non-oppositional continuity, where it is assumed that there are no unsurmountable obstacles. Such processes, like the family trees so close to Saint-Simon's heart, take for granted the existence of "cabals" within a larger formation: broadly speaking, everyone inside it is agreed on basic questions.

Political science, we know, has often taken inspiration from the natural sciences. Concepts based on social class and the class struggle (Guizot, Thierry, Marx) are, of course, linked to various phenomena in antiquity and modern history: the census by "classes" of Servius Tullius in Rome; the "classes" in the registration of sailors before the French revolution; or the tax divisions suggested by Vauban and others—"taxpayers of the first class", "the second class", and so on. And then there are the classification systems of Linnaeus, Buffon, and Tournefort, applied to plants and living creatures. Such notions of class, with the often rigid distinctions that they imply, whether in sociology or zoology (birds and mammals, bourgeoisie and proletariat, etc.) raise problems of frontiers and overlaps, especially in the field of anthropology, which are not easily solved even by the most subtle of marxists.

More recently, American sociology, which is in fact of European or rather East European origin (Sorokin), has adopted geological parallels. The concept of social "stratification" may bring a degree of flexibility to the analysis, since the geological strata which in this case provide the image for the model, can be overturned, faulted, folded, impacted upon one another, and rolled away in massive rock movements. When all is said and done though, geology has to do with lifeless, inert matter: there can be no real fusion, synthesis, or exchange between these dead layers. That is why I must confess that the geological-stratification ideas of Sorokin and his American disciples leave me almost as dissatisfied as the botanical-zoological classifications of Thierry, Guizot, Marx and Tournefort.

Lucien Febvre appreciated this problem; he was irritated by the stratification model, since it rested essentially on notions of an upper and a lower layer (even if they might become mixed up in rock movements). He suggested that it might be more useful to compare the social structures one wished to study, to the complex structures and infrastructures of a big city: the networks of water, gas and electricity mains that reach into every corner and every level, uniting upper and lower layers, and different districts and central points, by the most unexpected connections, thus abolishing both the upper-lower hierarchies of stratification and the rigid divisions of botanical-zoological classification.

Saint-Simon looked at it yet another way. As one of his admirers, Ernst Jünger, has remarked, his approach was unconsciously close to that of a science such as organic chemistry or molecular biology. "Saint-Simon studies the Court as if it were a vast molecule in organic chemistry. His was a very modern mind", Jünger writes. And indeed as we can see from the text produced here, Saint-Simon does not confine himself to distinguishing between cabals and factions. He also notes the "valencies" of all kinds which may link the member of one group, for instance, to a member of another. He also notes the negative forces of repulsion within each cabal: Pontchartrain the elder is on bad terms with Madame de Maintenon, or at any rate he has fallen from favour. But he remains, nevertheless, within her cabal. In this way Saint-Simon contrives, over and above his definition of the three cabals, to give a concrete description of a concrete situation: the main outlines of the picture do not obscure secondary (and sometimes contradictory) details. The Court was, to be sure, a comparatively closed and circumscribed unit, with only a few hundred important participants, and only a few thousand people in all. That made it easier to write about.

This brings us to the point at which we should move from the field of natural sciences towards that of the social sciences, and pass on to the rigorous disciplines of anthropology and the study of small communities. Evans-Pritchard's work on the Nuer comes to mind, or at a less abstruse level, Laurence Wylie's portrait of a French village.

THE CLOCK AND THE BILLIARD TABLE

But Saint-Simon, of course, had never heard of anthropology, any more than he had of organic chemistry. His personal references were different, and his models tended to be watchmaking or the manufacture of clockwork toys, for these represented the modern technology of his day. And the little duke also used analogies from games.

Clockwork: Here is rather a nice extract, from a time when Saint-Simon (who was really much better at analysing than at scheming) tried to set up his own cabal. In order to do so, he used the networks and connections provided for him by the three major cabals, described above as they appear in his writings. His aim in setting up this ephemeral construction (bearing on what he believed to be his future interests) was to marry "Mademoiselle", the daughter of the Duc d'Orléans, and great-niece of Louis XIV, to her cousin-german the Duc de Berry, son of Monseigneur and grandson of Louis XIV. (Another of those intermarriages.) Saint-Simon, in his efforts to engineer this wedding on which he founded certain hopes, sought to maneouvre certain ladies and a certain Jesuit by indirect means; and he described his activities as follows:

> Such were the mechanisms and combinations of mechanisms which my friendship for those to whom I was attached, my hatred for Madame la Duchesse and my concern about my present and

future situation, succeeded in discovering, assembling and setting in motion, in a regular and precise fashion, perfectly in accordance and with full leverage. It took only the space of Lent for me to initiate and perfect this machine, of which all the processes, breakdowns and progress were familiar to me, which responded to me in every respect, and which I wound up afresh in perfect cadence every day.

The Court, seen from this perspective, becomes a sort of clock or great turnip-watch, which Saint-Simon takes apart and puts together again for our edification, and in the interests of his cause. He realises, of course, the weaknesses of the comparison. Real clockwork mechanisms are made of metal, and last virtually for ever. But the mechanisms of the Court were unpredictable: they were like "ice-cubes" that melted in the sun. In the event, the Duchesse de Berry became scandalously drunk a few days after her marriage, and was to lead a dissolute life, greatly disappointing the hopes that Saint-Simon had placed in her. So, the cabal organized for the marriage of the Duc de Berry was later to be one of the memorialist's greatest regrets.

Saint-Simon also drew comparisons with the world of games: and in the first place with the wager. To organise or join a cabal was in fact to wager that the central figure of the cabal (Madame de Maintenon, Monseigneur, or the Duc de Bourgogne) would remain in power for some time (the first), or would either wholly acquire power, or achieve at least a share in power (the other two). Wagering was a familiar activity for Saint-Simon; indeed, his wager over the loss of Lille (which he predicted) was almost his undoing, as far as the King was concerned, and all for a few *pistoles*. And since at times he expressed some sympathy with the Jansenists, he no doubt knew of Pascal's famous wager.

Another game that invited comparisons was *billiards*: by the principle whereby ball no. 1 could affect ball no. 3 indirectly, through the intermediary of ball no. 2. We know that this popular game was played at Court: indeed Chamillart, who was very good at billiards, was launched on a brilliant ministerial career by his prowess at the game. And there is the story of the Bishop of Langres who, finding that he was hopeless at billiards when he played at Court, went back to his diocese to get some intensive practice and returned to Versailles, where he amazed all the courtiers by beating them hollow.

The cabal game was rather like a game of billiards. One can see this in the activities of Clermont-Chaste, for instance: remote-controlled by the Maréchal de Luxembourg, he became in turn the lover of the Princesse de Conti, and then of Mademoiselle Choin, in order to influence Monseigneur. Using two or three intermediaries, the Maréchal de Luxembourg was working, by various combinations of billiard balls, on the man he thought would be the next king: Clermont-Chaste and the Princesse de Conti; and Clermont-Chaste and Mademoiselle Choin.

Saint-Simon himself engaged in a game of billiards to engineer the marriage of the Duc de Berry: he used Père Tellier, the Jesuits, and a whole string of court ladies to influence the principals in the affair: the King and Madame de Maintenon. (Neither the future bride and bridegroom nor their parents, Monseigneur and the Duc and Duchesse d'Orléans, were likely to have much say in the decision.)

THE COURT GAME

From the point of view of a social or genealogical history, it appears that Saint-Simon's text, supported by our general acquaintance with his *Mémoires*, enables us to define a "political class", or at any rate the upper stratum or environment of the political class of the time, both men and women. Not that the Court was "in power"—it had no power. But it was from within the Court that one had greatest access to the levers of power, since all the ministers, the members of the great families of State servants—the Phélypeaux, the Chamillarts, the Colberts and the Louvois—were all present at court and arranged the marriages of their children there. There was a constant series of weddings, and people met each other continually, socially or otherwise. The two milieus of bureaucracy and aristocracy encountered and intermingled with each other. In the eighteenth century, an entire section of the higher aristocracy was descended quite simply from the "bourgeois" or so-called bourgeois ministers of the seventeenth century.

Another interesting aspect of Saint-Simon's text is that it uses genealogical analysis to the full: all three generations of the royal family, father, son and grandson, appear, with their wives. And one also finds the whole range of kinship combinations within the royal family and the great noble families: illegitimate children, princes of the blood, etc. Then there are the different ranks at court: of the royal bastards, the males tended to attach themselves to Madame de Maintenon, while certain of the daughters joined the princes of the blood, and were directly or indirectly linked to Monseigneur's cabal; and dukes could be found in the Duc de Bourgogne's cabal or Madame de Maintenon's (among others).

Inextricably mingled with these distinctions are more properly sociological analyses, since various forces (the Church, the higher aristocracy, financial interests and the army) took up positions in relation to the various cabals.

★

It would be interesting, in this context, to study the processes by which the chief pressure-groups were formed and took up positions; some of them are reminiscent, but only at some remove, of the social groups of marxist theory. I am thinking in particular of:

—the Marshals of France, who composed a sort of military pressure group, attached for the most part to the Maintenon cabal;

—the princes of the blood and the royal bastard daughters;

—all those who could be called "internal servants" at Court, and who carried out police functions;

—the dukes and peers, and the nobility in general;

—the ministers;

—the great dignitaries among the clergy and the Jesuits; the former had access to the Maintenon cabal, the latter to that of the Duc de Bourgogne.

However, this obviously takes us (hardly surprisingly perhaps) a long way from the categories of marxist analysis. The bourgeoisie is hardly visible at all. Financial interests do make an appearance in the Maintenon cabal through the Pontchartrain family, and in the Duc de Bourgogne's cabal, more or less, through Desmaretz. It was even said that Monseigneur was not entirely deaf to the sirens of high finance. But as important and perhaps more important than these in the power game at Louis XIV's Court were the great pressure-groups among the nobility and the powerful bureaucrats.

Similar patterns, but of a more "violent" nature, could be found in the time of Louis XIII: with Gaston d'Orléans, Anne of Austria and Marie de Medicis, and it should be possible to analyse the socio-political or socio-religious forces behind each group. The matrimonial and genealogical analysis favoured by Saint-Simon would be less applicable during the Fronde, since the revolutionary forces after 1648 were such as to disrupt family structures in the strict sense. Nevertheless, on one hand Condé, a prince of the blood and a very close relation of the royal family; on the other the Duc de Beaufort, son of a bastard of Henri IV; and, in the centre of the system, Anne of Austria and her friend, the minister Mazarin, not to mention "La Grande Mademoiselle", each played various rounds of the Family power game, with various supporting groups in each case (nobility, *Parlement*, "populace").

★

The significance of a work like that of Saint-Simon is that all these aspects are marked with great precision; thanks to the memoir-writing duke, it is possible to combine a modern "socio-economic" analysis with a "genealogical" analysis which is of ancient origin, and "ethnographically" inspired.

7

The Rouergue through the Lens[1]

In memory of Jeanine Field-Recurat

THE EARLIEST TRIBE

"THE Rouergue in photographs": this collection,* running from the last of the daguerrotypes to snapshots taken before and after the First World War, shows us how local photographers have looked at the region of southern France known as the Rouergue. They have left us these "true-to-life" images of an old province, one that was already settled in the last centuries before Christ, and which in 1790, with frontiers almost unchanged, became the *département* of the Aveyron.

A set of sepia-tinted photographs: like reflections in the many-faceted eye of a fly, they combine to give a particular, if composite, vision of the province. In itself this is only one way among others of viewing the subject; and one specifically dated in time. My intention in this foreword is not—or not primarily—to "introduce" the photographs. I shall do that very briefly at the end. In any case, they speak for themselves, and they are accompanied by a commentary. I should like simply to contribute as a historian: to describe in a few words, using concrete examples, how certain people have "looked at" the Rouergue over the centuries.

By exceptional good fortune, or rather thanks to remarkable powers of resistance, related perhaps to the conservationist virtues of its mountain race, the frontiers of the Rouergue region have remained the same since Roman or even Celtic times, surviving the transition into the *département* of the Aveyron (1790 to the present). In other words, the tribe of the Rutheni (the Rouergats of modern France) has preserved its ethnic and geographical identity vitually unchanged over twenty centuries or more. It was merely overlaid with a veneer in Gallo-Roman times: from this point of view, the most significant change occurred during the first half or

*Although this article was originally written to accompany a book of photographs of the Rouergue, a province of southwest France, it is concerned to show how eye-witnesses before the age of photography viewed the province, and can be read quite independently of the photographic collection.

174

two-thirds of the first millennium A.D. During this period, the Rutheni dropped their Celtic dialect and adopted, first under Roman, then under Christian influence, the local form of Spoken Latin, gradually to become the Rouergue version of *Occitan*—the language almost unanimously spoken in the region until the early twentieth century when French made rapid progress there; the age precisely of the camera, and the faded snapshots reproduced here.

Ways of looking may have changed; but the subject, the Rouergue, has remained to a remarkable extent the same. Such unity of content provides justification for looking, in turn, at a series of different views, bringing us eventually to the ultimate way of seeing—from behind a camera—which is the subject of this book.

My choice of views and viewers, from the earliest times to the nineteenth century, is as arbitrary as it is selective. This preface cannot pretend to be a "History of the Rouergue". So I have chosen to look (in chronological order): first, through the eyes of the antiquarian, Alexandre Albenque, whose intuitive vision of the Celtic, tribal and ancient beginnings of the Aveyron recreates its original unity for us. Next, after a glimpse of the dark age of the seventeenth century, I shall draw on the essentially local observations of a bourgeois ecologist of the eighteenth century, Jean Mouret, before moving on to the broader vision of a socially conscious bishop of the same period, Champion de Cicé, a lucid eyewitness of the terrible poverty in the Aveyron in the Age of Enlightenment. Lastly, some accounts from the nineteenth century will bring the reader up to the time of the early photographers with their quaint paraphernalia—black cloth, lens, tripod and exposure plates.

*

For a view of the Celtic and barbarian, not to mention Gallo-Roman versions of the Rouergue, then, taking one back to the times of primitive savagery, overlaid with a thin film of Latin culture, I have drawn on the work of Alexandre Albenque. Headmaster of the *lycée* in Rodez, and an Aveyronnais to the core (more of a Rouergat than the most colourful coal-merchant in the streets of Paris), Albenque was in his time (1948) the most knowledgeable expert on the antiquities of his *département*, in the deepest sense of the term "antiquity". His work is now rather dated, no doubt. It is not my purpose, nor am I qualified, to bring it up to date by comparing it with recent research. For me, the significance of his writing is that the outstanding unity of its field of vision makes it the most valuable "snapshot" we possess of the Rouergue in the early days.

The first thing that strikes one is the permanence of the frontiers. We do not know exactly what the territorial limits were of the Gallic "people", "tribe" or "civitas", the *Rutheni*. Did they coincide broadly with those of the Ruthenian *civitas* in Roman times? In this later period, at any rate, we are on fairly solid ground. The limits of the Gallo-Roman territory of the Rutheni correspond to what were later to become the boundaries of the diocese of Rodez, since these were traced, during the great invasions, on the outline of the administrative structures left by the Empire, which had in turn, no doubt, inherited tribal frontiers. These very ancient "borders" followed certain accidents of the terrain: the watershed of the Aubrac mountains to the northeast; the valleys of the Truyère and the Goul to the north; the valley of the Lot to the northwest; and the separation of the slopes down to the Atlantic and the Mediterranean to the south. The Causses (limestone plateaux) themselves, so useful for sheep and cereal-growing, had been shared out, to the south and southeast, among various proto-historic populations. "The Gabali (of Lozère) occupied the Méjean Causse and the Causse of Sauveterre. The Rutheni appropriated the western dependencies of the Causse of Sauveterre (the Causse de Sévérac and the Causse Rouge) and the greater part of the Causse Noir and the Larzac. The Areconian Volqui, who had settled in the Languedoc (in the present day *département* of Hérault) also needed transhumance grounds for their flocks of sheep; so they annexed the eastern part of the Causse Noir and the southeast of the plateau of Larzac."[2]

There was one amputation, over which we can quickly pass: in the early years of the first century B.C., a section of *Ruthenia* (Rouergue) was detached from the rest by the Romans, and annexed to the province of *Gallia Narbonensis*. This section rapidly lost its *rouergat* character, although its inhabitants were known for a while as "provincial Rutheni". It corresponds to the area south of the Aveyron, later to become the diocese of Albi and the departement of Tarn.[3]

Apart from this mutilation, the Rouergue remained administra-
tively and ethnically practically unchanged, from the earliest days
down to the beginning of the twentieth century. As we have seen, it
corresponded to the diocese of Rodez, but it was also identical, in
Merovingian and Carolingian times, with the *pays du Rouergue*
(*pagus rutenicus*), and the county of Rouergue (*comitas rutenensis*).
During the Middle Ages, particularly from the thirteenth century
on, the counts of Rouergue became, through a series of events,
satellites of the French Crown. Originally vassals of the Montforts,
they were "absorbed" by marriage into the Armagnacs. This period
saw the Rouergue become "French" for the first time. But the new
and enduring "Frenchness" was not translated into adoption of the
French language until much later (the twentieth century).

Meanwhile, the ecclesiastical diocese of Rodez kept its identity
unchanged until 1317, when the Aveyron parishes south of the Tarn
were detached from the old diocese, to make up the new, very small
diocese of Vabre. In spite of this ecclesiastical surgery, and the
"mitosis" between Rouergue and Vabre, the historical unit of
Rouergue, according to Albenque "was to survive in the minds of
its people": a striking example of *la longue durée* ("the long term"
in history), of "time standing still", or of "the stagnant society",
whichever term best accords with one's ideological preferences for
change or continuity. (Mine, in this instance, I confess, rather
favour continuity.)

The Rouergue was, under the French Crown, up to and including
the eighteenth century, a military command zone centred on
Rodez.[4] The command was attached to the general military administration of Guyenne and Gascony. The former "Ruthenia" was
also a *sénéchaussée* under the Valois and the Bourbons. The assembly of the three orders of Rouergue, later suppressed by the "modern" centralization of the French State under the *ancien régime*,
met regularly over a long period. The seneschalsy itself survived as
an ethnico-judiciary district until the French Revolution.

In 1790, the Constituent Assembly fully appreciated the real
vitality and potential of such an ancient and durable administrative
constituency; and so created the *département* of the Aveyron.
Geographically, this corresponded quite simply to the old *civitas* of
the Rutheni.[5] From the time of Bonaparte's consulate, then, the
prefect of this *département* and its departmental council were the

legitimate successors of the seneschals of the *ancien régime*—and the distant successors, too, of the *Rouergat* magistrates and notables of Gallo-Roman antiquity: the quaestor, aediles, curia and *vergobrets*, who were in charge of the "general administration of justice"[6] in the old Gallo-Roman *civitas*.

Are Alexandre Albenque's images of his Aveyron "tribe" in early history so very dissimilar in composition to those of the photographs of 1860–1950 (allowing, of course, for obvious differences)? In both cases, a superficial but prominent "modernity" appears to be occupying the horizon, unduly monopolizing one's attention—in the 1920s, this is the bourgeoisie of Villefranche; in 100 A.D., the small but conspicuous local Gallo-Roman *élite*. And in both cases one senses in the background, less spectacular but more fundamental, the enormous mass of peasants; they form the overwhelming majority, of course, but all evidence of their presence has been drastically reduced, both in the archaeological remains and, much later, by the photographer's lens.

According to Albenque, the Gallo-Roman *élite*, numerically in the minority among the Rutheni, had acquired a veneer of Latin culture over its original uncouthness; it occupied the centre stage. Rodez, or *Segodunum* ("citadel of the Rouergat people"), under the Later Empire possessed aqueducts, a network of Roman roads, an amphitheatre with seats for 15,000, and a number of fine suburban villas: the rich both lived in them and were buried in them. The Roman roads led to Lyon, Lodève, Périgueux, Cahors, and Bordeaux. At Graufesenque in the first century A.D. there was a pottery, making vases for export in their hundreds to both east and west. The craftsmen who produced these vases were among the most skilled in the ancient world; but they still spoke and even wrote the old Celtic or Gallic language. Lead and silver mines near Villefranche, state-controlled under Tiberias, were briefly worked. Throughout the area, Gallo-Roman houses, built of stone, were replacing the Gauls' huts of wattle and daub (though these were by no means totally eliminated). A thousand or so *villae* (estates)—any one of which might be up to 1,000 *hectares* in size—appeared on the Causses plateaux and among the fertile meanders of the Lot valley. They did not destroy but, on the contrary, absorbed into their system the little plots and cabins of the native dwellers.

For the indigenous population still survived. The mass of "savage" Rouergats were descended from local, largely pre-Celtic populations, which had settled all over the Causses long before, with their dolmens and tumuli. They had intermarried with their Celtic conquerors, who had given them a new language. They had cleared the land on the Causses, but hardly begun on the Ségalas. (These Ségalas were areas of primary, acid soil, not good enough to grow wheat but adequate for rye, hence the name (French *seigle* = rye.) The attempt, difficult and not very profitable, to bring some of this land under cultivation, had scarcely begun, with some small-scale clearings, in the Celtic or even Gallo-Roman period. Apart from the volcanic Aubrac range, much of the Aveyron is made up either of limestone *causses*, or of these primary Ségalas.)

Were the original Rouergats—essentially the old Rutheni with their own language, not yet Romanized—already being taken for *Auvergnats*(outside the Auvergne proper) during the early Christian era? For in the nineteenth and twentieth centuries, the Aveyronnais who came to Paris whether as coal-merchants, café-proprietors or professors at the Collège de France, were and are generally taken for Auvergnats by the Parisians, who do not bother with the finer ethnic or geographical distinctions. By Caesar's time, at all events, the Rutheni had become a client people, that is, dependent on and satellites of the Arverni of the Auvergne—the Auvergnats of Gergovie, of whom Vercingetorix was an illustrious example at about the same time. Their "satellization" was to be long-lasting. In Paris, whether one comes from Rouergue or Auvergne, one is generally labelled an Auvergnat. And in the true south, in lowland Languedoc or Spain, one would always be considered a *gavache*, a crude mountain-dweller from the Massif Central, whether one was in fact a Rouergat from the Aveyron, or a genuine *gavache* or *gabale* of the Gévaudan, i.e., the Lozère.

The Rutheni were peasants, farming both crops and livestock on their own account or for the owners of the *villae*. These were not very rich—the villas of the Rouergue are not remarkable for their works of art or inscriptions. The peasants of Gallo-Roman times grew wheat on the Causses, rye on some parts of the Ségalas, winter barley more or less everywhere, and oats not at all. They used the traditional implements of Gaul, with some Roman borrowings: the swing-plough, sickle, two-pronged hoe, scythe, and the pruning-knife for vines. For as early as the third century A.D., vines, which had been developed first in the Vivarais and Bordelais regions, were becoming acclimatized here and there in patches on the Causses. At about the same time, the wooden cask, as used by the Gauls, being more efficient for mass transport, was replacing the Roman amphora. In our own times, the unusual celebration on Whit-Monday, known as the feast of Saint Bourron (Bourron = *Bourgeon* = sprouting of the vine) at Marcillac in Aveyron, is a reminder of the pagan-cum-Christian feasts of the first vineyards of Rouergue: pagan in the first half of the first millennium, they were later converted to Christianity (their grapes being used equally well for communion wine or for secular drinking).

Christianity itself, when it was brought by Saint Amans in the latter part of the fourth century, made its own contribution to the "Rouergization" of the Rouergue. The new religion, as it sought to reach all parts of the area, completed the linguistic revolution. Celtic dialects disappeared and a local form of Latin entirely replaced them, becoming the general dialect in Rouergue, and one of the purest languages of the Occitanian community. Apart from this, though, there were a number of backward moves. An entire section of the thin Gallo-Roman crust which overlaid or cloaked the deeper identity of the region, cracked, crumbled and disappeared. Rodez withdrew to the top of its hill, and its population fell from perhaps 10,000 to 4,000. This re-ruralization wiped out some of the existing modest urban achievements. Saint Amans himself, the local apostle of Christianity, destroyed Roman idols and tried to protect the local populations from the police activities, and the judiciary, military and financial intrusions of what remained of the central powers of the Roman Empire. With this retreat to its parish pump, the Rouergue was tending more and more to slip from the grasp of the dying imperial institutions. Germanic influence, which might have attracted the regional entity in another direction, proved to be insignificant. The Rouergue was briefly and nominally attached during the second half of the fifth century to the "Visigoth" domains of King Euric; then to the Frankish state, enlarged under Clovis, and finally to Austrasia, of which Metz was the capital, in the sixth century. As one might expect, contacts between the Aveyron and Lorraine were not particularly lively. The Rouergue became, or remained, in many respects independent, since inter-regional state structures were so weak during this period: they were better at conquering and destroying than at achieving anything positive in

the way of administration. The province, therefore, became progressively more inward-looking, gradually withdrawing further into
its isolation, and developing inside the shell of its own identity
which thus became perfected and concentrated—like a Roquefort
cheese. The Rouergue *matured* internally, without outside aid.
Many things were to change concerning individual status and the
system of property in the course of the next thousand years or so.
But if one considers agricultural techniques, rural ecology, or that
mystical and physical bond between man and nature, species and
habitat, a number of things stayed remarkably the same: a whole
range of customs and behaviour, from the shape of ploughshares
and cheese-moulds, to the cult of stone axes and water-gods. Grégoire de Tours, writing about the lake of Saint-Andéol, on the
frontier between the Rutheni and the Gabali,[7] says that:

> "here at a certain period [about 500 A.D.] a multitude of
> peasants came to offer, as it were, sacrifices to this lake: they
> threw in linen and cloth used for making men's clothes; cheese
> and wax moulds, bread and all manner of things, each one
> according to his capacity—it would take too long to number them
> all. They came with carts, bringing food and drink with them,
> and would slaughter animals and organize banquets there for
> three days on end. On the fourth day, when they were about to
> leave, there came upon them a mighty storm, with terrible thun-
> der and lightning; torrential rain and hail pelted them, with
> hailstones as big as pebbles; those who were there feared for
> their lives. Every year the same thing happened, and these
> ignorant people continued to wallow in their superstition. After
> many years, a priest from the city, who had been appointed
> bishop, went to the shores of the lake and preached to the crowd,
> asking them to give up these practices, for fear of being struck by
> the fury of the heavens. But these stupid country folk would not
> listen".

In the end, the bishop had a basilica built on the lakeside, dedicated
it to Saint Hilaire de Poitiers, and put the saint's relics inside. The
people were converted, and from then on (or so they said) adopted
the custom of laying their offerings in the chapel. The annual storm
had been exorcised.

There is one thing wrong with the story: the happy ending is not
quite accurate. The peasants of Rouergue and Lozère, Rutheni or
Gabali, had not given up their habit of sacrificing to the lake at all:

On the second Sunday in August, even in the nineteenth century, people would come from all around to the lake of Saint-Andéol, and throw in coins, pieces of cloth, sheepskins etc. [just as they had in 500 A.D.]—hoping to be cured from illnesses or preserved from spells. And this went on until 1867, when there was a violent fight between some of the participants [plenty of wine was drunk on these ritual occasions] and the gendarmes of Nasbinal persuaded the public authorities to forbid the ceremony. The following year, armed troops broke up the meeting of the faithful, and since then only the occasional obstinate believer is to be seen taking a quick dip in the icy waters, throwing in a coin or sometimes a garment, and going away secure in his belief.[8]

What a splendid and fascinating example of pagan survival! Until "the gendarmes of Nasbinal" stupidly interrupted it, this ritual had lasted from (at least) the fifth or sixth century until the nineteenth.

ROUERGATS OUTSIDE THEIR PROVINCE

There are few general accounts of the social and economic (let alone psychological) state of the Rouergue in the Middle Ages. Only one major population survey claiming to cover the whole of the Aveyron has survived for the fourteenth century before the Black Death (1348). It suggests that the province was already as densely populated as it would be later, in the seventeenth century.

For the classical (or "modern") period—sixteenth to eighteenth centuries—there is a little more information. The survey of *Commodities of the Rouergue in 1552*, splendidly presented by Jacques Bousquet,[9] portrays what was, in appearance at least, a rich if not fertile country: it could boast 550,000 sheep and 70,000 cattle, either transhumant or in resident flocks. These are virtually record figures by comparison with other French provinces north or south. It produced cereals, of course, and also in various places wine, walnuts, fruits, saffron, cloth, leather, coal, and more besides. Fairs and markets were held more or less everywhere. The only form of transport was by mule; as a result of this backwardness, the entire region was by-passed as soon as good roads were built in the plains of Languedoc in the eighteenth century. Goods traffic carried by cart in these lowland regions, with their better roads, would then capture part of the transit trade previously handled by the mule-trains of the Rouergue.

But some problems dated from well before the capture of the trade; as opposed to the comparatively rosy picture to be found in *Commodities of the Rouergue*, there are many signs of fairly serious poverty or backwardness in the Aveyron; and this was to become, if anything, more marked, by comparison with neighbouring areas, during the seventeenth and even eighteenth centuries.

In the first place, this was a culturally retarded area: it is certainly worthy of note that the Rouergue should have been one of the last regions of the south to deign to accept the use of written French, at the end of the sixteenth century—whereas more developed parts of Languedoc, the Lower Rhône and Provence had admitted the use of the French language, in written form, as early as the end of the fifteenth or the first half of the sixteenth century. This cultural isolation enabled the Aveyron to preserve a very beautiful and pure version of the Occitan tongue, uncontaminated by the *langue d'oïl*. But such isolationism was also a sign that the Aveyron was cut off from the rest of the world. Without roads, and with no substantial network of trade and outside contacts, the area was doomed to remain archaic in its ways, and from now on this was a recipe for poverty and underdevelopment.

Indirect evidence on such poverty and underdevelopment can be found in Languedoc, in the records of the almshouses and parish registers of the lowlands, where the needy Rouergats came to die or waste away. Many set out for the south in the hope, not always a vain one, of improving their lot. During the great subsistence crisis of Louis XIV's reign, in 1694–5 for instance, travellers poured every day into the almshouses (*hospices*) of southern Languedoc, where they might spend a few days or a few hours. The administrators noted their names and their birthplaces in the registers, and the statistics which can be compiled from their files leave no room for doubt: there was indeed a massive emigration of poverty-stricken mountain dwellers, the ragged armies of the Massif Central and in particular of the Rouergue, into the Mediterranean plains.[10] The three poorest dioceses were Rodez (the source of 24 per cent of the migrants), Mende (12 per cent), and Saint-Flour (8 per cent)—in other words, the Rouergue was far ahead, with the Gévaudan and Cantal in second and third places. From these three centres of southward emigration, a mass of landless peasants and day-labourers streamed on to the roads. Uprooted from their native villages, they had no professional skills outside agriculture. But among them there were the elements of an artisan class and a proletariat, originating in the poorest layers of the population of the Rouergue. Such artisans, or semi-artisans might be assistants to barber-surgeons, sedan-chair porters, or weavers. The weavers of the Rouergue flowed in large numbers into the industrial town of Lodève in the Hérault, where they made up one-third of the immigrant population of textile workers.

Many of these Rouergats, travellers whom their empty bellies had driven from the hills towards the mirages of the south, never reached their destination, but died on the way of hunger, exposure, or disease: children of nine, twelve or fourteen years, exhausted and rickety old men "of small stature", from the Aveyron Causse. They collapsed from hunger in parishes at the foot of the mountains, a few leagues from the promised land. In the famine years of 1693–4 the beggars of the Rouergue and the Causse de Sauveterre took to the roads and flocked down into the plains of Languedoc. Mortality during the exodus was extraordinary. In one village in the Hérault, midway between the hills and the plain, where in a normal year there might be about 45 deaths (but 70 and 80 in 1693 and 1694) I have found records, between January 1693 and August 1694, of the deaths of 25 travellers passing through: mostly they had come from the Rouergue, Gévaudan and the Aubrac mountains, in particular from the hard-hit villages of Gabrias, Lastènes and Gillorgues. Almost all were under twenty or over fifty: "deceased, a little boy named Amans, 8 years, from the parish of Gillorgues, in the diocese of Rodez" (August 13, 1694); "a boy called Jean, aged about 13, who did not know where he came from" (May 18, 1694). Many children from the Rouergue, aged about ten or twelve, were wandering about on their own in the Languedoc, to die with no-one to care for them, whispering their names, "Jean" or "Jeanne" with their last breath. Old men, travelling on foot, collapsed and died by the roadside, like dogs. Whole families perished on the road. When it came to burying them in the lowlands, it was often impossible to find a witness to sign the register. Who cared about strangers? They were buried in a hastily allocated piece of land known as the "graveyard of the poor".

Not all the vagabonds of the Rouergue died en route, of course. Many succeeded in settling in some lowland village, resourcefully finding themselves a living before moving on again. Their children sometimes laid the basis of the family fortunes. A parish priest of the *garrigues*, the *abbé* Fabre or Favre, has left a colourful account of the doings of one of these migrant families of the early eighteenth century. Much abridged, it goes as follows: in about 1700, a Rouergat named Truquette left his native Aveyron and settled in the parish of La Vaunage, in a hollow in the *garrigues* near Nimes. Truquette was a likely lad, with hair on his chest and a twinkle in his eye; he married a buxom local girl, herself born out of wedlock. At the wedding feast, guests were offered a fox, some *courpatasses* (rooks), a bowlful of frogs' legs and an apparently endless supply of vegetables. The cost of the meal ruined the bridegroom, so he sold the trousseau. His wife set about him and, the priest tells us, there was a dingdong battle in the course of which Homeric insults were exchanged ("herring-face", "toadfish", "snot-nose", "clumsy oaf", "stupid rabbit", etc.). The young couple, having no money, were known locally as *les meurt-de-faim* ("the starvelings"). They had a son, Jean, as ne'er-do-well as his father and with the same appetite. It was not long before the father's trade collapsed and he was hanged for a thief. Jean, when he grew up, himself married a beggar-woman, Barbe-Garouille, "a regular repository of bad temper and shrewishness". Fortunately for him, she died in the alms-house. As it happened Jean, showing better judgement this time, had just seduced Babeau, the daughter of a landowner; when she turned out to be pregnant, he married her—and it was goodbye to rags and tatters at last.

Truquette and his family are merely one example among tens of thousands of others. The Rouergats, *gavots* or *gavaches*, in general contributed to the repopulation of a good part of Spain and the south of France; patterns of emigration were set for a long time, from the fourteenth to the twentieth century. For reasons partly, but not exclusively, connected with the poverty of the granite Ségalas, the Rouergue was, for half a millennium, a sort of anticyclone of emigration.

A CASE-STUDY: POVERTY IN THE ROUERGUE IN 1643

It could be argued that these observations on poor emigrants only show us "the Rouergat abroad" as he appeared to the communities, usually in the south, which were the destination of the traveller from the hills. So, let us look next at the Rouergats of the "modern" period, at home in the poverty and destitution which had been their culture for centuries. These peasants of the Aveyron, whose descendants appear in the photographs of a later age with the same rebels' faces, burnt black by the sun, are described to us as they were in the seventeenth century before the Fronde, in a document of exemplary authenticity which brings them to life—only to show us the more graphically the poverty, frustrations and motivations that sent them to their graves.

It was the year 1643, the year of the *Croquants'* rebellion: in the highlands of the Rouergue near Villefranche, Pierre de Molineri, and adviser to the king, was carrying out an investigation. Molineri, who had been delegated to this task by Monsieur de la Terrière, the Intendant of Guyenne, conscientiously surveyed a dozen or so parishes in the Rouergue. In each one, he questioned the farmhands, peasants, weavers, and "consuls" (i.e. magistrates). None of them, not even the consuls, could read or write, as Molineri found, encountering in his travels the total illiteracy of the Rouergue (scandalous even for this period) which indicated the complete absence of any educational provision. Only parish priests and notaries, who were by definition professional readers and writers, were able to sign their names. (It is true that the lack of schooling and literacy was the best possible means of safeguarding the Occitan language in its local and uncorrupted Aveyron form over a long period. An ill wind . . . ?)

The first thing his informants reported, unanimously, was that following floods, downpours, "ravines of water" and above all hailstorms, in the previous three or four years, the harvests had all failed. The year before, in 1642, "the inhabitants had been pelted with hailstones so often that they spent that year with no harvest at all." The notaries, Jean Garibert, of Savignac, and Antoine Tournemire of Martiel, were even more precise: they had noted disasters caused by hail in 1640, 1641, 1642 (three times) and 1643 ("for two days on end"). In 1642, not even the seed crop was recovered. This was reported by, among others, Gaspard Yssala, a bourgeois of Martiel, speaking of his own farm which he let out to a sharecropper, with four oxen. Apart from storm damage, the soil of the Rouergue, as we have already seen, was ungrateful and infertile, one of the worst regions of the *ancien régime*: the Ségalas especially, but the Causses too.

There was a bread shortage at the end of 1642, which became acute during the winter and spring of 1643. The price of wheat rose to four or five times that of normal years, whereas it only doubled in the lowlands, which thus suffered less, having a freer flow of money, better roads and access to Mediterranean or Atlantic ports. In three years, says the *recteur* of Savignac, wheat has gone up from 50 to 80 *sous* a *setier*, and this is confirmed by the corn-market records.

The local people, according to this report, *"sont à la faim"* (are going hungry). They eat bread only two or three times a week, apart from the charity of certain gentlemen or "well-off persons". In the hamlet of Saint-Georges, in the parish of La Chapelle, *"several inhabitants have gone fourteen whole days without eating"*, something of a record, as far as I know, in fasting and lack of nourishment—that is, if they survived.

"Many of the inhabitants", in the sober words of Antoine Carles, a peasant of La Bastide-Capdenac, "are going hungry, and are in despair that they cannot work their land, which they have abandoned, nor feed their families, whom they have to watch dying in front of them".

What were they to do? Sell the farm animals to buy bread? Impossible, the investigator was told by Gibergues, priest of Saint-Denis: "the said parishioners, having no other resource for buying bread than selling their animals, there came in the same year 1642 a contagious disease which carried off all the beasts, large and small, in the parish, and reduced all the residents to selling their furniture in order to survive, let alone satisfy the tax demands". Méjoul, the priest of Martiel, quoted the case of his own property. All the witnesses mentioned the death of the livestock: "it makes the markets empty and useless". These markets, or fairs, had been, in happier times, the pride of the Rouergue since the Renaissance; they made it possible for the livestock of the region to be disposed of and dispatched in all directions, at their proper value.

Another burden was that of excessive taxation, protested against by Lacassagne, consul of Labastide-Capdenac: "pressed by taxes and arrears, the inhabitants are selling all their possessions, and today they have to be content to eat bread two or three times a week". Roland Couderc, an illiterate labourer of Saint-Ygest, agreed: "the inhabitants are obliged to sell the most precious piece of furniture in their house, *even their own beds*, to meet the

charges". According to Antoine Carles, also an illiterate farmworker, "being unable to meet the tax arrears, and driven by
hunger, the parishioners are obliged to give up their lands, leaving
them untilled, and to go about the country seeking bread and
shamefully begging". No bread to eat; forced to sell all the furniture, including the bed, to leave the land and even the district—to
such straits were the peasants reduced by the heavy taxes, combined with the subsistence crisis and the natural poverty of the
region. And, looking beyond the taxes and dues, blame was naturally attached to the "partisans and their agents", as the priest
Méjoul (who had had to pay them "very high dues") called them.
The "partisans" were the tax-farmers and financiers, sharks with
big teeth or small, who farmed the various indirect taxes on behalf
of the king, and were traditionally hated by the people.

Like the fiscal "*taille*", land rents were also excessive. (Land rent
meant the tenancy dues, or the percentage of the harvest paid by the
tenant-farmer or share-cropper to the landowner). Individual calamities show what a burden it was; one among many responses
came from La Capelle where, according to the local notary, there
was "a drop of two-thirds in share-cropping tenancies". Even the
richer farmers, faced with huge rent bills, succumbed: "Charreton,
bourgeois of Caylus, was deprived of the agreement for the share-
crop holding of Gaspar".

As a result, there was much debt and mortgaging. The priest
Méjoul, ruined by a series of calamities, "has been obliged to
mortgage his land to buy seedcorn". There was a string of bankrupt-
cies, with unemployment. "The inhabitants", says Pierre Maille-
bion, an unlettered churchwarden of La Capelle, "are obliged to go
begging for bread, leaving their properties vacant, since they have
not the wherewithal to buy bread or to work their own land". The
most tragic feature of the destitution of these starving mountain-
dwellers of 1643 was the sale of their furniture, literally for a
mouthful of bread. Jean Coste of La Capelle testified to this, as did
a farm labourer, Jean Bous of Bès (both of them illiterate): "Most
of those with a respectable size of property *have to sell even their
own beds*, because of the charges". When there was no voluntary
sale, goods were seized and the owners forced to flee: "because of
the seizures of property, they are obliged to take flight to avoid
being put in prison", says Bernard Moly, a weaver of Bès. First-
hand witnesses, of course, were the bailiffs and their men who were

daily sent to "ransack the houses" of defaulters. One of these, Jean Leygues, was a *baille ordinaire* (that is, a seigniorial magistrate) in the village of Salles. He could barely sign his name (a bit steep, considering his position). This Jean Leygues, then, declared: "In cases of distraint for debt, when I arrive at the houses, all I find are the four walls, stripped of all the movable goods, which the tenants say they have sold or pawned to buy bread". Four bare walls, and no furniture. . . .

The notary Tournemire confirms this with further details: "The parishioners have been so completely ruined that when he (Tournemire) is employed to effect a seizure of property, he can find no furniture in the houses, no livestock large or small in the cowsheds or pastures, and he can get no reply from the debtors except that the hard times and the heavy charges have reduced them to hunger . . . and prevented them either from paying or having any goods left to seize; they can do nothing".

Hard times indeed, and heavy charges; and there was also a devaluation of copper coinage, which wiped out the savings of the humble. Individual disasters are profiled against a background of widespread poverty forced upon the Rouergue by an ungrateful soil and a high birth rate. There can be no doubt about the universally disastrous situation: the objective character of the Molineri report, which is our source, cannot be questioned. Molineri had been "deputed" to the task by the Intendant La Terrière, who was later in the same year 1643, to hang and subdue the rebels or "Croquants" of the Rouergue. La Terrière's subordinate was by no means systematically favourable to the peasants, far from it. He did not try to paint a gloomy picture of their poverty to attract sympathy for them. But he did want to bring to the attention of his master the real elements of a catastrophic situation.

In an attempt to solve their plight, to escape somehow from the despair described by everyone, the witnesses, who were themselves affected, seriously proposed three possible "solutions": death, beggary or emigration. One could beg on the spot, or one could leave the district "without consideration of land, wives and children", to join the army, or to go and work in the lowlands—a traditional solution for the Rouergats, which many adopted.

There was a fourth solution; one which was the basic reason for Molineri's arrival: rebellion, in this case the famous *Croquandage*. The willingness of the Croquants to challenge the authorities bears witness to the indomitable spirit of the Rouergue in the years before the Fronde.

THE CROQUANTS OF VILLEFRANCHE

From 1643, the Croquants were indeed beginning to show themselves in many villages of the Rouergue,[11] made desperate by so much misery. In June of that year, thirteen hundred of them marched into Villefranche-de-Rouergue, beating drums and carrying torches. Their leaders were artisans in the broad sense of the word: Petit was a surgeon, Bras (known as Lapaille) was a stonemason, who kept an inn. Lafourque or Lafourche was a master saddler. He was named by many rural parish assemblies (which were held almost everywhere in the space of five or six months) as "syndic of the poor inhabitants of the region of the Rouergue, united and joined together to inform the officers and powers of the taxes and surcharges". In short, Lafourche was the official leader of the "commons" of the Rouergue.

A prophetic aura surrounded the names of these three local leaders (Petit-small; Lapaille-straw; Lafourche-(pitch)fork). So-called verses of Nostradamus (the Provençal prophet and all-purpose source of authority at this period) were made up about them in 1643, for instance:

> Le *Petit* le grand surmontera
> La *paille* d'or et *la fourche* aiguë
> mettront à sec la mordante sangsue.

> (Approximately:
> The *Small* shall overcome the great
> The flaming *straw* and sharpened *fork*
> shall rid us of the bloodsucking shark.)

With a sure instinct, the Croquants of the Rouergue demanded that the *taille* be restored to 1618 rates, cancelling out Richelieu's "turn of the screw". That is, they wanted to return to the tax arrangements of the good old days, when the tax curve, while always rising, at least kept pace with price increases, and did not overtake them. That behind these "reasonable" demands were more subversive and concealed intentions, is not impossible. In Villefranche-de-Rouergue in 1627, during an earlier revolt (against the *regrattiers*, salt farmers) "rogues and seditious men boasted that property would soon change hands". (Though the Villefranche revolt of 1627 was somewhat misguided, anyway: one of the far-fetched rumours that started it off was to the effect that the king intended to tax every new-born child.[12]

In 1643, Petit, Lapaille and Lafourche confined themselves to protesting about taxation and nothing more. This enabled them in theory, thanks to widespread anti-fiscal feelings, to achieve a sacred union of all good Rouergats against the taxes. They were careful not to complain about other levies on the peasants: rent, tithes, usury, seigneurial dues, etc.

Their purely fiscal objectives won them, in the heady early days of the insurrection, the sympathy or neutrality of certain notables who were themselves inconvenienced by taxation. Young gentlemen joined the bands of Croquants in the countryside, and *"officers"*, that is holders of royal offices in Villefranche, were accused by the government of giving secret support to the *Croquandage*.

But this unity of the whole Rouergue did not stand the test for long. When the movement was crushed, the Croquants died alone, amid the hostility or indifference of the upper classes. It was the gentlemen of the Aveyron, mobilized by the Comte de Noailles, who arrested Petit and Lapaille, and handed them over to the executioner, who broke their limbs while they were still alive. It was the "respectable" bourgeois inhabitants of Villefranche, with the provost and canons, who launched the decisive sortie in October 1643: "They surprised a troop of these miserable Croquants in the vineyards of Puech de Penaveyre, as they were eating a dish of eggs". They put the rebels to flight and thus ended the revolt. All the leaders who were hanged for Croquandage in that month of October 1643 were men of humble birth—farmhands, weavers, a shoemaker, a saddler, a carder. Not a single gentleman or bourgeois went to the scaffold.

The tragedy of the starving people of the Rouergue and their brothers, the Croquants, is an exemplary one for the understanding of local and regional problems under Richelieu and Mazarin. The villagers and peasants of the Rouergue, who made up the over-whelming majority of the population of the region, were suffering the same fate as their neighbours in other southern provinces. They, too, were enduring the contradictions of the mid-seventeenth century. Their empoverishment was the result of the contrast between a still dynamic birth rate and a Malthusian economy. They, too, were groaning under an excess of charges of all kinds, for this was the apogee of rural taxation, "the golden age of rent". Among the people of the Aveyron—all good Catholics and therefore respectful of the tithe—pangs of hunger were easily converted into a single-minded resentment of taxation.

At the same time, one can see other, specific features: the indomitable originality of the Rouergue, a former tribe of Gaul and now an administrative division of the *ancien régime*; and the existence and persistence, in this region, of a "poverty culture".

THE ECOLOGY OF THE ROUERGUE DURING THE ENLIGHTENMENT:
DISTEMPERED AIR AND DISEASE

Between 1757 and 1765, a new "viewfinder" is trained on the ecology of the region. Its perspective has that essential unity and alertness which make it comparable in quality to Alexandre Albenque's retrospective view from the heights of the twentieth century over the antiquities of the Aveyron.

The "viewfinder" of 1760 is Jean Mouret. I discovered this document about twenty years ago, in the files of the *Société royale des sciences* of Montpellier, which are preserved in the departmental archives of the Hérault.[13] Marie-José Gordien, in a remarkable master's thesis of 1971–2 for the University of Paris-I, has extracted the essential data from Mouret's important work.[14] The following pages owe a great deal to Marie-José Gordien's excellent and thorough thesis, and I must express my gratitude to such an exemplary pupil.

Jean Mouret was a Protestant. He was the son of a master-hatter of Saint-Jean-du-Bruel, a little place in the south-east corner of the present *département* of the Aveyron. In about 1750, Mouret was pursuing a career in the French West Indies, as an administrator and a planter of coffee, cocoa and ginger. In the mid-1750s, he returned to his native land, and as a good Rouergat, a supporter of the extended family, he settled with his brother-in-law, a merchant, in Saint-Jean-du-Bruel. Here Jean Mouret became all eyes and ears: he observed nature all around him in the Rouergue, as well as his fellow-men's work, life, illnesses, and death. He was influenced by the doctors and naturalists of his time, possibly by Jean-Jacques Rousseau.

His observatory, then, was Saint-Jean-du-Bruel, a largeish village of some 2,300 inhabitants, in one of the less poor districts of the Aveyron. A good half of the *"saint-Jeantaise"* population at this time consisted of artisans, especially textile workers ("dyers, wool-combers, manufacturers of coarse cloth and stockings", says Marie-José Gordien). Agricultural labourers represented about 35 per cent of the population. They were mostly simple farmhands, but to avoid dying of starvation, they usually owned a small plot of land on the hillside, or a cottage garden. The *ménagers* (rich or well-to-do peasants) were only a tiny minority (2 per cent). In the upper echelons of the social scale, one finds about 4–5 per cent who were shopkeepers, and 4 per cent notables; the nobility accounted for barely 2 per cent. The land was unequally divided, though it would of course be incorrect to talk of *latifundia*: one-tenth of the landowners—the richest "decile", made up of absentee landlords (*horsins*), noble, bourgeois or merchants—possessed 45 per cent of the land surface, while 50 per cent of landowners, the smaller ones, owned only 12 per cent of the total area. The territory of the commune consisted partly of the infertile Ségalas. 28 per cent of the land was under cereals or fallow; 20 per cent was grassland and pasture; 9.9 per cent was wooded, 5.6 per cent grew chestnut trees, and the few vines accounted for 1.8 per cent. A whole third of the land was mountainous, uncultivated and unusable.

On this sometimes thankless region, Mouret tried the experiment of constructing a *visual ecology*. For the first time in history, an eye-witness was actually trying to look at the Rouergue of his own time, and to set down what he saw. These "newsreels" from 1760 follow the rhythm of the seasons and the farming year: in the manuscript, the cycle begins in the early spring of 1757:[15]

On March 21, 1757, there are kingcups in the fields of Saint-Jean-du-Bruel. Already the sap is rising in the vines and the chestnut trees, and children make cones from the bark. At the end of the month [of March] the box trees, almond trees and elms are in blossom. Ants are scurrying everywhere in the countryside. In the first week of April, the meadows are very green. There are daisies everywhere and the buds on the pear trees are opening. The country is full of wasps and flies and several kinds of butterfly, the apple-tree buds have blossomed and a few leaves are appearing. By April 9, people are wearing their summer clothes.

Bats appear during the middle third of the month. The flies are already becoming a nuisance. Apple and pear trees are in full flower. The rivers are swollen with melted snow. The toad is noisy, snakes come out of the earth and the cuckoo is heard.

After about April 20, there was an explosion of growth:

The plum, pear, cherry and apple trees are beginning to come into leaf. Swallows swoop close to the ground. The chestnut buds are beginning to flower. People no longer need fires for warmth. The peasants give the vines their first spring dressing. At the very end of the month, the hedges are in leaf and so too are the chestnuts, walnut trees and vines. The nightingale sings.

In the first week of May there is a crescendo:

Mulberry trees put out leaves, there are flowers on the broom, catkins are falling. The river is already dropping, the last snows are melting on the mountains. It is time to put the silkworm eggs to hatch, and to sow hempseed. Grapes appear on the house vines and then in the vineyards. The cherries are as big as sparrows' eggs, and apricots are as big as olives. The pear and apple blossom has almost all fallen and the fruit is swelling. Standing rye is about two feet tall, wheat is still low, but thick and green, and in general the cereals are beginning to flower. In mid-May there are fresh strawberries and mushrooms to eat. Mad dogs are roaming on the Causse de Blandas. [At the end of May 1757,] elder flowers are out and roses are in bloom, although there have been some late frosts which have frozen or blighted the hemp and silenced the nightingales.

June begins:

The rye is turning colour; peas are ready to eat; the second hoeing of the vines takes place. Summer [June 21] sees the seasonal harvest workers leave the Rouergue for the fields of Languedoc. [At home] flies are becoming very troublesome. The fruits on the chestnut trees are growing quickly and already they look like little hedgehogs; some of the corn has been scorched by the hot sun, and slugs [even so!] are damaging the beans and the kitchen gardens; the first cherries are eaten; at the end of the month the rye is cut; the wheat is turning golden and will soon be ready too.

Early July:

Not many flies now, hardly any wasps, but a great many fleas. [The villagers must all have been scratching like mad.] The wheat is cut, oats are turning colour, then it is the turn of the hemp and flax.

In mid-July, after the recent storms:

Male hemp is picked, there are many mushrooms to be found, pumpkins are flowering and the recently harvested fields are ploughed again immediately. The March-sown corn is cut in the valleys and the rye on the Causses.

At the end of July:

Raspberries, blackcurrants and string beans are ready to eat.

In August:

Flax is picked, rye is cut on the hillsides, and in the lowlands one can feast on the new season's plums.

The second fortnight of August, and it is already time for threshing the grain crops, if there is not too much rain:

Turnips are sown, and the first winter wheat is sown on the Causse; black grapes are almost ripe.

September, the end of summer:

One needs a fire sometimes now. Figs are good to eat; the second growth of hay is cut, and the female hemp is picked. The early rye is green on the hillside where threshing takes place once the sowing has been done.

The autumn equinox (September 21)

sees the departure of the swallows and the harvesting of nuts and apples. The first white frosts wither the pumpkins.

In October the frosts are twice as frequent:

They shrivel the acorn, turn the vine leaves yellow and wither the stalk of the grape. Brambles and mulberry trees are stripped, the new season's chestnuts are on the tables, and wheat is sown in the valleys.

In mid-October, comes the grape harvest:

There are greenflies on the turnips; lemon-coloured butterflies with black spots fly about.

November and December:

Moles are tunnelling in the pastures [while all vegetation gradually disappears. The mountains, covered with snow,] which sticks
to the trees like glue [are impassable.] Wolves are abroad in the
valley. At night they even come into the village street . . .

And so on, as Mouret continues with his visual ecology, month
after month, year after year, from 1757 to 1765.

Reading Mouret, who can write page upon page of this detailed
lyricism, charting the bounty of Nature and the rewards of Agriculture, one's impression of the Rouergue is of a luxuriant province,
with an extremely varied food supply, changing with the season and
based on polyculture, with market gardens and a great variety of
fruit trees. But certain passages should put us on our guard: the
delicious *poires de doyenné* (a variety of comice pears), whose
appearance makes Mouret's mouth water, were reserved for rich
men's tables. Wheat yields were low: four of five grains harvested
for every one sown. And such wheat as there was might be scorched, rotten, full of worms, weevils and other insects, or eaten on
the stalk by slugs. But to look at the quality of life in Saint-Jean from
another angle—that of disease—sanitary conditions in the village
were poor. Saint-Jean was by no means exceptional in Louis XV's
kingdom; but through Mouret's careful chronicle, more is known
about it. The germ-ridden mire in which Saint-Jean's inhabitants
paddled did not prevent the population from increasing, if a little
later than elsewhere, thanks to a high birth rate (35.6 children born
a year per thousand inhabitants) and a slightly lower death rate
(31.6 per thousand between the same dates, 1757–65). Things were,
after all, slightly better in Louis XV's reign than in that of Louis
XIV: the demographic surplus did not automatically find its way to
the graveyard. But mortality was nevertheless severe in this corner
of the provinces (and Rouergue was by no means the worst-off), as
it was in so many others. One can gauge something of its extent
from the seasonal attacks of death-dealing epidemics recorded in
the journal: in March 1757, an epidemic killed 30 people in Saint-
Jean. "The nature of this disease" Mouret says, "was not very well
known". It was said that "there were complications—pleurisy,
chest infections, putrid fever [i.e., intestinal infection], and malig-
nant fever. The patient's tongue went black, as did his lips". Many
of the victims, whether delirious or not "had worms issuing from the

mouth, nose and rectum. Purgatives were beneficial, but the effects of bleeding were inconclusive. Some of the sick had a flux of the belly [diarrhoea] this was salutary in the young but did not help the old, few of whom recovered and many of whom died." Some of these recent corpses "turned purple in the space of two or three hours, others swelled up extraordinarily, and all of them soon became foul-smelling". Mortality was highest on about April 25. According to Marie-José Gordien, whose work I am drawing on once more, some of the symptoms mentioned might indicate that during the second part of this epidemic cycle in the spring of 1757, there was an outbreak of typhoid fever, characterized by a high temperature, discoloration of tongue and lips, and diarrhoea.

During the winter of 1757–8, there were a number of eye-infections; in some cases the sufferers could not distinguish dark from light; "and then catarrhal fevers affecting first one ear then the other" (probably a few harmless cases of mumps[16]). Then came attacks of hydrophobia, fits, and intestinal fevers combined with pleurisy, which carried off a number of people in the Saint-Jean area. These intestinal outbreaks indicate the generally unhealthy environment, and in particular the prevalence of food poisoning, since food kept badly. These villagers would have been most grateful for the hormone-fed battery chickens we grumble about today. The digestive organs of the Rouergats of 1758 were greatly tried by the "putrid" fevers (i.e., with foul-smelling intestinal wind). Sixty people died of such diseases in Saint-Jean between January and June 1758. Meanwhile, children were still, as summer approached, suffering from the eye complaints that had begun in the winter. During the summer of 1758 the putrid fevers, obviously a feature of that year, struck yet again. But this time there were fewer victims and the symptoms were different, too: there was no pleurisy, but instead complications took the form of colic, kidney pain and headaches. These dangerous infections did not disappear (and then for how long?) until the last fortnight of December.

The months of July, August, and September 1759 were notable for a high number of deaths—over 40 in Saint-Jean. A human variety of foot-and-mouth disease, characterised by mouth ulcers, attacked the village children. They caught it from cattle or pigs, or through carriers such as "men, dogs, dung, dust and above all milk". By the end of July *as many as five children a day were dying*". Putrid fevers again complicated this epidemic, but this time, most alarmingly, they were accompanied by real dysentery, especially among children, who were again singled out as the little victims of 1759. The characteristic symptoms were "intestinal pain, diarrhoea, with sometimes fatal complications such as intestinal occlusions and perforations or haemorrhages".[17] This points to amoebic dysentery. It should, perhaps, be recalled that in the higher primates, as among French villagers of the eighteenth century, dysentery is an essential element in population control—a barbaric epidemic method of reducing the increase in numbers to more reasonable proportions.

Combined again with pleurisy, "putrid fevers" were still active in the region after September 1759, but they were no longer fatal, except for a period in January 1760 when once more some elderly people died.

Smallpox appeared in the hamlets around Saint-Jean in April 1760, where several children died. The other "catarrhal" or "putrid" fevers went underground for a while—they would be all the stronger for biding their time.

On August 12, 1760, smallpox made its triumphal entry into the village of Saint-Jean itself (note the important distinction between *village* and *hamlet* in the Rouergue, where distances were often great, and settlements scattered). This outbreak brought in its train a whole range of putrid dysenteries, colds, eye infections and in the autumn, pleurisy. In September, October and November, raging smallpox, (the centre of which was Saint-Rome-du-Tarn, a "settlement about 50 kilometres west of our parish") killed "about forty children under ten, including about twelve babies; this smallpox outbreak corresponds to a peak in the death rate and in fact it accounted for fifty per cent of deaths in that year".[18]

This, then, was how the demographic pattern of villages in the *ancien régime*, in the Rouergue in particular, operated in real life. Under the impact of waves of epidemics ("typhoid in 1757, broncho-pulmonary diseases in 1758 and 1762, foot-and-mouth disease and amoebic dysentery in 1759, smallpox in 1760"[18]) the population of Saint-Jean fell very slightly "between January 1, 1759 and January 1, 1763", from 2,255 inhabitants to 2,244.

This slight population loss continued into 1762, with about 100 deaths, significantly above average. They were caused principally by intestinal fevers in the spring, when the outbreak was so serious that the people of Saint-Jean stopped tolling the churchbells for funerals, since they were ringing all day and alarming the sick. In August 1762, these putrid fevers (dysentery?) moved on to the chest, according to Mouret, and the summer ended with an epidemic of colds, which proved fatal to many. As a result, the commune of Saint-Jean again saw a net decline in its population, with an excess of deaths over births.

Then things improved. In 1765, the Saint-Jean population was approaching 2,500, so it must have risen, making good and even better the losses of the bad period 1757–62. But life was not all roses between 1762 and 1765. Food was dear (rye went up 75 per cent) in the spring of 1764, as a result of the poor harvest of 1763, but no one died. For this was the eighteenth century, thank goodness. The general context was one of demographic increase, interrupted only by epidemics—a far greater threat then than they would be now— which from time to time imposed a "stop-go" or zigzag pattern of population growth. Periods of stagnation or even slight decline in the population curve were accounted for, as we have just seen, by bronchial or pulmonary infections, intestinal fevers, typhoid, small-pox—and also by mumps, measles and erysipelas.

To Mouret's mind, since he was a devotee of a certain Enlighten-ment philosophy of medicine, namely the "air" school, one single principle governed both orders of phenomena described in his notebooks: the two orders being Agriculture and Nature on one hand, and sickness and health on the other. The governing princi-ple, which was the true dictator of the Rouergue, was *air*.[19] Hot or cold, thick or thin, dry or wet, calm or windy, heavy or light, it was air that brought things forward, or held them back; it fixed the dates when roses bloomed, mushrooms were gathered, and hemp was picked. The air also inflamed the delicate pulmonary or bronchial membranes of the Rouergats, bringing catarrh and chest diseases; and, of course, it was responsible for the foul wind that inflated the bowels of the poor villagers. Air was the dealer of life and death in the Aveyron—or so thought those who believed eighteenth-century medical theories, now long forgotten.

A POVERTY CULTURE

I am more interested in the earth than in the air. With the acid soils of the Ségalas, and the only slighty more fertile—but too dry—Causses, the Rouergue in the modern period was not a likely

candidate for agricultural prosperity. All the signs in the eighteenth century were already suggesting that the region was doomed to remain poor. An extraordinary document of 1771 provides positive proof of the enduring misery of the Rouergue. Ten years after Mouret was writing in Saint-Jean-du-Bruel, the bishop Champion de Cicé set down a precise and frightening account of destitution in the Aveyron. With the aid of surveys carried out for him by the parish priests, the new bishop had an overall view of the whole Rouergue. Hardly had Champion de Cicé taken office before he was ordering the priests in the diocese of Rodez, his direct subordinates, to fill out in detail, with facts and figures, all the items in the questionnaire he sent them. In every parish, the questionnaire referred to the *seigneurie* or feudal estate, the tithes, the population, the clergy, the almshouse, the school if there was one, the "poor", that is beggars, able-bodied or not, etc., agricultural production, skilled trades, the local church—and so on. The replies the bishop received, in so far as they bear upon paupers and poverty in the Aveyron in the last third of the eighteenth century, are both fascinating and tragic. The archivist Louis Lempereur published the text of Champion's survey, with the replies of the parish priests, in 1906. The worthy editor was so horrified by the references to poverty in the documents he was publishing, that in his preface, he chose simply to evade the issue altogether: "the sections of the questionnaire relating to the poor", Lempereur wrote, "are somewhat complicated and lack clarity. The answers to these questions consequently reflect this and are not always as interesting as they might be"[20]—a rather bland comment, to put it mildly.

In fact, the extremely detailed and careful analysis of the Champion survey undertaken by Alain Guéry[21] is most eloquent on the "social question". The sample consisted of 162 parishes, scattered throughout the region, "totalling 96,593 inhabitants", or almost a third of the population of the Rouergue at the time. So, it is a very representative sample. Of the 96,593 inhabitants, 25,827 (families included) were poor, that is, dependent on the assistance of others for survival. Of these, 19,000 were "able-bodied poor", whom we would today describe as unemployed: though poor, they were fit enough to work. In addition, there were at least 8,119 beggars, generally reckoned over and above the 25,827 "poor", usually with no fixed dwelling.[22] Twenty-seven per cent of the population was, therefore, defined as poor, including 20 per cent who were totally unemployed. And as many as 8 per cent were literally beggars (in most cases they were counted in addition to the "poor"). So taking "paupers" and beggars together, 33 per cent of the population might be regarded as living in poverty. Imagine the France of today with close on a third of the total population (15 million) in families whose head was either unemployed, or a beggar: ten million people, counting dependants, would be affected by unemployment, four million reduced to begging. That may give some idea of the wretched state of the Rouergue under the *ancien régime*; and make it easier to understand the countless emigrants driven from their homes by want, the acute famines from the time of Louis XIII onward (admittedly less of a problem by the time of the Enlightenment); and also some of the rebellions of the seventeenth century; not to mention epidemics. The primary zones of Lévezou and the Ségalas of the north, centre, west and south were, of course, the areas most affected by the triple phenomenon of poverty, unemployment and beggary. In these five regions, Lévezou and the four Ségalas, 35.2 per cent of the inhabitants were poor (over a third of the population), including 25.4 per cent who were able-bodied but unemployed; and often another 12.2 per cent on top of that were beggars.

The record, so to speak, was held by the village of Sainte-Radegonde, in the present-day canton of Rodez (possibly the poorest village in France in the eighteenth century, though one has to exclude Brittany). Out of a total of 400 inhabitants, the parish priest wrote, "at least three quarters of the parishioners are paupers, whether able-bodied or handicapped. All require the helping hand of charity. There are about twenty families who have virtually no means of support. Because of our proximity to the chief town (Rodez), besides having a third of our own parishioners going begging, we receive "outsiders" (beggars) every day".[23] This unfortunate village brings to mind the wretched region of Las Hurdes in Spain, about which Luis Bunuel made the unforgettable film *Land without Bread*.[24]

This is not to say that the whole of the Rouergue was necessarily poor, even in 1771. From this time on, in fact, it seems probable that, apart from certain particularly acute local difficulties, the majority of people in the Aveyron could be described as "non-poor". To take the case of the Villeneuve region and Villefranche-de-Rouergue, one finds that it was relatively well-off in Champion de Cicé's time; it possessed a large slice of the Causses, which helped to make ends meet. The poor amounted to "only" 30 per cent in 1771; (17 per cent unemployed). Another 13 per cent were beggars. These rates would be enormous today but they were moderate compared to the rest of the Rouergue at the time.

But setting such nuances aside, and taking it all in all, one is entitled to say that under Louis XIII, Louis XIV, Louis XV and Louis XVI, the Rouergue came firmly under the heading of what twentieth-century sociologists would call a poverty culture.[25]

THE END OF THE TUNNEL: THE NINETEENTH CENTURY

So, it is interesting to ask oneself, for comparative and perhaps pedagogical purposes, how the Aveyron pulled through, during the period roughly corresponding to the nineteenth century (1780–1914). For pull through it undoubtedly did, while still retaining its own identity, and remaining fully integrated into Occitanian culture in the deepest sense. Our photographs of the Rouergue of the Belle Epoque, with their sleek bourgeois, and peasants who certainly do not look destitute, show that there was at least a partial victory over poverty.

The year 1800: and the Revolution (or at least its most dramatic phase) was over. The Rouergue would now join other French provinces launching into the adventure of modest but undeniable economic growth. It already had a number of resources:[26] its agriculture, on the Causses, in the "Rivières" (alluvial water-meadows), and in the vineyards was (comparatively!) prosperous. It was in a position to welcome certain inevitable kinds of progress. But there were still, alas, a number of dead-weights, drags on growth: for instance, the backwardness of the Aubrac mountains in the north of the *département*; and above all the grinding poverty, already mentioned here so many times, of the Ségalas. Their inhabitants, the *Ségalis* were derisively referred to as *ventres noirs* (black bellies) or *pétaris* (windy-guts). But nothing, not even and indeed especially not the Ségalas, could withstand the forces of change in the nineteenth century. The flood-tide floated all the boats, whatever their shape and dynamic capacity—or lack of it.

It should be said that the ground for this nineteenth-century growth was undoubtedly prepared by the gradual improvement in living conditions (despite the still frightening beggary) of the eighteenth century. Proof of this improvement is that under Louis XV and Louis XVI, famines were no longer killing people in the Rouergue, as they had under Louis XIII and Louis XIV. Epidemics were now the only major cause of death, breeding in the pockets of poverty still left.

To return to the nineteenth century in the Rouergue: agricultural growth took place against a background of traditional techniques and production: based on rye and chestnuts. What innovation and expansion there was, entered the Rouergue by a number of sometimes roundabout ways.

Firstly, there was a decisive improvement in the cycle of vegetable production. By the second half of the nineteenth century, cartloads of lime, manufactured with the aid of coal (another novelty of the age) and taken aboard at Carmaux and elsewhere, were trundling towards the Ségalas: the lime was to correct the acidity of the primary soil, immediately making it much better suited to the production of cereals, potatoes and hay. Other fertilizers which helped to increase agricultural productivity were not far behind. In 1902, the Carmaux-Rodez railway line opened. Indeed, the Third Republic was quite kind to Occitania, treating it by no means as badly as is sometimes suggested. The volume of lime, now carried in goods trains, doubled—and the battle was really won. The poverty of the empty bellies of the Ségalas had been overcome for good. Dysentery disappeared.

Other innovations in the same line of country were introduced from about 1856–1900: harrows, ploughs with mould-boards, swivel-ploughs (still pulled by oxen, though). They competed successfully with the old swing-plough (*araire*) favoured by the Rouergue farmers, but never drove it out entirely.

At the other end of the grain cycle (harvesting), mechanical harvesters and above all steam-driven threshing-machines enormously increased the productivity of labour when the crops were brought in. These technological breakthroughs—harvester and thresher—were crucial. They first appeared in about 1900, but did not become widespread until between the wars or even later.

Technological change from 1850–1950 coincided with a particular revolution in the vegetable world: the arrival of the potato. This plant from the Americas was brought to the highlands from about 1840–50 to enrich the harvest: it complemented the diet of the people of the Rouergue with filling carbohydrates. The "potatoes of the Aveyron" saved many inhabitants of southern France from going hungry during the Second World War.

But the Aveyron is principally, as it always has been, a land of livestock. In this, a second major area for improvement, one advance was the gradual elimination of wolves; they disappeared for good during the latter half of the nineteenth century. This may have been an ecological disaster, but it was a triumph for the sheep-farmers. The dangers, and in particular the cost, of guarding and maintaining the flocks decreased proportionately. Selective breeding of the Aubrac cattle (towards 1890), the regional development of dairies for Roquefort cheese (from the nineteenth century), and the opening up of national markets to both this and the Laguiole cheeses after 1900, completed the string of victories for the stock-farmers of the Rouergue.

Further "gateways" to progress in rural Aveyron were the development of a road network which was built, repaired and maintained. Pack-mules now gave way to the far more efficient horse-drawn carts. And there was a decisive change in the way of life for the great mass of small farmers (a population of hundreds of thousands, counting men, women and children) with the coming of public education. Though the provision was not as great as elsewhere, at least people now learnt to read, write and count: *Comptez, comptez vos boeufs, comptez, comptez-les bien*, as the rhyme goes. ("Count the cattle, count them well".) National education was gradually overcoming illiteracy, which had affected half the population before 1850, but only a quarter by the end of the century—a triumph, indeed, for the Enlightenment. Though it has to be said that much greater progress was being made at the same time in other regions such as the Marne and Calvados.

Any appreciable amount of growth should be accompanied by a rise in consumption. As we have seen, the villagers of the Rouergue in the 1840s augmented their diet with potatoes. That in itself is not perhaps very impressive, since potatoes are a poor man's food in any case. But other, more or less positive signs were appearing: mutton would be replaced on Sundays and special occasions by a stuffed chicken and cakes. Coffee ("Caiffa") made its appearance—at first for medicinal purposes, then for daily use. Forks appeared on tables, and the iron cooking pot replaced the earthenware crock. Among men, alcoholism was seen for the first time, though it was fortunately moderate compared with the provinces of the west and north. Apart from food, consumption of textiles rose too: true, the fabrics used to make villagers' clothes were tending more and more towards that funereal black (instead of the old reds and blues) as the nineteenth century went on. But on the other hand, marvel of progress, trousers definitely replaced the traditional breeches worn by the men of the Rouergue countryside—picturesque though they were, with their monumental codpieces ("like drawbridges to be raised and lowered").

The elimination (at least in part) of pauperism, which had been the scourge of the Rouergue in the seventeenth and eighteenth centuries, seemed to be well on the way after 1800–50. It was facilitated in villages and farms by the very considerable rise in real wages of farm labourers. In 1900, 20,000 people in the *département* of the Averyron were, according to the administration, eligible to receive "free medical care". This number would certainly have been very much higher—four times as high perhaps—in 1771, if free medical care had existed. The improvement, in the space of a century, in the lot of the poor, and the mobility of many descendants of poor families into the ranks of the "less poor", the comfortably-off, or even the well-to-do, are social phenomena of prime importance.

Developments in the Aveyron in the nineteenth century were not on the whole the result of capitalist stimulus (although this was directed at the *département*, but only from *outside*—one has always to look outside the Rouergue for some things). Rather, they were channelled by a *family*-based system of *agricultural* and *domestic* activity. This is a useful, even necessary truth for third world countries seeking to escape from underdevelopment, and it is a truth not always recognized by technocrats who always assume that what was good for the Ruhr or Lancashire will be good for the Rouergue or Sri Lanka. The family system in the Aveyron was based on the *ostal* or household. In Occitan, *ostal* signifies a whole set of meanings: house, farm, property, kitchen, family, married couple with children and perhaps grandparents, clan—and the continuity that comes when two or three generations, or more, have been living on the same land. So, it is a concept uniting past and present, tradition and progress, continuity and change. The *ostal* would not be the centre of a large estate, but of a holding that might be middling-sized, or even "piddling"-sized (*une "pissade" de terre"*). It would form part of the communal system of the Aveyron hamlet of about 30 to 50 inhabitants grouped in several *ostals* or *ostaux*. I do not wish to idealize the *ostal* system, which was often harsh on farmhands and servant girls, but merely to note its comparative efficiency as a farming unit, and its progressive capacity after 1880 or so, for population control, both by limiting births and by emigration. Zero population growth (as favoured by present-day Malthusians, on a world scale at least), had already been quietly achieved by the Rouergats by the end of the nineteenth century. At the same time, contrary once again to all fashionable theories, a deproletarianization of the region was taking place. In 1800, the majority of the Rouergue population consisted of rural proletarians, with a minority of self-employed farmers (about 50,000 to 40,000, according to Béteille). By the end of the nineteenth century, these proportions had been reversed in country areas. Rural society, as organized by the *ostal* system, was becoming not ideal (far from it) but distinctly better balanced and less wretched—and that, after all, is what matters.

No marks for Marx then, but no marks for Weber either, with his Anglo-Saxon-Germanic obsession with the regenerating and fertilizing effects of Protestantism. The Rouergue was blithely ignorant of such things. Until recently it remained part and parcel of an essentially Catholic culture: the Pope's little acre in the Occitanian south, a Catholic enclave like Poland or Ireland, but more fortunate than either of these. The Rouergue benefited from an appreciable rise in living standards, accounted for by its whole-hearted participation in the career of a comparatively privileged and highly developed country like France. The Catholic culture of the Rouergue produced a remarkable number of local vocations to the priesthood or to convents, thus making it easier for the *ostal* to pass to a single heir, from one generation to another. Such an heir, who had to be a dedicated non-priest and non-celibate, could thus with a clear conscience take on the heavy responsibilities of marrying and founding a family. The Blessed Virgin of Lourdes herself, with all her rosaries, grottoes and statuettes, graciously lent a hand, during the Third Republic, in maintaining the fertility of the farms and vineyards of the Rouergue—Our Lady of the Vines, one might say, who did her best to aid the growth of the Aveyron. A flask of Lourdes water was the surest guarantee of prosperity for the vine-grower, if he wanted to see his cellars crammed with casks and bottles of wine.

And those other vital factors in the development of the Aveyron, past and present, should also be mentioned: emigration to Paris; that rendezvous of the coalmen and café proprietors of the Rouergue; the growth of the industrial and coalmining sector at Decazeville; and the modest but undeniable urban expansion of Rodez, Millau and, indeed, Villefranche.

★

We have arrived at last at Villefranche-de-Rouergue, the town whose self-portrait in photographs, from the Belle Epoque to the 1930s, Bernard Dufour has put together for us. I must insist once more that this brief introduction (primarily concerned to show something of the Rouergue as a whole, since it is so unfamiliar to most French readers) cannot offer anything like a history of Villefranche—which is still to be written. Villefranche is built in the form of a quadrangular *"bastide"*: the "New Town" (Villeneuve) or boom-town of the eleventh, twelfth and thirteenth centuries, dominated by the massive belfry of Notre Dame; and in 1800 someone did look at it with the anthropologist's eye. This was the young Alexis Monteil, writing during the reign of Bonaparte:

> Villefranche is incontestably less ancient than Rodez, but of the two sisters, the younger is prettier and more pleasant. The town was founded in the Middle Ages by the Counts of Toulouse. Its position and privileges soon drew a large number of inhabitants. In 1779, when the provincial administration of Haute-Guyenne, which embraced the Rouergue and Quercy, was established here, Villefranche became the capital of the two provinces. Its wealth and population were increasing rapidly, when the Revolution came, and with it the "Boundaries Commission" which redrew the old administrative map of France and divided the country into 93 territorial sections or *départements*. . . . The capital of the Rouergue and Quercy was reduced to being a mere *commune* [municipality] in the département of the Aveyron: it sought in vain to be chosen as departmental capital: but Rodez won the prize. The latter town, situated in the centre, and unmoved by the activities of its rival replied to all attacks by the pen simply by pointing to the compass. Since then, Villefranche has looked for compensation for its losses in industry.

Alexis Monteil goes on to point out the internal contrast within the population of "eight thousand souls" which, according to him, composed the most concentrated section of the Villefranche community. Half the population, he writes, is made up of vine-growers and peasants; the other half of artisans and shopkeepers—and, it appears, never the twain shall meet. They keep themselves apart, dress differently; and though all speak the Occitan dialect, their knowledge of French is not the same. The former, the peasants and vine-growers, are more austere and hard-working; they make their wives toil like donkeys on the hilly slopes where the vines grow in terraces. The latter, the artisans, are more given to amusement, more familiar with the French language, more open to the ideas of the Revolution; and their wives rarely leave the household or shop.

A hundred years later, in the 1900s, P. Joanne, author of a gazetteer of France, engaged in an extraordinary flight of civil-servant's prose to describe Villefranche, of which the following is an extract:

> Villefranche-de-Rouergue, Aveyron, municipality of 9,730 inhabitants, 4,595 hectares . . . situated 624 kilometres from Paris. Telegraph, post office, toll house. Administrative centre [*Chef-lieu*] of the district [*arrondissement*] and canton. Sub-prefecture. Three urban, three rural parishes. Carmelite convent. Magistrate's court. Primary school inspectorate. One boys' high school. Two Catholic secondary schools. One public elementary school for girls. Six primary schools. Two private schools. Library comprising 15,000 books. Police superintendent. Captain of *gendarmes*, two sergeants, one mounted. One tax officer, one tax inspector, one tax collector, one official for Registration [property, etc.] and loans. One collector of indirect tax. Two clerks of the Highways Department. Two civil engineers for local roads. A Chamber of Agriculture; an annual agricultural show; a stud (four stallions); a wolf-control officer; several solicitors, notaries, bailiffs; a departmental prison; a general hospital (50 beds); an old people's home [*hospice*, formerly almshouse] with 117 beds; the orphanages of the Holy Family (55 children), the Good Shepherd (16 children), and of the Sisters of Nevers (30 children); a charity bureau. . . .
>
> Mines: copper, lead, tin, iron, phosphates, some stone-quarrying . . .
>
> A small spa, for bathing and medicinal waters, with three cold springs containing salts of sulphur and calcium, and two other springs: 300 litres per minute.

Local products: cereals, vines, fruits, mushrooms, young nuts [*cerneaux*], cheese, livestock, hams.

Nursery gardens and horticulture.

Local manufactures: bell-founding, copper hammers, cooking pots, rat-traps, plaster, wax, clogs, soap, hemp-spinning, bonnet-making, local fabrics, oils,—especially nut oil, liqueurs, mineral waters, chemical products, phosphates and superphosphates, brewing, flour mills, leather, tanneries, saddlery, dyeing, cane-weaving . . .

Fairs: on the 22nd of the month. Market-fairs: on the first Thursday in January, February, March, October, November, December. Ordinary markets on Monday, Thursday and Saturday.

Churches: Notre Dame (XIII-XVIth century) with tower (58 metres high); Old Charterhouse (XVth century), now used as almshouse . . .

Reading this list with its extraordinary jumble of girls' schools and stud farms, hemp-spinners and civil engineers, not to mention the wolf control officer, one does have an impression of shoes and ships and sealing-wax—but it sums up very well in its own way the extremely varied *functions*—agricultural, commercial, artisanal, industrial and administrative and bureaucratic—of Villefranche: a complex urban unit, dominated by a fairly prosperous bourgeoisie. Politically, the left, an active force since the nineteenth century, is in lively opposition to the traditional clerical right, for which the Aveyron is very much home ground.

The collection of photographs brought together by Bernard Dufour concerns particularly the *social occasions* in Villefranche during the heyday of the Third Republic: whether religious (processions of penitents, the funeral of the arch-priest); military and patriotic (the march-past of the regiment); or folklore (carnival); occasions for eating and drinking (the café or the banquet); the pseudo-rustic (picnics); traditional-medical (the crowd surrounding the tooth-puller).

School (church or state), local trade, the nut-sellers' stalls, cattle and poultry markets, the shapes—in stone or water—of houses or fountains, the modern age whether really experienced (railways, fertilizers, bicycles) or still a fantasy (aeroplanes) provide the field of images for pictures. The cameras of the photographers of Villefranche, rich and poor, have been trained on these and similar scenes. This kind of selection leaves out many aspects of urban reality, showing only certain elements deemed to be representative by the "artists" of the dark room. Their selection is doubly significant—both for them and for us, for producer and consumer.

The *countryside*—the vine-growers with their casks, the blacksmith shoeing the oxen, the autumn threshers, with their flails and the first steam-threshing machines (which were a great occasion for rural get-togethers)—only appears in these photographs as a background, occasionally noticed, but never the major phenomenon, in inverse ratio to the actual overwhelming preponderance of peasants over town-dwellers in the Rouergue at this time. And the *family* is firmly at the centre of the consciousness of these bygone photographers: from these faded sepia prints, which one can imagine smelling of rose-water, one has a very strong sense of the sturdily entrenched *ostal* or family-household. In the twentieth century, as in the fourteenth, in the Rouergue as in the Béarn, it remains the most solid and central structure of Occitan culture.

To sum up? I will not deny that I am a supporter of the Rouergue: I like the Aveyron. I like the way that this little province has been able to shake off its poverty and underdevelopment in the space of a century and a half, without creating pollution, without a great to-do or fuss, without overpopulation and mushrooming new towns; without too many smoking factory chimneys. And it has done so while respecting its own structures: the basic unit of the *ostal*; and the pagan-cum-Papist folklore which is the corner-stone of its intense religious sentiments. There is a risk that today's industrial and post-industrial civilization may destroy this culture of the Rouergue, which was able in the past to use the capitalist environment as a foil to define more clearly its own identity, both innovative and traditional. Such destruction would be heart-breaking. I have been looking at the past in this essay, the better to prepare for the future. Why not turn the picture upside-down? (Though not, I confess with very much hope). My wish for our planet, where the majority of people are poor peasants, is the opposite of most futuristic Utopias: namely a rural and probably impossible one. I should like, in the twenty-first century, to see the whole world looking more like the Aveyron in about 1925. It would not be at all bad as a brave new world.

8

Rétif de la Bretonne as a Social Anthropologist: Rural Burgundy in the Eighteenth Century[1]

Any study of rural society in the last hundred years of the *ancien régime* is likely to remain abstract, unless it includes the country-man's own unique perception of himself, of others, and of his world. In the diary of Gilles de Gouberville, I discovered a por-trayal, fresh, direct and full of life, of sixteenth-century Normandy, which I have described elsewhere. For an equilavent view of the last century of the *ancien régime*, I intend to turn to Nicolas Rétif "de la Bretonne" (as he called himself). Perhaps I should explain my choice. Rétif is not what Paul Bourget was determined to make him: an anti-Michelet, a reactionary apologist for prefabricated happi-ness, with an idyllic and rose-tinted vision of village life. Nor is he, except superficially and incidentally, as sentimental as the reputa-tion of *La Vie de mon père*[2] might suggest. Tears were indeed plentifully shed in the last third of the eighteenth century, whether by "Monsieur Nicolas" or in the paintings of Greuze; but we must try to look beyond the tales of woe. Rétif gives us an eyewitness account of the way of life of the well-off peasantry, for whom the idea of happiness was a new but real one. He was well aware, however, as his writings prove, that such happiness was making only tentative advances in an environment of poverty—still the familiar state of most country people.

Let me begin by situating the Rétif (or Restif, or Rêti) family, and in particular its central figure, Edme Rétif, the patriarch, both in his native village, Nitry, in lower Burgundy, and in his adopted parish, Sacy, near Auxerre. In Sacy, Edme and his son Nicolas, representatives of the better-off peasants, moved in a society of small cereal-farmers and vine-growers. Among these people, the typical figure (or head of family) appears to have been the *suitier*: a peasant who owned some sort of draft-team—or at least a fraction of one, since he might possess his own horse or donkey, or even a pair or a "half-pair" of oxen. In almost all cases, the *suitier* had to join forces (*suiter*) with one or more families in similar circumstances, to pool their draft animals and thus build up a complete ploughing team (*charrue*). Hence the forms of association, and indeed the extended family, which remained a significant phenomenon in a huge area stretching from the Auvergne to the Nivernais, and from the Morvan to lower Burgundy. As a boy, Nicolas Rétif tells us, he once knocked, at the end of a long day and a tiring walk, at the door of some *suitiers* of this kind—as it happened "three families who had joined together to make up a ploughing-team of three horses". The families had met under the roof of one of them to celebrate the end of the communal seedtime, with a meal of *petit salé* (bacon) and a great jug of wine, which was standing to warm in front of the fire.

Rétif makes no bones about the comparatively difficult circumstances experienced by such *suitiers*, and generally by the smallholders—holdings could be *very* small—who made up the bulk of the village population. He notes their poverty, or constant fear of poverty. With three *hectares* of land, under triennial rotation, one can just about scrape a living, he says in essence; but it is more a matter of surviving than of living. The peasant has to break his back labouring, to lease land from someone else *à moisson* (that is, paying rent or sharecropping, out of the annual harvest). Marriage is avoided like the plague. If a man allows himself to take the fatal step and be dragged to the altar, he does his best to see that it is as late as possible; there are few early marriages. As a result, by the time the children are born and start to grow up, the father's strength is already beginning to wane. It is only at the end of his life that he has sons old enough to work, and pay off some part of the parental debts. Well before this time, it is true, infantile and child mortality will have taken their toll, as a result, Rétif says, of the poverty and hardships of the father and mother. The wife, to help eke out a living, takes in babies to wet-nurse, and during such periods, in order not to affect the health of the nursing baby, in theory at any rate, she and her husband abstain from sexual relations.[3] It was not only a hard life but, *morguienne!* as Rétif says, one from which even the comforts of marriage were removed.

Of course, except in cases of extreme destitution, people managed to get through the year and to make ends meet somehow. After all, this was the eighteenth century. In certain families in

Sacy, the breadwinner had two hats: one villager was both stonemason and vine-grower; another smallholder was also a weaver; a third
mended shoes when not working his land. Blaise Guerreau, a man
of few words, combined farm labouring with tiling.[4] His son,
Jacques, was Edme Restif's herdsman—that is, he was in the lowest
category of male workers, ranking below the ploughmen and vine-
tenders in prestige, and higher only than the two servant girls, the
farmer's bitch, Friquette and his horse, Bressan. As a rule, it was
only by working as a day-labourer for the richer peasant, or by
sending a son out as a farmhand, that the *suitier* made ends meet at
all. Those who managed a little better, or even achieved a degree of
comfort, like Covin the tall and boastful militiaman and his young
wife, Marguerite Miné, owed their good fortune to their versatility:
their two *hectares* of land provided some of the grain for their bread;
their half-hectare of vines gave Covin a little spending-money and
wine to drink (Marguerite only had a drop of wine in water); and the
income from the tiny vineyard also helped to pay taxes. Weaving,
done at home by both man and wife, paid for the occasional luxury.
Marguerite, who had been married for love, since she was poorer
than Covin, also earned something by spinning, by selling "the eggs
laid by her ten hens, the wool of her seven sheep and the milk,
butter and cheese provided by her cow."[5] Then there were vegetables in the kitchen garden; and this couple had the advantage (not
everyone did) of owning a house, albeit a small one.

Such families, those of the poorer smallholders and vine-growers
who made up the majority of the inhabitants of Sacy, did not,
however, have much in the way of furniture, in the accepted sense
of the word. Inventories list about 200 *livres tournois* worth of
moveable goods: a bed, an old chest, a kneading-trough, a few
casks, some pewter vessels and iron cooking-pots. The economic
growth of the eighteenth century had provided these country people with iron and pewter, but not with comfort. In 1789, they
doubtless welcomed, or indeed drew up, the demands made by the
tiers état of Sacy, of which an early version can be found in *L'Ecole
des pères*, in the mouth of the rich farmer Touslejours (who is
himself another Edme Rétif, with less resourcefulness and sophistication). "Squeezed dry by the tax-collector", the *Saxiates* (inhabitants of Sacy) demand "reduction in the *taille* and the excise duties
on wine"; they grumble about "seigniorial dues"—probably the
tithe of one-twelfth levied on the grain harvest by the bishop and

chapter of Auxerre. "Without religion", says Touslejours, "life in Sacy would be hell on earth". What a good thing, then, that in this region, the Christian faith was still the tranquillizer of the parishioners!

There is nothing very extraordinary in these observations on the poverty of certain milieus in the eighteenth century—less cruel than in the seventeenth century, but more keenly felt because of the peasants' rising expectations. One finds very much the same kind of thing in the early chapters of the memoirs of Captain Coignet. Information of this kind is, nevertheless, essential for our purpose. Within the archipelago of poverty, very faithfully charted by Monsieur Nicholas, it enables us to pinpoint the little island of well-being which the Rétif family had succeeded in building for itself. According to J.-P. Moreau, who has studied the geography of this part of Burgundy, the family at the peak of its prosperity owned outright about fifty hectares of land within the large farm of La Bretonne. It was not El Dorado. But it was at least ten times the size of the fair-sized plot of a peasant "*à flot*" (one with his head above water), that is with a minimum of independence; and twenty-five or thirty times more than the "pocket-handkerchief" owned by a mere *suitier*, not to mention the poor day-labourer. Edme Rétif, then, when he bought La Bretonne, had realized the ideal to which so many tenant-farmers, though rich in horses and money, did not even aspire: to become a landowner oneself, with a place in the sun. An accumulator of land, exempted from taxes because of his fourteen children, Edme Rétif can be seen as the equivalent, on a more positive and sympathetic level, of the wealthy farmer in the Bresse, near Chalon, who in 1720, after thirty years of tenant-farming, had "acquired all the best lands from the poor inhabitants who dared not say anything"; he too had obtained tax exemption on account of his twelve children.[6] It is obvious, in other words, that the prosperous Rétif family were not exactly run-of-the-mill peasants of the region. Whereas everyone else in the village was known by his baptismal name only, Edme was the exception: he was called *Monsieur*, for he had, as they said, *du répondant*: he was a man of substance, the possessor of various status symbols. His house had a tiled roof and a carriage entrance (*porte cochère*). His second wife, originally a servant-girl whom her late first husband had got with child before marrying her, "now wears a dressing-gown"—that is, she was a woman of consequence in village society. Edme, who was an official of the local noble landowner, was *Monsieur le Lieute-nant*, and Barbe, his wife, *Madame la Lieutenante*. His sons—priests or clerks on the whole—were *Messieurs*, too. The author, as we know (from his book, *Monsieur Nicolas*) was so called because he was "a little better-dressed" than the other ragamuffins of the parish. As for the daughters of Edme's first marriage (whom Barbe in any case succeeded in expelling from the house, after a domestic scene which established her authority), they, poor girls, did not have the right to be called "demoiselle"—because *their* mother (an illiterate country woman, though the daughter of a rich peasant) "had never worn a dressing-gown".

There was, to be sure, an economic dividing-line between the independent peasant (5 hectares) and the dependent (one hectare). But more noticeable was the social difference which distinguished the *Monsieur* of the village from the non-Monsieur, who was mere Tom, Dick, or Harry (or rather Jean, Paul, or Pierre). Nicolas Rétif, who is indeed an anthropologist after his own fashion, com-plains that the Parisians, who have heard about the customs of the Iroquois, the Hurons, or the Algonquins, know nothing at all about the subtleties of a French village. *Monsieur le Lieutenant*, a pa-triarch in his own parish, enjoyed a prestige that set him apart—in the same way, but on a different level, as the Sacy midwife who, though possibly less than competent, was universally known among the villagers as *Bonne-Mère* (Good Mother). Patriarch and midwife had each, in his or her own sphere, reached the proper "level of incompetence". (Edme after all, although his son paints a flattering picture of his prowess as a husbandman, never harvested more than six quintals of grain to the hectare.) Such village notables, solidly entrenched, basked in the general esteem and consideration of their fellow citizens.

For all his airs, Edme Rétif cannot really be called a bourgeois. He was certainly not in a different *class* from his less well-off brothers. He remained, although at the pinnacle of village society, a peasant still; one who knew, as his son points out, how to talk to the other farmers, to his labourers, and to his horses, dogs and bulls. This privileged position, allowing him to participate without any complexes in the ever-open network of communication with other country people, also enabled Monsieur Nicolas, who was himself equally well-placed in the green purgatory of rural society, to give us his splendid first-hand account.

A prominent figure in his own village, in his parish, and indeed in the cluster of parishes that made up the district, Edme was the grandson of a modest cooper. His grandfather, who died in 1687, already had a position as informal arbitrator in his native *commune* of Nitry: he settled disputes, reconciled the opposing parties, and was known in Nitry as "the just man".[7] As members of a dynasty of leaders—one was either born a Rétif or one was not—Edme and especially his father, Pierre, built up a number of myths around the cooper, discreetly omitting any mention of barrels. They constructed a fabulous genealogy for him, claiming descent from the Emperor Pertinax, and from the Knight Templar Jean de Montroyal, nicknamed Rétif ("resistant") because of his tenacity.

Pierre Rétif, the son of the cooper and the father of the patriarch, was both a prefiguration, and at the same time a negation, of what Edme later became. Like his son after him, Pierre who talked (or so we are told) exactly like a physiocrat,[8] was a prosperous village peasant; but a tenant-farmer rather than a landowner. Somehow or other he contrived to rise above the modest level of the cooper. Pierre, it is true, had that irresistible charm which seems to have been a family trait: it was to surface in his grandson Nicholas in an extraordinary fashion, dazzling all the women who (he says) surrendered to him. Pierre, then, made use of his charm and his capacity to please everyone, of both sexes, to build up his position as a village statesman. The landlord's man, provost of Nitry, as Edme was to be of Sacy, Pierre acted in his parish as "tax-collector for part of the *seigneurie* of the said place"; and at some time he was also the *procureur fiscal*. The combination of these offices made him simultaneously public prosecutor at the seigniorial court of justice, and the receiver of the same seigneur's dues, quit-rents, tithes and lease payments. A man of power, influence, substance and pleasure, Pierre was popular in Nitry. His funeral, a supreme celebration of his standing, was an unqualified triumph: the entire village joined together with a hearty *Amen* (the equivalent of three rousing cheers) to commend his soul to the paradise he so clearly deserved. There was good reason for his popularity. Pierre, like Edme after him, dealt straightforwardly, and without a hint of chicanery, with the cases before him. He dispensed justice between a glass of wine and a bite of bacon, and he offered drinks to all petitioners, whether clients or culprits, since in Nitry there was no tavern in the town: "the hearing was held in his house and always at his own expense. In

Nitry no one except the judge served drink." Out of pocket (but then who was not in the years after 1709–10?), Pierre died in 1713, leaving his heirs a rather dilapidated succession.

Something of a rake, and open-handed to his friends, Pierre the lady-killer was a domestic tyrant behind his own front door. Terrorizing the household was apparently second nature to him. His harassed wife (who claimed, however, to come from a family of magistrates) was shamelessly ill-treated by him, but nevertheless worshipped her lord and master to such a degree that the slightest civil word would bring her purring round his feet like an affectionate cat. When he died, her only prospect of happiness was to join him in the tomb, her vision of bliss to be at his side in paradise (where else would he be?). As for his daughters, the trouble with them, according to Pierre, was that they belonged to the "unruly sex which resembles the most obstinate of animals". They were, therefore, brought up extremely strictly by their father (who, like most French peasants of the eighteenth century, was a male chauvinist of the most unbending kind). Going in dread of Pierre, they were instructed never to answer yes or no, but always to say "I should think so", "it would seem so", "perhaps" and so on. Their mother for her part bade them "be gentle and hardworking, and say nothing" (though this does not appear to have stopped some of the daughters from quarrelling with their husbands in later life). For this harsh upbringing of female children, justifications were easy to find, at least in the Rétif family tradition. One of its articles of faith, firmly supported by Pierre, Edme and Nicolas, was that "in all nature there is nothing more abhorrent than a headstrong girl; she is a monster". Towards his son Edme, Pierre Rétif, whose authoritarian personality was no doubt typical of French rural society, behaved as an archetypal castrating father. The most harmless word or sign exchanged by his son with one of the buxom village beauties would earn him a lashing from the father's whip, that bloodied his shirt. (One might note, incidentally, and it would also be true elsewhere, that austerity of morals was generally enforced in this parish by the father rather than the mother—although it was more a question of preaching than of practising.) Such paternal punishments did not obliterate affection between father and son however; in Nitry the verb "to fear" was generally taken to be synonymous with "to love": "it is common parlance in the district when speaking of God or of one's parents".

Edme certainly claimed to have loved his father, whose death he took as a personal tragedy, shedding over the newly-dug grave a stream of tears which the villagers compared to a torrent of holy water. In this rich peasant's home in Burgundy, the formidable father-figure inspired in both wife and child a fear which was not incompatible with love. But the focus of real affection within the household was the mother, Anne Simon, morally if not physically battered by her husband, but showing tenderness to her children and receiving it in exchange. The couple later formed by Edme Rétif and Barbe Ferlet was, in theory at least, founded on the same principle: a father who brandished his authority (though becoming more indulgent in his old age), and an affectionate mother (though a bossy little body at heart, and very down-to-earth).

But the archetypal authoritarian father, a stern patriarch towards his sons and even more so to his daughters, was not the only model to be found in the Auxerre countryside at the time. Barbe Ferlet (known as Bibi) for example, born in 1703, was adored by her own father, a vine-grower and a tenant of the château of the lords of Accolay. At home, Bibi was the spoiled darling and little princess of the family—a role she repeated with her elderly lover and first husband, Boujat, a bourgeois of Auxerre. Only too glad to have his own shortcomings overlooked, he too spoiled Barbe, the fresh young bride he took as his second wife. Nicolas Rétif, the son of the later marriage between Barbe and Edme, does not conceal his disapproval of the easygoing upbringing received by his mother. Edme, having married the much-indulged Bibi, was to school her in other habits: he impressed upon her the harsh anti-feminist principles of the peasants of Burgundy, who were quite obsessed—as any number of quotations would show—with paternal and marital authority. "Woman, go fetch your daughters", "Woman, fetch me some sausage", as the farmers, described by Monsieur Nicolas are always peremptorily shouting.

As regards the children, the indulgence which the ageing Edme showed towards the younger children of his second marriage did not find favour, either, with Nicolas, Barbe's eldest son. "The Rétif family character", he writes, "is too wilful" to derive benefit from a lenient upbringing. Like a rebellious vine-shoot, it needs a bit of firm pruning. To spare the rod, Nicolas says, is to depart from the proper pattern of the countryside. (Burgundians, please note.)

All in all, though, if Pierre was an only partly successful prototype for Edme—more authoritarian and less fortunate financially than his son—he had undoubtedly provided his heir with a model of the prosperous peasant-cum-tax-official, parish notable and domestic tyrant, a model to which Edme would willy-nilly conform, smoothing out some sharp corners and adding something in the way of money bags. The Nitry-Sacy region was a very different matter from the more feudal structures of the Puisaye, a wooded and backward region in the southwest corner of the present day *département* of the Yonne. Here, there were still "gentlemen who went hunting in their leggings and hobnailed boots, who still carried rusty old swords and, though starving to death in their tumbledown castles, were too proud to work". Pierre, by contrast, can be identified as a commoner who had got on: a village elder, a peasant farmer and judge-provost of the parish, quite integrated into the *seigneurie* and doing very well out of it; working hard, ploughing the land himself, sowing with his own hands, paying his taxes (not over-paying though, since he had friends in high places). Pierre, in short, was a "member of the middling class, that precious class so beloved by good kings".[9] Edme had only to observe with piety the feared, but never consciously hated, image presented by his father. And when he had sacrificed his Parisian dreams of love and ambition, he too would reproduce this model, bringing it to fullness and perfection.

THE TWO VILLAGES

Edme Rétif, less tyrannical (in practice if not in principle) and more prosperous than ever his father had been, was like Pierre a *Nitry man* at heart. The contrast between the two villages of Sacy and Nitry was fundamental to the thinking of the Rétif family. Sacy, the home of father-in-law Dondaine, was virgin soil, raw material upon which Edme could practice his experiments, in the hope of rendering it fertile. Nitry, on the other hand, was home ground, the matrix in which the Rétif dynasty, to which Edme and Nicolas belonged, had been formed. The difference between "the Sacy way" and "the Nitry way" in spite of—or perhaps because of—its Proustian echoes, is worth considering.

An earlier writer, Noël du Fail had, in about 1540, compared and contrasted two neighbouring villages of his own time, Flameaux and Vindelles, which represented respectively two differenct conceptions of the world: Flameaux the old-fashioned golden age, Vindelles the contemporary decadence. But Rétif, who is as confident in the future as Du Fail is nostalgic for the past, uses the parallel between the two parishes to illustrate a very different theory of the passing of time. Sacy, embedded or encrusted in the past, is contrasted with Nitry, looking forward to development. Indeed Nitry provides Sacy with a beneficial transfusion of its own vitality of culture, provoking a revival there (while incidentally hastening its own decline). In Rétif's work, eighteenth-century optimism prevails over the pessimism of the impoverished Renaissance to be detected in Noël du Fail.

It was shortly before his death that Pierre Rétif, scornfully dismissing Edme's Parisian fancies and hankering for the girls of the city, had established the alliance between Sacy and Nitry (a meeting of nature and civilization, as it were) for the benefit of his son. It was to provide the take-off point for the career of the future patriarch. For Pierre had decided that Edme, a boy from the airy village of Nitry should marry a rich and down-to-earth girl from Sacy, the daughter of a local moneybags, one Thomas Dondaine, a merchant farmer and syndic in his commune, "a hard man, with a forbidding face, who was considered to have superhuman strength, even in his own district where all the inhabitants are as strong as oxen". Thomas Dondaine, whom Edme already knew, and did not like, owed his fortune entirely to the strength of his arm and to his qualities of hard work, common sense and thrift, which in his case did duty for hard-headed intelligence. The theme has been sounded, and Rétif often returns to the same notion: Sacy stands for the soil, for silence and vital life-forces, as healthy as black bread and as innocent as nature itself.

Having been introduced to his father-in-law, Edme had his first meeting with the bride, Marie, whom the Rétif-Dondaine or Nitry-Sacy agreements had bestowed upon him. The latter encounter was hardly any more exciting for him than the former. Marie Dondaine, glimpsed for the first time by her suitor as she was working in a field of hemp, was "a thickset girl, rather mannish in appearance", who was "gathering hemp in armfuls, with astonishing strength". She was a female Tarzan rather than a great beauty, but would undoubtedly "make an excellent housewife". The chief qualities of the young woman, who was as unlike the "Parisian hussies" as it was possible to be, are best viewed as aspects of the awe-inspiring silence of the illiterate. Other features characteristic of such a force of nature were modesty and kindness. So, having found a suitable match for his son and arranged the marriage, Pierre could die in peace. Marie was to bear Edme seven children; then, having completed what was practically a regulation *ancien régime* family, she died, her reproductive function loyally fulfilled. Her death ended the seventeen years' bondage of Edme Rétif who, throughout the time of this marriage had been living "in an extended family" under the oppressive roof of father-in-law Dondaine, bowing under his yoke without complaint. The departed Marie had, however, left imprinted on the faces of her children the indelible mark of "the earthy complexion of the Dondaines". The Dondaine family were unquestionably "members of the earth", wedded to the soil and incapable of heaving themselves out of it: the *abbé* Thomas Rétif, son of this first marriage, "had neither the soul nor the colouring of the Rétifs;[10] he had the earthbound soul and the earthen complexion of the Dondaines: . . . His skin was the colour of wood, sprinkled with dark freckles, and oily . . . He was compactly built and very strong, though he did not look it. He was a quick-tempered, passionate and lascivious man, but one who had achieved self-mastery through religious devotion". It took the harsh straitjacket of Jansenism, apparently, to control the earthy passions of this Caliban of the vestry, the *abbé* Thomas, a child of Burgundy's rich soil and forests. The only trouble was that the *abbé* tried in vain to inculcate the same Jansenism, with blows and lashes, into the young Monsieur Nicolas who felt no need for it at all, and would ever afterwards bear his half-brother the bitterest of grudges. The episode explains the persistent distrust, sometimes concealed under a flow of honeyed hypocrisy, that Nicolas Rétif was to feel all his life for the latter-day rural disciples of Saint-Cyran. On this point, Rétif de la Bretonne's religious opinions remained fixed from childhood on: "Jansenism is all very well for the Dondaines"—all very well, that is, for these yokels, who lack the polish and urbanity of Nitry families like the Rétifs and the Ferlets. For the latter, a more relaxed and easygoing religion was appropriate, one tolerant of folklore, so relaxed indeed as to verge on the anti-Christian, as practised by the good *curés* Foudriat and Pinard. To each flock its own shepherd—more of this later.

The Nitry-Sacy contrast, as it appears in Retif's writings, eventually transcends the opposition (followed by a marriage-alliance) between two families, and is developed into what amounts to a cosmic system of comparative ecology, after the fashion of the philosophy of airs and elements and constitutional medicine, favoured by Vicq d'Azir and the learned doctors of the late eighteenth century.

Rétif presents a series of geographico-medical contrasts. Nitry, round as a millstone, is an open-field village, surrounded by windswept plains. The air here is excellent: constantly moving and stirring, free from pollution. The trade in commodities carried on in Nitry helps to develop urban contacts and an acquaintance with polite society. The soil is fertile and the air is fresh; incomes are good and production is diversified; the villagers are well provided with eggs and milk and eat meat on Sundays and holidays. There is diversification, too, in Nitry society, which is not as exclusively devoted to farming as that of Sacy. Because of a range of outside contacts, the French spoken in Nitry is purer than that of Sacy. The women have better circulation here than anywhere else, because of the quality of the bread: so they speak in accents of "inexpressible grace". The men are exuberant and fun-loving, expressing themselves in a constant stream of extremely varied language, whether they are addressing their fellow-villagers or their horses.

Sacy is a very different kettle of fish. Here the hilly, wooded land, not unlike the *bocage*, is made up almost exclusively of "marshy valleys" and "rocky slopes". The former exude "foul and unhealthy" vapours; the latter cause the polluted air, which comes twisting up through the "deep gorges" of the valleys, to be drawn up in corrosive currents, which impart to all the Sacy-dwellers an insatiable appetite. So much so that neither sexual desire nor personal misfortune can make anyone, who is cursed with the voracity characteristic of the village, forget his ever-gnawing hunger. The unfortunate *Saxiates* are therefore condemned by their nature to consume literally tons of black bread, which in turn gives their bodies a viscous consistency, making them both heavy and swarthy. This is particularly unattractive in the young women, who look mannish and talk in harsh voices.The black-bread-eaters of Sacy are, moreover, indifferent to mature and subtle wines, which they regard as fit only for the tastebuds of town-dwellers or the delicate palate of such as Edme Rétif. His son reports that the yokels of Sacy, who are almost too earthy to be true, require a "wine that takes the skin off your throat",[11] a *piquette* or pressed wine, "strained through the scrapings of the grapes". For in Sacy, "the human race is of an uncouthness unparalleled even in Germany".

The Sacy-Nitry contrast (barbarians versus civilization) becomes, as it were, the microcosm of a comparison between France and Germany—not a flattering one, needless to say, for Rétif's imaginary version of Germany, for which Sacy (many miles from the Rhine) is taken to be the somewhat unlikely representative. An example of this Sacy "Germanism" (as ridiculous as it is offensive) is to be found in Germain, "the head ploughboy" at the farm of La Bretonne near Sacy. This huge fellow "has a truly Teutonic air". His face is half a foot across, without a scrap of fat. In spite of—or perhaps because of—his Herculean strength, the village giant is the kindest of men, adored by children who are always eager to draw him into their games. Germain speaks the language of children (as Edme Rétif speaks that of horses). Underneath its rather forbidding appearance, then, Sacy takes us back to the basic values of Mother Earth and the inexhaustible resources of nature, blessed with vital energy and close to childhood. Germain, the Burgundian ploughboy who never left France in his life, is promoted to the role both of noble savage and indeed of noble German. A gloomy, brooding and colossal figure, whether totally speechless or uttering clumsy inarticulate sounds, the Saxiate as depicted in *La Vie de mon père* is a heavy sullen creature, who has only just learnt to walk on his hind legs. But he is not without virtues: he works like an ox, and possesses enormous reserves of strength, which are to be unlocked by the sorcerer's apprentice, Edme Rétif. And he is capable, like a faithful dog, of strong devotion to his master. It was this unpromising human material that Edme, the patriarch of La Bretonne, like some imaginary Moses freeing Michelangelo's slaves from bondage, undertook to transform, in the course of a lifetime of labour and domestic economy. His father had prevented him from taking on Paris, which he would greatly have preferred; well, Edme would take on Sacy instead: "*A nous deux maintenant*".

One has to admit that the challenge was almost as great. When one has deciphered Rétif's schema of air versus earth as an explanatory medical framework, it is easy to recognize in Sacy the typical French village of the *ancien régime*, combining the features of both hill country and *bocage*. It was a village of illiterates, with a low standard of living: under their roofs of flat stones or thatch, the inhabitants, who had much in common with the neighbouring Morvan, were indeed eating a very unbalanced diet: stuffing themselves with black bread rather than with fresh meat and red wine. Among the 30,000 parishes of eighteenth-century France, there must have been at least thousands, if not tens of thousands, of villages like Sacy. Rétif (in *L'Ecole des pères*) is not far off the mark when he sees in the Sacy-Nitry contrast a "condensed version of the nation's agriculture"—for there was indeed a contrast between the developed regions (the minority) and the backward communities (the majority). Edme Rétif had to work hard on the heavy dough of the Saxiates. When he describes the labour of reclamation or transmutation carried out by his father, Nicolas expresses himself in words more fervent even than those used later by the writers of catalogues for the Colonial Exhibition, describing Lyautey's efforts to police Morocco, or Gallieni's to civilize the Malagasies.

The mission of development—or internal colonization—which Edme Rétif was destined to accomplish in Sacy had painful beginnings. For the seventeen years of his first marriage (blessed with seven children) Edme had to "break his back working" for his father-in-law, with whom the whole family lived. Then "the venerable Marie" died, liberating our hero, a widower at last, from his bondage to the old man. The conversion of Sacy could begin.

This conversion was, in fact, the direct or indirect achievement of three people: Edme whom we have already met; the local parish priest, of whom more later; and Edme's second wife, Barbe Ferlet.

Barbe Ferlet, "the adorable Bibi", who claimed descent from the noble house of Bertro, was in fact the daughter of a tenant-farmer on the estates of the Bertro family, Burgundian aristocrats. In the home of this farmer and vine-grower, Barbe was weaned on family affection and fairy tales; she grew up in a non-authoritarian and comparatively easy-going household, with none of the sergeant-major atmosphere that reigned in the Rétif home (to say nothing of the Dondaines). When the Ferlet house burned down, the only concern of the parents (who lost everything in the fire) was that it might upset Bibi, the unwitting cause of the accident.

Barbe was a determined young woman, with an appetite for love (Nicolas does not conceal that he was conceived by his parents with mutual pleasure). She had begun by getting into trouble: she bore a child by Boujat, a bourgeois of Auxerre, in whose home she was a servant: a youthful indiscretion. Nicolas, in *La Vie de mon père* sees fit to camouflage this episode with an imaginary marriage which in fact occurred only some time later. Once bitten, Barbe decided, young as she was, that it would be better to settle down, even if it meant accepting an old man. She wanted to "be established" and rejected any suitors who asked for favours without proposing marriage. "No kisses, sweetheart, without a ring on my finger". Barbe therefore married her old lover Boujat, now a widower, whom she promptly dispatched to his grave, collecting the inheritance. Little effort was then required to act the grief-stricken—but still beautiful—widow. She looked beseechingly in the direction of the kindly *curé* Foudriat—who married her without delay to the gangling Edme Rétif: a widower now for three years, he had been living first with his mother, then alone in the total squalor which can result, in peasants unused to celibacy, from the lack of a wife. His mother was a kindly soul, but no great shakes as a housewife, and after her death Edme was gradually sinking into a state of grime, looking like a tramp, with no one to wash his clothes or his linen. Barbe, offered as a wife by the parish priest, must have seemed like a gift from heaven: she was beautiful, or attractive at any rate, and she was a good manager—much better than Edme.[12] This thrifty housewife had the additional advantage of owning a house in Sacy, inherited from Boujat, and a godsend for her second husband. Always well-organized and punctual, she gave birth to the first child of this marriage nine months to the day after the wedding, which had been celebrated with dispatch by Foudriat.

But the new household was not without problems. "Bibi" felt very foreign and terribly out of place. Although she owned a house in the village of Sacy, it was not her native parish and she had neither friends nor family there. No doubt there was a certain amount of gossip among the village women about her earlier illegitimate child by Boujat. Even in her own home, faced with Edme's grown-up daughters by his first wife—they regarded her as a threatening stepmother—Barbe did not get her own way all at once. She suffered the daughters' hostility for a time, while she prepared the ground with a husband who was only too anxious to sympathize; then she effected her *coup d'état*, seizing power within the family. At her bidding, Edme showed on this occasion that he could be a cruel father in the best family tradition: he threw four of the rebellious sisters out of the house: one was married off, another dispatched to Paris, and the last two went to live with the dreaded grandfather Dondaine. It is reminiscent of another, more tragic expulsion in the same period: that of the young Coignet. He had been cruelly treated by his stepmother, and lived for years away from home, as a starving shepherd boy, covered with fleas, sleeping under hedges, hating his father and above all the wicked step-mother.

After her coup, Barbe was queen of the hive, though affecting to respect the henceforth casual reign of Edme Rétif. Together they brought the household to indisputable prosperity, punctuated but not damaged by the births of seven children. The babies were born at very close intervals, since Barbe handed them over to "sturdy" wet-nurses, and as a result was almost continuously pregnant. Edme, like most peasants of his time, does not seem to have thought much about birth control. This father of fourteen surviving children did not apparently belong to the rural minority who were, by 1750, party to the "sinful secrets" of a modest degree of con-traception.

EDME THE DEVELOPER

Married once more, established as his own man, settled on land and with a dowry originally provided by old Dondaine, and occupy-ing the property, the house and indeed the bed of the departed Boujat, Edme was free to turn to advantage not only the strength of his arm and his native intelligence but the real estate and moveable goods resulting from two marriages. He was soon to buy the large farm of La Bretonne; he would then introduce the inhabitants of Sacy to the benefits of his personal agricultural revolution. This was not, needless to say, an agricultural revolution on English lines (abolishing fallow land and replacing it with clover, turnips or some such). All Edme did was to roll up his sleeves and add to the usual practices an extra helping of human labour. He cleared land, planted vines and made minor improvements in a small way. All this was very characteristic of regions where there were small land holdings. The eighteenth century, without introducing any major innovations, was more adaptable, more efficient and more produc-tive than the seventeenth.

Edme's first step was to remove the stones from some of his land and build walls, known locally as *mergers*, with the stones: a classic solution throughout the southeast and central eastern areas of France. To meet the demands of increased population or market pressures, farmers tried to bring marginal land (usually stony) into cultivation. Many of these well-built *mergers*, still standing today in parts of Burgundy, probably go back to this *"belle époque"* of the eighteenth century. In the age of Enlightenment, removing stones was an inseparable part (for Edme or for anyone else in real-life Burgundy[13]) of the clearing of virgin soil. People were now bringing into use such stony ground as, with the price rises, market stimulus and population increase, could operate above the admittedly low threshold of small-farm profitability. Edme, as various passages from *La Vie de mon père* show, was a canny observer of grain prices and movements in the cost of land. On these rocky but sunny slopes, Edme and those like him grew, instead of grain which would not have been worth it, vines. The other *Saxiates*, whether in imitation of Edme or simply at the same time as him (for we are not obliged to accept Nicolas Rétif's hagiographical account of his father's pioneer role—which may be totally imaginary), planted vines as fast at they could between 1720 and 1780. This "clothing of the land", once started, was pursued to the point where the product of the Sacy vines eventually approached, or even overtook, that of wheat. Having begun the century as poverty-stricken beggars, the inhabitants of Sacy as a community moved into vine-growing and became more prosperous. One element in the change, which through Edme Rétif's initiative, stimulated viticulture in Burgundy was the growing demand of the Paris market. Wine-drinking among ordinary Parisians was slightly on the increase, and the decline of the vineyards in the immediate vicinity of the capital (where they were replaced by cereals) began, after the economic revival of the 1720s, to encourage the trade in wine from the Yonne valley and lower Burgundy. It should be noticed that this was a very positive example of regional specialization and optimum allocation of produce, since the overall figure for wine consumption in Paris hardly altered between 1635 and 1789, reaching a ceiling of 240,000 to 250,000 *muids*. (To this one should, it is true, add 10,000 *muids* of spirits, or the equivalent of another 60,000 *muids* of wine, on the eve of the Revolution.) Edme Rétif was an economist without realizing it. After the Law affair, he grasped the new possibilities opened up to local vineyards: in 1725, he went to Paris, "to take the first samples of his own wine and that of his neighbours" who had either followed his example or were simultaneously inspired. For the journey, Edme kept on his old wig and his countryman's clothes, which made him look just like "the other Burgundian peasants who sell their wine at St. Bernard's gate". With his weatherbeaten face and hands he must have been unrecognizable to his former Parisian sweethearts (if, indeed, such admirers, generously attributed by Nicolas to his father, ever existed). The Parisian samples were successful. The planting of vines which preceded and followed the trip had beneficial side-effects. For, we read in *La Vie de mon père*, in order to cultivate the new vineyards on the hill slopes, more beasts of burden were required. And the extra money derived from the sales of wine made it possible for the now somewhat richer peasants of Sacy to obtain animals at cash prices: cows, sheep and goats whose meat and milk "eased the life" or improved the diet of their owners, who had seen little of such luxuries before. The animals also contributed more manure for the crops. But, of course, they needed feeding too. That was no problem: Edme provided artificial pastures—but his method would not have been thought of by English-style agronomists (so fiercely criticized by Morineau): Edme and his neighbours simply sowed red clover (which does very well in Burgundy) during the long fallow period of seven to eight years allowed between the uprooting of one set of vines on a hillside, when they are too old, and the planting of young vines on the same ground.

Edme was not only interested in reclaiming rocky slopes: he also tackled marshy valleys. By building dams, he dried out meadows bordering running streams, thus ending the almost permanent flooding of such land, and turned them into hayfields. Since all his projects complemented each other, the stones from a cleared field were used to build a dam, while the field's productivity increased, and so on. Rétif does more than any other writer of the period to indicate the interconnection of minor agricultural improvements. Set in motion by the original stimulus of expanding vine-production, they rescued the villagers from grinding poverty, without necessarily eliminating hardship altogether. Innovation, as Edme conceived it, and as many parts of France must have practised it (for in the absence, now confirmed, of an agricultural revolution, the "mini-prosperity" of the eighteenth century can hardly be explained otherwise), consisted of selecting the most worthwhile elements in local tradition, in response to direct or indirect market pressures. One broke one's back labouring, digging out stones, building *mergers*; one increased the stock, drained fields and so on, thus bringing into use the impressive labour reserves of a population hitherto apparently slumped in apathy and inarticulacy.

This population was always ready in fact, at least in the particular instance of the Saxiates[14] and others we know of, to rush into harness and accomplish great feats of strength as soon as there was any work actually available, as a result of the innovations mentioned above.

I wanted to begin by setting Edme Rétif and his circle in the context provided by their genealogical background, by changing economic circumstances, and by the contrast between the two villages. We can now take a closer look at the daily life of the Rétif family. This will enable us to shed some light, from an anthropological point of view, on what intimate domestic life really was like in the household of a well-off peasant under the *ancien régime*. The results can legitimately be seen as typical, if not of France in general, then at any rate of a certain part of Burgundy—which is at least a start. History as it might be written by the bailiff's man is not to be sniffed at, and I shall indeed draw, if need be, on the inventory of furniture.[15] Edme's belongings were no different from those to be found in any wealthy peasant's house: twelve chairs with rush seats, two tables and two cupboards in the main room, together with a prie-Dieu and a picture of the Virgin and child; a great millstone standing in the yard; any amount of grain—wheat, barley and oats in the barn; *feuillettes* (casks) of wine under the vaults of the cellar, with the cooper's tools; silver was kept in the master's bedchamber. All such items, as Gilbert Rouger has ascertained so admirably after a fruitful exploration of the notarial records of the Yonne, commonly made up the worldly goods of the average prosperous peasant; something very comparable would be found in many regions of France, from Languedoc to Auvergne and from Provence to Picardy. One hardly needs to stress that the degree of wealth and comfort to be found in the Rétif household would not have been found in a similar social milieu in the age of the brothers Le Nain.

But how many could aspire to this privileged position? An enquiry, unfortunately dating from long before the 1770s (the time when the inventory of the late Edme's belongings was drawn up), might help us to form an opinion on this. In 1682, François Artaut, "general representative of the Third Estate", was riding through the region of Auxerre. On his travels, he conducted a close survey of the "way of living" of the inhabitants of the hamlet of Vermenton, very near Sacy.[16] Out of the 365 houses occupied by the citizens of this village, excluding forty deserted or "ruined" houses, nine were "properly furnished". Edme Rétif, had he lived a century earlier to have his inventory compiled, would probably have come into this category—the "happy few" indeed, since they do not even amount to 3 per cent of those visited. Then come twenty-seven "fairly well furnished" houses; but another 126 had no more than "some old bedsteads with wretched beds on them", and 133 houses contained only "straw mattresses and a few tattered blankets on roughly-fashioned couches". Finally in seventy households, the inhabitants slept on straw spread on the ground with no mattress-cover or blanket. This last group of seventy "houses" the poorest of all, would hardly have figured on any notaries' inventories, which tend to cream off the upper and middle layers of rural society.

What these seventeenth-century statistics on poverty in Vermenton tell us, then, is that in 1682, at least two households out of twelve corresponded to what present-day French people would describe as rabbit hutches or *bidonville* (shantytown) dwellings. The most elementary comfort, in the strict sense of the term, was entirely lacking. In the nine households out of every twelve where there were "old bedsteads" or "roughly-fashioned couches", the inhabitants lived near, or indeed below, a certain degree of poverty one associates with the peasant interiors painted by Le Nain. And finally barely one household out of twelve, in a hamlet which nevertheless did possess its petty-bourgeoisie, had some kind of minimal or even decent comfort. It is in this top twelfth, and probably in the top 2–3 per cent (although the 2–3 per cent of 1682 may have become a higher percentage by the time of our hero's gilded old age in 1770), that such rural notables as Edme Rétif and his friend, the parish priest Antoine Foudriat, must be classed. The latter, indeed, must have had quite a bourgeois interior with his four-poster bed, mirror in a red frame, some engravings, and a barometer. So Edme Rétif is both typical and atypical. He is atypical because he provided a striking contrast to the poverty which predominated in the village, and which the respectable growth of the rural economy since 1682 had not yet eliminated: for proof of this, one has only to read the descriptions written by Jaimerai Duval, a poor boy who became a child prodigy, and who knew what he was talking about. According to him, visitors to Arthenay-en-Tonnerrois in 1752 would have seen only a few thatched cottages (just about fit for cattle) inhabited by villagers in rags and reduced to beggary. As for rural Burgundy in general, in the last century of the *ancien régime*, as described in its tragic particulars in a recent thesis,[17] the picture was a pretty black one.

And yet Edme is typical, too: although well-to-do, he was a real peasant, not a landowner with soft hands who walked round his estates with a walking stick. As a cereal-grower, he practised what he preached. Every morning during the long ploughing season, he drove one of his own teams. He combined being a horny-handed son of toil on weekdays with his weekend occupations. From mid-day on Saturday he fulfilled the role of judge and community leader: he busied himself being the local magistrate and notary, giving consultations and pronouncing judgment. But he never gave up his physical labour, and died in harness at the age of 73, from a chill caught when he got his feet wet cutting grass in a flooded meadow.

A man with a double identity, both typical and untypical, of the village and yet something above the village, Edme also had a double role in private life as a husband and father. A widower with a "divided family", he was a totally representative case of *ancien régime* demography: the children, who all lived together in the second home until some of them were driven out, were a mixture: the offspring of the first marriage; the natural son of the second wife by another man; and the children of the second marriage. Typical, too, are the ages of the various spouses on marriage: Edme was 23 when he first took a wife—a little young, but that is explained by the sudden death of his father into whose shoes he had to step right away. Marie Dondaine was 25—virtually the norm for girls at this time. The second marriage between the widowed Edme and Barbe took place, of course, when they were over 40 and 30 respectively, in 1734. Extremely typical too are the close intervals between the pregnancies with which Edme Rétif bombarded both his wives. A man who must have been, in relation to his milieu, intelligent, rich and cultivated, Edme does not appear to have shown any inclination to limit the number of births. The sturdy country girl he married first bore him children in 1714, 1715, 1716, 1718, 1720, 1723, 1727, and 1730: six weeks after the birth of the eighth and last child, the mother died. As for Barbe Ferlet, she had already experienced motherhood, both in and out of wedlock—one bastard child who survived, and two legitimate children who died in infancy. She was closely acquainted, then, with the high mortality of the *ancien régime* which had already robbed her of two babies and which made her, in 1733, the widow of a widower. After her remarriage in 1734 at the age of 31, she again had a very typical conjugal record, representative in particular of the well-to-do woman who could afford wet-nurses, and thus did not breastfeed her babies. Between the ages of 31 and 41 she had eight pregnancies (including twins): in 1734, 1736, 1737, 1738 (twin girls), 1740, 1741, 1743, 1744. Having reached the age of 41, a typical age for the last childbirth among mothers in the non-Malthusian villages of France, the charming and fertile Barbe hung up the cradle, so to speak, and produced no more. Edme was by then 54, an age at which many husbands were already declining into old age. So far then, the record fits the norms of the century—one might even say the centuries—of *ancien régime* demography. Barbe, for example, when she put her children out to nurse, was not simply indulging in a rich woman's whim: she had to care for house, garden, food and farmyard. Undertaking a heavy workload at La Bretonne, she relied on other women, since she could afford it, to relieve her of the labour which was so costly in terms of working hours—that of feeding her latest-born.[18]

But when one turns from birth and fertility rates in Edme's household to the problem of mortality, one no longer finds such a predictable pattern, but encounters, instead, certain specific signs characteristic of an avant-garde. While it is not exceptional for the eighteenth century, the late age of mortality among the Rétifs tends to classify the family within a (fairly large) *élite* and no longer in the traditional masses. Of Edme's seventeen children by two marriages, only three died before the age of one year[19]—an infant mortality rate which is low for the period and for France, but not negligible (176 per thousand). Much more remarkable, however, is the almost total absence of juvenile mortality (between one and twenty years), whereas in the age of Louis XIV it could be as high as 250 per thousand in more than one region. Of Edme's children, we should set aside the case of Charles Rétif (1743–60), a clerk to a Parisian notary and then a soldier in the regiment of Auvergne, who was killed in Hanover at seventeen, since his death really counts as a military statistic. His case apart, the only natural death that comes under the heading of juvenile mortality, among all the seventeen children, is that of Jean-Baptiste Rétif (1740–55) who died at the age of fifteen. In the Age of the Sun King, two children had to be born for every man or woman who reached adulthood.[20] In the Rétif family, seventeen births produced twelve adults: the average life-span of the seventeen individuals was 50 (62 for the first marriage and 40 for the second).

These remarkable scores are interesting: they are probably representative of *optimal* achievements by the families of working farmers. While not always as outstanding as those of Edme Rétif, such achievements contributed to the demographic takeoff of the eighteenth century. Can they be attributed to better medical care in the eighteenth century? It seems very unlikely. Sacy may have honoured the local midwife, whose level of competence or incompetence is not known. (She was *la Bonne Mère* to whom her fellow-villagers accorded deference, respect and "tender veneration".)[21] But real medicine, with the seal of the university medical schools— no thank you. The backward Saxiates were supported in this by Edme from sophisticated Nitry. However enlightened he was supposed to be he, like Molière, had the same low opinion of doctors as he had of women. Sacy, like Nitry, wanted nothing to do with medicine. In the course of a conversation with his wife about money, Edme wanted his children to economize, amongst other things "by giving up all confidence in remedies and doctors".[22] Medicine may well have played its part in reducing mortality rates in the early part of the eighteenth century; but the medical impact was much more evident among the real *élites* such as princely families (whose demographic and medical habits have been studied by English demographers, and described by Saint-Simon),[23] than among the peasants, where, in Burgundy at any rate, prejudices against doctors, rightly or wrongly, seem to have reigned. In fact, if mortality rates among such well-off or "advanced" peasants as the Rétifs declined in the eighteenth century, it was probably, setting medicine aside, the result of improved diet and, more generally, of living standards and a way of life rather superior to those of the past. Nicolas Rétif certainly thought so: the high mortality among children of needy peasants in his native district was, he reckoned, the result of the parents, whether through avarice, poverty or ignorance, bringing up their children "in want".[24]

And indeed Micheline Baulant's studies of the Meaux region,[25] and Pouyez's work on villages near Lille[26] have shown that infant and juvenile mortality was higher among the children of working peasants than among those of day labourers. This tells us that in the absence of a Pasteur-type revolution, which is now saving the lives of many children in the Third World, modifications and changes in living standards and diet "made all the difference" where mortality was concerned, between one class and another, one period and another.

Fortunately we know quite a lot about the diet of the Rétifs who were so resistant to death; and we also know something about the eating habits of those who were not as well off. Monsieur Nicolas, in *L'Ecole des pères*,[27] describes the precarious life of the poor, or as he calls them the "not-well-off" peasants: such people normally ate "barley- or rye-bread, soup with oil made from walnuts or hemp-seed" (walnut or, if the worst came to the worst, hempseed oil, seems to have been a basic ingredient in the cooking among the poorer country people of middle France, in provinces such as Burgundy, Anjou, Auvergne).[28] "Some poor-quality drink", says Nicolas, "and that is all they have to sustain a life devoted perforce to continuous heavy labour". It will not do, then, to accuse the writer of viewing the world through rose-coloured spectacles. But Rétif knew very well, of course, that the richer peasants, a non-negligible minority of the population, ate fairly well: an interesting factor related to the spread of improved eating habits among the masses. At five in the morning, which was breakfast time,[29] the master, his sons and his farmhands, before setting out to plough, would sit down to "a broth in which salt pork, cabbage and peas had been cooked, followed by a slice of the pork and a plateful of peas and cabbage". (Salt pork, or bacon, and cabbage was also the usual meal—using just one cooking-pot and one plate a day, and the services of a neighbour woman to wash up—consumed by a certain country priest, an abstemious one it is true, described in passing by Nicolas.) This meal at daybreak, eaten by the ploughmen, could also consist, on fast-days or when there was no bacon, "of a soup with onions and butter, followed by an omelette or hard-boiled eggs, or *herbages* (garden vegetables), or quite a good *fromage blanc* (a kind of curd cheese)". Thereafter the other meals, which were more in the nature of snacks, were: first, "dinner", taken at various times. (Ploughmen ate their "dinner" sometime in the morning, often taking it out to the fields; at eight o'clock on work-days and at ten on Sundays. It would correspond to what peasants and workers would today call a *casse-croute* or "ploughman's lunch", half-way through the morning.[30]) The next meal, still for the ploughmen, was *le goûter* (nowadays the name for an afternoon meal like the English tea), which took place at midday.[31] We do not know very much about the contents of these two meals: but we know that the "dinner" (or elevenses) of a Rétif child, who was sent to watch over grain spread out to dry on sheets in the fields, included some soup made with milk and a fresh egg.[32] As for the dinner and *goûter* of the ploughmen, "at autumn sowing time or in the spring, when one stays at the plough until four or five o'clock" it apparently consisted of "bread, some nuts and a piece of cheese to eat, and a *demi-setier* per man of wine in a wicker bottle, with an earthenware bottle full of water, because the fresh air makes one thirsty".[33]

A precious share of the bread and water, moreover, went to the horses: "at midday when it is time to eat, before giving the horses their oats", the ploughmen of Sacy "would pour water from their bottles into their hats, and crumble in some bread to make a sort of broth for the animals to refresh them". The horses would then munch hay and oats, while their masters "pick in hand, were breaking up clods of earth and taking out the stones, all the while eating their black bread". This refreshment, eaten at what we should call lunch-time, was therefore an extremely frugal meal, snatched on the job: the men went on breaking the ground with one hand, while eating bread from the other. If they were lucky, the break was cheered up with some nuts or a piece of cheese.

Frugality (but with more nutritional value than at midday) remained the rule at the third (or fourth) meal, taken in the evening. Supper was supposed to take place "at the end of the day in the summer and at eight o'clock in winter". Burgundian sobriety seems to have ruled: Edme Rétif, as the master of the house, was in theory the best provided with food and drink of all those who worked on his land; and yet he was well-known, like his grown-up sons, for having a small appetite. He was content in the evening to eat "a single fresh egg and about four ounces of bread, washed down with two glasses of a good old wine". On social occasions, supper might be more substantial. Nicolas one day found himself sitting down with three families of *suitiers*, smallholders who had joined forces to make a ploughing team of three horses. They were "celebrating the end of seedtime", and were therefore eating *petit salé*[34] (fat salt pork) "with a big jug of wine which was warming in front of the fire". To put on a bit of a show for the visit of the son of the revered Edme, their friend and benefactor, they served black pudding and fresh pork all round [35] ("Woman, fetch the black pudding"). Social distinctions as between the meals of smallholders and those of richer peasants, both based on eggs and salt pork or bacon, were marked by the colour of the bread: black for the humble, but white in Edme's house for the whole family, servants included. "For the bran, which is the coarsest part of the grain, is needed for the horses, for the daily-herd, for pigs being fattened and even ewes after lambing".[36] As this clearly indicates, in northern France white bread was not simply a luxury, indicating conspicuous consumption, but could also, on large farms, be the by-product of a by-product—in other words, white bread was the consequence of using bran as animal feed, one of the minor improvements in stock farming (especially of pigs) during the eighteenth century.

Among the richer members of rural society, well illustrated by the Rétif family, one has the impression, therefore, that meat consumption was adequate but by no means excessive. It was thoroughly chewed too, for the peasant, Rétif says, was as slow in eating as he was in talking and walking (and in the latter activity after all, it was prudent to save energy when one had to walk over the fields, sometimes for very great distances, before reaching one's workplace).

Having noted these descriptive references, we should now take our courage in both hands and try to quantify: in *La Femme du laboureur*, in which Nicolas portrays his father,[37] the latter estimates the meat consumption of the household at La Bretonne at four pigs per annum, each of which gives 120 lbs (60 kilos) of meat (not counting bones); plus ten adult sheep eaten at the time of the grape-harvest: 20–25 kg per animal; and five pounds of beef a week. A maximum in all of 600 kg of meat a year, shared among the twenty-two permanent residents at La Bretonne, to whom one has, of course, to remember to add the many seasonal labourers, who were very fond of meat, especially during the grape-harvest. The maximum ration possible for the permanent residents[38] (family and servants) would be about 27 kg each then, per annum, which is only half the figure for Paris in 1789, and for developed countries in the present day. And one should bear in mind that much of this meat ration was in fact bacon, which is richer in fats than it is in protein.

To the meat ration one should, it is true, add eggs (one per person per day in season, or 182 eggs per head per year); and dairy products. There were about twenty cows on the farm:[39] they provided nourishment for the family and especially for children; and they also, when sold at market, brought in an income in cash of 936 *livres tournois* per year.[40]

Taken together, the rations of eggs, dairy food and meat, while not eaten in such quantities as at present by a long way, were sufficient to protect children and farmworkers from serious under-nourishment. And again, at La Bretonne, the vitamin intake seems to have been adequate. When Edme Rétif came home dripping with sweat,[41] Barbe immediately gave him a "great silver goblet full of wine", and in addition "the refreshments he loved, dairy foods and fruits; for this good husbandwoman had managed, after a few years of marriage, to stock her garden with all kinds of fruits to tempt the appetite—strawberries, raspberries, gooseberries, pumpkins, melons, pears, apricots, blackberries, apples, chestnuts and fruits for cooking". And all the year round, salad dressed with walnut oil was served, less prodigally than today, perhaps, but regularly all the same.[42]

The development of gardens in the eighteenth century among richer villagers like the Rétifs, is of course nothing compared to the present. But it prevented deficiency in vitamins A and C, thus alleviating certain patterns of mortality for the members of the family and servants who ate at the same table. There was no need of an agricultural revolution for this. We know that "garden-mania" in the seventeenth and eighteenth centuries (as evidenced by books and almanachs full of instructions about sowing vegetables) was, long before "agromania", the sign of a gradual and profound change in habits that took place over a couple of centuries. The eighteenth century literally harvested the first fruits.

The cities and the middle classes, with their growing appetite for fruit and vegetables which brought about a change in eating habits, were beginning to have an influence on more advanced country-dwellers who, like Edme and Barbe, had frequented the towns in their youth. Nicolas liked fruit—he tells us that he often had indigestion after eating the refreshing blackberries which he picked whenever he could. And Barbe on baking days (twice a week) made spinach tarts for her family and leek tarts for the farmhands; hot cakes made with leavened dough for the vine harvesters and *galotes* made with a milk batter in early summer for the threshers.[43]

Barbe, who had been born into a family of vine-growers ready to accept the changes of the time, and who later worked as a maid in a bourgeois household, may have lived in Paris for a while. She became the wife of a petit-bourgeois and eventually of a rich farm-er. Hers was by no means an isolated case. Many other young women went into service in the town as a sort of transitional vocation before returning to the land. They came back to the villages with a veneer of manners newly-learnt from the (sometimes very modest) *élites* they had frequented. Such acculturation had demographic repercussions, through the improved quality of meals. Not, of course, that all the peasants of Burgundy in the eighteenth century were dining like lords or eating lashings of melon and spinach tart (the latter a rich source of iron, trace-elements and vitamins which are not destroyed by cooking). Such phenomena as I have described were strictly marginal—the margin was narrow and precarious, but it did make all the difference compared with the seventeenth century.

The same could be said of the clothing of country-dwellers, whether the Rétif family or the villagers of Sacy. It was certainly still much too light and did not protect the wearer from the cold. Nicolas notes somewhere that the peasants and dependents in his family, rich as it was, were habitually, "too lightly clad in cotton material" and all the more appreciative of the big fire at the back of the room which kept them warm in the evenings, "stoked up with bundles of oak branches, vine twigs and shoots and charcoal".[44] Edme the partiarch, himself, normally wore cow-hide breeches during the week, with a long smock or *gannache* of grey canvas. Only on Sundays did he change these shabby garments for his "suit of Elbeuf cloth, his muslin cravat and his shirt with silver buttons".[45] But in this respect too, and not only on Sundays, there was a gradual progress away from the patched garments of Le Nain's figures. When a young Rétif went (on foot) to Paris, he wore a grey linen smock, gaiters, no stockings and hob-nailed boots with a triple thickness of soles; in a bag on his back he carried "six coarse shirts, a few cravats, handerkerchiefs and cotton stockings for Sundays". Another time, the young man again had a knapsack, but this time, we are told, it was made of kid, to keep off the rain, and his spare linen consisted of "a clean suit, two jackets, two pairs of breeches, eight shirts and several pairs of stockings". When he had arrived or settled in Paris, Nicolas-Edme received a letter from his mother saying "My dear Edmond, I am sending you some silk hose, with homespun leggings, two jackets and the goat-hair coat, so that you will look smart on Sundays and holidays. I embrace you with all my heart, Your mother, Barbe". To this peasant girl who knew a little about city ways, loving her son meant seeing that he was well-dressed. Barbe Ferlet, the woman of the world, was as different in this respect from her late mother-in-law, Anne Simon, kind-hearted but slovenly, as a Greuze figure from a Le Nain.

Clothing brings us to hygiene, and to problems of differential mortality rates over time and in different social strata, problems that are raised but not answered by our anthropological study of the Rétif family. Nicolas is strangely silent on personal hygiene and the subject of washing. One suspects that not very much of it went on. The family no doubt gave off that specific aroma which one doctor of the period would have greeted with delight as "an agreeable scent in a healthy man".[46] The same doctor, incidentally, considered that the rich (who were—for reasons that had more to do with the desire to please than with hygiene—beginning to take washing more seriously and as a result were actually becoming healthier) "were, by cleaning themselves in this way attempting to drive out the odour of masculinity . . . in the name of luxury and soft living".[47]

The Rétif family fitted firmly into the social category of the "unwashed rich",[48] but they did have the singular virtue of changing their linen (two servant girls were kept to do the washing and mending). They were therefore protected against the vermin that attacked the poorer peasants in Burgundy.[49] Halfway between the flea-bitten poor and the already rational hygiene of the rich, the Rétifs were comfortably ensconced in the "odour of masculinity" of their own habitat. They correctly defined themselves as what they wished to seem: men of the middling class.

In the absence of washing, changing the linen was one of the cornerstones (not yet very firmly fixed) of their minimal personal hygiene. When in winter, Edme came home from one of his trips as tax-collector for the *seigneurie*, Barbe would be warming clogs (instead of slippers) for him with hot coals, so that he could thaw out his feet; and a glass of hot wine would be ready for him.[50] But when he came in soaked in perspiration at harvest-time, she would have "fresh linen for him, if he should be in a sweat[51] . . . She makes him change his shirt and put on a jacket". As for the two servant-girls,[52] "their mistress has them mend the linen and working clothes for the men". We do not know of any of the details of the laundering, but unquestionably Barbe was more concerned about clean linen than a housewife would have been a hundred years earlier. And another detail tells us something of the comparatively advanced hygiene of the Rétif family. Present-day medical historiography[53] has suggested that it was commonplace in peasant families, even during the latter half of the eighteenth century, to sleep in close proximity with others, on mattresses soiled by incontinent invalids, children, etc. But this was not so in the Rétif family. Nicolas, as a child, wet the bed until he was twelve. He was teased about it by the other boys, but also as it happened met with kindness, sympathy and enlightened understanding from his older sisters. There was never any question of another child sleeping with him, or after him, in a wet bed.[54] The ban was not considered at all exceptional or progressive. And it proves, if proof is needed, that 'modern' notions about hygiene in bedding had already penetrated to the heart of the provinces and to the milieu of the rich peasant. It is true that the ignorant, dirty and backward peasants of Brittany and Poitou, like the poorer inhabitants of Burgundy, were still on occasion sleeping on mattresses soiled by their bedfellows.

Meat, vitamins, clean linen and bedding are all visible factors which explain, at least in part, why the Rétifs and those like them had such a healthy record of births and deaths. Underlying all this was undoubtedly an acculturation process, ultimately derived from the urbanisation and indeed embourgeoisement which had reached even the green heart of the Burgundy countryside. Actual medical care, however, remained the privilege of the very highest *élites*; doctors were unlikely to condescend to treat the local stratum of well-to-do peasants. They in turn distrusted the medicine men of town or city.

Thanks to social imitation,[55] the Rétifs and their associates were copied, imperfectly perhaps, by other peasants of the neighbourhood less prosperous than they. Such efforts contributed to the improvement of the general lot, and to the greater survival rate of children. Paragons of rural virtues, Edme and Barbe were also models who set the pattern for their fellow villagers.

When children survive to adulthood, their parents have to establish them, or help or encourage them to find a situation. And Edme Rétif had ambitions to suit his paternal success. As the father of a large and surviving family, he was eager that his children should be both geographically and, if possible, socially mobile. The family estate, according to him, would accommodate only one of his sons. The other sons and all the daughters would have to seek their fortune—and why not in Paris? In Edme's opinion, the capital had the advantage both of its ancient and of modern connections: "there is more religion, but also more equality, better health (?) and science" there than in other cities. Edme was not fond of small provincial towns: according to him, a handful of local bigwigs— magistrates, noblemen or office-holders—were enough to ensure that the rest of the urban population was trampled underfoot or despised. "Either Paris or our village, my children; but better Paris than the village". As one who had joined the rural exodus but had never taken root elsewhere, Edme was ambitious that his children should succeed in the Parisian career he had failed to achieve in his youth. Was he typical of the thousands of fathers who encouraged their sons for better or (more often) for worse, to go to Paris in the age of Louis XV? That I cannot say. But one thing is certain—the Rétif children did, on the whole, follow the counsels of geographical mobility suggested by the paterfamilias in their conversations round the fire on winter evenings. These mobile children were doing no more than adapting to the new trends of the eighteenth century: in these modern times, unlike the seventeenth century, a comparatively large number of young people were tending to marry and settle down outside their native parishes. Of the fourteen Rétif children of whose careers we have some minimal knowledge, (including Edme Boujat, Barbe's illegitimate son, Nicolas' half-brother), only one remained firmly entrenched in the family home: Pierre Rétif, 1744–78, "farmer and merchant", who succeeded Edme on the La Bretonne estate. Five (four daughters and a cleric) settled in villages or small towns near Sacy, engaged upon or "marrying into" the secondary sector (cooper, blade-maker) or the tertiary (teaching in dame schools, village priest, housekeeper for the priest, or trade). Eight children, (including four boys, who benefited from the longer-range geographical mobility of the male) went to seek their fortunes in Paris or the Paris region. Five did not come back: Nicolas, a typographer who became a famous writer; a brother who became a surgeon; two girls who married (one a jeweller, the other a pastry-cook); and one girl who became a sister of mercy. Two others (one, the wife of a coachman who returned to the land, the other, a schoolteacher) came back to the district of Auxerre or indeed to Sacy itself; and the last, who was a notary's clerk in Paris, was killed in the army.

This, then, was a social and family milieu with a high rate of geographical mobility. Though the attribute of a minority, as compared to the population at large, such mobility was by no means untypical. One has only to think of the vast emigration into Paris from the open fields of the Paris basin between the sixteenth and the eighteenth century. What is remarkable is that the departures took place not in opposition to the father, but with his wholehearted consent and indeed at his request—which amounted to a command. (One might find something similar today in, say, Corsica, a place with a strong tradition of emigration.) All the Rétif migrants severed their connections with agriculture permanently (or in the case of one exception who failed, temporarily). None of them, not even the writer, whose extraordinary talent did not receive proper recognition until after his death, had any outstanding success. None of them was to experience, either in town or village, the exceptional moral prestige of the father, a recognized leader of his rural community. The flight from the land, as is well known, tends to engender frustration. When he leaves, the migrant can climb a notch or two up the social scale, simply by moving from country to town. But as a first-generation immigrant, he finds himself on the bottom rung of urban society, whereas his father may have been a man of importance back home in the village. That is why, as Edme found and Nicolas realized, the pleasures of rank gave way to calls for equality in big cities. In such calls there is an element of nostalgia for the community life, symbolized by the family gathering round the big farm table or even the indiscriminate paternal hidings.[56] Rétif in this respect echoes Rousseau, without the false consciousness.

It is the structure of this family gathering, or more generally the "domestic group" that we should now examine. In the peasant world as described by Rétif, the family is always something more than the family. Peter Laslett[57] was, of course, quite right to expose the myth of the extended patriarchal family, which had wrongly been considered the predominant pattern of rural life in past centuries. But the nuclear family, reduced statistically to four or five persons, was too small to meet the demands—the ploughing, for instance—of a farm of any size. The nuclear family, if taken too literally, can equally become a myth, a trap for the unwary demographer who is taken in by lists of names. In fact, among smallholders it was normal, for a family too poor to afford the luxury of a plough to link up, as we have seen,[58] with two, three or even four other households of *suitiers*. Pooling labour, tools and animals, they could between them provide a ploughing team which could then work the land of all in turn. The sons, or *suitons*, of the families

associated in this way would each take turns on certain days of the
week to serve the "cooperative" and lead the horses. Meanwhile
the head of the nuclear family, replaced by his son, could devote
himself to his own backyard, so to speak, and get on with the
threshing, vine-dressing and so on.[59] When seed-time or any other
major seasonal labour was over, all the members of a group of
suitiers would meet together to drink, feast and generally make
merry.

If one turns to a big farm like La Bretonne (which, with about 50
hectares, was fairly typical of the average *large* landholding in
France in the eighteenth century), one finds a domestic group of
necessity larger than the nuclear family. At La Bretonne, the group
was made up of a good score or so of individuals: the parental
couple, ten to twelve children (the eldest having already left the
nest), and the farmhands and serving-girls. The children's hierarchy
was naturally one of age, which determined each child's place at the
supper table. Of the farmhands and servants, the ploughmen had
most prestige, in order of seniority. Then came the vine-handlers,
who worked in the vineyards during the growing season, and
threshed the grain during the winter months. Lowest in the pecking
order at La Bretonne, which was as rigidly organized as the court of
Louis XIV (all those duchesses with their folding-stools)—came the
cowherd, the shepherd, and the two servant girls who brought up
the rear. Various other divisions cut across this little society,
quartering it like a coat of arms: there was a male/female division
for instance. Edme used the familiar *tu* to his sons and male workers, and they did the same in reply; but he used the more formal
vous when addressing his wife and daughters, and vice versa. And
there was an ethical grading of the various tasks to be done: in the
scale of moral values, the ploughmen, the NCO's of the farm squad,
were considered as having "better morals"[60] than the vine-handlers,
who in turn were thought superior in virtue to the young lads
assigned to animal management. Highest among these stood the
cowmen; then, really at the bottom of the heap as regards reliabil-
ity, the shepherd-boys, suspected of witchcraft and black magic;[61]
they were "even less honest and innocent than the cowherds". So
even the "natural world" could be good or not so good: there was a
step down from cereals to vines (and yet vines are very difficult
plants to look after); then again from the vegetable to the animal
kingdom; and finally down once more (reversing the order of both

pre-historic and historic chronology, as regards domestication or harnessing) from horses to cattle, and from cattle to sheep.

The descending order of prestige, depending on whether one worked with:		
cereals vines	vegetable products	
	animal products	plough-horses
		oxen, cows, sheep

At the very bottom of the scale as one reads it in Rétif—and on this point he was merely reproducing the conventional wisdom of his native region—came the servant girls, whose duty it was to "mend the linen and working clothes of the men". All the men, without exception, enjoyed greater prestige than the female workers on the farm.

Status could also be measured by a third distinction: the drinking of wine. Edme, at the age of twenty, drank only milk or water. He had been drinking wine only since becoming the head of the household. Children and young men did not drink wine. Young women, even during childbirth, were also obliged to abstain. Older mothers, over forty, were allowed to have "a few drops of wine in water". The workers drank *piquette*. And yet wine, in moderation, would have been beneficial to these villagers—instead of water which was often polluted (in the Languedoc, for instance, working men and women regularly and traditionally drank a litre of wine a day and were all the better for it). But in Burgundy, where less wine was produced than in the south of France, people preferred to put the wine aside for sale or for special celebrations like harvest, or simply to use it as a status symbol: wine for the paterfamilias, water for the women and young people, *piquette* for the labourers.

There was also a hierarchy of tasks around the farm. Children, Monsieur Nicolas when small for instance, went with the shepherd to help with the sheep, or on their own to see to the bees. "When a country child is seven years or more, he can be employed in the country on small tasks which do not require a great deal of strength.[62] He is given a cow to look after or a few sheep; he gathers kindling and grass to make bundles of firewood; his body gradually becomes accustomed to stooping; he practises carrying loads and acquires strength; at fifteen he is already a farmworker and at twenty-five he marries"—so says a report of the Year XIII on country children in the Paris basin.[63] The lot of the children in Burgundy was not very different. As for farmhands, we have seen that they had a clear division of labour, with ploughing as the noblest pursuit. Edme himself, as a member of the ploughing status group, was always up early to set his own hand to the plough and he was proud of it—whereas he did not himself touch his vines: he merely visited them to cast a master's eye over the work from time to time. This curious distinction is easily explained. Throughout the vine-growing area of the Paris basin, work in the vineyards was considered second-class labour—much more tiring and demeaning than ploughing which, if it did not exactly ennoble the ploughman, at least gave him some dignity.[64] In the present day, distinctions equivalent to those made by Edme can still be found. A rich farmer of today would by no means be ashamed to be seen driving his own tractor—on the contrary. But he has the fields of sugar-beet hoed by seasonal labourers, immigrants from Portugal, just as Edme left his vineyards to the vine-workers.

Female labour, too, had its own hierarchies. Of the girls who did the mending, one also helped in the vineyard, while the other "saw to the cows and milking", a duty traditionally left to women on all French dairy farms. Weeding and milking: once more (see the table earlier) we find women confined to these less noble areas of work. They were also subject to the possibly despotic power of their mistress, who was herself at the beck and call of the master of the house.

The duties of wife and mother were back-breaking, and can be summed up in the single word: food. The servant-girls—in contrast to all our bourgeois and petit-bourgeois traditions which would be out of place in this prosperous but rustic Burgundian farm—were exempt from all cooking and preparation of food, and were wholly occupied with the cows, the vineyard and the linen. The mistress of the house, with the occasional help of her daughters, was responsible for all the cooking, the gardening, and the orchard (where the children helped out). An additional burden was that she was also expected to feed at least some of the animals (Nicolas does not say how many). Edme the patriarch only had to do with the "higher" animals—dogs, horses and bulls, which in his estimation came immediately after the lowest farmhands and girls, and before cows, pigs, sheep, chickens and bees which were looked after by children and young cowherds. And indeed for Edme, his wife was both as it were an extension of himself and a sort of top-level animal (one day he remarked in all seriousness that an attack on his wife was just as bad as laying hands on his pet bitch.)

In this system, at once highly hierarchical and minutely structured, problems of resistance by the young to the old, by farmhand to employer or by women to men, hardly ever arise. The peasant family was not exempt from quarrels between mistress and servant,[65] or domestic scenes between husband and wife. The *curé* Meslier, who listened to people's secrets and collected gossip in his own village, noted more than one incident of the kind. But in the end, it was always the man who wore the trousers in his own house. Nicolas Rétif, just as much a male chauvinist as his father, speaks scornfully of the noblemen or rich bourgeois of Paris, who allowed the maid to tell the dinner gathering (and this incidentally is evidence of the greater feminism of urban society,[66] facilitated—it is true—by having servant-girls to do the cooking) "Madame is served". In Edme's household on the contrary, Madame did the serving. She was more of a maid of all work than a sex object.

Even if it was tending to disappear, or rather to lose its former predominance,[67] the patriarchal family model—Edme as paterfamilias with his back to the fire and his paunch against the table, watching over his household—remained a pattern very present in peasant consciousness. We know that Edme had twice lived in an extended family: first under his father-in-law, then with his mother. After Edme's death, Barbe Ferlet took over the sceptre of authority formerly wielded by her husband, and it remained in female hands till her death. The Rétif children, of whom one at least still lived with his mother, never permitted themselves to split up the inheritance during her lifetime. In this they were only conforming to the custom in Burgundy, which was to pass on successions undivided, a custom which the seigniorial judges as interpreters of tradition, strove with greater or lesser success to maintain. Matriarchy certainly existed, but it was never more than a transitional regime between two male reigns—a regency.

The power of the rich peasant, as head of the household, was expressed in particular in his dominion over children. Nicolas Rétif had a happy childhood, close to nature and mingling normally with the villagers and other children of his age. But from his earliest years, when he was fiercely scolded by his father, he was to retain the memory of a long-lasting aversion to men, and feelings of complicity with the gentler world of women—mother and sisters were more openly affectionate than the remote and admired father and the whip-happy brothers. In the previous generation, relations between Edme and his father Pierre had been much worse. For carrying on a modest flirtation without permission, Pierre beat his grown-up son till the blood ran; then, overcome with contrition, hurried into the kitchen garden to shed tears of remorse.

But in Edme's case, the upbringing of children by rewards and punishments was firmly ritualized. The father never beat a child in the heat of the moment. Punishment of his sons (for it was the mother who beat—or rather usually failed to beat—the girls) was only administered a week after the offence; and there might be a reprieve. But Edme, too, could persevere until there appeared blood, or at least "lasting marks". As for rewards and praise, a child could earn these by acting as watchdog against intruding animals: chasing away a wolf or someone else's stray cattle, or by showing kindness to a poor man or a gleaning woman—both of whom were thought of as images of Christ on earth.

More generally, the patriarch had the monopoly of speech. Mealtimes or evenings round the fire meant a virtually uninterrupted flow of talk from him—the volubility in inverse ratio to the volume of food (adequate but not over-plentiful). While the Rétif family was thus under the spell of the paternal monologue, everyone would be occupied with some work: the boys "sharpening stakes," the girls "cutting hemp or spinning," the mother "mending while she listened". Occasionally tiring, Edme might hand over to his wife for an interlude: she would recount something she had read (for Barbe was a literate woman, familiar at least with the pious or popular tales of the chapbooks); or some gossip about her female relations.

Edme's quasi-monopoly of words in his house was rarely challenged. The farmhands were local Saxiates, as dumb as doorposts, who never opened their mouths at La Bretonne except to talk about vines, ploughing, sheep or rat-traps. The Rétif children ate in silence, as was proper. Edme therefore fulfilled in some ways the role of today's mass media: he entertained the household rather like a one-man television set, giving weather forecasts and comments on agricultural affairs; passing on local news he had picked up in Auxerre, Vermenton, or Noyers; he was an indefatigable reader of both Old and New Testaments which, as he gravely informed his family, gave him a direct line to the Holy Spirit; he also delivered the longwinded prayers at bedtime, and was the folk singer who at Christmas time would strike up the old songs from the popular broadsheets. His verbal and musical repertoire came mostly from the chapbooks or similar literature represented, on the shelves of what it would be presumptuous to call his library, by the *Vieille Bible gauloise*, and the *Grande Bible des Noëls de France*, the family bible and hymnal, in editions piously preserved and dating back at least to the seventeenth century.

THE PATRIARCH'S RELIGION

Edme, a heavy-handed father and a patriarch in the Old Testament sense, was also a priest in his own household; of that there is no doubt. In France in modern times, or to be more precise in the twentieth century before Vatican II, religion has often appeared to be the province of women, who form the bulk of the congregation. In the secular civilization of the nineteenth and twentieth century, men have been on the whole fairly indifferent to religion, if not indeed freethinkers. But matters were rather different in the seventeenth century, and to a lesser extent in the eighteenth.[68] Religion, especially among country people, was—indeed perhaps predominantly—a male affair. Edme Rétif was the one at home who read the Bible, sang at Christmas or recited the Lord's Prayer, while his wife, on her knees by the bedside, combined private prayer and household duty by putting the warming-pan in the conjugal bed where her august spouse would take his ease.

What was true of religion was also no doubt true of ethics. It seems, at least in this corner of Burgundy so well described by Rétif, that the great age of moral, particularly sexual austerity which is to be found in the seventeenth century, and attenuated somewhat, in the eighteenth was principally the result of what might be termed male terrorism—paternal or fraternal. Had religion been more of a female affair it might have been less harsh. It was Pierre Rétif who, despite the timid remonstrances of his wife, Anne Simon, ("look what you have done to him!") thrashed his son Edme to remind him that outside a marriage arranged with paternal permission there was no legitimate occasion for sexual activity—even the most hesitant—on the part of a young peasant bachelor-boy. As for Edme Rétif, he impressed upon his children his taste for an Old Testament kind of religion, and an ethical code that was not to be trifled with. (But his wife Barbe, who had something of a past, represented the hidden principle of sin, now cloaked in latter-day piety, nourished on much devout literature which she consumed after the age of thirty.) Nicolas' brothers too beat the future author as a small boy, simply to teach him that morality could not be conceived of without repression, without the thrasher and the thrashed.

Underlying this austere code of ethics was of course a particular brand of Christianity—but which one? The author of an excellent introduction to *La Vie de mon père*[69] has suggested that Edme was in fact a Protestant: for he loved the Bible, was Hebrewphile, and skipped services and feast days. And it is true that one Rétif, of Auxerre, had been a Huguenot in about 1580—of course, at this rate half of France could have been called Calvinist at one time or another. The truth is, I think, more complex. As I see it, in the real-life culture of his time and his milieu, two paths were open to Edme Rétif's religious development—again the contrast between Nitry and Sacy, village of the Dondaines.

Over Nitry there still hovered, even in Louis XV's reign, the memory of the beloved *curé* Pinard,[70] who in the early part of the century had allowed the village boys and girls to play together and who tolerated races, dancing and wrestling matches on the school field. Pinard looked benignly upon the village school which was mixed—to the annoyance of the bigoted townsfolk from Noyers who had settled in the parish. The Pinard tradition was carried on, and indeed liberalized even further by *Messire* Antoine Foudriat, who became the curate at Sacy. With Edme, he embarked on civilizing the village.

Born in Burgundy and sent to the Collège Sainte-Barbe in Paris before returning to his native province as a *curé*, Foudriat, despite his inclination to chase petticoats, was adored by his parishioners, male and female. They would have gone through fire for him, and certainly stood up to the hierarchy on his behalf when anonymous letters about him were sent to the bishop. Foudriat was an atheist, a materialist and a disciple of Bayle—another *curé* Meslier, in short—but easy-going, fond of life, and with no communistic ideas.

He too tolerated the games and merriment of his parishioners. He considered his colleagues, who remained orthodox, as holier-than-thou brethren who deceived the people with their pedantries. He made no secret of his anti-clerical—anti-Christian even—opinions, which he professed openly round the supper table in front of Edme and other friends in Nitry.[71] The priestly office, which he continued to discharge, remained for him a means of educating his country flock, and of introducing them to a code of ethics rather than of binding them to a particular form of worship.

Edme was fond of Foudriat, who had found him a wife, and who continued to support him when the parishioners complained that their seigniorial provost absented himself too often from services, to deal with his magistrate's caseload. But in spite of their friendship, there was certainly nothing of the atheist about the patriarch with his prayers twice a day, his authoritarian recitals of the catechism and his interminable readings from holy scripture. The easy-going Christianity of Pinard may have suited him, but Foudriat's atheism was not at all to his taste. In fact Edme, through the intermediary of his two eldest sons by his first marriage— Nicolas-Edme, the parish priest of Courgis, and Thomas, a tonsured cleric who became a schoolteacher—was strongly attracted by the Jansenist model. Nicolas, as we have seen, considered Jansenism admirably suited to the stubborn idiosyncracy, which had to be overcome, of the Dondaine family. The Augustinianism of Thomas Rétif the school-teacher took a brutal and aggressive form. And the sermons of the *curé* of Courgis were interminable: they made the most pious listeners nod, and were too much for even the strongest bladders. All the same, there was something admirable about the courageous insistence of both these sons of Edme on developing the education of the peasants round about. And it was an education certainly superior to that dispensed by the uncaring teachers whom Nicolas remembered from the days when he sat in the classroom, with one eye on his work and the other on the hemp he was cutting or the vine-stakes he was sharpening. Thomas Rétif founded schools that were non-paying, though not mixed. Without knowing it, he was a living reproach to Voltaire and Rousseau and other apologists of rustic ignorance. His wish was that the poor should have access to that enlightenment of which they had originally been deprived by their lack of fortune, and that thus they would receive here on earth some equivalent of the beatific vision of the next. There is something moving, too, about the unbounded charity of the *curé* of Courgis who led a strictly ascetic life as a country priest, dining on bacon and cabbage soup. The two brothers between them made up, as it were, an image of forbidding austerity but touching piety, which Edme, proud of his eldest son who was set up as a model to the family, was not displeased to contemplate among his offspring. At the same time, the old man was, as one might expect, a careful politician. He took care not to upset the Jesuits who owned a farm at Sacy, and when necessary he gave their bursar sage advice on farming matters. But deep down, Edme was a Port-Royal man, and on the best of terms with the party of Mgr de Caylus, the ultra-Jansenist bishop of Auxerre.

Edme's religion did not take the form of frequent attendance at mass or taking the sacraments, but rather consisted of withdrawing to the privacy of the family for individual or communal meditation, and the reading of the holy scriptures—mostly the Old Testament— so much so that Edme, like many of the less sophisticated and even convulsionary Jansenists, had become personally pro-Semitic. The religion of the patriarch of La Bretonne was unquestionably cast in the mould of a kind of village Augustinianism, very widespread in France in the second quarter of the eighteenth century.

Michel Vovelle has shown that during the Age of Enlightenment, the path towards religious indifference and even the dechristianization of the countryside could either follow quite simply by way of gradual disaffection (the model implicitly proposed by the priest Antoine Foudriat), or it could take a course through the Jansenist preference for simplicity and opposition to the sacraments. This too, over a very long period, could encourage religious indifference, to the extent that it gradually transferred the practice of religion into the stifling cocoon of the family and household. Both models were evidently present during the years 1730–60 in the Rétifs' part of Burgundy, just as they were in Provence which M. Vovelle has studied. Edme may have hesitated a little before embarking on the road to godlessness indicated to him by *curé* Foudriat; then, under pressure from his older sons, finally settled for a solution tending towards Jansenist intimism. In this respect, Edme was a typical child of his century. He was already *en route*; he was becoming alienated from the Counter-Reformation, if indeed it had ever struck any roots into this part of Burgundy. He was moving, without realising it, towards what was still no more than the Jansenist attitude of the early eighteenth century and towards what would become—in straight succession to all that had preceded it—the indifference and dechristianization of the peasants of the Auxerre region in the nineteenth and twentieth centuries.

We can at any rate, thanks to Nicolas, see how a large peasant family and its head related to the cultural developments of the time. Not that every family in Sacy had as intense a spiritual life (based on the Bible) or an intellectual life (based on the chapbooks of the *bibliothèque bleue*) as we find in the Rétif clan. But because Edme was the seigniorial judge, and because he was regarded as a good and a just man, the Rétifs were taken as a reference group. Modest *suitiers* did not hesitate to send their sons to La Bretonne as trainee ploughboys, so that they could learn their craft and also so that they should pick up a little learning and morality. "In Edme's house, they will be given good habits; a smattering of culture; and spinach tart"—something of the sort, depending on their appetite for things material and things spiritual, seems to have been unwritten wisdom among the villagers of Sacy.

FAMILY SOCIALISM

The Rétif family was indeed taken as a model—not least in the visionary ideas of its hagiographical chronicler. Rétif, along with Morelly and a few others, is known as one of the precursors of Utopian socialism, which made its first appearance in the eighteenth century. It is tempting to think that the ideal social organization of the future, as suggested in *Le Paysan perverti*, was inspired by the democratic structures of the peasant community, functioning within the overall village environment, as Nicolas had seen it operate in his youth. Such a peasant community is itself conceived, by the historians who have interpreted Rétif in this sense, as a distant but plausible descendant of some kind of "primitive communism" (the actual existence of which, in historical or prehistoric times, is in fact questionable).

But in reality, although Rétif certainly professes Utopian socialism, the actual model for his futuristic Erewhon is not the village community at all, but quite definitely the close family unit. The imaginary "village of Oudun, composed of the R. family living together", (Nicolas's much more austere version of the Abbey of Thélème) is simply the family of the patriarch Edme, indefinitely

extended, expanding to occupy the space required by its own demographic increase; and fixed for all eternity on the model of the
fraternal units of the Auvergne and Morvan. Nicolas would have
been familiar with these since they were close both geographically
and chronologically to the groups of *suitiers*, of whom there were
large numbers to be found near the border of the Morvan.

After the deaths first of Edme, then of Barbe, we know that the
Rétif children proceeded to divide up their parents' property
among themselves: the division ended "badly rather than well". So,
in his fictional village of Oudun, Nicolas imagines that this division
does not take place: the brothers and sisters "decide" to live com-
munally on the very large Oudun estate which, with the births of
their many children and grandchildren, is soon transformed into a
village.

Over the territory of Oudun there floats the mighty shade of the
dead patriarch, who remains moral overlord. The customs and
habits of both La Bretonne and lower Burgundy, as Nicolas ex-
pressly stresses, are preserved in the communal refectory, where
bacon is eaten on weekdays and beef on Sundays. The four meals,
breakfast, dinner, afternoon snack and supper, are taken at the
sacrosanct times. Women and girls are forbidden wine, and have to
drink plain water, while the older men are allowed their half-bottle
of wine. The system of rewards and punishments so dear to Edme is
in force: the bigger boys play quoits, discus, and *paume*; the
younger ones play games of tag. Girls, who form part of the system
of rewards, dance with deserving boys to the sound of bagpipes.
Older women, on these occasions, sit and chat over their embroi-
dery. Something of the primogeniture rule seems to survive, since
the priests of this big family are chosen systematically from among
the elder sons of each of the couples in Oudun. These older sons—
who are a sort of collective embodiment of Edme Rétif—are regarded as the "communal fathers" of the village. Agriculture in
Oudun is not carried out on the pattern of a collective farm in the
strict sense: each couple has a hereditary and inalienable right to
twenty *arpents* of land, half in cereals and half in vines. Communism
is confined to consumption: it begins at the refectory door. Needless
to say, strict male supremacy is the rule: the choice of wife is entirely
at the discretion of the men. The annual election of two syndics, or
councillors, replaceable every twelve months, introduces a whiff of
democracy into the community. But the real power remains in the

hands of the sons of the patriarch's eldest son, and their descendants. The decision-making process therefore remains patriarchal by proxy, and not communal. Between this kind of socialism—male dominated, hierarchical and rural—and the bourgeois-peasant ambitions of Edme according to which "a man shall be absolute owner of his wife, children, houses, estates and money" there is in fact no contradiction at all, and here I part company for once with Gilbert Rouger, who has on this occasion allowed himself to be too influenced by modern, and in this case anachronistic categories of "socialism" and "capitalism". In fact the classic and rigidly authoritarian communism of Rétif is merely a device to confer eternal life on the mortal remains of Edme's father, by substituting for them the mystical body of his descendants, within which all the Rétifs would become *suitiers* together—and also, according to Rétif's sexual philosophy, an incestuous community.

One has to say that Nicolas, as one of his own letters proves, would have been bored to death in this rural Utopia dedicated to the memory of his father. He had therefore wisely decreed that those of the Rétif clan who had already been corrupted by the polluted atmosphere of the cities would automatically be excluded from the village of Oudun—himself in particular, naturally.

Nicolas' vision of peasant society is not, however, merely confined to an elucidation of the family unit, whether on a realistic or a Utopian level. The sociology implicit in his writing also embraces the village as a whole. Whatever its assumptions, in no way could Rétif's "sociology" employ categories such as stratification, whether into orders or *estats* (estates). Such categories, while valid on a general plane, do not make much sense in a village case-study (like Wylie's, for instance). In Sacy in 1730, there simply was no important landowner—let alone one who was noble, lay and resident. Even if one could be traced, that particular individual with his family would not be sufficient to account, on his own, for the noble or landowning *estate* within the community of Sacy. By the same token, the resident presence of the *curé* Foudriat in the parish by no means guarantees the local existence of the *estate* of the clergy. And indeed Foudriat, the parish priest, was a very complex individual: close to the peasantry with his cows and his vines, nearer the petty-bourgeoisie or the bourgeoisie in his life-style, and even to a sort of philosophical sub-*élite* of the Enlightenment through his atheism, supposedly inspired by Bayle.

Rétif does not altogether ignore the sociology of estates. But his version of it is closer to mythology (cf. Dumézil) than to the pains-taking monographs of, say, Mousnier. When Edme dies, the young village priest, Foudriat's successor, turns the late patriarch into a sort of folk-hero, directly in line with Indo-European archetypes. Edme, the curé says, has founded a dynasty of all three orders: *oratores*, *bellatores*, *laboratores*. He has engendered valiant war-riors, pious priests and good citizens of all classes (not to mention fertile women).[72] When Rétif does mention the division of society into three or four orders (including peasants) this is only with reference to the nation, not the parish, and it concerns a proposal to call the Estates General.[73]

PEASANT POWER

The sociology of the village, as Rétif records it, describes a magnetic field, so to speak, which is not fully provided by the diagram of the estates. It is more concerned with the structure and distribution of power, both above and within the peasant com-munity.

The most traditional and important power, for the Saxiates, was that exercised by the "three *seigneurs*" of the higher clergy: the bishop of Auxerre, his canons, and the Knights of the Order of Malta. The bishop and canons had jointly imposed an exorbitant and unpopular tithe: one sheaf out of twelve, plus one sheaf per *arpent*. (Fortunately this harsh levy did not operate on vines; which constitutes an even more pressing reason, if one were required, for the boom in vine production recorded in Sacy in the eighteenth century.

The Knight Commander of Saulce-lèz-Auxerre[74] on the other hand (as overlord of one-third of the territory) only asked for a very small quit-rent (*cens*) of 6 *deniers* per *journal* (an area correspond-ing to one day's ploughing), which the inhabitants appeared to endure without complaint. Once more, in the seigniorial structures of the *ancien régime*—lay, but above all ecclesiastical—one finds a clear distinction between the tithe, a heavy burden, and the *cens*, a light one.

These three ecclesiastical landlords were necessarily absentees. Their direct contact with the village was either episodic, or by correspondence. As a consequence, Edme became the *de facto* intermediary, the essential go-between for the powers that be and the parish. On this foundation he built his career as a magistrate and even, one might say, as a local politician. For although he was a representative of the *seigneuries*, the landlords' man, he was no man of straw. During his bondage under Dondaine, he had acted as the neighbourhood lawyer, thanks to his contacts, his modest fortune and his beautiful handwriting,—that of an educated peasant who had seen something of Paris. Then he moved up to become *procureur fiscal* (his function was to prosecute defaulters before the seigniorial judge). And eventually, taking up in Sacy the position his father had held in Nitry, Edme in turn himself became seigniorial judge, (seigniorial) provost of the village, tax-collector for the bishop of Auxerre and, to crown it all, the representative of the three *seigneurs*; thus combining within a single judiciary *seigneurie* the three separate powers (bishop, canons, knight-commanders) who between them ruled the territory of his *commune*. The striking thing about his appointment as judge-provost is that this was not an arbitrary decision by the Commander of the Order of Malta, but was earnestly pleaded for, on the death of the previous judge—who had been in office for forty years—by the *cens*-payers of Sacy themselves. A petition requesting his appointment and signed by twelve prominent inhabitants of the parish was presented to the Knight Commander. This indicates the ambiguous nature of seigniorial powers as they might be exercised by a rich peasant like Edme. They derived from the surrounding society, outside the village world; but they were also firmly in the hands—under the vague supervision, weakened by distance, of the absentee landlords—of a prosperous countryman who thus managed to reintegrate the judiciary *seigneurie* into his own world. It was all the easier for him since the *procureur-fiscal* (his successor in the post) was a nephew of Marie Dondaine, Edme's first wife: the *procureur* did whatever his uncle told him, without much interference from commander, bishop or canons.

At the end of this *cursus honorum* which made Edme first lawyer, then *procureur*, then judge, our hero had acquired the real power within the village: in his role as provost he was, like his predecessor, virtually irremovable; he dispensed justice according to his conscience and his acquired experience. The *seigneurie* allowed him to exercise his function as judge and arbiter as he pleased, so long as he regularly provided it with the receipts from tithes and other dues it required him to levy from the taxpayers of Sacy. It let him preside and dominate the community assemblies. The landlord had the rent, the provost had the power. Viewed from inside the village, the "little judge" takes on a very different character from that of the abstract figure he cuts in the seigneurial documents. These reduce him to his humble post as collector of taxes: they do not give an adequate picture of his power and prestige. Edme wisely avoided fleecing those to whom he dispensed justice and who were his masters' subjects, in order to retain their confidence. Acting in collaboration with the *curé*, his friend and accomplice, he looked into all family affairs; at his little tribunal, he would arbitrate between mother and sons. While respecting the time-honoured local laws, in particular the redemption of a family's estates, he would from time to time (privileged as he was with inside information about the financial fortunes, or misfortunes, of his fellow-citizens) buy up the odd piece of land that was part of some transaction. He had no wish, nor was he powerful enough, to destroy by land-grabbing the village community under his leadership, from which he himself came, and which was his power base. But he lent money to his fellow-villagers, using such small loans as a means of power and influence, rather than as a pretext for usury. Edme, pillar of the community, eventually built up, in his own village where he sat in judgment on Sundays and feastdays, and in the villages round about as well, a reputation as an arbiter second to none. He was flattered by the Jesuits and cajoled by the Jansenists. The representatives of the *Intendant* (if not the *Intendant* himself, as Nicolas boasts) effectively released him from the major part of his taxes, as a father of fourteen surviving children (in Spain, he would have qualified as an honorary nobleman, one of the "knights of the numerous family"). And on Sunday evenings, supreme token of local esteem, the farmyard at La Bretonne would be in chaos: the newly arrived hens and chickens and poultry of all sorts, offered as gifts to the judge, would be trying to find themselves a perch.

Edme was not the only leader in the village; far from it. Nor was he the only repository of local power: he had to share this with several others, whence, no doubt, a certain amount of friction. As the landlord's representative, he was of course automatically chairman of the parish assembly, summoned by bells after high mass on Sundays. But here he had to contend with the other parochial officials: they had been democratically elected by the villagers, not simply appointed by an overlord. Among such more "democratic" officers were the two syndics, elected, like Roman consuls, for twelve months; the parish clerk; the *messiers* (crop-watchers); the communal stockman; and the *taille*-collectors. So Edme's power was nibbled at from below; and could in the last resort be challenged from above—since any decision of importance by the parish assembly had to be approved by the *Intendant*.

We can guess at some of the conflicts: while extremely deferential towards his own overlords (ecclesiastical), Edme waged a legal battle against the neighbouring (lay) landlord. He embarked upon a lawsuit to recover some woods belonging to the community of Sacy, which had been seized by the ancestors of the present incumbent. Having won the case, the Sacy villagers used the produce from the wood to build a communal fountain, which provided purer water than the wells, for all the villagers (a hygienic measure typical of the period). Edme was indeed adroit in his use of carrot and stick in his relations with this landed gentleman: in return for the wood, which reverted to the parish, he offered a special pew in church to the lord who had lost the case.

Apart from such external quarrels, which indicate certain limited possibilities of challenging the seigneur, various internal conflicts raged beneath the surface of village life. They are only obliquely referred to by Nicolas, but even so they indicate a certain pattern of social forces within the community, a pattern by no means unique in northern France. Very similar phenomena figure in Georges Lefebvre's *Les Paysans du nord*.[75] The collectors of the *taille* in Sacy, representatives of the corporate community (that is, the mass of middling peasants and richer *suitiers* who formed the electorate), several times tried to tax Edme Rétif, the landlord's man and village elder. At the same time, striking at the poor as well as at the rich, they also extorted taxes from the poorest of the villagers. Edme's fiscal tactics were the exact opposite: first, he obtained exemption directly from the *Intendance* as a father of fourteen; secondly, and with the support of the parish priest Foudriat, he secretly helped the poorest peasants, overtaxed as they were by the collectors, to pay their *taille*.

Studies of the distribution of power in a rural community under the *ancien régime*, falling as they do halfway between anthropology and political science, are not exactly plentiful, and we are on uncharted territory here. Let us say then that as an anthropologist,

Nicolas Rétif presents us with a more complex model of his community than one normally finds. Against the power of the local elite (the seigniorial magistrate, the rich farmer, the parish priest who, in Rétif's Utopia is supposed actually to replace the seigneur) are ranged, in a discreet set of counterbalances, the more temporary and less spectacular powers of that middling class which provides the municipal officers. And even the very poorest of all (humble labourers and vine-tenders, impoverished *suitiers* and beggars) are called upon from time to time to furnish the rich with a political base, as well as forming a clientèle for charity. Let us for the moment then put aside the over-simple picture of a peasant community exclusively dominated by the richest farmers, or even carved up by the bourgeois of the towns (as if the village were not essentially a *community of inhabitants* in an agrarian world where the low productivity of labour makes expropriation possible, but precludes the expulsion of individuals). This image has too often been accepted by historians of rural society. Rétif's anthropology, which is more authentic than many of the documentary records (often tampered with) of municipal debates, replaces it with a three-fold stratification: at the top are those who wield power in the absolute sense (group A); then come those who have *some* power (group B, the municipal or intermediary stratum); and lowest of all those with *no* power, the poorest stratum (they may nevertheless be used as a clientele by group A in the course of a joint conflict over taxes, with A and C opposing B).

Towards the institutions of the *ancien régime* and the surrounding society, this peasant power, subtly distributed within the village, maintained an ambivalent attitude: distrust of the nobility went hand in hand, in the few villagers who did accede to the power *élite*, with the snobbery of inventing titles for themselves (which may have been a by-product of downward mobility, the memory of which was dimly kept alive in family tradition, dating back several generations). The Rétifs often described themselves as *de Montroyal*; Anne Simon as *de Coeurderoy*, Barbe Ferlet as *de Bertro*, and Nicolas for good measure called himself Rétif *de La Bretonne*. More understandably, these local power-holders were sullenly hostile to the oppressive tithes and to encroachments upon common woodland, while accepting the *cens* which was not a burden. Seigniorial justice, despite its feudal and even ridiculous aspects, in fact delegated a degree of power to certain peasants; it was more willingly tolerated by both judges and even by plaintiffs than might usually be imagined.

Peasant power, fairly widely distributed throughout the villages, received a further boost from the opportunities of communication through dialect or patois, and from the patterns of kinship within a parish or group of parishes. Rich or poor, whatever the degree of the actual relationship, knew that they could almost always say to each other: "You and I are of the same blood". Urbanization, in every sense of the word, was however threatening peasant power, to the extent that the seigneurs were tending (and this happened for the first time in Sacy after Edme's death) to transfer the function of judge from the rich peasant to more educated "experts" who came from the small towns. These experts, to the great regret of the villagers who preferred to keep secrets in the family, began settling affairs concerning the peasants without consulting them.

Edme Rétif, then, represents a situation comparatively favourable to peasant power: in a province where the seigniorial presence was very evident, certain groups within rural society had nevertheless succeeded in gaining access to some of the control levers of an institution which oppressed them. Elsewhere the situation was often less favourable for peasants. The fact remains that *some* power was wielded by the 20 million or so country-dwellers apparently vegetating in eighteenth-century France. A good deal depended on the way in which the State, *Intendants*, officials, etc., chose to approach the power of the peasants, and to order their relations with it: under Richelieu and Mazarin, this approach had been absurdly brutal. It gradually became more intelligent from the time of Colbert, whose administration often took the part of the communities against their highly-placed creditors in *parlements* and elsewhere. There were, in fact, plenty of men like Edme Rétif in the French peasantry before 1789. They acted as a link, an unavoidable bridge: honest brokers between peasant society, including the very poor, on one hand, and society at large (State, Church, nobility, notables, etc.) on the other. The Revolution did not take such "honest brokers", the local leaders, by surprise: Edme, like almost all French peasants, nursed some deep-seated anti-fiscal grudges, passed on to him down the ages.[76] He sometimes concealed them under earnest exhortations to others—entirely platonic, since he was exempt from the *taille* himself—to pay their taxes. If he had lived to see the French Revolution, which he did not, the patriarch of La Bretonne would probably have welcomed it, once the first reaction of shock and scandal had passed. One can easily imagine him buying up the *biens nationaux*. In other words, the *seigneurie* in Burgundy, as in England, was a good breeding-ground for rural capitalists. They prospered under its wing, but were quite capable, if need be, of taking care of themselves and surviving after it collapsed.

Having followed the Rétif family and its head, the working peasant proprietor, on a tour of the problems of society, family and power in a French village of the *ancien régime*, we shall now turn briefly, still with the sharp-eyed Nicolas as a guide, to questions of love and sex, folklore and local culture.

MORALS, FOLKLORE AND CULTURE

First of all, how did people make love in Sacy? ("Make love", that is, in the sense explained by Trévoux' *Dictionary*: "to seek to please someone and to make oneself loved by another: to *make love* to a girl or a woman is to seek her hand in marriage").[77]

Monsieur Nicolas, a bright and precocious little boy, very aware of himself and of others, was well acquainted from the first with the innocent paradise of childish love; and problems of infantile sexuality did not escape him. This was given free reign, through being allowed to observe or even take part in sexual activity, precisely because in a child it was not taken seriously, whereas young people were kept under extremely strict supervision, since for them sexual activity could have serious consequences. Monsieur Nicolas recalls having been present, as a very small child, while a young married couple, peasants who were neighbours of La Bretonne, engaged in a sexual flirtation, hardly stopping short of intercourse, before his eyes and without the least embarrassment. As a child, under orders from his older sister, herself barely into her teens, he had simulated copulation with a little girl in the vineyard at Sacy. He also admits that he let his hands wander more often than he should have under the dresses of the village girls, who kissed and pampered him,[78] showering him with caresses after mass on Sundays. They were giving him a generous foretaste of the favours which they could only bestow on the young men of the parish sparingly and with prudence.

But this age of innocence did not last long, and it would be wrong to interpret it as a sign of the freedom of morals in the countryside— it points rather in the opposite direction. After fifteen or sixteen, the facts of life were taken more seriously. Relationships between young people of oppostite sexes became cautious; in high summer, Fanchon, who is "choking with thirst" feels she must apologise for asking water from a boy, although she knows him: "Pardon me, Edmond, but I was so thirsty". Rites of passage, both masculine and feminine, marked the transition to adolescence and the beginning of the post-pubertal age. All village girls aged fifteen went, on special feast-days, to the *offerte*, in church, and gave their coin (*liard*). Nicolas mentions in this connection "the custom in ancient Sparta when all young girls who were fully grown were made to dance naked in the middle of a circle of all the young men seeking a bride". Sacy was not quite Sparta in this respect, though the intention was no doubt the same. The "fully-grown" young girls of Sacy would, after the *offerte*, file slowly out of the nave (reserved for women) while "the men of the village standing in the choir and the transepts" could watch the file-past of local virgins, rather as if they were judging a beauty contest. Under the piercing eyes of the males, the girls went one by one to place their *liard* on the altar and to kiss the paten. The parade was an occasion for experts and interested parties to work out at a glance the medium-term prospects on the marriage market. Although this ritual took place in church, it has a touch of folklore about it that is incongruous in a holy place. The Jansenist priest of Courgis, Edme's eldest son, was aware of this. He stripped the premarital marchpast of its meaning and usefulness by restricting "the right of making an offering" to girls who were taking communion that day. This was one way of gradually uprooting folklore; for Thomas Rétif, a rigorist priest and a faithful disciple of Jansenist theology in this respect, was not in favour of frequent communion.

Fifteen, then, was the age of the *offerte* for girls; for the boys of the Auxerrois, it meant the pilgrimage to the Mont Saint-Michel, a Mecca of masculine puberty: 142 leagues there and back.

Then, between the ages of fifteen and twenty, after this ritual initiation by travelling to the famous Mount-in-the-Sea, the boys found themselves in a sort of closed group of young males; during this time, any pre-marital flirting with the girls on the other side of the fence was strictly limited, if not forbidden. At twenty there was another ritual: calculated to postpone the inevitable weddings: in return for a subscription of one *livre tournois*—which, given the shortage of money in the district, might mean a whole year's labour and painful saving, the young man of twenty gained admission to the group of "older boys". After nine in the evening, the hour of the bat, the werewolf and after-dinner fun, they were allowed to go "courting the girls". Even here there was a strict ritual, at least in theory (one supposes that in practice there were plenty of departures from the norms laid down). Each boy would choose (or where there was rivalry, draw lots for) the village girl whom he intended to woo. Choice, as almost always in Sacy and in Rétif's little world, was a male prerogative—not that that necessarily prevented a shrewd girl using subtle means, such as a certain graceful pose when taking communion in church, to steer the choice in a certain direction. Once he had staked his claim, the boy would use all manner of tricks, expedients, and transparent manoeuvres to gain entrance, say, to the cowshed where his beloved worked, if she was a dairy-maid, and finally to the house where she lived. If there were no hitches, marriage would be mentioned in the second year and perhaps celebrated in the third. The girl's parents were free at any moment to intervene in the courtship, initiative belonging to the father, who might undertake to bring the affair to a dramatic end by thrashing the ex-future son-in-law. When the path of true love ran smooth, kisses would be exchanged on Sundays. Most girls remained chaste until marriage, emphasizing their determination on this point by a pilgrimage to Sainte-Reine d'Alise, patron saint of local maidens.[79] The entire ritual corresponds to a ceremonial, or an "orchestration", as it were, of the system of late marriage, accompanied by premarital chastity, a system which has now been quantified and described in detail by historical demographers. Another effect of the system was that, within the endogamous community of the village, it prevented socially undesirable matches—say between the daughter of a rich tenant-farmer of a nobleman's estate and (heaven forbid) a former lackey who had been a servant in town, or the son of the bakehouse tenant (who would be considered the "tenant's tenant", and therefore very low in the ranks of marriageable persons, living as he did in a most undesirable environment for an aspirant to the hand of a prosperous peasant's daughter). It is indeed on occasions when such mésalliances are embarked on within the village that signs of deviancy from the system appear, such as the infrequent illegitimate births where there was no prospect of a solution by marriage.

Another aspect of the courtship ritual was that it reinforced the idea that a girl was a precious piece of property which the would-be sweetheart or suitor had to seize or attack in some way: to demonstrate his love, the *grand garçon* might roughly grab his beloved's ring or bunch of flowers, or the basket of fruit she was picking. Only refined, romantic and town-bred lovers *gave* their sweethearts flowers or fruit, instead of taking them from her. Somewhere between the rape of the Sabine women and the American panty-raid, these would-be or partial ravishments of the village girls enacted by the young males of Burgundy could not prevail against the rule that the girl in question "can only be given away to her suitor by another man", her father, or if necessary her brother. The infrequency of premarital conceptions is indeed explained, not so much by any considerations of religious morality, as by the fact that the fathers of unmarried girls were jealous guardians, watching with eagle eyes over their daughters' chastity and even over their sons' virtue. At the least sign of an illicit seduction, like so many Cerberuses they reached for their cudgels. The chastity of the *ancien régime* was based on the maxim "Lock up your daughters." And a possible explanation of the slight liberalization of morals at the end of the eighteenth century is a degree of relaxation in paternal vigilance.

At the end of the courtship comes the formal request by the future son-in-law for the daughter's hand in marriage: it is celebrated with a meal—perhaps a bacon omelette, some cream cheese and a half-glass of Chablis or mulled wine; and often by a promise by the young man that he will live under the father-in-law's roof and work for him. A formal betrothal is followed very shortly by the wedding: this is a feast such as Flaubert described in *Madame Bovary*: a real banquet with bacon, sirloin of beef, goose, turkey, jugged hare, and even leg of fox, "a tasty morsel when it has been hung up for two weeks out of doors in frosty weather, from a plum tree"—all eaten to the sound of bagpipes and recorders. The traditional dances of Burgundy were invariably part of the wedding feast: they had the added charm of allowing a close embrace every few minutes; the young girls "spring like zephyrs" and their red petticoats "billow like parasols". The bride wears black—the same dress that she will wear for mourning or when she is laid in her coffin. After marriage there will be no more dancing for her: "when she marries, a woman gives up everything to immerse herself in the sorrows and hardships of the household: her only music is the crying of little children, her only dancing when she dandles them; her conversation is to chatter with them as she carries them in her arms wherever she goes". In short, the laughter and games, after fulfilling their function which is to tempt the young girl into a suitable match, stop short after the wedding: there is no further use for them. Rétif's Utopia is just as firm on this point as was real life in Sacy.

But there are other kinds of amusements and games, less closely tied to the necessities of marriage, though they may make humorous references to the philosophy of conjugal life: that is folklore in the very general sense of the term—songs for instance, children's or young people's games, stories and folktales.

Nicolas mentions several country songs commonly sung or, rather, bellowed in Burgundy: a young girl's love-lament, a hymn to the nightingale, a ploughboy's *Deo laus*, which is in fact a rather pagan ode to the sun, expressed in dialect. Then there are the canticles from the great *Bible des Noëls* or some such book, religiously passed on from father to son, as in Edme's family. These popular songs of Sacy and Nitry seem to date back in general to the sixteenth century, an age that witnessed both the formal establishment of customs, and a renaissance on new lines of peasant music and folklore.

Children's games were often explicit and of almost perverse crudeness: the "maiden" for example was a game which disappeared when a stricter priest succeeded Foudriat: the group of boys who amused themselves this way had to try to kidnap a girl who was hidden and not allowed to move ("in the tower"). After being captured, married and delivered up to her husband, she is told that she will be "stripped like the rose, shaken like the damson tree, eaten like the fieldmouse and withered like the windflower". The game of "wolf" was like the maiden the other way round: the wolf was tied up in the dark and not allowed to move: he had to guess what kind of clothes a girl was wearing, to win the reward of being able to feel them for himself. Again, the strict *curé* Jolivet who took over from Foudriat forbade the game of wolf (*le loup*) although it had been played in Sacy "for 500 years". (Apparently, then, some of Sacy's folklore was, by the eighteenth century, in the course of disintegrating under the double impact of militant Catholicism and latter-day Jansenism.) Another game known as "the step-mother" enacted not the preliminaries of marriage nor the superficial appearance of rape, but the tribulations of a marriage severed by death, that of the mother, and the entrance at the beginning of the game of a cruel step-mother: she persecutes her poor daughter and makes her eat mouldy bread. In lighter vein, the swing on which boys and girls took it in turns to be pushed (*brandillé*) might also fall foul of strict moralists, especially when scamps like Nicolas, now a big boy, tried to make the girls fly up high enough to provide "very immodest views".

Finally "the goat" (throwing sticks at a target) and quoits were considered to be purely sporting pastimes by Nicolas. When he himself was a child he had the rather exceptional privilege[80] for this country village of owning some toys: a Paris coach and a cardboard horse.

It is particularly interesting for the sociology of peasant culture to study the folktales from far and near which were in circulation in Sacy; and to study, too, the story-tellers and the audiences. Two social levels can quite clearly be seen in this oral literature known to the Saxiates.

The basic level is that of traditional folklore, passed on by women, whether young mothers or old grandmothers; and by those strange members of the farm workforce, the shepherds. Talkative, unlike the silent and unresponsive labourers, the shepherds would tell Nicolas, while they were minding the flocks, about their adventures in love, and the violent reactions of the father or brothers of the girls they had seduced. They also told stories of "enchanters, of ghosts, of pacts with the devil, of the excommunicated who turned into animals and ate people, and stories of shepherds who could do magic: one man made himself some wings and flew like a hawk".

From the never-empty magic barrel of oral literature came the ghost stories, told by old women and listened to by the young, on the evenings when everyone sat stripping hemp, with only the burning hemp-straws for light. One of the most frequent themes is that of a ghost in animal form. If some man (or woman) had been dishonest when alive (a peasant who had cheated the clergy of tithes, for instance, a miller's wife who robbed the poor by returning short measure, or perhaps a woman who had secretly sold her soul to the devil in exchange for riches or pleasure) the devil would come to claim the body of the guilty person, dead or alive. If the priest, who of course had his book of incantations to drive away the devil, did not intervene, the wrongdoer's body would be transformed into a part-time or full-time beast. A man might become a werewolf, indestructible and with a savage appetite; a woman, a snake or the devil's black mare. Intervention by a man with the slightest bit of courage would break the spell—which in less serious cases turned out to have been a practical joke (the story of the robber dressed as a ghost). These stories from Sacy, and the Morvan and Burgundy in general, with their unvarying structure, seem to me to bear out with convincing crudeness Propp's[81] theory that the original purpose of the folk-tale was to narrate the journeys of souls after death, in some corporeal or transmigratory form. In spite of vague attempts by the Church to appropriate these stories (cf. the tale of the tithe-stealer who was turned into a werewolf for his crime), their flavour is much more pagan and diabolical than really edifying and Christian. The Christianity is no more than a veneer. Sometimes they were incorporated into true stories, macabre in themselves perhaps, but even more macabrely interpreted. Jean Piot, the son of Jean Piot the blacksmith, had cursed his parents, "sworn" at his mother, and beaten his two sisters, who had taken refuge in their mother's arms. Some time later he died and was buried under the wall where girls came to pick violets in spring. One day they found some of Jean Piot's teeth in the ground over the grave—teeth that had bitten the breast that suckled them. One of the girls was foolish enough to tell the parents who immediately fell lamenting: "Hola mon gieu, noute poure gasson ôt-i damné" ("Ah, *Mon Dieu*, our poor boy is damned"!)

In the churchyard where the dead were buried in shallow graves, to make their resurrection easier; in the ghost stories round the fire at hemp-cutting; or late at night at La Bretonne, when—after Edme had gone to bed—the shepherds took the chance to tell Nicolas stories to make his hair stand on end, the village of the dead remained very close to the village of the living, embracing it in a tight clasp. And the devil was never far away: as a change from minding his sheep, Pierre Courtcou, who had a taste for obscenity, tried to conjure up the Evil One with a recipe from the chapbooks, like the shepherds of Brie.

This, then, was the basic bedrock of oral literature in the village, whether cried aloud or whispered from ear to ear. But there was another cultural level, higher in tone and more formal. Its relationship with the older, underlying folklore of the people was not always an easy one.

This second level is to be found among the more educated peasants like Edme; and also among the young notables of the village, who might have been away to school. Among these were the son of the *bailli*, the son of the notary, and the *curé*'s nephew, who sometimes dressed up as ghosts to mock the ghost stories and frighten old women. Or they would tell unlikely tales about a man who turned into a donkey. Edme himself told stories that came, not from the great store of folk memory, but from popular literature, i.e., the chapbooks, like *Robert the devil*. His stories were distinctly more "modern" than those previously mentioned: they had their origins not in some vague antiquity but in the literary Middle Ages. The old wives' tales at hemp-cutting were several thousand years behind high culture; Edme was only about five centuries out of date. Children like Nicolas, who liked to be scared, in any case preferred the obscene or tall stories told by the shepherds to the more staid adventures narrated by the more educated patriarch.

Still at this higher level, we come to the question of "libraries"—a word that seems absurdly pompous in this context: but it was not as rare as all that for peasants—including Edme Rétif, his father and even his stolid father-in-law Dondaine—to possess, or to have possessed, a few books. Mostly these were works of piety—the *Hours* or *Offices* or *Lives of the Saints*. Those who owned such books were participants in a Christian culture which might be more or less Jansenist, depending on the preference of their parish priest. They had turned their backs on superstition and folklore, but knew nothing of Latin civilization, of the classical agronomists for instance, Cato and Varro, or of secular history. Edme and his fellows were totally ignorant of such things. He did like to impress his wife though—like a priest who enjoys making his rustic congregation open their eyes wide at his sermons. He solemnly told Barbe, making it all up as he went along,[82] how the Roman Emperor subdued the Cappadocians (hidden meaning: Me, Emperor—you, Cappadocian). Edme had also compiled a so-called experimental calendar, after the fashion of the almanacs. It was supposed to forecast, for himself and the other vine-growers of Sacy, the droughts and spring frosts, the best grape-harvests, and how many casks to buy. His culture thus embraced meteorology, which like other peasants, he worked out for himself.

The third cultural level, that of the Enlightenment in the full sense, was virtually absent from the village. The fable of the fat pig and the lean pig in any case warned the peasant, even when he was rich, not to set himself up as the equal of the nobles, who would mock him for his lack of sophistication. Foudriat alone read

Bayle—but that was in the enthusiasm of his college days at Sainte-Barbe in Paris, or in the silence of his country retreat. Did Foudriat's atheism infect any of the country folk of Sacy or elsewhere? There is nothing in Rétif's writing, where details of this kind are usually abundant, to suggest any evidence for such a view. It might be noted that Level 3 (Enlightenment) in the person of Foudriat, good-naturedly accepted Level 1 (traditional folklore) while Level 2 (culture of local *élite*), though closer to popular folklore, displayed an unmistakable aversion for it. "Show me your nearest neighbour and I will show you your worst enemy".

9

The Crisis and the Historian[1]

In what follows, it is not my intention to refer directly to the future, or to the present. I shall be more concerned with the "past historic". In any case, it seems to me that knowledge of that past can contribute to an understanding of present-day events, or indeed those of the future. Viewed in this sense, the historian's perception of the present crisis can without difficulty, though I make no claim to be a Bossuet, turn into a Treatise on Universal History.

Another preliminary remark: the word "crisis" has such a general meaning that it is becoming overworked—and as a result, losing its usefulness. So, I should like to restrict my analysis of the concept of "crisis" to the economic or demographic senses generally accepted (in history). This restriction need not rule out a few glances at future developments in our culture.

To an economic and/or demographic historian, a "crisis" always represents some kind of break—a negative, short-lived phase within a long-term trend or tendency. It may refer to a slowdown, a period of stagnation or a collapse, during a general period of growth. Or it may correspond to a (reversible) decline during a period of stability. Such phenomena (slowdown, stagnation or collapse) can, of course, affect prices; but they also, sooner or later, affect production and other indices of activity. The crisis, in these various cases, may be set in motion in several ways: perhaps by a fall in prices, which discourages producers and is then reflected in other elements in the economy—as was the case in 1929. And in earlier periods, one thinks of the crisis caused by the low wine prices during the 1780s, described by Ernest Labrousse, or the deflation under Colbert during the 1660s and 1670s. We might note that this deflationary type of crisis has become very much more serious in recent times, since 1929. It was much less harmful in the seventeenth and eighteenth centuries, when it was worrying, but not tragic. In those days (and in a context frequently characterized by wars and epidemics) it was the *bad harvest*, or series of bad harvests that created the most dramatic "crisis" situations (cf. the *cereal deficits* during the Wars of Religion, the Fronde, or the famine years

270

at the end of Louis XV's reign). It will be noted that the present crisis (1973–75), seems to have been connected, at least in part and in the early stages, to a temporary, perhaps artificial, but undeniable shortage in the supply of oil. This shortage provided the initial stimulus (it was far from the only cause, of course) for the present worldwide depression. In this sense, the post-1973 depression is not a case of insufficient demand, as in 1929, but of a blockage (if only a temporary one) in the oil supply. Paradoxically, this is something it has in common with the old-fashioned subsistence crises, which were also the result of shortages of supply (cereals, in their case). If the forecasts of the Club of Rome turn out to be correct, we are likely in the future to move increasingly towards crises caused initially by a shortage of supply in one or other strategic sector (food, oil, fertilizers, phosphates, raw materials of various kinds): in other words, back to the old régime.

Whether caused by deflation or by shortages, the various types of crisis, seventeenth-century or twentieth-century-style, are translated into an absolute or relative fall in the *gross product* of the society as a whole. Such decline in gross product may last no more than a year; or more seriously, for several years; or even in very long-lived crises, for decades, and sometimes a century or more.

Moreover, the crisis may conceivably, though not in every case, affect population numbers. In other words, the economic crisis may be prolonged, or reflected, or exacerbated, by becoming a demographic crisis. The connection is plain to see at present in western society: the depression, originating in 1973–74, has accentuated the decline in the birth-rate—a decline that had begun independently of the depression. A demographic crisis can also be caused initially by non-economic factors like epidemics.

In many cases, a demographic crisis is reflected in an increased mortality rate, resulting from famine and/or war or pestilence; or possibly from temporary impoverishment which may have led to physical deprivation, as in the most recent economic crises, and in others in the past. Alternatively, demographic crisis may be the consequence of the voluntary limitation of population in societies using various forms of birth control; or it can be caused by a high incidence of late marriage or celibacy.

I shall now move on to a chronological study of crises, looked at both in the long-term perspective of possible typologies; and in the short-term circumstances of their dramatic appearance.

1. CRISES BEFORE THE EIGHTEENTH CENTURY

a. *Crises Extending over Several Centuries*

It is essential for our purpose to distinguish between several different time-scales. Certain "crises", which lasted for over a century or for several consecutive centuries, are sufficiently long and serious to be considered equivalent to the collapse of a civilization. The most spectacular and tragic of these was the ecological catastrophe which hit the Amerindian continent during the "long" sixteenth century (1492–1650). Over this period, something like 90 per cent of the native population (and even 100 per cent in some places, in the Caribbean) was wiped out by diseases imported from Europe.[2] It would be extremely hard to find any equivalent for this hecatomb in the Old World, at least during the last millennium. This gigantic crisis, or chain of crises, led to a total restructuring of the Mexican and Peruvian cultures, on a new foundation of mixed race. The new order was creative in some respects, it is true; but the price paid at the outset was horrifyingly high—too high by any standards.

A different crisis, less devastating in terms of epidemics, but longer-lasting in time than the American Indian tragedy, was the crisis that coincided with the collapse of the Roman Empire under the impact of the invasions. It was a phenomenon that occupied, one might even say blocked, several centuries. The first signs appeared in the third century A.D. And it was to be a very long time before the "invasion complex", with all its forces, both destructive and creative, was overcome. The trauma was finally "shaken off" in about the eleventh century, once the raids of the Norsemen were over, and as the greater explosion of medieval growth got under way. The time of troubles which delivered the *coup de grâce* to the achievements of the Roman Empire was marked, during the long early phase, by a fall in population and in production. Over and above the fall itself, it was also characterized by a dislocation of the socio-cultural system, and by the creation of new, or relatively new socio-political structures: one thinks, among other things, of the rise of feudalism. And in northern France (the *langue d'oïl*) it is possible to see the appearance of a new culture through the Germanization or "Frankization" of Latin which was now turning into French. The sociologist Jean Baechler[3] considers that the successive collapses of the great Roman and Carolingian Empires provided the creative foundation in which feudalism took root (and few would contradict that). But he also sees in this the origin, in the very long term, of the modern bourgeoisie and capitalism. In any imperial society (whether Roman, Soviet or Chinese), with its "normal" forces of order, the cities and the merchant classes are, in fact, generally kept in their place, which is a modest and subordinate one. But in Western Europe, from the eleventh century, groups of merchants began to take advantage of the independence or autonomy of urban units, achieved at the expense of the disintegration of the Imperial super-structures. These prolific groups were, before long, multiplying like catfish in streams. And in the long run, after continuous if sometimes uneven progress, they succeeded—much later—in converting a large part of the globe to their own "capitalism".[4] The great post-Imperial crisis of the second third, or second half of the first millennium A.D. was, therefore, the matrix of a radically new socio-economic pattern: one that looked beyond the medieval period, prefiguring and laying the foundation for the capitalism of modern times.

b. *Examples of Century-long Crises*

I shall turn now to crises of shorter duration—about a hundred years, or perhaps a little longer. The most celebrated episode on this kind of scale occurred at the end of the Middle Ages (fourteenth to fifteenth century). It can be fairly simply characterized. Rural Western Europe as a whole had been experiencing demographic expansion since the seventh century A.D.; to a pronounced extent since the tenth to eleventh century. It was in the years after 1300, and more generally in the first half of the fourteenth century, that certain adverse factors which were to cut short this growth, *in the shape of crises*, first appeared. In the first place, Western Europe, with its expanding population, had come to seem like an exploding galaxy: offshoots had been sent in all directions, even to central Asia and towards China (itself in a state of expansion at the time). Meanwhile, between Europe and China, straddling Siberia, Russia and Turkestan, Genghis Khan's Mongol and universal empire had been created—guaranteeing security of communications. This empire thus facilitated contacts and short cuts between the West and the Far East. Contingents of Mongolian soldiers and caravans, organized by the silk merchants of Genoa, made their way over the vast expanses of Eurasia, passing through zones where plague was endemic, in Turkestan and neighbouring regions. And one day, the inevitable happened. These imprudent excursions set up a bacteriological short-circuit: the Black Death of 1348 spread from Central Asia to the Genoese trading-posts of the Black Sea, and from there to the cities of Italy and thus to the whole of Western Europe, cutting a swathe through the population of Italy, France, England etc., from 1348 and over the next hundred years, as successive waves of plague invaded our continent in the wake of the Black Death. The demographic crisis was, moreover, seriously aggravated in France by the Hundred Years' War. For armed conflict in this period had catastrophic consequences; not so much in terms of military casualties, which were never very great, but as a result of the epidemics carried by soldiers, and by the hordes of refugees fleeing from the fighting. Their fleas carried plague, and their lice, typhoid. Not only that, but armies also requisitioned horses, destroyed mills and annihilated a large amount of agricultural capital investment—thus causing famines. In short, this amounts to what one medievalist has described as "the Hiroshima model". The population fell dramatically: within what are the present frontiers of France, the population fell from 17 or 18 million inhabitants in 1330, to under 10 million (and perhaps much less) by 1440—a massive collapse between the age of Philip the Fair and the time of Joan of Arc.

Did this crisis, which lasted over a hundred years, lead to any innovation or creative achievement? One can attempt to answer this question, it seems to me, in three different ways:

(a) One answer might be to consider that the blow, or rather series of blows, that the crisis dealt to the demographic and economic aspects of society, slowed down by a whole century the entire historical process that was to follow, after 1500. In other words, if it had not been for this crisis and the successive blows (or "bloodlettings" which weakened the organism), all the phenomena of demographic and economic growth, which our society has now experienced for several hundreds of years, would have begun distinctly earlier—in 1600–20 let us say, instead of in 1715–20, as actually happened. That is, the accelerated pace—or headlong rush—of history, which we are now somewhat anxiously contemplating, would have originated further back in time. According to this theory, "we", or rather humanity, would now be wrestling with the (perhaps insoluble) problems that the futurologists tell us are in store for us in the twenty-first century. (I do not subscribe to the somewhat over-simplified analysis offered by the Club of Rome. But everyone agrees that certain very serious contradictions and distortions, created by unregulated bouts of growth and consumption, will make their presence felt between now and 2050–2100— with a degree of acuteness not experienced hitherto, although warning signs are already beginning to appear in our time.)

(b) But perhaps such a "counterfactual" analysis is both mechanical and illusory. It is as difficult to visualize what did *not* take place, as it is to carry out a human heart transplant (cf. the criticisms aimed at Robert Fogel in the *New York Review of Books* 2/10/75, p. 34). Let us look instead at the crisis of the fourteenth and fifteenth century, *as it really was*. The dramatic fall in population was accompanied, contrariwise, by the survival of considerable agricultural capital; that is, the vast areas of cultivable land which were abandoned in 1348. They had hardly had time to revert to their wild state in 1450, and were therefore much easier to clear than the virgin forest. This being so, the crisis by 1450–1500 had created a remarkable surplus of land-capital, thus bringing about a substantial rise in the standard of living and a diversification of the urban and maritime economy etc.—which would from now on be concerned to satisfy the increasingly complex material and cultural needs of western society, from Portugal to Germany.

The Turkish conquests (accomplished during the demographic vacuum caused by the crisis) also, as is well known, disseminated Greek scholarship and Hellenic manuscripts to the West. It was in this context that the three phenomena, of varying importance, which were to change the face of Europe and the world in the fifteenth and sixteenth centuries, took place: the intellectual Renaissance; even more significantly, the invention of printing; and the discovery of America. So, on this occasion, the crisis performed a creative function, which is sometimes the case. The reduced population of fifteenth-century Europe was no longer obsessed by the problem of subsistence, as previous societies living on the same territory had been in the thirteenth and early fourteenth centuries. This late-medieval population, as a result, revealed an unprecedented capacity for renewal, as well as for initiatives in new directions.

And, of course (though here we are on familiar ground), the crisis was also a source of significant cultural phenomena, like those described by Huizinga in *The Waning of the Middle Ages*—including the well-known obsession with death and corpses which gave a particular cast to the mentalities of the late medieval period. There were many reasons for this obsession, some of which persist in our own times since, although we have succeeded in postponing death, no one has managed to conquer it. Some of these reasons, though, have to do with the very specific conditions of the fourteenth and fifteenth centuries. People living in this period, even those with a high standard of living, knew that many of them were doomed to die within a few years during some inevitable outbreak of plague. As Philippe Ariès has remarked,[5] it was as normal for men and women during the "waning of the Middle Ages" to reflect on death—the ultimate failure—as it is for our contemporaries, when they reach the age of say, forty, to reflect on their own lives in terms of the failure of their youthful ambitions.

But did the crisis of the fourteenth and fifteenth century only affect Europe? Apparently not: Ping Ti-Ho's historical studies on the population of China[6] have shown that in about 1400 the Chinese population, like that of Europe, reached an all-time low (60 million), as opposed to the 130 million registered during the peaks recorded respectively in the twelfth and the seventeenth centuries. The situation is broadly comparable to that of European demography over the same long time-span. But it appears that this substantial drop in the population of the Celestial Empire in 1400 did not bring to the Far East the beneficial consequences which we are inclined to attribute (see above) to similar phenomena in Europe at the same time. The civilization of China was still, during the late Middle Ages, capable of some remarkable achievements. But despite a number of advantages (if I may state the obvious, and remind the reader that the Chinese were the first people in the world to possess the compass and the art of printing) the Middle Empire did not make that vital breakthrough which gave the West, in about 1500, its "vocation" (a questionable one, needless to say) of taking over other continents and imposing its stamp upon them. Among such breakthroughs, we might class the discovery of the New World; the increase both of the means and the objects of communication by the mass medium of the time, viz. the printing-press; and the intellectual and later scientific revolution, partly resulting from the reformulation of certain concepts, which was brought about in the West by the classically-inspired Renaissance.

This foray into comparative history inclines me to query some of the ideas I have previously, rather timidly, suggested as to the innovating role of the fourteenth/fifteenth-century crisis. It is true that this long drawn-out episode was fruitful to the extent that it raised considerably, though briefly, the living standards of the western populations, thus affording them the respite and the elbow-room necessary to develop certain projects which were to go far beyond the mere reproduction, even with increased numbers, of a subsistence economy. But it is striking how these opportunities were seized only here in the West: the crisis of the end of the Middle Ages must, therefore, have acted merely as a catalyst, stimulating into activity structures previously dormant, but which nevertheless lay in waiting. In China, although the catalyst (the crisis) was similarly present, the underlying context which might have led to the creation of a Chinese-inspired world-economy, and to a society at once communicative, industrial, capitalist and scientific, was lacking. (A definition and description of such a "favourable" context ought to be given here in the interests of greater clarification; but that would take us outside the limited scope of this article.)

★

After 1500, one encounters no eco-demographic crisis in Western Europe comparable in catastrophic intensity to that of the four-teenth-fifteenth century. There is one exception though, to prove the rule: a massive but unique case, that of Germany during the Thirty Years' War, in the seventeenth century. The German population fell by roughly one half during the second and third quarter of the seventeenth century—because of the war, of course; but also, and in particular, because of the epidemics and famines it engendered. The crisis made possible a reorganization of Germanic society, thus fulfilling a role that was on balance positive—if one takes a Panglossian view of the world. Can this "crisis-type" reorganization account for the brilliant rococo period in certain parts of Germany at the end of the seventeenth century, and in the eigh-teenth, when the time was approaching for a thoroughgoing recon-struction? It is not impossible. But we should note all the same, in order to keep this idea within proper proportions, that seventeenth-century Russia too, during the "time of the troubles", saw an alarming collapse of its population: this did not prevent eighteenth-century Russia from rebuilding itself, and developing once more along the lines of certain authoritarian models and constants which had been, and would remain from the Mongols to the twentieth century, characteristic of Russian society. Crisis proposes, culture disposes perhaps?

c. *A Combination of Medium-Term Crises and a Secular Crisis: The Seventeenth Century*

The earlier mentions of the Thirty Years' War in Germany, and the Troubles in Russia, bring us directly to the problem of *the* (secular) crisis of the seventeenth century, and the *various* crises (lasting a decade or two, or more) of which the entire hundred-year period is made up. In fact, the "extended" seventeenth century, in France at least, runs from about 1560 to 1720. This was an age of stagnation, and sometimes of decline, in population levels and in the gross agricultural product, whereas industry—and especially the cities, the State and Science—continued, on the contrary, to develop between 1600 and 1700.

Looking at the period in more detail, one can distinguish three long phases of difficulty or crisis, each clearly defined, which help to account for the economic and demographic stagnation of this "extended" century (1560–1720).

The first crisis coincides with the wars of religion, which lasted thirty or forty years depending on the region: roughly from 1560 to 1595.

The second corresponds to the Thirty Years War, devastating in eastern France and Alsace; and, more particularly, to the disastrous effects of the Fronde, which were catastrophic in the Paris region in about 1560.

The third accompanied the end of Louis XIV's reign and lasted a good twenty years (1692–1715).

Each of these three episodes had the effect of reducing the population of "France" possibly by one or two million inhabitants; perhaps, in some cases, even more. At the same time, agricultural production was tending to slow down temporarily, and this, combined with several years of bad weather, prepared the way for shortages and famines. Then, after each of these major long crises, one finds phenomena of revival, or rather of recovery, both in the economy and demography. The first phase of each crisis—the decline—is dominated by fallout from three wars being waged at the time (Religion, Thirty Years, and Spanish Succession). And one has to bear in mind the train of destruction, especially the epidemics and the tax burdens, which these wars brought with them. These great crises, which served to lay bare deep-lying structures, occasioned major social conflicts: troubles, risings, even revolutions. I am thinking in particular of the famous "popular rebellions before the Fronde" (in France) studied by Boris Porchnev and Roland Mousnier, as well as the Fronde itself, and the revolutions in Naples, Catalonia and Portugal, and above all in England, in or around the decade 1640–50.

Can one say that these seventeenth-century crises were in any sense creative; leading, that is, to innovations?

While one cannot provide a really satisfactory answer to this question, it is at least possible to make one or two points. In the first place, the seventeenth century (taken to be 1560–1720 in France, but with different dates elsewhere) was *on the whole* an age of crisis: both structurally and through the accumulated effects (in France, at least) of the three episodes already referred to. Secondly, and this is by no means incompatible with the first statement, the seventeenth century was also an age of major intellectual creativity. Pierre Chaunu, for example, has written forcefully about this paradox. So we have the juxtaposition and apparent divergence of two phenomena: high cultural, but poor economic and demographic achievement. The tragic and inhospitable seventeenth century nevertheless produced Descartes and Newton and the great scientific breakthroughs, especially in mathematics. The famous "crisis of European consciousness" to quote Hazard, occurred precisely between 1680 and 1720—exactly the period when population figures and gross product were at an all-time low. It is as if there sprang from the ashes of the economy an intellectual renaissance of phoenix-like brilliance.

What is more, it was during the two or three most difficult decades, 1680–1720, that the foundations were laid for a radically new phenomenon, one for which there had possibly been no equivalent since the eleventh to thirteenth centuries! That is, *real growth*, both economic and demographic: this was no mere recovery after a depression, but growth that broke all previous records; and it began after 1720 or so, in France (the date may vary somewhat elsewhere). This wave of *real growth* was to last, not without interruption, but to last all the same until our own day—until 1973, to be precise. And it is by no means impossible that it will be resumed for a while before very long.

To return to the "classical" period, let us say, then, that it was during the crisis itself (that of the seventeenth century as a whole, but the 1680–1720 crisis in particular) that the conditions which would ultimately lead to the end of the crisis were unobtrusively brought together; thanks to them, innovation and growth would begin after 1720. The economic and demographic revival—a creative revival, not a mere "recovery"—was thus being prepared in the throes of *an economic crisis on a worldwide scale* between 1650 and 1715. Take the case of the American Indians, in Peru and especially in Mexico: they had been annihilated (up to 90 per cent of the inhabitants of pre-Columbian Mexico) by cruelty and above all by viruses, foreign to the native peoples, which the Spanish colonists carried on their skin, in their blood, and in their baggage. In 1650, this indigenous population (having already to some extent been mixed with the Whites) touched rock bottom in numbers, then began to climb back—though very slowly—from a baseline that had fallen temporarily to zero in mid-seventeenth century. At the same time, the inhuman slave trade had begun to transport black captives from Africa to Brazil and the sugar-producing islands of the West Indies.

Thus, simply through an upturn in demography, new consumer markets were set up in America for European textiles, which could be exported to the New World. The Indian population, now once more increasing, no longer went completely naked. Even wearing the lightest of clothes, this population, simply because it grew larger, enabled the French, Catalan and other textile industries, or "manufactures" to get going again—or to start up for the first time in the eighteenth century, or even as early as the latter half of the seventeenth, despite the "crisis". In addition, the newly-available Indian or half-breed labour in Mexico, and the black slaves in Brazil, afforded the means (for the first time, or once again, depending on circumstances) of mining precious metals in these countries. Mexican silver—back in production—and Brazilian gold, discovered by the Portuguese during the crisis years of Louis XIV, were to revitalize the entire European economy, and this renewal was felt everywhere in the eighteenth century, from the Iberian peninsula to the British Isles, by way of France. Before long the importing, refining and re-exporting of sugar from the West In- dies—where it was cut by black slaves—was bringing new life to the great ports on the Atlantic seaboard of France, Nantes and Bor- deaux, which were to be so prosperous in the Age of Enlighten- ment.

So it was that the elements constituting a "critical mass" were produced in the course of the long stagnation of the seventeenth century—sometimes amid general indifference or even hostility. They included industrial and urban development; the continued growth of taxation and of the State under Richelieu, Mazarin and Louis XIV; the development of primary and secondary education— the nursery of the new *élites*. And one should, at this point, mention the creative influence of the Church in Latin countries (as for the Protestant north, the creative influence of the religious ethic needs no further demonstration, thanks to the work of Max Weber).

The Catholic Church had changed a great deal under the in- fluence of the Counter-Reformation. Seventeenth- and eighteenth- century priests, trained and shaped in the seminaries at the height of the crisis (like the French primary-school teachers of a later age turned out by the *écoles normales*, the training colleges) tended, in certain regions at any rate, to devote themselves to the moral and intellectual education of the peasants—if only to a limited extent. At least they could teach them to read. Max Weber's theory of the stimulating role played by the Protestant ethic in the development of capitalism during the extended crisis of the seventeenth century could be applied *mutatis mutandis* to the cases of the Jansenist and even the rococo-baroque varieties of Catholicism during the classi- cal and Enlightenment periods. Under the influence of these dif- ferent factors, the period 1600–1750 had already seen not only the material, but also the spiritual and intellectual development of various sectors of the bourgeoisie: the merchants, the state- mandarins, the original technocrats. And the nobility, too, was evolving—becoming a more intellectually open and creative class. Lastly, there was development, too, in the depths of the country- side, among the peasant *élite* composed of rich tenant-farmers and well-to-do peasants, who were becoming better educated, more competent and prosperous, and therefore more efficient. All these phenomena put together, combined imperceptibly to form a "snowball", or a *critical mass*, even during the period of economic and demographic stagnation of the seventeenth century. But that stagnation was *confined*, I must stress, to the economic and demographic spheres.

To this must be added the simultaneous appearance of ferments, more strictly—or more narrowly—cultural, listed by Paul Hazard: critical reading of the scriptures, the challenging of Catholic dogma; the emergence of new trends in philosophy with Bayle and Fontenelle, etc. For religion (although a force for progress among the people and in rural areas, as we have seen) was at the same time either being transcended or contradicted by the spread of irreligion or even anti-religion. Both irreligion and anti-religion were productive too, but this time at the "loftier" level of the *élites*. In the end, the tide lifted up all the boats—the fisherman's smack and the rich nobleman's yacht. Whatever metaphor one uses, apposite or not, all these very diverse phenomena, which reinforced and multiplied each other, and which had already increased in importance during the phase of crisis, were to produce their full effect as that crisis drew to a close—after about 1715—20, the Age of the Regency and of Law's economic experiments. This "critical mass", accumulated during the period of crisis, exploded once it had passed; yet the explosion was not a single event, but a phenomenon that went echoing on down the years. For what emerged after 1715–20 was sustained, or rather *self-sustaining* growth—radically different and new compared to the seventeenth century, and indeed the whole period from 1300 to 1700.

We should also note, or repeat, that the initial date of this unprecedented "upsurge" fell earlier in England, Belgium, Catalonia and in the major French sea-ports (Marseilles, Saint-Malo) than in the inland regions of France.

Perhaps this is a good moment to pause and ask ourselves, apropos of the seventeenth century, what the creative possibilities of the long crisis really amounted to. Let us say that during this period, a type of growth in the spiritual, intellectual, scientific, cultural, administrative, urban and even industrial spheres, was able to distribute its increasing *per capita* benefits to a population which, precisely because it was horizontally "blocked" by the depression, or by the eco-demographic crisis, happened to be, without realizing it, ideally placed to take advantage of the very particular phenomena of this type of growth. If in such a situation, the crisis made possible certain changes and encouraged the accumulation of a "critical mass", this was not because of the crisis *per se*; but because, as a crisis, it lent particular force to certain phenomena in those sectors which happened, during the crisis, to find themselves in a situation of unilateral and asymmetrical expansion.

2. CRISES IN THE PERIOD 1720–1973

The period 1720–1973 was an age of general growth: in Europe and Asia, and in extensive areas of America, North and South. It was, nevertheless, punctuated by crises of various kinds and various lengths—although they never lasted anything like as long as a century. (And that marks the essential difference between this period and that of 1300–1720.)

Viewed within the two- to three-hundred-year framework (1720–1973), these crises were all, by definition, "crises of growth". But one can draw certain distinctions between them. Firstly there were subsistence crises—in 1740 for example. These were short, lasting only a year or two. Their incidence and gravity progressively diminished, and they gradually died out or at any rate became mild or harmless for a long stretch from 1740–94. (The Revolutionary period was marked by a relapse and a near-famine in 1795.) The creative effect of such crises or mini-crises was virtually nil. But they did contribute, within the context of rising expectations in the eighteenth century, to encourage the emergence and development of new kinds of political agitation—such as the *bread riots*: these were frequent in eighteenth century England and France, and promoted a new consciousness of social problems among the popular masses—in the countryside to some extent, but more especially in the towns. Such riots are a direct link in the chain of events leading to the Revolution in France and to radicalism in England.

Secondly there were, even in the eighteenth century, examples of a type of crisis which would become increasingly common in the nineteenth and twentieth centuries: the cyclical economic crisis of the industrial and commercial establishment. This kind operated on the deflationary principle, whereas the subsistence crisis was inflationary (with soaring grain prices). Cyclical crises of this kind are known to have a potentially progressive content, in as much as they contribute to the modernization of industrial structures.

A third kind of crisis, to be found in the eighteenth as in the twentieth century, is much more serious, long-lasting and extensive. This combines in varying proportions: the problems of subsistence (of the "old-fashioned" or pseudo-old-fashioned type), an economic depression (of the modern variety), epidemic, war, and a fall in the birth rate.

Such crises are, or can be, situated at certain nodal points, at the strategic crossroads of social history, or of History itself. Because this was an overall age of growth, development in the eighteenth, nineteenth, and twentieth centuries contained possibilities hitherto unexperienced, leading—for better or for worse—in new directions. The outstanding examples are the French Revolution and the Russian Revolution.

To take the French Revolution first: this took place within a period which was neither one of intense poverty, nor with a trend towards pauperization (although there still were considerable numbers of poor people in *ancien régime* France). On the contrary, the fifty or sixty years preceding 1789 were characterized by a modest but unquestionable rise in the admittedly low standard of living. They were equally characterized by an inflationary rise in popular hopes for the future—the famous "rising expectations". The economic crisis of the 1780s dealt these hopes a severe blow, triggering off a revolutionary reaction which was considerably sharper than it would have been in the seventeenth century, when expectations were not rising at all, and when people were simply dying of starvation, and so were less likely to revolt. Their path led to the graveyard, not to the barricades.

Economically and socially, the French Revolution also took place during a long period of increased prosperity for the great estates owned by the aristocracy and the church, and farmed by capitalist tenants. These estates served "objectively" to provide the towns with cereals. The Revolution also occurred against the background of a secular phase of growth in the manufacturing and commercial economy. Lastly, this was also a period that saw the emergence of a liberal aristocracy among the *élites*.

It was this entire system, rather too briefly described above, which entered upon a crisis, at different levels, during the 1780s and 1790s. A number of epidemics slowed the rate of population growth between 1775 and 1790; and an economic depression, described in Labrousse's masterly pioneering study, began during the 1780s. To make matters worse in the short term, the 1788 grain harvest was very bad; and the latent subsistence crisis provides one of the keys to the popular discontent, which was to culminate in Paris on July 14, 1789.

Certain choices were made at this juncture, during the French Revolution—a time of popular rising and war, both of which followed close on the heels of the crisis, and were an integral part of it. These choices would by no means put an end to long-term growth, but they certainly interrupted it, partly and temporarily, in both the short- and the medium-term. They would determine its future direction and guide it according to new models. (When I use the word "choice" in this context, I am, of course, using it in the historian's sense, that is, allowing that a very large, perhaps preponderant proportion of its content may originate in the collective unconscious.)

"Choice", then, in agriculture for instance, meant a move from the capitalist-farmer type of development (by noblemen and physiocrats before 1789), to a pattern where the small peasant holding— the family farm—was to make a come-back in the nineteenth century. Against all expectations, the peasant smallholder succeeded in holding his own, and more, against the great capitalist estates once owned by noble landlords. And this victory was due, at least in part, to the form the French Revolution took in the countryside.

We should therefore note, in passing, that to talk of an antagonism between feudalism and capitalism in this period does not make much sense, in the countryside at any rate (in the cities it would be different). Far from being antagonistic, these two modes of production were actually moving closer together during the eighteenth century and putting up a united front against the peasant-smallholder family-farm economy; they were in league. In this respect, then, the French Revolution faced them with a setback: not a fatal one, but a severe and unmistakable one.

The revolutionary crisis in the decade 1789–99 also meant a separation in the destinies of the *élites* and the masses, or at least of certain sections of them. There was a rise, not of "the bourgeoisie" in general, but of a legal bourgeoisie, which was of greater historical importance at this time than the industrial or commercial bourgeoisie (the typically capitalist section). One has therefore to discard the "vulgar marxist" explanations (which do not, I recognize, necessarily represent marxism as such).

The revolutionary crisis was also disastrous for the liberal aristocracy: the group was not wiped out completely, but would never again occupy the politically prominent place that it had held in 1787–90. On the other hand, the Revolution's novelty was to inject into the veins and arteries of the national body politic its own long-lasting invention: Jacobinism.

Innovatory with respect to the development of small-scale family or artisanal production, the revolutionary crisis cut right across certain capitalist trends which formed part of economic growth in general. I am thinking, for instance, of the development of industry, of the great manufacturing establishments and external trade: this development was slowed down considerably by the Revolution and its aftermath over the next few decades. It is for this reason that François Crouzet and Maurice Lévy-Leboyer have been able to describe the French Revolution as a *national catastrophe*. It undoubtedly was a catastrophe (though a short-lived one) for large-scale enterprise of the modern type; not so for the small-scale unit of production, the artisan's workshop and, above all, the peasant's smallholding.

So, the decade 1789–99, or perhaps to extend it, 1789–1815, proved to be the critical crossroads. From this point of view, major crises, during a period of growth (differing in many respects from major crises during a period of stagnation) may have a creative function that is potentially quite considerable.

There have been other, later turning-points: the Russian Revolution seems to me to be absolutely typical in this respect. It took place following a period of extremely rapid growth, which had taken effect in Russia since the last third of the nineteenth century (at least). This growth, as is only too often forgotten, was on American lines, although its baseline was much lower, and its achievements therefore regularly fell short of those of the United States. And this growth was just as rapid, perhaps even more rapid, and certainly less costly from every point of view, than that of Stalinist Russia. The chain of growth-crisis-revolution as it occurred in Tsarist Russia between 1900 and 1917 is therefore comparable to what happened in eighteenth-century France before 1789. Comparable—but because this was the twentieth century, much more accentuated. The *revolutionary crisis* in Russia was essentially linked to war (in 1905 and again in 1914–17), and to the problems of subsistence, morale, and indeed everything else related to the war. Crisis and revolution brought innovation in every sense of the word, good and bad. For the 1917 revolution made possible a genuine choice for society (choice here does not, of course, mean *freedom* of choice). It was a choice which was equivalent to the creation of a radically new model of social development. At a second level of analysis, the new model was accompanied by a powerful reassertion, and an incredible recovery, of the most authoritarian tradition of the Russian past, paradoxically promoted during the years 1930–50 to the rank of symbol and standard of world revolution—with twentieth-century embellishments, of course. The crisis/turning-point, missed in 1905 but successfully taken in 1917, appears, with hindsight, to have been an event of fundamental significance for the whole of mankind; or a least for the millions who were absorbed into this regime, or the various other varieties of it.

As for the world economic crisis of 1929, if it had not happened, Hitler would probably never have come to power. Nazism, then, was also the result (an "innovation" undoubtedly, in the worst sense of the word) of this terrible crisis: it cut across, though without completely stopping it, more than two hundred years of long-term growth. Supposing, which God forbid, that Hitler had won the war, the consequences of the turning that Germany took in 1929–33 would still be with us, terribly with us, in Europe today; just as the results of the crisis-turning that Soviet Russia took in 1905–17 are still with us in 1975.

In conclusion, we should try to look ahead: I have already suggested that the present crisis (1973–??) presents certain Ricardian-cum-Malthusian aspects, since it was sparked off, at least in the early stages, by a temporary shortage of oil—an artificial one from a certain point of view. All the same, the end of the twentieth century, and above all the twenty-first, are likely, as certain essential primary materials run out, to confront humanity with more than one episode of this type, again Ricardo-Malthusian in nature.

The "shortage" crisis, which it was thought had been overcome for good since the eighteenth century, may therefore reappear. It may once more replace, or combine with, the periodic deflationary crises (slumps) which have characterized our brave new industrial world since 1800 or 1830. Will the effect of such shortage crises be to "innovate", if that is the right word, in an authoritarian direction, as has been the case in most major revolutions in the twentieth century? This is a question that can legitimately be asked, though one would not claim at present to provide any answers. Are crises subject to the same rules as money? Will a bad innovation inevitably chase out a good? Not necessarily: crises of the future will no doubt tend to reinforce authoritarian regimes, and reduce the areas of the world still held by the supporters of liberalism. This may not be an unmitigated evil, if, as seems possible, certain of the authoritarian regimes are actually better placed than liberal systems to provide the people with bread, peace and order (take the Chinese example). But we should not forget that liberty is the mother of innovation: by increasing the grip of authoritarianism, one might be in danger of killing the goose that lays the golden eggs: the combination liberty-innovation. Our aim should, therefore, be to avoid becoming too alarmed in advance about the possible authoritarian outcomes of future crises (which will in fact be "reincarnating regressively tendencies formerly repressed"); while at the same time seeking to preserve, in all areas where it is legitimately possible, opportunities for creative solutions of libertarian or liberal inspiration, according to our personal creeds.

Of all the metaphors used of crises, those drawn from geology have always appealed to me most. A crisis[7] is something like the San Francisco earthquake of 1906. This earthquake was the product, first, of the tension building up in the rock masses on either side of the San Andreas fault; and then, of the release which accompanied and followed the sudden terrifying readjustment. Earthquakes do not themselves create anything: they reveal underlying forces, regressive or progressive as these may be. They cause widespread destruction, laying waste the existing superstructures—and they unquestionably give builders freedom to indulge every fancy in their choices and designs for reconstruction.

This is the pattern of events we shall no doubt see when the next major earthquake strikes a city (Los Angeles, they tell us, is the most likely site). And it is also the kind of pattern that will emerge during the crises which will undoubtedly threaten our civilization over the next hundred years.

The train of thought pursued in this essay may be clearer to follow at the end than it was at the beginning: it is now clear that I started with what was merely a symptom: a break in economic and/or demographic continuity;[8] a rather clear and more readable symptom on the whole than those ever-controversial phenomena such as "the crisis of the novel", "the crisis of faith" or similar cultural crises. And this discontinuity, which turned out to be no more than a symptom, has led me gradually towards the heart of the phenomenon we call a "crisis": it represents, in the most classic fashion, the outward and momentarily visible sign of the clash between mighty and invisible forces.

Notes

1 History That Stands Still

1. "L'Histoire immobile", inaugural lecture given at the Collège de France, November 30, 1973, (revised for publication).
2. Paul Bois, *Les Paysans de l'Ouest*. See *The Territory of the Historian*, I, chapter 7, for a thorough discussion of this book.
3. Censier and Jussieu are two university faculties in Paris.
4. J.-P. Enthoven.
5. The reference is to the Marxist philosopher Louis Althusser, author of *Lire le Capital*, etc. and, a teacher at the Ecole Normale Supérieure in the rue d'Ulm, Paris (translator's note).
6. Robert Fogel and Stanley Engerman, *Time on the Cross*, Boston, 1974.
7. J.N. Biraben, *Les Hommes et la peste*, Paris, 1975, vol. I, p. 142.
8. See Guy Bois, *Crise du féodalisme*, Paris, 1976.
9. *Les Fluctuations du produit de la dîme*, collective work edited by Joseph Goy and E. Le Roy Ladurie, Mouton, Paris-Hague, 1973.
10. Pierre Goubert, *L'Ancien régime*, vol. II, Armand Colin, Paris, 1973.
11. François Lebrun, *Les Hommes et la mort en Anjou*, Mouton, Paris-The Hague, 1971.
12. See studies by Michael R.A. Chance.
13. For convincing evidence of this, see Jean-Marc Debard, *Subsistances et prix des grains à Montbéliard de 1571 à 1793*, published in Société d'émulation de Montbéliard, *Bulletin et mémoires*, vol. 71, fasc. no. 98, 1974–5.
14. Maurice Garden, *Lyon et le Lyonnais au XVIIIe siècle*, Les Belles Lettres, Paris, 1970.
15. See for example, J.-A. Ganiage, "Structures de la natalité dans cinq villages du Beauvaisis" in *Annales de Normandie*, March 1973.
16. Pierre Chaunu, *La Civilisation de l'Europe classique*, Arthaud, Paris, 1966.
17. J. Dupâquier and M. Demonet, "Ce qui fait les familles nombreuses", *Annales, E.S.C.*, July-October 1972, p. 1025 ff.
18. Wilhelm Abel, *Crises agraires (VIe-XIXe siècles)* (French trans. of German original), Flammarion, Paris, 1974.
19. See studies by A. and J. Gordus, for example in *Annales*, December 1972.
20. P. Goubert, *L'Ancien Régime*, Paris, 1973, vol. II, p. 136.
21. This highly debatable assumption is virtually explicit in M. Morineau's book, *Les Faux-semblants d'un démarrage économique* (Cahier des Annales, no. 30) A. Colin, Paris, 1971, p. 366: "Taking into account the exceedingly high mortality rates almost everywhere between 1680 and 1700 (I would say 1680 to 1715—L.R.L.) it may be assumed that the population of France on the eve of Revolution had returned to its 1670 level".

2   A Concept

1. *Revue suisse d'histoire*, vol. 23, part 4, 1973.
2. J.N. Biraben and J. Le Goff, "La peste du Haut Moyen-Age", in *Annales E.S.C.*, 1969.
3. See articles by J.P. Goubert, J. Meyer and J.P. Peter in *Médecins, climat, et épidémies à la fin du XVIIIe siècle* by J.P. Desaive and others, Mouton, Paris-The Hague, 1972.
4. Elizabeth Carpentier, "Autour de la peste noire", in *Annales E.S.C.*, 1962.
5. R. Pollitzer, *Plague*, Geneva (World Health Organization), 1954.
6. Abbé A. Tollemer, *Un Sire de Gouberville, gentilhomme campagnard au Cotentin*, Mouton, Paris-The Hague, 1972.
7. J.F.D. Shrewsbury, *A History of Bubonic Plague in the British Isles*, Cambridge University Press, 1970; and J.N. Biraben, *Les Hommes et la peste*, Paris, 1975.
8. For these various references, Shrewsbury, *op. cit*, p. 12.
9. Biraben and Le Goff, *art. cit.*
10. *Ibid.*
11. The pre-plague population of England is a matter of some dispute among the experts. I can express no opinion on this thorny problem: the figure quoted here is that advanced by one of the best demographic British historians: E.A. Wrigley, *Population and History*, 1969, p. 78.
12. M. Morineau, *Les Faux-semblants d'un démarrage économique: agriculture at démographie en France au XVIIIe siècle*, A. Colin, Paris, 1971, p. 83 (Cahier des Annales, no. 30).
13. J.N. Biraben, "Conceptions médico-épidémiologiques actuelles de la peste", in *Concours médical*, January 26, 1963.
14. Quoted by C.S. Bartsocas in *Journal of the History of Medicine*, vol. 21, no. 4, 1966, p. 395, according to Philip Ziegler, *The Black Death*, Penguin Books, 1969, p. 113 and p. 296.
15. Biraben, *art. cit.*, 1963, p. 622.
16. For much of this section I am indebted to Biraben and Le Goff, *art. cit.*
17. Biraben and Le Goff, 1969, p. 1493.
18. On these complex ecological conditions, see Biraben, 1963, p. 620–1, in which he claims that plague is permanently endemic in central Asia, but intermittent in the Far East.
19. The sixth-century plague only minimally affected the Rhineland.
20. For a good comparative assessment of the two plagues, see the maps of Biraben and Le Goff in *Annales*, 1969, p. 1500–2 (the sixth-century plague), and Carpentier in *Annales*, 1962, p. 1017 (the plague of 1348).
21. At least if one accepts Shrewsbury's theory.
22. Poland was comparatively spared by the Black Death: Carpentier, *art. cit.* 1962. Bohemia likewise: Frantisek Graus, "Autour de la peste noire au XIVe siècle en Bohème", in *Annales*, 1963, p. 720–5.
23. Biraben and Le Goff, *art. cit.* 1969.
24. Biraben and Le Goff, *ibid.*
25. Pollitzer, *op. cit.*, p. 15 and p. 269; Biraben, *art. cit.*, 1963, p. 620.
26. Pollitzer, *op. cit.*, p. 269–71.

27. Pollitzer, *ibid.*, p. 335–6.
28. Biraben, *art. cit.*; Baltazard, quoting G. Girard, "Peste tellurique et peste de fouissement", in *La Presse médicale*, May 30, 1964.
29. R. Grousset, *L'Empire des steppes*, Paris, 1939; for a fuller bibliography see Louis Hambis, *Genghis-Khan*, Paris, 1973, and Chantal Lemercier-Quelquejay, *La Paix mongole*, Paris, 1970.
30. Lemercier-Quelquejay, *op. cit.*
31. G.I. Bratianu, *Recherches sur le commerce génois dans la mer Noire au XIIIe siècle*, Paris, 1929, p. 219.
32. Lemercier-Quelquejay, *op. cit.*, p. 46.
33. For a fuller bibliography of the silk trade route see J. Heers, *Gênes au XVe siècle* (full text), Paris, 1961, p. 366–7 (the map in particular); Robert Lopez, *Naissance de l'Europe*, A. Colin, Paris, 1962, p. 298–9; Francesco Pegolotti, *La Pratica della Mercature*, ed. Allan Evans, Cambridge (Mass.) 1936, p. 21–2.
34. Pegolotti, *op. cit.*, p. 21–2.
35. Heers, *op. cit.*, p. 367
36. Encyclopedia Britannica, 1960 edition, article "Plague"; John Stewart, *Nestorian Missionary Enterprise*, Edinburgh, 1928; Stewart made use of a series of articles that appeared in three volumes of *Mémoires de l'Academie de Saint-Petersbourg* (VIIth series), from 1886 to 1896, especially vols. 34–5 and 37–8.
37. Pollitzer, *op. cit.*, p. 14.
38. Heers, *op. cit.*
39. For a chronology of the spread of the plague see J. Glénisson, *Le Temps des périls, 1300–1500*, p. 67ff. in the collection *Les Métamorphoses de l'humanité*. Glénisson believes that even if the plague had not come to Europe from Caffa, it would have reached us anyway in the end from central Asia by way of Antioch and Asia Minor.
40. I make no claim to have shed new light in this essay on the *événementiel* aspect of the spread of the Black Death (the conventional name for the plague of 1348). In this connection see F.A. Gasquet, *The Great Pestilence*, London, 1893, republished in 1908 under the title *The Black Death*, London, together with a number of other accounts up to the previously mentioned study by P. Ziegler. For a critical appreciation of these studies see W.M. Bowsky, *The Black Death*, Holt, Rinehart and Wilson, New York, 1971, p. 126–8.
41. F.A. Gasquet, *op. cit.*, 1908, p. 39.
42. Édouard Baratier, *La démographie provençale du XIIIe au XVIe siècle, avec chiffres de comparaison pour le XVIIIe siècle*, Paris, SEVPEN, 1961.
43. Readers will note with some surprise that the places which were affected by *one* plague only, that of 1348, suffered more heavily, losing 54.9 per cent of their population, than those of the second group which underwent *two* outbreaks (1348 and 1361) but nevertheless lost only 48.2 per cent. The reason is that the places for which it was felt necessary to make a recount of households in the years immediately after the 1348 plague were probably among those most seriously affected. Hence, possibly a certain false "weighting" in our first group. But in any case, from all the existing data, it seems clear that when both plagues, 1348 and 1361, had run their course, the population of Provence had fallen by at least 40 per cent.
44. Guy de Chauliac, *La Grande Chirurgie*, ed. by E. Nicaise, Paris, 1890, p.

167–70. (The editor uses an old translation—from the Comtat dialect—of Chauliac's text.) Cf. also the detailed letter sent from Avignon quoted by J. de Smet, *Recueil des chroniques de Flandre*, Brussels, 1856, vol. III, p. 15.

45. My thanks are due to Professor Mollaret of the Pasteur Institute in Paris, an expert on bubonic plague, for the suggestions he kindly offered in the course of several conversations I had with him.

46. It is not impossible (nor, on the other hand, is it certain) that the plague was pneumonic when it reached Constantinople on its way from the Crimea. In this connection, cf. Jean Cantacuzène's text quoted by Gasquet, *op. cit.*, ed. 1908, p. 12–3. See also C. Anglada, *Étude sur les maladies éteintes*, Paris, 1869.

47. The winter lasting from December 1347 to March 1348 is not mentioned as being either mild or severe in C. Easton's *Les Hivers dans l'Europe occidentale*, Leyden, 1928. The few years *preceding* the plague in Montpellier were wet (for three years, according to the possibly simplified account by an anonymous doctor: *Tractatus de epidemia*, 1349, Bibliothèque Nationale ms. Latin, 7026, f. 86; and 227, f. 209 verso). It would be interesting to know what the weather was like in the months of January and February 1348, around the shores of the Gulf of Lions.

48. Therese Sclafert, *Cultures en Haute-Provence, deboisement et pâturages au Moyen Age*, Paris, 1959.

49. *Histoire du commerce de Marseille*, published under the direction of Gaston Rambert, Paris, 1949–59, vol. II, p. 261.

50. On this question of chimneys and fireplaces in medieval times see F. Braudel, *Civilisation matérielle et capitalisme*, A. Colin, Paris, 1967, p. 223ff.

51. My thanks to Gabrielle d'Archimbaud who pointed out to me, *in situ*, archaeological work carried out at Rougiers.

52. Pollitzer, *op. cit.*

53. *Histoire du commerce de Marseille*, *op. cit.*, vol. II, p. 304–16, text and tables.

54. J. Duvernoy, *Inquisition à Pamiers*, Privat, Toulouse, 1966, chs. iv and ix. The original texts were published by J. Duvernoy, *Le Régistre d'inquisition de Jacques Fournier*, Privat, Toulouse, 1965 (3 vols).

55. A. Montel and P. Lambert, *Chants populaires du Languedoc*, Paris, 1880.

56. *op. cit.*

57. E. Le Roy Ladurie, *Les Paysans de Languedoc*, Paris, SEVPEN, 1966, vol. I, p. 141. See also W. Abel, *Crises agraires en Europe*, Flammarion, Paris, 1973, p. 61 and note 1.

58. This hypothesis is based on several leading texts in B. Bennassar's *Recherches sur les grandes épidémies dans le nord de l'Espagne, à la fin du XVIe siècle*, Paris, SEVPEN, 1969, p. 53 *et passim*.

59. *Histoire du commerce de Marseille*, *op. cit.*, vol. II, p. 39; Baratier, *op. cit.*, p. 81; G. Lesage, *Marseille angevine*, E. de Boccard, Paris, 1950, p. 165.

60. See anti-usury texts quoted in Sclafert, *op. cit.*, and Baratier, *op. cit.* These texts show the anti-semitism of the times.

61. Lesage, *op. cit.*, p. 164 (low pre-plague wages).

62. G. Prat, "Albi et la peste noire," in *Annales du Midi*, 1952; Philippe Wolff, "Trois études de démographie dans la France méridionale", in *Studi in onore di Armando Sapori*, Milan, 1957; and by the same author, *Les "estimes" toulousaines des XIVe et XVe siècles*, Toulouse, 1956; E. Le Roy Ladurie, *op.*

cit., p. 142; *Documents de l'histoire du Languedoc*, published under the direction of Philippe Wolff, Privat, Toulouse, 1969 (Collection Univers de la France), p. 159–61.

63. Chauliac, ed. 1890, p. 172, Chauliac, who prescribed this treatment, was originally a farm lad in Aveyron. He later became the foremost surgeon of his time (Chauliac, *ibid*, p. LXXXIX).

64. *Documents de l'histoire du Languedoc, op. cit., ibid.*

65. De Smet, *op. cit.*, vol. 3, p. 16–7.

66. E. Fournial, *Les Villes et l'économie d'échange en Forez aux XIIIe et XIVe siècles*, Presses du Palais-Royal, Paris, 1967.

67. Fournial, *op. cit.*, p. 303–4.

68. Fournial, *op. cit.*, p. 305–8; and p. 721.

69. For eye-witness accounts of flagellants in and around Avignon, see J. De Smet, *op. cit.*, vol. III, p. 17; for the Forez flagellants, there is a somewhat less reliable text in Fournial, *op. cit.*, p. 311.

70. 102 households in Saint-Pierre in 1352; 244 households in the seven parishes in 1352.

71. Pierre Duparc, "Démographie de paroisses de Savoie," in *Bulletin philologique et historique (jusqu'en 1610), du Comité des travaux historiques et scientifiques*, 1962, p. 247, 275. It is also possible, as Duparc remarks, that the average number of households in Savoy had also decreased.

72. Texts collected by M. Costa de Beauregard, "Conditions des Juifs en Savoie au Moyen Age", in *Mémoires de l'Académie de Savoie*, 2nd series, vol. II, 1854. Later authors have not produced any further information on this point, e.g., V. de Saint-Genis, Gerson, etc.

73. In Saône-et-Loire, administrative district of Chalon-sur-Saône.

74. 310 households in 1360, according to P. Gras, "Le registre paroissial de Givry", in *Bibliothèque de l'Ecole des chartes*, vol. 100, 1939, p. 307 (the whole of the paragraph above, relating to Givry, is taken from this article).

75. E. Carpentier, in *Annales E.S.C.*, 1962, p. 1073, quoting the works of H. Van Werveke.

76. Baratier, *op. cit.*, p. 142–3: there was either a slight fall in the number of households in Tarascon, or the numbers remained as before, in 1316, 1319 and 1352, but the evidence is not altogether reliable, chronology suspect, and perhaps the 1352 figures are a copy of some unpublished pre-1348 records).

77. P. Tucoo-Chala, *Gaston Fébus*, Bière, Bordeaux, 1959, p. 221; and by the same author, "Peste noire en Béarn", in *Revue regionaliste des Pyrénées*, 1951, no. 111–2. I derive my references from E. Carpentier, *art. cit.*

78. E. Le Roy Ladurie, *Paysans de Languedoc, op. cit.*, p. 142–3, and note 1.

79. Damouzy, in Coville, *Histoire littéraire de la France*, vol. 37, 1959, p. 529.

80. Cf. the works of Peter, Goubert and Meyer on the XVIIIth century, in Desaive, *op. cit.*

81. See G. Fourquin, *Les Campagnes de la région parisienne à la fin du Moyen Age*, Paris, 1964, p. 227–8; B. Geremek, *Le Salariat dans l'artisanat parisien aux XIIIe-XVe siècles*, Paris, 1962, p. 123. See also J. Favier's remarkable study *Les Contribuables parisiens à la fin de la guerre de cent ans*, Droz, Geneva, 1970, p. 10 and note 22 (chronological span: 200,000 inhabitants in *1328*, 100,000 inhabitants in about *1421*).

82. R. Cazelles, in a study published in the *Bulletin philologique et historique (jusqu'à 1610) du Comité des travaux historiques et scientifiques*, 1962, demonstrated convincingly that the *élites* in the north suffered fewer casualties than their opposite number in the south, in 1348.

83. *Chroniques de Guillaume de Nangis, et de Saint-Denis*, quoted by A. Philippe, *Histoire de la peste noire*, Paris, 1853.

84. B. Guenée, *Tribunaux et gens de justice dans le baillage de Senlis à la fin du Moyen Age*, Strasbourg, 1963, p. 48–9.

85. Archives Nationales, Paris, S2620 and S2621 (rent records of Garges); Fourquin, *op. cit.*, p. 349; Dominique Vincent-Bocquet, *Garges-lès-Gonesse, 1273–1400*, unpublished doctoral thesis, University of Paris VII, 1973.

86. Cf. in this connection, texts quoted in my *Paysans de Languedoc*, 1966, p. 195 and note 1.

87. Text quoted by Coville, *op.cit.*, p. 390.

88. Biraben, *Les Hommes et la peste en France et dans les pays éuropéens et méditerranéens*, Mouton, Paris-The Hague, 1975, vol. 1, p. 120 (table).

89. F. Lot, "L'état des paroisses et des feux en 1328", in *Bibliothèque de l'Ecole des Chartes*, 1929.

90. M. Reinhard, A. Armengaud, J. Dupâquier, *Histoire générale de la population mondiale*, Paris, 1968, p. 90–1: data calculated by me from the totals in the table on p. 91.

91. P. Goubert, in F. Braudel and E. Labrousse, *Histoire économique de la France*, P.U.F., Paris, 1970, vol. II, p. 13.

92. Guy Bois is emphatic on this point in his *Crise du féodalisme*, Paris, 1976.

93. Baratier, *op. cit.*

94. E. Le Roy Ladurie, *Paysans de Languedoc, op. cit.*, 1966, at the start of part 2.

95. See the article by L. Binz, "La population du diocèse de Genève à la fin du Moyen Age", in *Mélanges Anthony Babel*, vol. i, Geneva, 1963.

96. *The Autobiography of Thomas Platter*, English trans., London, 1839, p. 3.

97. A. Fierro, *Les Enquêtes de 1339 en Faucigny*, unpublished thesis of the Ecole des Chartes (1964–5); and by the same author, "Un cycle démographique en Dauphiné", in *Annales*, 1971, p. 959.

98. J.M. Pessez, *Archéologie du village déserté*, A. Colin, Paris, Cahier des Annales, no. 27, p. 97.

99. Martin-Lorber in *Annales de Bourgogne*, no. 117, 1958.

100. H. Dubois, "Chalon d'après les cherches de feux", in *La Démographie médiévale, sources et méthodes*, published by Congrès de l'Association des historiens médiévalistes in the series *Annales de la Faculté de Nice*, 1971.

101. Marie-Thérèse Caron, unpublished thesis on *Le Tonnerrois au XVe siècle*, University of Nanterre, 1972.

102. G. Fourquin, *Campagne . . . , op. cit.*, p. 364–5; Guenée, *op. cit.*

103. Guy Bois, *Crise du féodalisme*.

104. *Histoire de la Bretagne*, published under the direction of J. Delumeau, Privat, Toulouse, 1969, p. 182 and p. 206 (H. Touchard).

105. R. Boutruche, *La crise d'une société: seigneurs et paysans du Bordelais pendant la guerre de Cent Ans*, Bordeaux, 1947.

106. J.M. Pesez, in *Villages désertés et histoire économique*, SEVPEN, Paris, 1965, p. 170. The author uses and quotes a work (unpublished) by A. Bocquet, 1956.

107. H. Neveux, in *Annales de démographie historique*, 1971, p. 269.

108. M.A. Arnould, *Les Dénombrement de foyers dans le Comté de Hainaut (XIVe–XVIe siècles*, Brussels, 1956, p. 278–9; G. Sivery, "Hainaut et peste noire", in *Mem. et publ. de la Soc. des Sciences, des Arts, et des Lettres du Hainaut*, vol. 19, 1965, p. 433 (cf. E. Carpentier, in *Annales*, 1968, p. 646).

109. On the subject of the Black Death in Hainaut (drop of 48.5 per cent in the number of households between 1286 and 1365), see Sivery, *art. cit.*

110. J. Cuvellier, *Les Dénombrement des foyers en Brabant*, quoted by Reinhard, Armengaud, Dupâquier, *op. cit.*, p. 98 and p. 107.

111. H. Neveux, *Les Grains du Cambrésis*, thesis, University of Lille III, 1974.

112. S. Guilbert, in *Annales*, 1968, p. 1283–1300.

113. Le Roy Ladurie, *Paysans de Languedoc, op. cit.*, vol. III, p. 942.

114. Biraben, *op. cit.*

115. See Overbeck's pollen graphs, 1557, reproduced in *Annales*, 1962, p. 445.

116. See. W. Abel, *Crises agraires en Europe (IXe–XIXe siècles)*, Flammarion, Paris, 1973, p. 61–70.

117. Soetber, in *Pet. Geog. Mitt.*, quoted by Borah, *New Spain's Century of Depression*, University of California Press, Berkeley, 1951.

118. S.F. Cook and L.B. Simpson, *The Population of Central Mexico in the Sixteenth Century*, Yale, New Haven, 1948, quoted by Borah, *New Spain's Century of Depression, op. cit.*, p. 3.

119. W. Borah and S.F. Cook, *The Population of Central Mexico in 1548*, 1960.

120. See S.F. Cook and W. Borah, *Essays in Population History: Mexico. . .*, vol. I, Berkeley, 1971; Borah and Cook, *op. cit.*, 1960, p. 114; Cook and Borah, *The Indian Population of Central Mexico, 1531–1610*, 1960, p. 48.

121. S.F. Cook and W. Borah, *The Population of the Mixteca Alta, 1520–1960*, 1968.

122. P. Chaunu, *L'Amérique et les Amériques*, Paris, 1964, p. 104.

123. S.F. Cook, *The Extent and Significance of Disease among the Indians of Baja California, 1697–1773*, Berkeley, 1937.

124. N. Wachtel, *La Vision des Vaincus*, Gallimard, Paris, 1971, p. 140–50.

125. W. Borah, "America as model: the demographic impact of European expansion upon the non-European world", in *Actas y memorias del XXXV congresso internacional de Americanistas*, Mexico, 1962.

126. P. Chaunu, "La population de l'Amérique indienne", in *Revue historique*, July-Sept. 1964, p. 112 ff.

127. S.F. Cook and W. Borah, *Essays in Population History: Mexico and the Caribbean*, vol. I, Berkeley, 1971.

128. C. Verlinden, "La population de l'Amérique pré-colombienne. Une question de méthode", in *Mélanges en l'honneur de Fernand Braudel*, vol. II, Privat, Toulouse, 1973, p. 453–62. This article, while occasionally discussing Mexico, mentions neither the work nor even the name of W. Borah, whereas Pierre Chaunu seeks only to be as faithful an interpreter as possible of the American historian. Readers will be hard put to understand this omission on Verlinden's part.

129. Ibid., p. 45.

130. Ibid.

131. W. Borah, *art. cit.*, 1964, p. 387.

3   The Aiguillette: Castration by Magic

1. This article appeared in *Europe*, March 1974.
2. Cf. in particular Migne, the 1846 edition, the article "ligature"; and A. de Chesnel, 1856, article "aiguillette" (in Migne).
3. The first edition appeared in 1679; I have in the main used the 1700, 1704, and 1777 editions.
4. Févret, *Traité de l'abus*, book 5, ch. 4, no. 6, quoted by Thiers, ed. 1777, IV, p. 505.
5. De Lancre, 1622, p. 316.
6. Montaigne, *Essais*, book I, ch. xxi.
7. Noël du Fail, *Propos rustiques*, 1547.
8. Crespet, 1590.
9. *Ibid.*, p. 17.
10. According to Migne, 1846 and 1866 editions.
11. Bodin, 1580, II, i.
12. Bodin does not agree with Févret on this point (see above).
13. Bodin, 1580, p. 59.
14. Texts taken from Crespet, 1590, p. 276, and Bodin, 1580, p. 59.
15. Bodin, 1580, p. 58–9.
16. Bodin, 1580, p. 58; Bodin, quoted by P. de Lancre, 1622, p. 316, marginal note.
17. Bodin, 1580, p. 207.
18. Platter, see below, note.
19. Bodin, 1580, p. 57.
20. Crespet, 1590, p. 276.
21. Thomas Platter, *Journal of a Younger Brother*, ed. and trans. S. Jennett, Muller, London, 1963, p. 90.
22. Ibid., p. 171.
23. Bodin 1580, p. 57; De Lancre, p. 316.
24. De Lancre, 1622, p. 314.
25. *Ibid.*
26. *Ibid.*, p. 322.
27. *Ibid.*, p. 320.
28. *Ibid.*, p. 323.
29. Albertus Magnus, *De Animalibus*, book 22, tract 2, cap. i, Munster ed. 1920, p. 1411.
30. Chapter I, quoted by Migne, 1846, article "ligature". col. 1007.
31. All this information is taken from a research study by Géraud, Fēstal and Delorme (Arles), quoted at some length in article "Bistournage" in the *Grand Dictionnaire Universel du XIXe siècle* (Larousse, Paris). Cf. also from the same source the articles on "castration" and "fouettage"; and Olivier de Serres, Théâtre d'agriculture, 1600, IV, 9.
32. The sexual meaning of the word *Bourse* is well attested in the sixteenth century, notably Montaigne (cf. the texts quoted by Littré: *la Bourse des testicules*, *la Bourse des génitoires*, etc.)
33. Le Goff, no. 158.
34. Himes, 1963, p. 6 and p. 9.

35. Thiers, 1704 edition, IV, p. 588; cf. also P. de Lancre, 1622.
36. Thiers, *ibid.*, p. 588.
37. *Ibid.*, IV, p. 504.
38. Platter, as quoted above.
39. Thiers, 1704 edition, IV, p. 585.
40. Thiers, *ibid.*, p. 509 ff.
41. *Ibid.*, p. 515 ff; cf. also in the same vol. IV of Thiers, numerous synodal ordinances dating from the sixteenth and seventeenth centuries, relating to superstitions concerning marriage. The chronology suggested by Thiers antedates a little that suggested by M. Caumette, as quoted in J.L. Flandrin's important article, "Mariage tardif et vie sexuelle", ("Late marriage and sexual life"), *Annales*, 1972, p. 1368.

4 French Peasants in the Sixteenth Century

1. This article first appeared in *Conjoncture économique, structures sociales, hommage à Ernest Labrousse*, Mouton, Paris-The Hague, 1974.
2. Cf. Dupâquier, *Annales E.S.C.*, 1969.
3. J. Jacquart, *La crise rurale en Ile-de-France*, A. Colin, Paris, 1974.
4. A letter from Jean Correro, Venetian Ambassador in Paris, in 1563; 15 to 16 million people in France in the boundaries as they then existed (*Relations des ambassadeurs Vénitiens au XVe siècle*, published by N. Tommaseo, vol. II, p. 149, 1838 edition, in *Collection des documents inédits historiques de la France*).
5. All sources, as a matter of fact, indicate that the population of France in about 1550 was in all regions greater than that of 1700, when it exceeded 19 million.
6. A study on this subject by Dupâquier appeared in *Annales E.S.C.* (4), 1972.
7. These figures are taken from M.H. Neveux's thesis, *Les Grains du Cambrésis*, University of Lille III, 1974.
8. Graphs and tables reproduced in M. Reinhard, *Histoire générale de la population mondiale*, 1968, p. 133.
9. *Les Fluctuations du produit de la dîme*, ed. by J. Goy and E. Le Roy Ladurie, Mouton, Paris-The Hague, 1972. (Volume published under the aegis of L'Association françaises des historiens économistes.)
10. Ramsey, ed., Methuen, London, 1971; M. Baulant in *Annales E.S.C.*, 1971.
11. *Op. cit*
12. In *Scandinavian Economic History Review*, 1957.
13. Articles in *Revue du Nord*, October 1953 and January 1954; and in *Revue historique de droit français et étranger*, 1952, no. I, p. 18–9.
14. J. Jacquart, *La Crise rural en Ile-de-France*, Paris, 1974.
15. Although these still existed on a large scale, note that 30 per cent of the total land acreage consisted of seigneurial *réserves*. Under the Carolingians in the same regions around Paris, 50 per cent of the land was taken up in seigneurial *réserves* (Halphen's statistics). Disintegration of the *réserves*, as we see then, was not rapid!
16. For further information on this subject, see my contribution in *Histoire économique et sociale de la France*, vol. II, tome I, ed. F. Braudel and E. Labrousse, Paris, 1977.

5 Balzac's Country Doctor

1. First published as preface to a re-edition of *Le Médecin de campagne* by Honoré de Balzac, Gallimard "Folio" collection, Paris, 1974.
2. The novel is set in the neighbourhood of the Pre-Alpine Massif of the Chartreuse.
3. Maurice Garden, *Lyon et les Lyonnais au XVIIIe siècle*, Les Belles Lettres, Paris, 1970.
4. See Pierre Jourda's edition of Noël du Fail's *Propos rustiques* in *Conteurs français du XVIe siècle*, Gallimard, Bibliothèque de la Pléiade, 1965.
5. Albert O. Hirschmann, *The Strategy of Economic Development*, Yale University Press, New Haven and London, 1958; Clifford Geertz, *Peddlers and Princes*, University of Chicago Press, Chicago and London, 1963.
6. Mandrin was a famous outlaw and smuggler.
7. The Beauce is a cereal-growing plain south of Paris.
8. Michel Vovelle, *Piété baroque et déchristianisation en Provence au XVIIIe siècle* (*Les attitudes devant la mort d'après les clauses des testaments*), Plon, Paris, 1973.
9. With reference to the attachment of Balzac's peasants to their homes and households, see the extraordinary passage in the novel about the expulsion of the poor and the cretins.

6 Versailles Observed

1. Written in collaboration with the late Janine Field-Recurat. The article printed here is a fuller version of the one which appeared in *L'Arc*, no. 65.
2. Saint-Simon, *Mémoires*, Pléiade edition, vol. III, p. 206 ff.; or Boislisle edition, vol. XVIII, p. 5–19. Much of what follows relates to this passage. Footnotes giving page references to French editions of the original have been omitted; readers who wish to follow them up are referred to the French edition of this book, p. 275 ff. An English version of the passage referred to here will be found in *The Historical Memoirs of the Duc de Saint-Simon*, ed. and trans. by Lucy Norton, London, Hamish Hamilton, 1967, vol. I, ch. XIX, esp. p. 454 ff. Since Lucy Norton's translation is abridged and does not contain all the extracts quoted here, they have been re-translated in this version. We have used the same system of nomenclature as the English edition, for convenient reference, i.e.: Madame la Duchesse de Bourgogne, the Duc de Maine, etc.
3. D. Van Elden, *Esprits fins et géométriques dans les portraits de Saint-Simon*, Nijhoff, The Hague, 1975.
4. Hence the links between Torcy and Pontchartrain the elder, who was also a gallican.
5. See the diamond-shaped diagram above, p. 000.

7 The Rouergue through the Lens

1. This chapter originally appeared as a contribution to Bernard Dufour's *La Pierre et la seigle: Histoire des habitants de Villefranche-de-Rouergue racontée par les photographies d'amateurs et les albums de famille 1860–1950*, Editions du Seuil, Paris, 1977.

2. Alexandre Albenque, *Les Rutènes*, Carrère, 1948, p. 43–4.

3. *Ibid.*, p. 40

4. Abbé Expilly, *Dictionnaire géographique, historique et politique des Gaules et de la France*, Amsterdam, 1770, vol. VI, article "Rouergue".

5. The only difference was that the *département* lost the canton of Saint-Antonin, which was transferred to the Tarn-et-Garonne *département* in 1808 (Jacques Bousquet, *Enquête sur les commodités du Rouergue*, Privat, 1969).

6. A. Albenque, *op. cit.*, p. 35.

7. Gregory (Grégoire) of Tours, *De gloria confessorum*, the chapter on St. Hilaire; contained in Grégoire de Tours, *Le Livre des miracles*, Paris, 1860 edition, vol. II, p. 344.

8. E. A. Martel, *Les Cévennes . . .*, Paris, 1890, p. 271–2; and P. Joanne, *Dictionnaire géographique et administratif de la France*, Paris, 1902, vol. VI, p. 4036, article "Saint-Andéol" (lake).

9. Bousquet, *op.cit.*

10. From this point, down to and including the section on the *Croquants*, I have drawn on material published in the unabridged edition of my doctoral thesis, *Les Paysans de Languedoc*, Paris SEVPEN, 1966, p. 96 and *passim*. (English translation by John Day, *The Peasants of Languedoc*, University of Illinois Press, 1974.)

11. M. Degarne, "La révolte du Rouergue en 1643", in the review *XVIIe siècle*, 1962.

12. Y. M. Bercé, *Histoire des Croquants*, Paris-Geneva, 1974, p. 622.

13. Departmental archives of the Hérault, register D 150.

14. Marie-José Gordien, *Etude de Saint-Jean-du-Bruel-en-Rouergue (1757–1765) d'après les observations botanico-météorologiques de Jean Mouret*, D.E.S. for the history department of the University of Paris-I, 1971–2, unpublished.

15. The following passage is taken verbatim from Mouret's notes, which I have merely abridged.

16. M.-J. Gordien, *op. cit.*

17. *Ibid.*, p. 101.

18. *Ibid.*, p. 102.

19. Michel Foucault, *Naissance de la clinique*, Paris, 1963. See also J.-P. Dessaive, E. Le Roy Ladurie, *et al.*, *Médécins, climat, épidémies*, Mouton, 1972, p. 26.

20. L. Lempereur, *Etat du diocèse de Rodez en 1771*, L. Loup, Rodez, 1906, p. xi.

21. I am here drawing, therefore, not only on the original document published by Lempereur, but on the excellent research carried out by Alain Guéry: *Etude démographique du Rouergue de la fin du Moyen Age au XVIIIe siècle*, D.E.S. for the University of Paris-VII, 1970–1, unpublished.

22. *Ibid.*, p. 131.

23. L. Lempereur, *op. cit.*, p. 454.

24. See M. Legendre's substantial study *Las Hurdes*, Bordeaux, 1927.

25. Oscar Lewis, *La Vida*.

26. The following draws a good deal on R. Béteille's magnificently documented study *La Vie quotidienne en Rouergue au XIXe siècle*, Hachette, Paris, 1973, with a bibliography; see in particular A. Monteil, *Description du départment de l'Aveyron*, Paris, Year X; and A. Meynier, *Ségalas, Lévezou, Châtaigneraie*, Aurillac, 1931.

8 Rétif De La Bretonne as a Social Anthropologist

1. Originally published in the author's contribution to *Histoire de la France rurale*, edited by G. Duby and A. Wallon, Seuil, Paris, 1975.
2. Throughout this article I have used Gilbert Rouger's edition of Rétif de la Bretonne's *La Vie de mon père*, Classiques Garnier, Paris, 1970, hereafter referred to by the letter R. Most of the quotations in the text are taken directly from this work.
3. R., p. 185.
4. R., p. 194.
5. R., p. 186–7.
6. P. de Saint-Jacob, *Les Paysans de la Bourgogne du nord au dernier siècle de l'Ancien Régime*, Les Belles-Lettres, Paris, 1960, p. 187.
7. R., p. 56.
8. Nicolas puts the following words in Pierre's mouth; they may quite simply be taken *post festum* from Quesnay's writings: "The most worthwhile art of man is agriculture . . . wealth is not truly wealth unless achieved by this means", R., p. 56.
9. R., p. 57.
10. R., p. 288, note 104.
11. R., p. 131.
12. R., p. 84.
13. See P. de Saint-Jacob, *op. cit.*
14. Rétif stresses the specificity of Sacy.
15. R., p. 30 ff.
16. M. Quantin, *Recherches sur l'histoire et les institutions de la ville de Vermenton*, 1876, quoted R., p. 23, note 39.
17. P. de Saint-Jacob, *op. cit.*
18. On comparable practice in Lyon, see M. Garden, *Lyon et les Lyonnais au XVIIIe siècle*, Les Belles-Lettres, Paris, 1970 (Bibliothèque de la Faculté de Lettres de Lyon, XVIII).
19. Of the three who did not survive, two were stillbirths and the third a baby, Thomas-Pierre, who died aged two and a half months.
20. Pierre Goubert, *Beauvais et le Beauvaisis, de 1600 à 1730*, SEVPEN, Paris, 1960.
21. R., p. 188.
22. R., p. 84.
23. On the reduction of perinatal, infantile, juvenile and adult mortality from the beginning of the eighteenth century in royal families, see the research published in Glass and Eversley, *Population in History*. Saint-Simon in his memoirs refers to the persistent efforts of Doctor Fagon (unsuccessful in this case) to deter Louis XIV from wearing out his mistresses or the women in the royal family by insisting on unnecessary travelling when they were pregnant. It was often by simple, commonsense advice that medicine eventually succeeded in curbing the worst excesses of female and child mortality previously provoked by the brutal habits of individuals like Louis XIV, whose old-fashioned behaviour was more typical of the seventeenth than the eighteenth century, at least among the *élites* who took medical advice at all.
24. R., p. 185.
25. Thesis in preparation on Meaux.

26. Unpublished thesis.
27. R., p. 191.
28. R., *op. cit.*; J.-J. Hémardinquer, *Pour une histoire de l'alimentation*, A. Colin, Paris, 1970 (Cahier des Annales); A. Lebrun, *Les Hommes et la mort en Anjou aux XVIIe et XVIIIe siècles. Essai de démographie et de psychologie historiques*, La Haye, Paris, 1971; *Les Cahiers du capitaine Coignet*, Hachette, Paris, 1968, cf. the first chapters, p. 3–45.
29. R., p. 191.
30. The curé of Courgis, on the other hand, a peasant by menu, but a bourgeois by mealtimes, had his dinner at midday or one o'clock.
31. R., p. 183.
32. R., p. 145.
33. R., p. 192.
34. *Petit salé* contains more fat than lean.
35. R., p. 149 and p. 186.
36. R., p. 130.
37. R., p. 31, note 54.
38. Even an approximate estimate of the average food rations on the Rétif farm is of particular interest, since it is absolutely exceptional to find data of this kind for a farming unit entirely in peasant hands.
39. The number is not certain, R., p. 31.
40. The estate was self-sufficient in wine and grain, and sold any surpluses; walnuts (100 *écus* per annum) and eggs (144 per week) were also sold, and the proceeds bought salt and spices.
41. R., p. 190.
42. R., p. 31.
43. R., p. 191 and 289.
44. R., p. 189.
45. R., p. 32.
46. J.-J. Hémardinquer, *op. cit.*, p. 153.
47. *Ibid.*
48. One of the rarest sets of statistics on the advancement of hygiene in the eighteenth century is R. Lick's work on Coutances: "the china jug and basin", almost non-existent in 1750–3 (it appears on only 2 per cent of household inventories in this small country town) figured in almost all the households of councillors, nobles or rich merchants (14 per cent of inventories) on the eve of the Revolution. In spite of this remarkable increase, the fact remains that 86 per cent of inventories, that is, the majority of ordinary people and even a section of the middle class, were still without a jug and basin in 1788 (R. Lick: Inventaires après décès de Coutance", *Annales de Normandie*, no. 4, Dec. 1970, p. 293–316).
49. Cf. Coignet, *op. cit.*
50. R., p. 140.
51. R., p. 190.
52. R., p. 131.
53. J.-P. Goubert and J.-P. Peter, in *Médecins, climat et épidémies à la fin du XVIIIe siècle*, a collection of articles edited by J.-P. Dessaive and E. Le Roy Ladurie, Mouton, Paris, 1972.
54. *Monsieur Nicolas ou le coeur humain dévoilé*, Paris, J.-J. Pauvert, 1959, vol. 1.

55. Maurice Agulhon, *La République au village*, Paris, Plon, 1970.
56. R., *passim*.
57. Peter Laslett, *The World We Have Lost*.
58. R., p. 184.
59. *Ibid.*
60. R., p. 130.
61. R., p. 225.
62. But both Rétif's *Monsieur Nicolas* (vol. 1) and the opening of Coignet's book indicate that poor children were employed from the age of ten in manual labour, such as threshing.
63. Agnès Souriac and Catherine Rollet, *Démographie et société en Seine-et-Marne au début du XIXe siècle*, Thesis (*3e cycle*) Paris-Sorbonne, 1970, vol. 2, p. 359.
64. Quite the opposite is the case in vine-growing regions today: the vine-grower (a landowner of the petite-bourgeoisie in his own eyes) would be ashamed to be taken for a "peasant"—i.e., a cereal-farmer. And a finer distinction should be made apropos of ploughing: if it was not *ignoble*, it certainly was not a noble activity. A genuine nobleman of the sixteenth century, like Gilles de Gouberville, never set his own hand to the plough. But he did prune and graft his apple trees, since in this field he considered himself an innovator. Snobbery can take many forms.
65. N. Mogensen, *Le Pays d'Auge au XVIIIe siècle*, Thesis (*3e cycle*), Paris-IV, 1972.
66. On the greater status of women in urban society, contrasting strongly with the male dominance in the countryside, see *Monsieur Nicolas* (vols. 1 and 2): the young Rétif is sarcastically greeted by the city girls (in Auxerre and Paris) when he tries to impress upon them his (rural) prejudices about male supremacy.
67. Peter Laslett, *op. cit.*
68. M. Vovelle, *Piété baroque et déchristianisation en Provence au XVIIIe siècle*, Plon, Paris, 1973 (in the series *Civilisations et mentalités*).
69. Gilbert Rouger's introduction to R.
70. R., p. 164–5.
71. R., p. 86, 164–6, 256.
72. R., p. 152.
73. R., p. 249.
74. R., p. 86.
75. Georges Lefebvre, *Les Paysans du Nord pendant la Révolution française*, 4th ed., A. Colin, Paris, 1971.
76. Cf. Touslejours (another incarnation of Edme Rétif) in *L'Ecole des pères*, and Brasdargent in *La Vie de mon père*, R.
77. Trévoux' *Dictionnaire*, quoted in R., p. 197.
78. It seems fairly clear that these childhood amours were accompanied in Nicolas' case by a strong Oedipal attachment to his mother (see *Monsieur Nicolas*, Pauvert edition, vol. 3, p. 215–30): the girl "Nanette", whom the author claims to have got with child in the stables at La Bretonne when he was only ten years old, is later provided with a biography (maid-of-all-work in Paris, servant-mistress and virtually wife of her elderly employer), extremely similar to that of Barbe Ferlet in her stormy youth. This supports the theory that Rétif identified Nanette with his mother.

79. In the seventeenth century, they used to make the pilgrimage to Sainte-Reine accompanied by their sweethearts; but a parish priest put a stop to this towards the end of Louis XIV's reign or the beginning of Louis XV's. A compromise was then introduced: two girls would leave Sacy, each accompanied by the other's suitor; once they were away from the village, they changed partners again—one way of evading the new puritanism of the Church (see *Monsieur Nicolas*).
80. R. Lick, *op. cit.*, p. 308.
81. Vladimir Propp, *Morphology of the Folktale*.
82. R., p. 138.

9 The Crisis and the Historian

1. This article first appeared in *Communications*, 25, 1976. I should like to thank André Béjin for the valuable help he gave me during its preparation.
2. See chapter two in this book.
3. *Archives de sociologie éuropéenne*, 1968, 2.
4. Immanuel Wallerstein, *The Modern World-System*, Academic Press, New York, 1974.
5. *Essai sur l'histoire de la mort en Occident, du Moyen Age à nos jours* Seuil, Paris, 1975.
6. Ping Ti-Ho, *Studies on the Population of China*, Cambridge (Mass.), 1959; see also Pierre Chaunu, *Histoire, science sociale*, SEDES, Paris, 1974, p. 303.
7. The reader will note that I have included the war-phenomenon in my definition of the crisis-phenomenon: this is, of course, the action or reaction of a historian, not of an economist.
8. I have not touched on the specific problem in many under-developed countries of today, with their soaring population figures. In so far as this is *ipso facto* accompanied by an interruption to economic advance, which has an inverse relationship to demographic expansion (automatic reduction of per capita resources), this too represents a genuine case of long-term crisis.

Glossary

Weights, measures, money

livre tournois	:unit of account in France under *ancien régime*, minted at Tours and orginally worth a pound of silver, but devalued so much that it was worth under 5 grams by 1801 when the decimal franc was introduced.
sou	:there were 20 *sous* in one *livre* or franc.
denier	:there were 12 *deniers* in one *sou*.
setier	:grain measure, somewhere between 150 and 300 litres.
muid	:hogshead.
hectare	:land measurement = 10,000 m² or 2.47 acres.
arpent	:land measurement = approximately 1 acre.

★

arrondissement	:subdivision of a *département* or large town (e.g., Paris).
ancien régime	:used of the historical period and system of government in France before 1789.
Annales	:*Annales: Economies, Sociétés, Civilisations*, to give it its full name, is the journal founded by Marc Bloch and Lucien Febvre, which has given its name to a school of historians in France.
bailli	:magistrate, or functionary administering justice on behalf of the Crown or of a noble.
bailliage	:territory under the jurisdiction of a *bailli* ("bailiwick").
bastide	:a fortified town, especially in Languedoc.
bibliothèque bleue	:a popular collection of books with blue covers, usually containing adaptations of medieval romances and tales of chivalry; first published in Troyes in the seventeenth century, and widely read until about the middle of the nineteenth.
biens nationaux	:the property, owned privately or collectively (e.g., by the Church) appropriated by the State during the revolutionary period.

307

bistournage	:a method of castrating animals, by twisting the testicles.
bocage	:the landscape typically found in northwest France, where the fields are divided by many hedges and woods (hence, by extension, any similar landscape).
canton	:administrative subdivision within the *département*, usually for electoral purposes in modern times.
cens	:quit-rent, i.e., dues paid by landowner to feudal overlord.
champart	:right to a share of the crop, exercised by feudal landlords.
châtellenie	:a chateau and its land, under the jurisdiction of the *châtelain*, or lord of the manor.
Chouan	:Royalist rebel against French Revolution. The Chouannerie was an uprising in western France, one of whose leaders was nicknamed "Jacques Chouan" (= "owl").
commune	:the smallest territorial and administrative division in France: approximately "parish" or municipality.
Croquant	:peasant rebel, especially during reigns of Henri IV and Louis XIII. The name may come from *croc* = pitchfork.
curé	:parish priest.
curé assermenté	:priest who had taken the oath of allegiance to the State at the time of the Civil Constitution of the Clergy after the Revolution.
département	:administrative division of France, introduced in 1790 and administered by the prefect; very approximately equivalent of a county.
événementielle (histoire)	:literally, the history of events; often used of the traditional narrative or biography, as opposed to quantitative and interdisciplinary research in history. Sometimes, but not always, derogatory.
fouettage	:method of castrating animals, using a cord (*fouet*).
gabelle	:salt tax under *ancien régime*.
garrigues	:scrubland, especially of the rocky and infertile limestone plateaux of Languedoc.
gavache (gavot, gabale)	:variants of name given, usually pejoratively, to the mountain people from the Pyrenees by lowlanders,

or by people of the *langue d'oc* to those from the *langue d'oïl* (see *oc, oïl*).

garde-champêtre	:rural constable.
Gautiers	:peasant rebels in Normandy, 1587, from La Chapelle-Gautier.
Grande Armée	:Napoleon's army.
Intendant, Intendance	:the royal administration under the *ancien régime*; the *Intendant* had very wide-reaching powers over one of the old provinces.
Jacques, jacquerie	:Jacques was the traditional name for a peasant and became particularly associated with the peasant risings in the fourteenth century; later used generally of peasant revolts.
laboureur	:literally one who ploughs and can mean ploughman or farmer who works with his own land. Often found meaning "well-off peasant" as opposed to poor peasant or day-labourer.
langue d'oïl, d'oc	:see *oc, oïl*.
maître de requêtes	:official in judiciary hierarchy, often sent on missions under *ancien régime*; today, counsel at *Conseil d'Etat*.
manouvrier	:labourer, who works for others, as opposed to *laboureur*.
notable	:a person of note, influence and standing, usually used of local rather than national figures.
Nu-pieds	:peasant rebels, literally "the barefoot", in Normandy in 1639.
oc, oïl	:literally the forms of *oui* = yes in the dialects of southern and northern France respectively. The *langue d'oc* refers collectively to the south, hence *Languedoc*, where all the *occitan* dialects are, or were spoken. (In recent years there has been a revival of regional interest and culture in *Occitanie*.) The *langue d'oïl* refers to the dialects and territory of northern France, where the language eventually became close to standard French.
offerte	:collection for the parish priest, given by the congregation in a procession at the moment of the offertory.
ostal	:family or household in southern France: see chapter seven for full discussion of meaning.

parlement	:of the provinces, under the *ancien régime*, refers to assembly with primarily judiciary functions, meeting at fixed times, rather than a parliament in the modern sense.
paume	:a game like tennis.
piéton	:foot-soldier.
piquette	:drink obtained by straining water through grape residue from wine-making.
poilus	:originally "brave soldier", used especially today of the French soldiers who fought in the First World War.
poujadisme	:political movement launched in the 1950s by Pierre Poujade on behalf of small shopkeepers and businesses opposed to taxation; right-wing in tendency.
précieuse	:originally used of a movement of fashionable women of the seventeenth century who sought to influence taste through their salons, especially in literature and culture. Caricatured by Molière among others, and thus sometimes used pejoratively to mean pretentious.
procureur fiscal	:representative of the fiscal authority, whether of the State or of a seigneur.
regrattier	:retailer of goods, especially salt; usually used pejoratively.
réserve	:the part of a *seigneurie* which the lord owned outright, and usually worked, or had worked, for himself. The "home farm"—but usually a large one.
sénéchaussée	:district corresponding to jurisdiction of *sénéchal*; under the Merovingians a household officer in the palace, later a royal agent.
seigneurie	:the area over which the feudal overlord (seigneur) had the rights to ask for *cens* or *corvée*, even if he did not own or work the land himself.
taille	:tax under *ancien régime*, paid mainly by commoners.
tard-venus	:literally "latecomers"; used of highwaymen especially in eastern France in the fourteenth century.
tiers état	:the Third Estate (the other two were the nobility and the clergy) under the *ancien régime*.
vergobrets	:annually elected magistrates in ancient Gaul.